NIGHT PEOPLE

BOOK 1

THINGS WE LOST IN THE NIGHT

LARRY J. DUNLAP

Copyright © 2015 by Larry J Dunlap.

All rights reserved. No part of this publication may be reproduced, distributed or transmitted in any form or by any means, including photocopying, recording, or other electronic or mechanical methods, without the prior written permission of the publisher, except in the case of brief quotations embodied in critical reviews and certain other noncommercial uses permitted by copyright law. For permission requests, write to the publisher, addressed "Attention: Permissions Coordinator," at the address below.

Claremont Village Press
5352 Algarrobo Street, #P
Laguna Woods, CA 92637 USA
www.claremontvillagepress.com

Publisher's Note: The author has attempted to recreate events, locales and conversations from his memories of them. In certain places, time has been compressed to fit the approximately three years this book covers. Interactions between the author and friends, band members, acquaintances, family members, celebrities, and others in this book, etc. are as true as the author's memory recollects. Liberties have been taken with dialogue, as remembering word-for-word what was said fifty years ago is impossible. But the actual connections that instigated the dialogue happened, and the conversations convey the truth as the author recalls it. In a very few instances, not material to the story, the author may have changed the names of individuals and places in order to maintain their anonymity.

Cover and interior design by Damonza.com
Proof editing by Katie Stirling, Eschler Editing
Author photograph by Studio 1921, Montclair, CA

First Edition Jun 2015, v 1.2 Oct 2016
Dunlap, Larry J.
Night People: Things We Lost in the Night, A Memoir of Love and Music in the 60s with Stark Naked and the Car Thieves / [by Larry J. Dunlap].
pages cm.

ISBN 978-0-9906279-0-6

1. Dunlap, Larry J. 2. Rock musicians——United States——Biography. 3. San Francisco (Calif.)——Biography. 4. Hollywood (Calif.)——Biography. 5. Las Vegas (Nev.)——Biography. I. Things We Lost in the Night : A Memoir of Love and Music in the Sixties with Stark Naked and the Car Thieves. II. Title.

ML419.D835 D86 2015
787.87/166092 —dc23

in memoriam to my mother

IVY WRIGHT BUTCHER-DUNLAP

Dedicated to

my children

&

my band brothers

DAVID DUNN, MACARTHUR J. BROWN, and LES SILVEY

including Joan Brown & the members of

The Aristocats, The Reflections,

The Checkmates,

and

Stark Naked and the Car Thieves

And especially for LAURIE

> "There's no safety in writing well. There is no way to be naked, which is what you have to be to be a good writer . . . and still be safe. What is truly naked is emotional exposure."
> — Dorothy Allison

PREFACE

MOST PEOPLE WHO pick up this book will never have heard of Stark Naked and the Car Thieves even if they're familiar with the better-known groups of the 60s. This book wasn't written because this band was one of the nationally famous bands of its era. Otherwise it would have been a much different book, and probably less interesting.

Some people might think that this group, which rose about as far as rock performers can without a successful national recording career, just missed the brass ring. But in my mind, those of us who came of age together and transformed ourselves from callow and irresponsible youths to self-disciplined and professional entertainers—with the perseverance to stick together through the tumultuous times of this story—did catch brass rings. Rings that have bound us together in long-lasting relationships we've maintained to this day. Most of us close our conversations with, "I love you, brother." I consider the riches of these lifelong connections as precious as gold—and I call that winning. If the two books that tell of my six years in the 60s with Stark Naked and the Car Thieves read that way to you, then I've accomplished at least one of my goals.

Memoir is the recollections of a writer as he or she recalls them, and that's certainly true with me, but I've also carefully researched the events related here. It has required compressing certain events and using some fictitious names for names I can't recall or for people I have no hope of locating. And I'll freely admit I use any tool or method I can to best describe the feelings and emotions of the people in this book as I experienced them. That includes reconstructing conversations that I would have no hope of remembering word-for-word.

As Jack Hamann, a documentarian who writes in Writer Magazine about transcribing the spoken word from his interviews says: "Few of us speak with clarity and precision. We start and stop. We digress. We interrupt. We assume unspoken thoughts or truths. We mangle phrases and screw syntax. Our rambling conversations switch tense, switch gears, switch directions. The way we talk rarely resembles the way we write. And nothing rings less true—in fiction or nonfiction—than articulate dialog."

I would add that the state of the physical environment around the speaker, the attitude of the listeners, the circumstances of the events surrounding the conversation, and other subtle nuances add many layers of context to the spoken word that do not easily translate in narration. So I chose to surround conversation with quotation marks to distinctly represent the emotions and communication between people from narration and description in this story. The statements between the quote marks should not be considered sacred for the reasons above, and for the pure and simple fact that they happened forty to fifty years prior to this writing. Common sense should prevail.

If you have taken the time to read this, thank you. And if you're ready to begin reading, find a comfortable spot, maybe grab a snack or drink, and join me at the beginning of the story where in a low point in my youth, I thought all of the most important things in my life were coming to an end. However, like most ends, it was simply the Universe making way for a beginning.

Table of Contents

Preface vii

Part One

Introduction: Change. 3
1: Orphaned. 5
2: Family Matters. 11
3: The Ticket 17
4: Through The Rabbit Hole. 21
5: Déjà Vu All Over Again. 27
6: California Checkmates. 33
7: No Plan B 41
8: Six Months In A Dive Bar. 47
9: Marie. 53
10: Changing Checkmates. 59
11: The Pharmacist And The Nurse 67
12: A Message In The Desert. 75
13: Bear Anxiety 81
14: A Call From Indiana 87
15: Pat. 95
16: Delta Moonlight 103
17: Star Crossed. 109
18: I'm Late, I'm Late 119
19: Pat And Marie. 125

20: Love, And Other Casualties..............................131
21: Night Falls...141
22: Losing The Briefcase....................................147

Part Two

23: The Name Game...159
24: Herb Caen Says Naked's Hot............................167
25: Naked On Broadway......................................173
26: Galaxians..181
27: Leonard..187
28: Adoption...195
29: The Dime Bag...203
30: Mother's Milk...209
31: The Goomba...217
32: Torchie And The Pru....................................225
33: Twin Peaks..231
34: The Galaxie Girls...237
35: Hollywood After Hours..................................241
36: Piano Player..249
37: Mattress Diving..253
38: City Of Illusions..263
39: Two-Night Stand...271
40: Backstabbed..279
41: Across The Street, Across The Musical Universe.......287
42: Negotiations...293
43: The Sunset La Brea Travelodge........................299
44: Rock Fight...309
45: A Casino Christmas Carol...............................319
46: Rag Doll...325
47: Martoni's..331

48: Welcome To The Big Time.................337
49: Hollywood Sessions......................343
50: The B3................................349
51: Inducted..............................355
52: The Prophet And The Lawyer..............363
53: Gay In La.............................369
54: Get Me To The Cat On Time 379
55: Larry Lamb............................387
56: Bonnie Springs Ranch...................393
57: The Colonial House Debacle 401
58: Two Bricks And A Hundred-Dollar Bill 407
59: Viking................................415
60: Missing Morrison 423
61: My Father And The Cat..................429
62: Serial Monogamy.......................437
Acknowledgements 443
Before You Go............................445
Important Information:....................447

PART ONE

I am always doing that which I cannot do, in order that I may learn how to do it.
— Pablo Picasso

INTRODUCTION
CHANGE

WE HUMANS DESPERATELY seek stability, in hopes, I think, that we can control our lives, though that isn't the way things work. Everything is in flux; we are dynamic beings born with expiration dates into an uncertain Universe. We live on the thin skin of a planet that rotates at about a thousand miles an hour, travels sixty-six thousand miles an hour around a gigantic gas fire, in a galaxy of a billion more wild fires moving at 1.3 trillion miles an hour across a barely comprehendible Universe. Forget the mission of the Starship Enterprise; we are unwitting galactic explorers traveling into uncharted territory at terrifying speed in every second of our existence. Cataclysmic events can happen at any moment. The winds of potential change blow constantly through our existence altering potentialities until a tipping point or nexus shakes our thread into a different weave, a new existence. It is our pattern-sensing consciousnesses that tricks us into believing remaining static is an option, that this day is like the next or the one before, as if the chaos that change will inevitably bring can be avoided. It's a comforting lie . . .

1
ORPHANED

Victory has a thousand fathers, but defeat is an orphan.

— John F. Kennedy

April 9, 1965
Indianapolis, Indiana

IT WAS ONE of those Indiana skies an early spring can produce. A late morning sun, flickering through patchy fast-moving clouds, illuminated the neighborhood in erratic patterns of startling color and somber grays. In an open field, you could lose your balance under an unsettled sky like this. I tucked my hands into my armpits as Dave 'pulled his 63 Ford convertible into my parents' driveway. Despite my irritation, his grin forced me to smile as he unfolded his lanky frame to hang over the idling car's door.

"You know, this isn't going to make any difference. I told you on the phone I can't go with you guys." Dave Dunn and I had been best friends since our junior year in high school, on into college, and afterward as we fumbled our way into real life with sketchy success. He'd stood up for me when I married Pat. We'd named our oldest son after him.

"No excuses. Just grab your toothbrush and a change of clothes and get in the damn car. We got a long ride ahead of us." The convertible's engine ticked over quietly. The tang of unburned hydrocarbons caught in the back of my throat and made my eyes water.

Mac Brown peered out from the passenger seat. Les Silvey—male-model handsome, not a hair out of place—rolled down the rear window.

He didn't speak but his restrained impatience was obvious. The three of them were the other members of my disintegrating vocal group, the Reflections. Except for a couple of phone calls from Dave, I hadn't spoken to them since the last time we'd sung together in Fort Wayne. Next to Les, sat a moon-faced guy I didn't know named Mickey Smith, an unexpected guitar-player friend he'd invited to go with them.

"Come on, man," Mac wheedled in his soft, Cincinnati south-side, drawl. Like a goateed Cheshire Cat's, his toothy smile appeared over the car roof. "Let's get on out to that Golden Gate, bub. Go to the beach, get an eyeful of them foxy California honeys in their teeny-weeny bikinis."

MacArthur Jesse Brown, at five eight, was about my height though just north of skinny instead of stocky like me. His mother named him after General MacArthur and Jesse James—men she admired for their independence, he'd said. He'd started singing with us late last year, and he was very different from the other guys I'd sung with as my group flickered in and out of existence since high school. For starters, Mac was a professional.

"Already told Dave I couldn't leave." I shrugged in frustration. "You guys do get that my entire life's fucked up beyond belief, don't you? Should be pretty clear I can't go anywhere." Two months ago they'd been with me dressing for a show in a Saint Louis hotel room when Pat called threatening divorce.

"Best reason to go," Mac said. "Thing is, your life can still be fucked up in California if you want. Least the weather'd be better."

I glanced in at Les in back. He was why they were leaving. When he'd joined the Reflections in January—even more recently than Mac, he'd said unless something spectacular happened before his twenty-first birthday, he planned to go play guitar with a guy he knew in California. He'd hit that milestone yesterday, and appeared antsy to make up for the lost day. *Bad enough to lose him, but after Fort Wayne, no surprise either.* What I hadn't expected was, like the Pied Piper, he'd convinced Dave and Mac to go too. It killed me to see the three of them leaving.

"Gotta hand it to you." I nodded in reluctant admiration. "Going out West just like you said you would."

Mac shrugged, and ducked inside the car. He must've known their detour to offer me a second chance was no more than a gesture. Dave wrapped me in a bear hug and slipped back into the driver's seat.

As Dave's ragtop shrank into the sharp-edged morning, another big part of my life calved off like an iceberg. I imagined them heading west toward Plainfield, gathering speed as they picked up Highway 40 toward Saint Louis. I'd never thought much about the West Coast before Les brought it up. California was some exotic, far-off country that exported movies and surf music to places like Indianapolis. I trudged to the house feeling hollowed out. In the first three months of this year I'd lost things I would've sworn in December were impossible to lose: my home and wife and two little boys and now, my group, my closest friends, had taken off to somewhere so far away it might as well be the moon.

Inside, the house stood quiet, redolent with aromas of a home that hadn't been mine for years. I drifted aimlessly through the living room touching furniture, lampshades, running my hands across the spines of my mom's books as if they were museum exhibits. For a moment, I imagined piling into Dave's car and riding off with them. I might have been more tempted if that Mickey Smith guy hadn't been with them. Five of us crammed in Dave's convertible would have made for an uncomfortable two thousand miles. Maybe they knew that. Maybe it was only a token visit, and they didn't really want me along at all. I'd been pretty crappy company lately. But that didn't mean I wanted them to leave and abandon the group. Abandon me.

Standing there, with no one to witness, the truth slammed into me; *I was more relieved than devastated*. How is that possible? When those guys drove away, the last shovelful of dirt fell on the Reflection's grave; it was the end of an era for me.

Eight years ago, at the beginning of my junior year in high school, the compulsion to sing hit me like a fire bolt. My dad had made it clear I'd have to improve my grades if I ever intended to use the driver's license I wanted more than anything else. Some of the kids at school said listening to popular music made doing homework easier. Hoping it was true, I convinced my mom to let me study with the radio on in their second floor bedroom. Anything, we tacitly agreed, to get me off to a better start this year.

Sprawled across their bed one fall night, struggling to conjugate Spanish verbs, I drifted instead into steamy daydreams of the college girl next door. From my bedroom window one morning, I'd seen Sheila's nightgown slip exposing the pebbled center of a creamy white breast that sent puzzling shudders through my body. I rolled over onto a pillow, slip-sliding back to Reggie Riley's birthday party last summer. I relived intense embraces with two of the neighborhood girls, remembered the tactile sensuality of their soft adolescent chest bumps as we took turns slow-dancing in the dark. Each of them, hot breath in my ear, pressed their uniquely own warm groins into my embarrassing, celebratory, and painful rigidity while The Penguins sang, *Earth Angel*, over and over. Before I could begin thinking about Susie, the girl from church camp who let me feel up her breasts, though, disappointingly, not under her bra—the static from Randy's Record Shop on the Nashville station I'd tuned to suddenly cleared. The music that broke through chased all other thoughts from my overheated mind.

It wasn't the lyrics that left me breathless; I barely noticed or cared what the song was about. It was the words, the way they sounded when the singers' voices blended them. It seemed to give expression to the raging emotions and confused longings coursing through my young brain since grade school. The chorus began, and though I wasn't entirely sure what a silhouette was, the sound of it being tossed back and forth between the background singers and the main singer amazed me. A rising cascade of voices before the last verse—what I would later understand was a modulated key change—lifted the song in some mystifying way. The vocal harmonies triggered an unexpected response to my seething hormones that would change everything. *Tomorrow*, I decided, *I'm going to find some guys and learn how to sing this* Silhouettes *song*.

I didn't have idea one about how I was going to do that, but ignorance rarely deterred me from jumping into things full bore. Outside of some failed piano lessons, I hadn't shown any musical inclination or interest, let alone talent, before that night. Stubborn persistence drove my obsession to form and keep a group together as we figured out how to sing the rock and roll songs made popular by the vocal groups of the era. I lost myself in the companionship of singing with my friends, and best of all, it led me to the girl who rescued my teenage years, the girl I was sure I would spend the rest of my life with. Pat. Without any intention to, I finally found the place where fit in, though I'd had to create it myself.

The hurricane of change ripping away these anchors rooted in my life—my little family and the fellowship of singing with my friends—had begun at our annual New Year's Eve party three months ago. Sloshed to the gills, several of the guys voiced a usual complaint about money being tight, and a good job impossible to find. Mac suggested a way we could make a few bucks singing around town. He'd been in a successful nightclub group when we'd met him and, *it would be dead simple*, he claimed, *to mold the Reflections into a show band*. As midnight rolled us into 1965, I'd found myself reluctantly agreeing to a plan I didn't believe for a moment could happen. *Drunk talk*, I assured Pat. *How could it? We're singers, honey, we don't even play instruments. We almost never sing in public.* We'd had an astonishing brush with recording success last year, sure, but the group was mostly a companionable pastime left over from high school and college. *How could I have failed to realize what I was risking? How had I been so blind?!*

Within a few short weeks, the Reflections became the Checkmates, a nightclub show band, and a booking agent Mac knew had us booked out of town to shake out the kinks. In the four weeks that followed in Birmingham and Saint Louis, and our final disastrous night in Fort Wayne, I learned one thing—I wasn't cut out to be a nightclub performer. I froze stiff as a trashcan-snacking possum caught in headlights before I could force myself to sing. While I considered myself pretty agile on a basketball court, I danced like an unstrung puppet.

Worst of all, with our voices submerged beneath drums and electronic instruments, I couldn't hear us when we sang. I couldn't lose myself in the vocal fusion of tone and rhythm that was my abiding passion for singing. *That's what I missed*, I thought, as I brought a glass of milk to the captain's table, oversized for its space in the kitchen. *I'm not going to miss being a clumsy dickhead in a show band, that's for sure.*

All significant family events took place at this table, and my place here had always been this wooden chair beneath the wall phone. Family and close friends were gathered here in our kitchen's intimacy, while acquaintances and visitors politely relegated to the living or dining room. Over the years, innumerable bridge and board games had been fiercely contested across this tabletop. Here, my family enfolded Pat into the Dunlap clan. Five years ago, my mom sat at this table listening to Pat's mother, Mary Lou, inform her in a phone call that I'd impregnated her sixteen-year-old daughter, and dictate what would follow.

I'd worshiped Pat from the beginning. Before I met her, it was as though I'd missed an orientation meeting on how to survive being a teenager. She'd given me a reason to live, and even thrive, and I fell into a love with her beyond reckoning. In the years following our first son's birth, and the arrival of our second boy, she became a wonderful wife and mother. Despite a constant stream of negativity from her mother and family, we'd always been each other's favorite companion, faithful cheerleader, and trusted confidant. Yet somehow, here we were, our marriage tangled into a complicated mess.

So much change, so much loss. Everything's fallen apart so fast. Sometimes it seemed as if I inhabited an alien skin, existed in some incomprehensible parody of reality. I glanced at the star-shaped, bronze clock concoction Mom had let the builder install over the kitchen sink. *Time to go. Thankfully.* I longed for the mindless activity of the RCA assembly line, and the music in my headphones to ease my panicky emotions.

If I'd hoped burrowing into my parents' home would let me take a time out, slow the torrent of changes, give me a chance to find my feet, that hope was already vanishing down a rabbit hole. The Tarot cards of my life were about to be reshuffled again by a phone call.

2
FAMILY MATTERS

*There is a theory which states that if ever for any reason
anyone discovers what exactly the Universe is for and
why it is here it will instantly disappear and be replaced
by something even more bizarre and inexplicable.*

— Douglas Adams

April 19, 1965
Indianapolis, Indiana

"WHO IS IT, Mom?" I glanced up from my book. Outside of my tiny bedroom, the one place I could curl up undisturbed was in the unlived-in living room. What the rock hard couch near the fireplace lacked in comfort, was made up for in peace and quiet. In times of stress and confusion, I could nearly always find escape between the pages of a book. I'd uncovered Isaac Asimov's Foundation Trilogy in a forgotten box of my old paperbacks in the attic. I was deeply immersed in the rise of the Mule in the second volume, *Foundation and Empire*, comforted to revisit an old friend.

"Dave Dunn," Mom said. "I thought you said Dave had gone to California? You should turn on another light if you're going to read in here. You'll ruin your eyes."

We were both sixteen when Dave came to audition for the Aristocats, my vocal group's name in its early years. He never failed to remind me what a jerk I'd been. How I'd shown up late. How—after he'd chugged away, shy and acne-ridden, in his '47 Dodge with a Broad Ripple High bumper sticker—I told the other guys his voice wouldn't work for us. Fortunately, my opinion had been overridden. A few months after Dave became an Aristocat, his voice was maturing into the strongest, clearest falsetto I'd ever heard, with an equally impressive first-tenor full voice. By the end of our senior year he was our fulltime lead singer.

Hearing Dave's voice from California on the phone was terrific, if unexpected. Long-distance was expensive. I didn't see how he and Mac could afford to call just to say hi though Dave did wonder if I would ever consider coming to California. I fantasized about driving off to some exotic adventure out West after we'd hung up. But only for a moment. I'd lost any desire I might have had to sing on stage. My mind was made up. I would stay here in the real world, not chase after some Disneyland fantasy of Les's.

Dave's animated call Sunday evening a few days later was even more surprising. "We need you. We've got a big opportunity to work in a nightclub, man, but we need all our voices to get it. You'd love this place, Larry. Sun, palm trees—music everywhere, all the time."

Once my parents heard about Dave's second call, an impromptu family meeting materialized the next night after dinner. My soon-to-be sixteen sister, Cheryl, disappeared to the telephone extension in the back bedroom while my dad and I cleared the kitchen table.

"So," Dad said, munching one of Mom's lacy, raisin-free (in deference to me) made-from-scratch oatmeal cookies. "Dave's positive about this nightclub job out in California? He did say for sure and certain, did he?"

My parents were both Irish; Dad originally from upstate New York, a product of a stormy Catholic and Protestant marriage, and Mom, from a large, second-generation Protestant family in Burlington, Vermont. Dad's wiry hair atop his athletic six-foot frame was graying at the temples but he still kicked my butt in every sport. With a touch-of-the-blarney, as he'd say, his independent insurance agency kept us in comfortable middle-class comfort.

I nodded. "Yes. He says the contract is already signed."

"And those musicians they told you about, with them there would be enough people to form a band?" My mother had pulled in her chair after putting a kettle on to boil. Her red hair had faded a little, but she'd always maintained her cute, compact figure. Though hidden now, her mischievous Irish smile lingered just out of sight.

"Yeah Mom. Guitar, bass, drums, and three singers—counting me."

"Um, hmm." Dad exhaled and glanced up from his cookie. "Son, how do *you* feel about this?"

I stared at them in confusion. My father's question smacked me in the face like a missed basketball pass. I'd been waiting for them to tell me what to do. Five weeks ago, I let them catch me after I'd free-fallen from Fort Wayne, my marriage in ruins, the crazy idea of a nightclub band torn to shreds and my vocal group along with it. They gave me my old bedroom and enough money to get by until I found the assembly line job at RCA. I accepted every condition, spoken and unspoken, without question, trying to anticipate and do whatever they suggested. A relief, considering the disastrous results of my own decision making.

"If this turned out to be a golden opportunity," Mom emphasized *golden opportunity* as if it was in capital letters, "and you missed this chance, how would that make you feel?"

"I'm not sure." I dropped my face into my hands. The secret truth was, if I'd wanted to go to California, I could've gone with the guys when they left town two weeks earlier. "I can't see how it's even possible. Their contract is supposed to start soon. I have a job here. And how would I even get there?"

"Not much sense worrying about how to get someplace unless you're sure you want to go." Mom studied me in a sideways gaze.

I was shocked. I'd expected a simple, *No Larry, you idiot, of course you can't go to California*, and we'd be done with this.

She took a cookie with a wistful little smile and nibbled a tiny bite. The kettle started a breathy low-pitched whistle.

"You're worrying me, son," Dad said. "There's times I've wanted to snatch you bald-headed, try to knock some of that stubborn, know-it-all attitude out of you. But considering the state of things—maybe you need to get some of your gutsiness back."

"But I'm trying to please you guys . . ."

"Larry," Mom said, covering one of my hands with both of hers. "What we want is for you to be happy. That's all we've ever wanted. We know you want to please us, but you need to be yourself, too. Since you were a little boy, you've been consumed by one grand project or another, flinging yourself into this or that. You just seem so lost . . ."

"You guys are killing me." My fingers wriggled like trapped animals. "I thought I was being responsible, being mature, doing the right things . . ."

"I know, I know," she said, hands retreating. "But you're twenty-three, and leaving important decisions up to us." Mom glanced at Dad. "And I don't know if that's the best idea. We've tried to do what we thought was best for you and Pat in the last few years, but I'm not sure we've always used the best judgment. We might need to accept some responsibility for . . . well, all that's happened."

I glanced up in surprise. My mother's brow was furrowed and my father's face, grim with introspection. Neither of them looked at me or each other. Mom's statement was lighting a fuse to emotional dynamite.

I'd never mentioned how much I'd resented them, particularly my father, for allowing Pat's mother to shame Pat and me into marriage and disgraced exile to a distant college in Kentucky. Or their passive acceptance, if not silent agreement, with Mary Lou's constant disparagement of a son who would never be forgiven for loving her daughter too much, too soon. *No way did I want to open this bitter can of worms right now.* I lowered my eyes and waited. The explosive moment passed.

"Anyway," Mom mused, "maybe this trip to California could bring back your joy of living." She rose to pour hot water into her mug and sighed. "I'm not certain what we should do, but I don't believe we can oppose it, not even for Pat and the boys." She glanced at me. "Have you talked to her since you've gotten back?"

I shook my head. I hadn't, but she hadn't called me either. If we talked, and she wanted me to come home, I doubted I could resist. I missed everything about being home with my family. I was miserable without them. But eyes opened now, I feared returning to the trap my mother-in-law had set in motion with the most precious people in my life. An impossible, no-win situation that could only get worse. I tried not to think about the looming disaster ahead.

The dismay on Mom's face was painful to witness. Pat was family and she adored her two blond baby grandsons. "Well, we won't interfere. We've done enough of that and look how that's turned out."

"Maybe," Dad said, "there's a way to find out whether this opportunity of Dave's is genuine, and get you to California if it is." He dusted cookie crumbs from his lips with a quick brush of his fingers.

"Your mother and I think you should ask them to send you airfare to San Francisco."

"Airfare?"

"First-class airfare," Mom said. "You need to ask them for a first-class ticket. That will tell you whether the offer is substantial or not." She sipped tea and peered at me over the edge of her mug.

"But they don't have any money. Pretty obvious they won't be able to do that."

"Well then, son," Dad said, reaching for another cookie, "the answer's simple. You won't be going anywhere."

Dave's third call came late Tuesday evening. The house was quiet and cool, everyone asleep but me. I answered before the ring disturbed anyone.

I took a breath. "Well, here's the deal. You know my folks took me in and have been helping me, so I've got to consider them in this decision." I hesitated. "They think I should go, but there's a condition."

"Yeah? Well, okay. I mean, that's actually fantastic!"

"Wait, wait. Don't get too excited. This is one humongous condition."

"Doesn't matter. We agree."

"They want you guys to send me an airline ticket, paid in advance. They want to be sure the nightclub gig is a solid opportunity, plus flying is probably the only way I could get there in time."

"What? How can we do that? We're barely getting by. People have been giving us money to buy sandwiches. We're sleeping on a floor in some girls' apartment. I . . . How do we do that, Larry?"

"First-class, man. Got to be a first-class ticket, Dave." I was feeling really rotten now.

"Might as well ask to sit up with the pilot."

"Look, I get this is impossible. I don't see any way you can buy me a ticket. It would cost a fortune. How could you guys come up with money like that? But you have to understand, my folks won't agree unless there's something concrete. And I couldn't leave, even if I had a way, without their blessing."

Dave was quiet on his end.

"I thought they'd say no, maybe even be pissed off that I would even consider leaving with so much crap up in the air here, but they were completely cool. They want to be sure there's a solid opportunity before I give up what I've got started here."

I didn't want to lose what I had going here, either. After being left behind, I realized going to California was the last thing I wanted. What I really wanted was a fresh start, a Mulligan, a do-over. Pat had always believed in me, no matter what crazy dream I followed, regardless of what anybody else thought. I didn't know how, or if, I could ever get that back, but without her, I couldn't keep swimming upstream against everyone's disapproval. I'd crossed a line I hadn't seen, opened a crack in her faith that let her mother come between us. Maybe this clean sweep was necessary for me to change, to become what everyone here expected me to be.

I didn't have a clue how to do that, but for now, I was amazed to discover I liked my assembly-line job. The repetitive motions of building record players let me slip off into some kind of Zen state, pushing my worries aside. Or I could distract myself with music or the radio on my headphones. A couple of weeks ago, Dad cosigned on a loan to help me buy an older, but very cool little Chevy II convertible. I'd made a few friends on the line, and even met a girl who seemed interested in me, a gratifying, if puzzling, sensation.

I felt bad about the sanctimonious and insurmountable requirement I'd given Dave, but my folks, though they didn't know it, had handed me the perfect out. Purchasing a first-class airline ticket was out of the question for guys who couldn't afford to buy me lunch at White Castle. They'd never have to know I'd let them down.

Anyway, they didn't need me; I just sang harmony. I would miss singing with them, but in all honesty, that had ended when we tried to make ourselves into a band. No. I'd stay here and figure out how to be a normal guy and live an ordinary life in Naptown.

3
THE TICKET

*It's true that we don't know what we've got until
we lose it, but it's also true that we don't know
what we've been missing until it arrives.*

— Unknown

April 22, 1965
Indianapolis, Indiana

THURSDAY AFTER WORK, I opened the front door to my sister dancing pirouettes and arabesques around the living room off into the dining room. My dad had *I've Got a Secret* on the television. I tried to watch, but, restless, I got up to take an evening walk through the neighborhood. Saplings, planted when my parents had this house built, were now young trees coming in green. Though it was a tract, the big lots and lack of sidewalks gave the homes a pleasant, rustic setting. Rodger Ward, an Indianapolis 500 winner, and Bill Vukovich II, son of my favorite 500 driver, owned homes nearby—big celebrities in a town where the Indianapolis Memorial Day race and high-school state basketball tournament were the two biggest events of the year.

After a late dinner, I burrowed back into *Second Foundation*, the third book of Asimov's trilogy. Isaac knew how to distract me. Even knowing how it turned out, I was drawn in again by the author's inventive twists and turns in revealing where he'd hidden the Second Foundation.

The phone rang.

A few minutes later, Dad turned down Steve Allen when I walked into the wood-paneled family room. Everyone's eyes turned to me.

"They got the ticket," I said, in helpless shock. "I don't know how they could've, but they got it. I'm supposed to fly to California Saturday afternoon."

"Are you going to go?" Cheryl asked.

"Well yeah. Of course I'm going. They got me a first-class ticket. On American Airlines. It cost somebody an arm and a leg."

"What about Pat? And little David and Danny?" Cheryl said, smoldering eyes challenging me. Pat had always been my kid sister's shining princess, which made her emotional relationship with me, the older brother she'd always looked up to, complicated and awkward. We'd clumsily avoided talking about it. At least I did. I didn't know how to explain it to her, and had little solace to offer.

"Good God, Sis." I hadn't considered the consequences. This wasn't supposed to happen. "I don't know. It's out of my hands for now. Have to deal with it later, I guess."

"Saturday," my mother said, "the day after tomorrow. We haven't much time to get you ready."

"Can I have your car then?" Cheryl asked.

I gaped at her. "What? My car?"

"Don't be silly, Cheryl." Dad said, "We'll have to sell the car. You aren't old enough to drive anyway.

"I'll be sixteen in two days." She pouted.

"That's enough. We can't afford to keep it, and you haven't cared enough about driving to even get your learner's permit."

"I've got to pack," I said in panic. "And Dave said not to forget my black suit."

"I'd get a license if you let me have the convertible," Cheryl muttered until Dad shushed her.

"We've time to get your suit pressed," Mom said, all business. "You can wait until Saturday morning to pack. Go through your clothes and pick out what you want and I'll get them washed and folded for you. Pack light, you won't be sure where you'll be staying at first so you should stay flexible. We can ship anything else you need later."

At the American Airlines counter, I checked the oblong piece of punched cardboard. There was my name. Destination: Oakland, California.

Somewhere near San Francisco, I supposed; I'd meant to check the Americana Encyclopedia but hadn't found time.

Yesterday had been a madhouse. The lady in personnel at the RCA plant was understanding about my lack of notice after I explained I was leaving to join a band in California. Surprise was still evident in my voice when I told Rita, the pretty, shaggy-haired girl on the assembly line. She asked to come to the airport to see me off.

I'd gone to bed early, hearing the television, muffled through the walls, unable to fall asleep at first. Tomorrow, the security blanket my parents provided for me would be ripped away like a scabby bandage off my broken life. I couldn't decide whether to be petrified or excited. I'd put an impossible, irresponsible task out into the universe and it had responded with a minor miracle. It was a signal. It had to be. My entire fate seemed to hang in the balance. This wasn't something I could reject; I had to go.

I stared into the dark, thinking, *Pat is just a few miles away in our bed. If I were there, I could roll toward her, run my hands along her . . .* But then I pictured her slim figure on the tiny porch of our duplex, holding Danny on a hip, little David standing beside her, waving as Dave and I drove away to Birmingham, Alabama, none of us suspecting I wouldn't be coming home again. I wedged knuckles into my eyes trying to shut out the anger and fear in our voices on the phone three weeks later, the last time we'd talked.

In the morning, Dad wanted a final conversation with me at the kitchen table. "Son," he said. When he started with son, I knew he wouldn't be giving me a pep talk. "We're not opposing you going to California to sing with your friends. You do understand that?"

I nodded.

"But you're leaving a whale of a mess behind, and your mother and I are going to bear the brunt of some of it."

I nodded again.

"You do realize, we can't afford to support you, I hope. You'll have to make your own way. You can't call home for money. Is that clear?"

For the third time, I nodded.

"Okay. One final thing." Dad stared me dead in the eyes. "You can always ask us for help to get home. Your mother and I will never leave you stranded. We'll figure out some way, if need be."

"Yes, Dad, I understand. I appreciate everything you guys have done—everything you're doing—for me. Can't imagine what comes next." My jaw dropped open into a stress yawn. "Anyway, guess this proves something's going on out there even if I don't know what."

"Well dammit, Son," he said, grinning as though his marbles had been jarred loose. "Get the hell out there and find out!"

I stuffed the ticket into my windbreaker pocket and turned back to the family. Rita had joined them. She smiled and waved. *Weird*, I thought, returning her smile, but also nice in some indefinable way. The boarding call came, and they walked me onto the tarmac. The plane loomed huge and propeller-less. I'd been on an airplane once before, on a day trip to Coney Island in Cincinnati. There'd been four propellers on that plane, and we'd bounced all over the sky; a pudgy little puddle hopper compared to this sleek, powerful jet.

Patches of hardened late-April snow glinted harsh sunlight into my eyes, and a stiff breeze cut through me at the top of the boarding stairs. Dad grinned like a monkey below me. My face must've reflected the same pained, grin-to-hide-your-feelings smile, as his. Though they'd just met, Mom and Rita wept, hanging onto each other as if saving themselves from drowning. Cheryl stood with arms crossed, looking half-angry, as if she couldn't reconcile her emotions. In leaving, I was further defiling the cherished ideal my relationship with Pat had always been to her.

An attractive stewardess in a blue suit and soft cap welcomed me into the luxury of the airliner's first-class section by handing me warm slippers to replace my shoes. A troubling lump of uncertainty mixed with a breathless sense of adventure settled uncomfortably into my stomach. I leaned back, engulfed in the huge window seat. The jets wound up to a mighty roar. I'd sleepwalked through getting ready to leave never really convinced I'd actually get on an airplane, until now. Take off was no longer a daydream! Reality settled around me like a straitjacket. Ready or not, right choice or wrong, this powerful machine was preparing to hurl me into the sky to my friends halfway across the country in the next few hours.

Nothing in my life could have prepared me for the experiences ahead. Highs so high I'd think my heart might stop or my head detonate, lows so low my very life and sanity would be at risk. But never once could I bring myself to regret leaving on a jet plane that April afternoon.

4
THROUGH THE RABBIT HOLE

It's a dangerous business, Frodo, going out your door.
You step onto the road, and if you don't keep your feet,
there's no knowing where you might be swept off to.
— Bilbo Baggins, LOTR: The Fellowship of the Ring

April 24, 1965
Oakland, California

I FROZE AT THE top of the boarding stairs, lost in a life-changing moment. A fiery sun, reigning above a darkening city, spread a glimmering diamond-studded pathway across the open ocean bay toward me. Soft breezes off the water smoothed playful kisses across my face, tickling the hairs at the nape of my neck with fairy fingers. I knew at once the Universe had been right. Despite my earlier fears, I'd arrived right where I was meant to be. I blinked away moisture, trying to absorb this indescribable vision through every pore.

"View's impressive, Larry," Eve, my stewardess from first class whispered behind me. "But I've got a couple of hundred passengers who'd like to get off the airplane, if you'd let them."

I two-stepped down the stairs, trying to keep the spectacular view in sight. An inner voice paraphrased Dorothy from *The Wizard of Oz*: *I'm never going home again, I'm never going home. How could I after finding this place?*

Across the tarmac, I caught a glimpse of Mac's grin and, over his shoulder, Dave's. We ran together into a back-pounding group hug.

"Would you look out there?" I gazed out over the water, still amazed. From here, the swollen sun blazed in frustration, reluctant to fall behind the distant city as lit windows poked random holes in its silhouette. "It's like a living painting, only who could paint that?"

I stopped at the look on their faces. "Oh. Sorry. Really glad to see you guys. What an amazing trip. I don't know where to start . . ."

"Start with how much money did you bring," Mac said, with a lopsided smile. He turned toward the terminal. "C'mon, meet Sandy." Near the doors, a young girl in a light turquoise cardigan, with blond hair yanked up into a severe ponytail, waited with a hesitant smile. "Sandy and her roommate Robin been keepin us alive. Weren't for them, we'd be sleepin on the streets somewheres."

"Not sure why they put up with Mac and Mickey but I sing to them," Dave said.

I disclosed my $32.89 in the backseat of Sandy's yellow Volkswagen Beetle. Dave gave me back two dollars and the loose change and took the rest. We drove to a Safeway grocery where we splurged fifteen dollars on bread and sandwich fillings.

I'd hoped to get another glimpse of San Francisco or even Oakland, but instead Sandy turned toward the eastern hills. Her little car transformed the country highway into a roller coaster, as we twisted through headlight-pierced tunnels in the gathering dusk. We spilled out onto a huge divided highway running inland to the city of Concord and Sandy's one-bedroom apartment, which smelled a little like too many people living in the same small space.

Mac motioned toward a single mattress wedged in a corner of the living room. "Used to be Les's room, yours now, I guess."

"Where is Les, anyway?" I dropped my small suitcase and myself onto my new bedroom.

"He's stayin with his friend Jerry over near the bay. Got himself a little trio playin' somewhere around there. Think he woulda liked to play in Jerry's band but they're tight, no room for anyone else." I wondered why he hadn't included Mac and Dave in his new group, but decided now wasn't the time to ask.

Mac eyed me from his nearby mattress. "Things any better back in Naptown, with your wife and your boys?"

"No, not really." My mind shied from those troubles the way a silvery fish slips past a shark.

"I know brother, I know. Tryin to figure out my own thing with Joan and my sweet baby girl, Dani. Miss 'em somethin fierce." I nodded. I was curious about Mac's wife and daughter, though. He hadn't talked much about them in Indianapolis.

Dave and I met Mac for the first time in November. One or the other of us had read in the paper that Neil Sedaka was appearing at the Rat Fink Lounge, located north of downtown's mile square on Meridian Street, and we'd gone to see him. I was excited. I'd never been to a nightclub before, and I'd never seen anybody famous in person, either. We must have gotten the date wrong, because a six piece, high-energy vocal band from Cincinnati called the Casinos—including Mac Brown—performed on the stage instead. Seeing a live band sing some of the same songs we did was almost as good as seeing Neil Sedaka.

When we heard a few days later that there'd been a disagreement in the Casinos and Mac planned to leave his band and stay in Indianapolis, Dave, Chuck, and I talked it over. Though we couldn't think of a reason why he'd want to join a bunch of living-room singers, we needed a new voice, so we decided I should slack off one afternoon from selling ads for the *Indianapolis Times* to at least go ask him.

When Mac wanted to know who the Reflections were, I told him we mainly sang for fun, but last January, songs we'd recorded in a local studio had either gotten released, or somehow escaped. Our up-tempo cover of the Five Satins' *In the Still of the Night*, had inexplicably become a featured hit on WLS in Chicago, one of the nation's most powerful rock stations. We'd hit the charts at number twenty-seven and risen to sixteen before our joyride ended. Somehow, the master tape had gotten lost or destroyed. Without it, no more of our records could be manufactured.

I didn't tell him how hard the four-week fantasy-turned-nightmare had hit us, as we slid helplessly back into obscurity. One of the guys quit singing altogether—the reason I was here in this luxurious home, where Mac and two young women seemed to be living together, trying to recruit him. Though we'd considered our near brush with recording success a major disappointment, it must have appealed to Mac, maybe in the optimistic way a green cow patty implies there's fresh steak walking around nearby. Soon after he'd agreed to sing with us, the lifestyle he led here, within blocks of the governor's residence, revealed a slice of Indianapolis society I'd never imagined existed. Whatever else I thought of Mac's personal life back then, it hadn't included a family.

It was Saturday night. Everybody wanted to go out to clubs and see some bands. I hadn't slept much the previous night and was still three hours behind, but after a quick shower, somebody's used towel, and a sandwich, I was ready to go.

A slender, raven-haired girl with a preoccupied expression rushed through the apartment and disappeared into the single bedroom where Sandy was getting dressed.

"Robin?" I guessed. "The other roommate?" Nods all around. "Pretty girl."

"Yeah, she's a stone fox," Mac said. "Sposed to be engaged. Seems kinda flirty to me, though."

"Everybody ready?" Sandy said, popping out of the bedroom. Robin had plans with her fiancé and wouldn't be joining us. Good, because I don't where we'd have put her. The five of us jammed ourselves into Sandy's little Beetle where I was allowed a window seat in the back so I could see out. Sandy drove us through the San Leandro Hills until the lights from San Francisco, simply "the City" to the locals, were visible across the water.

Dave pointed out the Town Club as we skimmed down Mission Boulevard through a little city called Hayward, one of many small towns strung out along the east side of the San Francisco Bay.

"That's where we met Sandy and Robin," he said. "Mac walked up and said 'Hi, we're singers, we're new in town.' They tried to brush him off, but Mac just kept talking."

"That's what he does," I grinned.

"He was kind of cute, so we bought him a beer," Sandy said. "We yelled to the band that we'd found a new singer in the audience. They wanted him to come up on stage. He said okay, but Dave, Mickey, and Daddy Bear had to go up there with him."

"Daddy Bear?"

"That's the nickname these girls give Les." Mac said. "Anyway, figured I couldn't do too much harm to *Kansas City*. Dave put in some harmony at the right spots. Band let us use two guitars so Les and Mickey both played and traded licks."

"He ripped it up," Sandy said. "Mac sang, and danced up onto his toes, and ran up and down the stage. Everyone loved it."

"It was good he didn't fall off the stage," Dave said. "Wasn't his first beer of the night."

"Everybody was wanting another song. What'd we do next, bubba?" Mac asked Dave.

"You convinced me to do *Walk Like a Man*, and for some insane reason I agreed."

"Yeah, right. Them people never heard a falsetto like you gave 'em."

"Mac's right, Dave, you were amazing," Sandy said from the driver's seat. "I've never heard anybody sing like you do. Everyone around me stopped talking and stared up at you. At the end, they all stood and clapped and yelled."

"What happened next was pretty funny," Mickey said. "These guys wanted Les to sing. He didn't want to but somehow Mac got him to start that *Pappa Oom Mow Mow* song."

"Les didn't say nothing at first," Mac said, "didn't even look at us. Then all of a sudden he leans into the mic and starts in—'Papa oom mow mow, papa oom mow mow'—singing the bass line 'til the band catches on and Dave jumps in on the lead."

"You guys were such showmen," Sandy said craning her neck toward Mac causing the Volkswagen to swerve. "I mean, people were going wild for you." The car thumped over the bumps between lanes and she yanked the wheel back before we hit, or got hit by, anything.

"That's when the girls started calling Les 'Daddy Bear,'" Mickey said.

"'Cause he sounded kind of gruff like a big old scary bear. But really, he's a sweet guy," Sandy said. "He just seemed like a Daddy Bear to Robin and me." I tried to imagine Les as a Daddy Bear.

That night at the Town Club was also when Carlos and Reno, the two guys we'd be meeting at our first rehearsal tomorrow, heard Dave and Mac sing and Mickey play. They'd approached them afterward with an offer to form a band with Mac, Dave, and Mickey to save an engagement they would otherwise lose because two of their players had been injured in an automobile accident. And that, of course, is what brought me to California.

We went from club to club, seeing bands from Fremont to Berkeley. A power guitar band in one club rattled my teeth; a party band played at another place so wall-to-wall with people, I could barely get a glass up to my mouth. Horn bands, folk trios, funk bands, Beatle bands, country-rock bands; some with matching outfits or shirts, most in everyday clothes, and some sleazy. Live music rang out everywhere up and down the East Bay that night, but one thing stood out; none of them sang the tight harmony our vocal group did.

I collapsed onto my bare mattress and light blanket, exhausted, as daylight began to grow in a new sky. Music rushed through me like blood through veins; my head spun from all the different clubs and night-madness. As time slowed for the first time since I'd gotten off the plane, all I'd left unresolved in Indianapolis rose to haunt me. *This is where I belong, anything's possible here*, I thought, before sleep overwhelmed my apprehensions. *I can figure everything out if I can just find a way to stay.* The Pied Piper had captured me, too.

5

DÉJÀ VU ALL OVER AGAIN

Life isn't about waiting for the storm to pass . . .
It's about learning to dance in the rain.

— Anonymous

April 28, 1965
Oakland, California

"SO LEMME GET this straight" Reno Bassi, our new drummer, held his palms out as if he held an invisible box. "You guys do ten songs, just ten songs all night—while we back you up? Then me and Carlos, and Mickey here, as a trio, we gotta play dance music for the rest of the night? Yeah?"

I was meeting Reno and his bass player buddy, Carlos Crawford, in the Hilltopper for our first rehearsal Sunday afternoon. The Hilltopper, an isolated roadhouse, set on the side of a back-country road outside of the little California delta town of Pittsburg, was bright and clean; surprisingly, based on my limited experience with nightclubs. An elevated entryway stepped down to a long sleek bar across the back with wine-red leather booths lining the side walls. Down another level to the main floor where cocktail tables hugged a parquet dance floor in front of a large, low stage.

Mac shrugged, his expression a tight grin. The original notion of simply snapping the singers and musicians together into a band wasn't turning out to be as simple as conceived. He and Dave assumed we'd do the same show format we'd done at the clubs in Birmingham and St.

Louis two months ago. But Carlos and Reno were hearing about this for the first time.

Reno thought about what Mac told him, sliding his hands through his lank, just-out-of-bed hair. He slapped a knee in decision. "Okay, guess we can do that." At Reno's acceptance, Carlos's stolid, Native American countenance slipped into an infectious grin. Mickey's face showed concern now. Though Mickey knew from Les that we did special shows, and that he'd have to sing at least the simplest of Les's parts, the realization of how much responsibility was falling to him had just begun to hit home.

"So hold on," he said, tilting his head at Mac. "Trying to get this straight. We three musicians gotta play something like—a minimum of thirty dance songs on our own, besides backing up you guys?"

"Yeah, sure," Mac said. "You guys can come up with a bunch of dance songs pretty quick, can'tcha?"

Mickey caught Carlos's eyes. "How many songs you think we can get together right away on, man?"

I glanced at Mac and Dave in shock. "Uh, these guys are just finding this out now?" They gave me a glum look. "Couldn't Mickey have started rehearsing dance music with these guys before I got here?"

"Hey man, why you got to be so critical?" Mac said.

"Seems like somebody's got to be. Jeez, guys."

I couldn't criticize, though; none of us, not even Mac, knew that much about putting together a rock band. We weren't musicians, and there wasn't a how-to book for learning how to do it. Les had handled all that for us back in Indianapolis when we formed the first Checkmates. He'd found the Zeb Miley Trio, who already had a repertoire when they agreed to back us up. We were starting from scratch here.

As our players started pitching song titles at each other, I knew Mac and Dave wondered the same thing I did: *With only today, Monday, Tuesday, and Wednesday afternoon before we opened, could a band materialize out of this chaos in time?* It would be devastating to call home for rescue, to suffer another bitter defeat. I couldn't lose what I'd found here. We had to make this work.

Three nights later, as our little trio of musicians prepared to launch our engagement at the Hilltopper to an empty room, the band was on life-support. Mac and I sat in gloomy silence as Dave doodled on a notepad between us. Starting with our first rehearsal three days ago, things had gone from very bad, to incredibly worse, followed by virtually impossible.

We watched Mickey, Reno, and Carlos stagger into *Stormy Monday Blues*. It was a travesty to call it blues. The song ground to a tragic ending in a silence so deep I expected to hear crickets. *Maybe no one will come in tonight*, I hoped, crossing my fingers. The players began a tepid version of *Tequila*, an instrumental featuring a sax, which Mickey unsuccessfully attempted to emulate with a lone guitar. It crawled along at an unhealthy tempo to finally expire. This was going to be a long, long night.

Our first rehearsal, last Sunday, had been spectacular in its lack of productivity. Mickey, in his new role of musical director, had become a bottleneck. Besides his vocal and musical responsibilities to the singers, he also had to pull together a dance playlist and rehearse the trio. It didn't begin well. The guitar, bass, and drums sounded thin and uneven with lots of starts and stops. With no real musical leadership, everything got discussed to death. So little got accomplished that doubt and fear began to ramp up until they owned us by the end of the day.

Our songs were arranged for four voices. Now we were three, and needed Mickey to fill the fourth voice in the harmony as well as play guitar. He was so wrapped up with the musicians, he hadn't found time to work with us during rehearsal. Outside of rubbing some of the rust off of our choreography, there wasn't much for Dave, Mac and me to accomplish. After a modest dinner Sunday evening, Mickey tried to learn our songs. We quickly realized he was more instrumentalist than vocalist and entirely unfamiliar with the more complex songs we sang. To help him work out the chord changes, and his parts, we sang our demanding songs over and over deep into the night as he struggled to figure them out.

The repetition scorched our voices, especially Dave's. If we'd been more experienced, we'd have thought to reduce the stress on our throats by singing down an octave, or in half voice. By the time we hit our mattresses late Sunday night, Dave's goodnight was a hoarse whisper. When he couldn't croak out a word Monday morning, Sandy volunteered to take him to a nearby clinic.

Dave returned holding a small notepad where he'd scratched out: *Doc says I can't talk. Have to write everything down.* He tried to scribble answers to our rapid-fire questions before crumpling up the notepaper in disgust and pointing to Sandy.

"The doctor says Dave's vocal chords are badly swollen. He said no spicy food, warm drinks are okay, but not hot, and no alcohol." Sandy spoke through clenched teeth, hating to relay the bad news. "Especially, he shouldn't talk. Speaking is harder on vocal cords than singing, he said. He'll check them on Friday, but if Dave tries to sing before then, he's risking permanent damage."

Friday! How could the band survive the first two nights on stage at the Hilltopper without Dave? With no alternative, Dave looked on in encouragement as Mac and I tried to put together a war plan. We couldn't do any of the songs featuring Dave's falsetto, so we tackled a couple of his other leads. Dave wrote out lyrics while we worked with Mickey to prepare for the next rehearsal.

Before sleep that night, my thoughts drifted back to two days before our new band planned to leave for Alabama. I'd taken Pat that Saturday night to see the Zeb Miley Trio close at Susie's Twist Club, a little dive on West Washington Street near the downtown Indianapolis, circle monument. Pat's eyes had sparkled with excitement. She'd never been to a nightclub before, and it was only the third time for me—an intoxicating walk on the wild side for young working parents and day people like us.

Our group had been invited on stage, as planned, so the newly minted Checkmates could try out some of our songs in a final dress rehearsal. The crammed-to-the-rafters crowd shouted and clapped for us, and we basked in their approval until closing. We accepted an invitation for a quick beer at a walking-distance after-party, arriving just in time to get caught up in an early morning confrontation between a police officer and a random drunk guy. Before we grasped the situation, all of us—band, singers, bystanders, and my innocent young wife—were swept up by an army of cops. Lying on my mattress, I pictured her pale face tight with anxiety that night, as she glanced at me before stepping into the female-only police van.

Pat's parents bailed her out the next morning. I told my dad not to waste bail money on me; I'd get out when court opened on Monday, anyway. The only thing we were guilty of was being in the wrong place at the wrong time. On Monday, without any testimony, the judge charged all the new Checkmates with a VAD misdemeanor, "*Visiting a Dive*," one of Indiana's old "blue laws," and fined us fifty dollars each. I was finally released late Monday afternoon; the next morning I left with the new band for Birmingham. *The timing couldn't have been worse*, I thought, drifting into a fitful sleep.

So here we are, I worried, as the opening set limped along, about to fail again, only this time, we're even farther from home, in California. At our last rehearsal the previous afternoon, the trio believed they had fifteen dance songs they felt comfortable with and another seven or eight they hoped they could fake. Cheat sheets of penciled lyrics and chord changes papered Carlos and Mickey's amplifiers and mic stands. A deepening sense of déjà vu from our collapse in Fort Wayne loomed in my mind.

The Midwest Checkmates had struggled through two rough engagements before we arrived in Fort Wayne, Indiana, to find that Zeb's drummer had turned south toward his home in Florida, instead of north with the rest of us. The local musicians' union sent us an emergency fill-in, a jazz drummer who hated rock and roll and would only play with brushes. But that wasn't even the worst problem. We weren't the right Checkmates. Unbeknownst to us, a local and well-loved band from Fort Wayne, also named the Checkmates, had recently left for the West Coast to find fame and fortune, leaving behind a legendary legacy in their hometown. And that's who the bozo club owner thought he had hired. Not only were we not them—we sounded pitiful. After the second set, the owner stormed to the stage cursing and screaming for Zeb to pack up and get the hell out. That was the last we saw of Zeb and Johnny Lamb, his keyboard player.

Dave, Mac, Les, and I didn't say much to each other driving home to Indianapolis. I hadn't talked with any of them since, except Dave, until they'd come to convince me to go to California. *Had that been only two weeks ago?* It seemed like months.

After the fifth song, Mac and I slipped unobtrusively on stage. We wouldn't be doing shows on the dance floor without Dave, but I still tried to swallow my nerves. Mac began the handclaps and started into the Dovells' *You Can't Sit Down*. Mickey tried to sing the background harmony with me but fumbled the guitar chords and dropped out to concentrate on playing. I felt silly singing background by myself. We managed to humble ourselves through four more songs before slinking off stage to a halfhearted boo from the bar.

As I headed to the bar for a soft drink after the set, Bill, the club owner, spotted me. I thought about pretending I hadn't seen him but instead I gave him a rueful grin. He returned the rueful part.

"You guys don't sound very good."

"It's early, there's a good chance we can get worse."

"Hard to see how."

I nodded at his refusal to accept my weak attempt at gallows humor. "We're having a tough time without our lead singer. We'll be better once we play together more."

"We can pray for a miracle," he said, before walking away.

The night wasn't half over before the trio began repeating dance songs that hadn't sounded good the first time. I hoped Bill wouldn't notice. The crowd certainly didn't—they stayed away in droves. For most of the night, the place remained empty as my billfold. Most people left at the door. Of those few who came in, nobody stuck around for a whole song.

The band was dangerously demoralized when the night ended. We'd stunk the place up so badly they'd probably have to fumigate before we played again. We agreed to meet tomorrow afternoon to work on the worst of the kinks, and add a few more songs. Mickey remembered some Ventures and Duane Eddy songs. Mac asked Mickey to run through Tommy Tucker's *Hi-Heel Sneakers* with him.

We'd suffered though our awfulness tonight, but we would try to get up off the mat and come back for round two tomorrow night.

6
CALIFORNIA CHECKMATES

*In the depth of winter, I finally learned that
within me there lay an invincible summer.*

— Albert Camus

*April 29, 1965
Pittsburg, California*

THE BAND'S PERFORMANCE improved a little Thursday, but there were still serious breakdowns. Mac and I had butchered the Temptations' *My Girl* opening night. Though she'd survived for another try tonight, we maimed her again to the point we were forced to stop and start the song over. Dave cringed when I stumbled over the same note I'd blown in *Stay* the night before. To add to my misery, I forgot the next couple of lines entirely. We were ugly bad.

People walked in and then back out of the club's entryway like a revolving door in a department store. There was a rare handclap and occasional boos. For the most part, our audience remained limited to empty tables and chairs, though I imagined if they could have animated themselves, they'd have left, too. We'd tried to improve some things at rehearsal, but our fixes were like peeing on a house fire.

At the service bar, a waitress with *Rosie* pinned on her blouse noticed my condemned prisoner expression. "Must be tough for you guys up there." She caught my look of glazed ignorance. "You do know why everyone is walking out, don't you?"

"The silence outside sounds better than we do? They heard someone fixed the jukebox anywhere else?"

"Oh, stop." She grinned at me like we were both in on a secret. "The place is trying to change over its crowd." She picked up on my incomprehension. "Don't you get it? Bill wants a rock club. You don't actually know, do you? Well, that's rotten. No one told you who closed here last week?"

"What difference would that make?"

"Try Buck Owens and the Buckaroos, darlin'. The pride of Bakersfield."

At first, I couldn't place the name. "The TV comedy show—Buck Owens was on *Hee Haw*, wasn't he? They're a famous country band. Why would we be following them here? We don't play country and western music. And we're nobodies."

I set my glass down before I spilled it.

"You seem like a bright guy. Figure it out."

I thought it through. "We aren't expected to be successful, are we? We're supposed to turn away the folks expecting to hear country music, right?"

"Yee haw."

"Then Bill must not be that upset about how crappy we sound."

"I wouldn't go that far. I'm sure he'd like you to switch some of these rednecks over to rockers." Her eyes danced before she turned to the tables below. "You're getting half the job done anyway."

Knowing the situation helped relax us a little. I still wouldn't have crossed the street to listen to us, but at least the music had a touch of life.

After the last set, Carlos told me Bill wanted to talk to him and asked me to go with him. I understood his nervousness; he'd been the one to sign the contract here. Bill waited outside his office as Carlos walked up stiff-legged, as if expecting to hear his run-over dog had died. Bill took a squinty look at us and said to Carlos, "I'll be frank. You boys sound like horseshit. I knew you'd be rough around the edges but Jesus Christ on a life raft!" We had no answer.

"You're here on a two-week contract with my option for another two. I can tell you're trying, so I'm telling you early: it's an opportunity I'm going to pass on. Gives your guys a little more time to find day jobs, or someplace else to play in case you've made the ill-advised decision to stay with music."

Just to confirm, I asked, "But we finish out this week, right? And we're here for the next one for sure?"

His eyes tightened in irritation. "This week and next, then you're out. That's the contract."

I glanced at Carlos before speaking for both of us. "This might sound stupid but—thanks. We're having a tough time right now. We're going to be better, a whole lot better, I promise. And, uh . . . if you could find another mic with a stand for us, that would help."

Bill offered a reluctant smile. "I appreciate your attitude." He hesitated for a moment. "I'm going to make a suggestion. The Town Club over in Hayward has an afterhours. You should consider showcasing yourself there this weekend, or find another jam session or afterhours in the East Bay. That's where the local clubs usually scout for bands."

A twisted little smile played along his lips. "Now get the hell outta here and try to get better before tomorrow night. I'll make sure you get an extra mic."

After spending more early morning hours refreshing harmonies when we got home, I managed to get my shoes and jeans off before falling onto my bare mattress. The loneliness and fears, banished during the hectic days and nights, invaded my thoughts before sleep as they'd done since I'd gotten here. Though thoughts and pictures of Pat and the boys troubled me, I wasn't homesick for Indiana. I didn't want to go back. But for someone who loved singing acappella in a tiled bathroom, and hated performing in public, it was a little weird to find myself trying so hard to create this band so I could stay here with my friends, and the new ones I was making. Being in the band was taking on another, deeper meaning. I dropped into exhausted, dreamless sleep before I could reconcile my incompatible thoughts.

We straggled into the club for rehearsal on Friday. The sound of someone washing bar glasses tinkled down to the tables where we gathered. Dust motes floated in the rays of afternoon sunshine streaking the dance floor. No joking or teasing—too quiet. Even though Dave had passed his medical checkup and would be singing with us tonight, heads were hanging. Almost without thinking, I called everybody together.

Beginning with the Aristocats, my original vocal group in high school, through all its kaleidoscopic versions that had evolved into this

California Checkmates band, I'd been the leader. Being the leader didn't mean telling everybody what to do—to me, it meant doing whatever was necessary to keep us together. The group's existence, so I could belong to it, and sing in it, had always been crucial to me.

I'd abdicated leadership staying behind in Indiana, of course, but Mac and Dave had wanted me here so much they'd worked magic to get me here. It was my responsibility to do all that I could to make sure we succeeded. And this band we were creating somehow offered me a lifeline to a new existence in this amazing place I'd landed in. So I stepped back into the job.

"Listen you guys, something I want to say." I waited while everyone shuffled around me, with questioning faces. "Getting the impression some of you think the Hilltopper not picking up our option is a bad thing."

"Well, it ain't good news," Reno said.

"Actually, it kinda is. Last gig the Indiana Checkmates played, we got fired after the second set. Since we've survived through the second night here, I'd say we're on a roll." Mac and Dave grinned.

"Look, Dave Dunn has the best voice I've ever heard." Mac nodded, others perked up. "When he's singing and Mac Brown's funky, when our harmonies come together, we're as good as any band I've seen around here." Faces registered more surprise than inspiration.

"Forget the last two nights, they don't matter. Nobody's heard the real band yet." I had their full attention. "We can't quit on ourselves because I'm telling you right now"—I pinned every set of eyes, one by one—"I'm not going back to Indiana. I don't think Mac and Dave are, either." Dave stood, steely-eyed. Mac stuck out his jaw, nodding.

"I'm here, man," Mickey said, stepping forward. "And I plan on staying here." Reno and Carlos's confirming nods were definite, if not emphatic.

"Okay. Our music's still a little rough." That brought a mordant chuckle. "So we've got to sell ourselves with energy and enthusiasm to buy time to tighten things up. Starting tonight, the singers will do a show four times a night instead of two. Means we'll have to repeat the shows every other set, because we only have two shows right now, but I promise you, we'll bring them with everything we've got." Carlos and Reno grinned.

"We need people to realize that Dave is a star and our vocal harmony is what sets us apart. Doing more shows will emphasize that and eliminate some of our crummy dance material at the same time. We'll still have some dogs, but if we let those dogs live a little while longer while we concentrate on Dave's songs and the shows, we'll be okay.

"One more thing, Saturday night we're going to the Town Club afterhours and burn that fucking place down. I know we can do it. You local guys, call your friends, get everyone you know to call their friends, and get 'em all to go. Our next gig is coming from that afterhours."

Heads went up, and I felt some energy in the room.

When the musicians kicked off Friday night, *Stormy Monday Blues* was more in the pocket, not that much better musically, maybe, but the laid-back tempo gave the tune a bluesier feel. Then Mickey began a guitar line from a popular instrumental by the Marketts that sounded like the theme from *The Outer Limits*, a TV show; Reno popped off his stool through the drum fills. I'd noticed at rehearsal the trio pulled together more. They recovered faster from a messed-up chord or a blown drum beat, not worrying about being criticized, encouraging one another instead.

I found a spot near the front door to gauge how we looked and sounded to people as they entered. An off-duty waitress settled herself at a table in the entryway with a cash box and propped up a hand-printed sign reading *$5.00 Cover Charge*. Crap—people have to pay to get in? Man, could we not catch a break?

A couple came through the door. They eyed the stage and the girl began to sway to the music. She smiled at him and he reached for his wallet. *Okay, good.* Next, a guy came in alone, appraising the room like a hunter scouting game. A quick glance at the sign and he left. Another couple paid the cover, and then two girls walked in. After a quick, covert glance at the bar, the waitress stamped their hands without taking money. *Cool, girls will attract guys.* They giggled as they stepped down to the bar. A group of four or five people came in together and forked over the entry charge.

An unexpected picture of me screwing turntables into record players a week ago on an Indianapolis assembly line popped into my head. *Why in hell would anyone pay five bucks to see me?* I was nobody. The last time I'd been on a stage, they'd closed the place rather than listen to us. I shuddered and tried to brush the image away. I'd just have to pretend to be the professional entertainer they'd paid to see when the show started.

Mac, Dave, and I, wearing the cleaned and pressed matching black suits Dave's dad had bought for the original Checkmates, with dark ties on white, freshly ironed dress shirts, and coordinated boots, ran to three microphone stands on the dance floor. Dave, in the middle, nodded in time to the clicks from Reno's drumsticks. We began clapping out a beat. Dave leaned into his mic:

"Hey pretty baby . . ." Dave broke into the Dovells' East Coast rocker, selling the song. We worked it, performing like the place was full to the rafters. Behind our mics, Mac and I broke into our little kick steps and twirls with energy and flair. I felt the musicians play to our enthusiasm, lifting us. *Careful, Reno*, I worried, *don't rush the beat*. After the second verse, we were into the bridge; I listened for a flub, but when it didn't come, I smiled wider. We made it through the last verse, into the turnaround, and out. No boos—well okay, one from some ten-gallon hat at the bar—and a smattering of applause. We weren't going to win anyone over with one song, but goddamn it, now we were giving the best we had.

"Good evening, ladies and gents," Mac said, smiling out at our meager audience. "Happy you came out to the Hilltopper in downtown Pittsburg tonight. Here's a Four Seasons' tune, *Walk Like a Man*, which you'd actually have to do for a coupla miles to get to downtown Pittsburg."

Dave sang Frankie Valli under the table with a voice fresh as daybreak and clear as a lake of glass. Next up was the Temps' *My Girl*. While Mac and I strolled the Temptation Walk, clicking our fingers as we crooned the background parts, Dave took the microphone out of its holder and stepped out and wowed 'em. Mickey came close on his vocal part, but he sang with confidence, so it wasn't that bad.

You Really Got Me Now, the Kinks tune we did next, wouldn't impress anyone vocally, but our dance moves were crisp and we kept the intensity going into the closer, *Stay*. Mac and I hit our marks and parts on the numbers while Dave caressed the lead vocal. When his falsetto ripped into the last verse, I knew we'd done a decent show set. We bowed and walked off to steady applause.

It was gratifying to detect the dawning realization of how good we might be in Reno, Carlos, and Mickey's eyes. I felt better than any other time we'd performed as a band, like I was part of building something special.

Though we were already exhausted, and Saturday would go deep into Sunday morning, we still met in the late afternoon. Our growing sense of confidence and commitment carried us; we were beginning to believe our fledgling band had possibilities, and the guys were listening to me for direction.

"Mac suggested we come up with our best possible five-song show, guys," I said. "Get it good and tight now, at rehearsal, and do this super-set twice to a live audience tonight."

"Our second show will have to be what's left over, you know," Dave said. "Might be pretty half-assed."

"Maybe, but we've only got another week here. Wowing 'em at the afterhours has to be our priority."

The crowd in the club at any one time on Friday night had probably never maxed out at more than fifty. Those who liked us stayed, which was about half of those who came in, while the other half, expecting country music, left, usually before paying the cover at the door.

Saturday night's start, with few people in the audience, was similar, but by the time we ran out to do the superset show we'd practiced at rehearsal, the ringside tables around the floor held a respectable crowd.

The first three songs we'd done in the early show Friday night paced together fine, so we started with them and added Randy and The Rainbows' tune *Denise* next. Its East Coast, street-corner, doo-wop sound was exotic here, and it went down great. The final song, the Isley Brothers' *Shout*, had been our only showstopper for the Midwest Checkmates. We got a solid ovation for it as we closed the set and came off the stage grinning.

At the service bar, Rosie from Thursday night stopped me. "What's got into you guys? Your little show was terrific."

"We're built around Dave's voice." I shrugged. "No Dave, we're like Sonny without Cher."

She giggled and poked me. "Heard you're gonna do the afterhours in Hayward?"

"We are. Going to do that same show at the Town Club."

Rosie's eyebrows popped. "That'll be hot. A bunch of us are going to go." She swept a hand around the room. "Lee and Robbie, couple of the bartenders, Raquel, Haylie, other waitresses, and a lot of their friends.

Also," she said, glancing behind her, "we're telling everybody who comes in tonight where you're going to be later, too. Can't wait to find out what they think of the Checkmates over the hill."

"Thanks Rosie, that's so cool." I was touched. We had allies we didn't even know about.

With all our effort going into the show sets, our players hadn't been given much opportunity to work on their dance numbers. We'd have to fix that. At least playing together seemed to help tighten them up. Mickey had come up with some neat guitar instrumentals like *Rebel Rouser* and *Pipeline* that sounded decent. By midnight, the house was full, busy with laughter and conversation, and the dance floor was crowded until closing.

We packed for the trip to Hayward as the thinning crowd worked its way outside into the cool darkness. Carlos passed out a hundred dollars in twenties to each of us, our pay for the last four days. Mac was riding with Reno, while Carlos took most of the equipment in his car. Dave, Mickey, and I accepted Sandy's offer to drive us. Bill stopped me as I was about to leave with them.

"Larry. When you get over to Hayward, talk to Bob, he's the owner. He's expecting you." He gave me a half smile.

"Told him you guys needed four mics and four stands to sound good."

7

NO PLAN B

To succeed in life, you need two things: ignorance and confidence.
— Mark Twain

May 2, 1965
Hayward, California

SANDY DROVE AND Robin rode shotgun. With the last minute addition of Robin, Dave, Mickey, and I were crammed into the Volkswagen's backseat. I scored a window next to Mickey, who was crunched into the middle. The ride through Crow Canyon's headlight-carved tunnels was exhilarating but spooky. God had flattened Indiana with a giant glacier in the last ice age down to where southern Indiana's hill country began. We had no concept of mountains and hills like these where I grew up in Indianapolis.

"Omigod, everybody's coming," Sandy said, looking back at us while negotiating a tight hairpin. "We called around like you asked. Everybody was dying for a reason to party." I wanted her to look at the road. Robin turned toward the backseat.

"A bunch of people are coming from my work. A lot of them have been following along on how we've been helping you guys. This is so supreme, now they can see who you are in person."

I'd been wondering about something. "Afterhours clubs don't open until two in the morning. How come so many people are out running around that late?"

Both girls started laughing. "Boy, the corn must be high as an elephant's eye where you're from," Sandy said, endangering us once again, as she turned to look at me. Her excited gaze returned to the windshield just in time to brake for a stop sign hidden by the curve we'd come through.

"Lotta people don't even get started 'til midnight," Robin said. "We go to an afterhours or two and if we're heavy into it, we go to a jam somewhere. It's party time 'til daylight on weekends around here, Daddy Rabbit."

"What? Who?"

"Yep, we decided your nickname is Daddy Rabbit."

"Daddy Rabbit? Really? Why?"

"We don't put a lot of analysis into this, you know." Sandy pretended to pout a little. "You just are what you are. But I think you're a Daddy Rabbit because you're sort of pink, and seem so young and—well, young." *She should talk; she looked like a teenager.*

"Especially when you blush," Robin said with a sly grin.

They both laughed uproariously. I didn't think I liked my nickname, but my opinion didn't seem to count.

We parked in the crowded lot across the side street from the Town Club. Loud rock and roll music rumbled through the brick wall of the building as we got out. Carlos pulled his car into the space behind us and caught up to me as the others went ahead. The more I got to know Carlos and his quiet self-deprecating manner, the more I liked him.

"Man, I don' like dealin' with the club owners and the money stuff. You, you're good with that stuff and everybody listens to you, so you talk to the guy here for us *esé*, okay?"

I shrugged. "Sure Carlos, I don't mind."

He gave me his wide open grin. "*Qué gracioso, hombre.*"

It was crazy in the room. Everybody talked or yelled or drank. The club had their interior lights up, and smoke hung in a lazy cloud hazing the industrial ceiling as if someone had set fire to the basement. I tried several times to catch a bartender's attention at the packed bar to ask for Bob. Finally, a harried service bartender with greased-back hair gestured toward where the wall and the bar met.

Behind the three-deep press of people at that end, I spotted a big man in a working-man's heavy-weave button shirt, open at the neck. He had to be who I was looking for.

"Hi, I'm Larry, with the Checkmates. Bill said to look for you when we got here."

He nodded. "Good. Talk to Jimmy Lee from the house band, he'll lay everything out for you. I figure you should go on about"—he tilted his wristwatch to see it better—"oh, a little before four; should be full then."

"This isn't full?"

"Nothin' like. This place gets packed. Lotta the big tables open in the back still."

Sandy and Robin had found a booth against the wall large enough for us all. I recognized a surprising number of people from the Hilltopper, including Rosie, who winked and smiled at me. I grinned back. Our contingent from behind the hills to the east had shown up.

"Reno," I shouted over the chaos, "you know the guys in this band, right?"

Reno raised his eyebrows and his hands began to work the air. "Yeah, Jimmy Lee and the Coolers. Me and Jimmy Lee got some history, and I'm tight with Danny Leone, his drummer."

"Would you figure out with them what equipment we need to bring onto the stage, and tell Jimmy that Bob said we should go on around four?"

Robin introduced me to her fiancé, Alan; I'd wondered about him, and how he felt about a bunch of itinerant musicians sleeping on the floor of his fiancé's apartment. He seemed like a good guy and happy enough at the moment.

The band on stage began playing *Louie Louie* too loud, even the intentionally unintelligible lyrics—rumored to be laced with obscenities—thundered out as raw noise. I hoped the PA would sound better for us because it sure sounded like hell right now. All around me, conversations took place at full shout.

The smoke grew thicker and the crowd denser. In some weird way, it felt like a *happening*, and that made everything okay. There wasn't supposed to be booze in here during afterhours, but several poorly hidden bottles splashed alcohol into the soft drinks the club sold. I waved off offers to spike my Coke. I was exhausted, but I couldn't sit still so I paced our little area. *Was there anyone here who might be interested in hiring us? God, what if there wasn't? What would happen to us? We had no plan B.*

Reno hollered in my ear. "Let's go man. Got to get set up and start in fifteen." I shook off my worries and picked my way forward.

The view from the stage was vastly different than at the Hilltopper. We were much higher; below us, people on the dance floor milled in amoebic pools, coalescing, swirling, and breaking apart to reform again. The garish house lights illuminated the place from the center out, leaving the room's edges mysterious and dark.

It would be too crowded to perform down on the floor, so Mac had modified our routines to the space available on the stage. Though well-rumpled now, we vocalists wore our matching suits and ties. At least the five-song set we had planned would seem more like a show.

We weren't sure how to get started. The audience ignored us. My stomach was jumping when Jimmy Lee, an angular guy in tight jeans with stringy, long dark hair, arm-hopped onto the stage. He gave us a friendly smile and, turning to the mic, hit a foot switch that turned on the spotlights. *Damn, hadn't even noticed those.*

"Ladies and gentlemen, boys and girls, we have the pleasure of hearing the Checkmates tonight. They've only been here from the Midwest for a few weeks, and they play over at the Hilltopper in Pittsburg. Let's make 'em welcome."

He took a step away and swept an arm in our direction to healthy applause. Pretty cool.

Dave stepped to the mic, took a deep breath, opened his mouth, and began to sing; it was clear sailing from there. We'd rehearsed these five songs this afternoon and done them twice earlier tonight. We didn't have to think about anything but performing. Almost everybody in the club stopped whatever they were saying or doing as we began, the dance floor turned into a sea of faces staring up at us as we went through our abbreviated dance moves for *You Can't Sit Down*. Though the song was a national hit and had a great beat, most West Coast people weren't familiar with an East Coast band like the Dovells.

Mac came to the mic after the applause died down. "That's for all of our friends here tonight from back east—back east in Pittsburg, Concord, and Pleasant Hill anyway." Yells and screams rose from near our booth in the back. "Thanks for being here for us, you guys. You treatin us like royalty and we appreciate it.

"Now we're gonna do a tune for our favorite gals, Sandy and Robin, and all their buddies. You babes out there somewhere? Lemme hear from y'all, now." More screams and yells.

Reno smacked a rim-shot to kick off *Walk Like a Man*. Though their records were big hits on the radio, we hadn't heard anyone around here singing the Four Seasons. Of course, I hadn't heard a voice like Dave's around here, either. The applause was deafening. *My Girl* gave the set a nice change of pace, and a few couples tried to slow-dance around on the floor overflowing with standees. *Denise*, a modern reminder of street-corner vocal groups was, once again, unique and well received. But *Shout* was the capper, and Dave and Mac fed off the audience's reaction as they worked the audience, getting everyone to shout, "Hey, hey, hey, hey." The crowd, everyone standing, responded with gusto, singing the simple lyrics with us right to the end. After a standing ovation, our first ever, we added the Seasons' *Stay* as an encore.

Jimmy Lee vaulted onto the stage before the applause died away. "Man, that was far out. Had no idea you guys sang like that." Behind me, Jimmy Lee's drummer said, "You got a hot band, Reno. Where you playin' again?"

When I got to the booth, I found that Bob had sent a round of soft drinks and a request for me to join him at the bar. I gestured for Carlos, but he shook his head and waved me on. I battled through the crowd. Everyone wanted to tell me they liked the band. It was gratifying in every way, but the buzz was leaking away. I was starting to feel shaky from the hour, the effort, and the strain of the last week.

"You guys show some promise, give you that. Lotta vocal talent." Bob perched on the same stool at the bar, up against the wall. A six-foot area around him, like the eye of a storm, seemed unnaturally quieter as the clamor of the crowded bar whirled around beyond us.

"Thanks, nice to hear. Been a challenging week."

He gave me a gap-toothed grin. "Bill says you're just ending the first week of a two-week contract with an option. He picking up the option?" *I guess Bill hadn't told him everything.*

"I think we're only going to be there one more week. Hasn't been easy following Buck Owens."

"He wants a rock club. Knew that would be tough on somebody." His brow furrowed. "Might be some folks in here who would make you an offer to play in their clubs, not likely enough for what a big group like yours needs, though. You be interested in playing here on a two-plus-two-week option when you're done at the Hilltopper, same money?"

"Even if it means starting in a week?"

"Yup."

A lot of people might consider the Town Club a dump. Okay, maybe it was. But Bob was the first owner who'd actually seen us and still offered to pay us to play music in his club. Ever. And the room seemed popular and welcoming enough to me. Bob explained we'd work five nights, 9 PM to 2 AM, and host two 6 to 10 AM jam sessions Saturday and Sunday mornings. Hosting, he said, meant we played the hours, but lots of musicians came in, and we could let them sit in and play and sing for as long as they wanted.

We had two weeks to turn this gig into two more, which was the closest the band had ever come to job security.

8
SIX MONTHS IN A DIVE BAR

*The problem with people who have no vices is
that generally you can be pretty sure they're going
to have some pretty annoying virtues.*

— Elizabeth Taylor

May 11, 1965
Hayward, California

WHEN I WALKED into the Town Club after we'd closed at the Hilltopper (on a high note), I noticed with pleasure that we'd have a nice-sized opening-night crowd. As I threaded my way toward the dressing room, Bob caught my eye and motioned me to his barstool "office."

"Couple items before you start tonight. First off, as you guys aren't local, you might not realize how heavily Latino Hayward is. We get a lot of Mexes in here. They consider this place part of their home turf."

I nodded, without much comprehension.

"And up the street, a contingent of Hell's Angels unofficially headquarter at the Doggie Diner." He referred to a fast-food hotdog stand built like a giant hot dog in a bun, about a block north on the opposite side of Mission Boulevard. You could see it from the corner outside the front door. "They share similar proprietary feelings, and these groups can get competitive around each other."

He squinted at me as if trying to see if he was penetrating my rock-hard skull. "We try to minimize the competition. For instance, we don't allow Angels to wear their colors in the club."

"Colors?"

"Hell's Angels' logos: on jackets, hats, shirts, bandanas, whatever might spark a flame just by seein' the damn things." I visualized images of Marlon Brando and Lee Marvin in *The Wild One*.

"Problems are most likely to arise when there's too many of one of these groups. Like, say we had an overabundance of Angels in here, they might feel like they had an edge, an opportunity, so to speak, to kick a bunch of beaner ass."

He leaned onto the bar and flipped his hand over. "Usually happens the other way around, though. Not meaning to sound racist but a lot of the Mexicans around here receive government checks on the first and fifteenth, and when they do, they pile in here to party hearty."

"I think I understand," I said, getting the drift. "There's more danger of a fight between these groups at the beginning and middle of each month, right?"

He nodded. "Course, a scuffle might break out anytime. Couple of individuals get plowed and decide to hold a punch party. That ain't no problem. Usually lasts less than a minute before my guys yank 'em outta here. But the situation can get serious when the Mexes outnumber the Angels. That has caused the Angels to show up in larger groups to protect one another. And the truth of it is, some of these people just like to fight. It's a blood sport to them."

"Man, sounds kind of dangerous."

"Which is why, if something starts, I want you to keep your boys on the stage and you'll be fine. That's the thing, stay on the stage.

"Point two: I know your band likes to do a little show out on the floor. Not the best idea here. We want folks to dance, seems to minimize the mayhem. Keep your singers on the stage.

"Final point: do not stop, I repeat, do not stop playing music if a fight breaks out. In fact if something happens when you're not playing, start playing. Comprende?"

When I'd finished laying it out for the guys on the first break, I added my opinion. "I haven't seen any other bands around here doing shows like we do, so I think we should consider all of us working on stage together all night anyway."

Personally, I wouldn't miss the shows. Despite the comedy bonanza of Les, Dave, and I trying, and usually failing, to do the splits in our little dance solos back in the Midwest, it would be too soon for me if we never did them again. We hadn't tried breaking out our individual moves in California yet, but I knew Mac itched to hitch up his pants and put his best James Brown wiggles on display. It would mean, however, that the singers would be standing around on stage a lot until we'd learned more songs.

"Me, I'm more worried about the Mexicans and Angels," Reno said. "I don't wanna end up the salami in a sandwich between those two." But no one fought anybody that night, and some guys at the bar, who Bob said were Hell's Angels, wanted us to know they thought the Checkmates were a hot band, and they'd be back.

We learned four songs during the week, picking up Don and Juan's *What's Your Name* for Dave and Mac, and *Big Girls Don't Cry*, which Dave, Mac, and I already knew from our Reflections days. Mac added *Walking the Dog*, a good soul tune from Rufus Thomas, and an easy party song, *Land of a Thousand Dances*, by Cannibal and the Headhunters. *Where do some of these bands get their names?*

Maybe learning the new songs impressed Bob; he picked up our two-week option before the end of the first week. Good. It was a relief, because I desperately needed to be distracted after a disturbing telephone call from Indianapolis.

"I know this will come as a shock to you, Larry," my mother's voice said through the receiver. "I talked with Pat. She brought the boys over to see me. I'm not going to talk about them right now, but she told me the divorce was final two days ago. I'm sorry to be the one to tell you, but there it is."

I hadn't even realized she'd filed the papers. I hadn't been completely sure Pat would go through with her threat. I'd been passive, I knew, letting things just happen, but how could someone get a divorce as easy as going to the grocery for a quart of milk? I tried not to let my mom hear the shock in my voice, holding in feelings being a family trait.

"Mom, how did Pat get a divorce without me knowing about it?"

"She said the attorney used some sort of abandonment clause when she told him she didn't know how to reach you after you'd gone to California. I'm so sorry, dear."

Who was Pat kidding? She always knew how to reach me—my folks always knew where to find me. Her mother must have pushed her hard while she was on the ropes. Maybe it shouldn't have come as such a surprise, but like a tooth extraction, there was a moment of intense pain and then a numbing sense of loss. I was officially unmarried. The last time I was single I was eighteen and in the second semester of my freshman year at Butler University. Despite my fears and misgivings, I guess I'd always believed, deep down, we'd find a way to patch things up and get back together.

After the second morning jam session of the weekend, I sat dog-tired, half-drowsing, on the curb outside the club smoking a cigarette, waiting for Dave and Mickey so we could go back to the girls' apartment. Warm, melancholy breezes off the bay tickled my cheek, wisped down my moustache, and teased my lip until chased away by the next zephyr. Hayward might have been considered a dangerous city in the East Bay, but it seemed peaceful and quiet in this Sunday's brilliant morning sun.

I tried to refocus my thoughts on my new life and quit brooding about what had happened in Indiana. Next week, the band was going to work on a solo for me. I'd chosen *Hang on Sloopy*, by the McCoys. I hadn't located a record player yet so I could listen to the record and learn the lyrics.

Dave winced in the bright sunshine as he came out of the club and held out his car keys. "Would you drive the car back to Concord? I've got another ride." He rocked his head toward an attractive dark-haired girl in sunglasses nearly my height standing discreetly behind him.

"Sure."

He nodded with a little self-satisfied smile and turned back to her. She grasped his arm and leaned into him as they turned up the side street toward the cars parked there.

As I drove Dave's car out of the parking lot, Mickey said, "Man, we've got to move house soon. Sandy's pissed. She got a phone bill with a bunch of Cincinnati calls Mac made to his wife. He got out one step ahead of the bill when he moved in with Reno, but I think she's pretty sick and tired of all of us."

"Robin's fiancé has probably had enough of us, too."

Mickey nodded. "Robin made that clear enough when she told me she saw some inexpensive apartments in Pleasant Hill. She said they looked pretty new. We should get some sleep, and go look later today with Dave."

Later that afternoon, we took a furnished apartment with three tiny bedrooms and an aroma of newness on Monument Boulevard in Pleasant Hill. We were excited to have our own place. I felt like we'd put down a taproot in California, but it was a big risk, not knowing where, or if, we'd be playing in the next few weeks. Dave had his own reasons for being pleased.

"Met this amazing girl in the club the other night, you know," Dave said, after we'd moved what little we owned on Monday afternoon. We could hear Mickey getting comfortable in his own room, playing his guitar.

"Oh? You really slipped that past me."

"Well yeah, I know. Anyway, she only lives about five minutes from here." He sat on the couch with a goofy grin on his face. "She's so cool, so smart, so together about everything. Besides, she smells really good. I really like her, Larry. I'm hoping I can keep her around for a while."

"What's this amazing girl's name?"

"Helen. Helen Nevarez."

"When do we get to meet her?"

"Tonight, I guess. She's coming over."

I'd only seen her at a distance, but close up, Helen was striking, breathtaking, a complex blend of health and beauty. For the first time, I understood how the phrase "a handsome woman" could be considered a compliment. Her face was classic, with a strong, straight nose and even, clean features, warm brown eyes, and full, dark lips. Thick, silky hair cascaded in dark waves over her athletic shoulders and flawless golden skin, her loose dress hinting at a voluptuous shape. Dave said she got a lot of exercise lifting her two bedridden brothers, stricken with MS, into the bath and their wheelchairs and beds each day. Her expression gave me the impression of calm and quiet competence.

When I saw how Dave's new girlfriend smiled at him, I couldn't help thinking that I should be looking for someone, now that I was officially single. Focusing on the desperate issues surrounding the band over the last several weeks had distracted me from the emptiness I felt reaching out in the night expecting Pat and finding no one. Now that I had an actual bedroom, an urgency was growing.

For the first set of the next week we opened with a couple of our newest songs. The harmony in *Let's Hang On* sounded a little iffy but not for long; after all, it was the Four Seasons, and we had their sound down pat. It only took about fifteen minutes for Carlos to have the band ready to play *Wooly Bully*. It was strictly a party tune, okay for this club, and it gave the singers a chance to rest our voices.

One night during the week, I swung onto a barstool with a questioning look for Bob. "Gotta proposition for you to run by your boys," he said, lighting up a cigar. "Suppose I offered you a six-month contract here, same money as now. I know you might get a bit more somewheres else but you might not, too."

I nodded, considering. "You could concentrate on your song list. I hear you repeating songs right now but I also noticed you're learning new songs every few days. In six months you could get the band tight, get enough songs so the singers are completely worked in all night. You'd have yourselves a big-time act. Be too expensive for me, but until then we'd both make out."

Dave had some reservations when I brought Bob's offer to the band. "I like the idea of having a steady gig, but this joint's kind of a dive, isn't it? And the jam sessions are killers. Couldn't we find something better in less than six months?"

Funny how perspective changes. A few short weeks ago when we played the afterhours we'd thought the place was a cool, exciting nightclub we'd only hoped we'd get to work in. Now, as Dave said, the place was a dive.

"Do we get more bucks, moola, jack?" Reno asked.

"No, no more money, but Bob's got a good point. We're vulnerable, kind of between being one thing and another. We're not a show band anymore but we don't have enough songs for our vocalists to cover a whole night, either. And the reality is, most of us are a long way from home if something goes wrong and we end up out of work. True, some low-lifers come in this place, but Bob's been straight with us. I think we should stay put, get ourselves together, be ready for whatever comes next."

9
MARIE

Love is a Naked shadow, On a gnarled and Naked tree.

— Langston Hughes, US poet.

May 28, 1965
Hayward, California

THE GIRL HAD her back to me when I slipped in between an occupied barstool and her. As the bartender came over to take my order, she gazed in my direction with exotic almond-shaped brown eyes shaded by long dark hair.

"Jake, I'd like a rum and Coke," I said over the crowd noise, trying my best to impersonate someone cool like Steve McQueen. "And maybe something for the lady I tripped?" *Did I really say something that idiotic?*

"That would be me, Marie." She pursed her buttery crimson lips in tired cynicism. "Tequila, Jake," she said, without taking her eyes from mine, "straight up with a lime."

I blurted out hello, retreating to the script, as Jake left to fill our order. Her cinnamon face puzzled for a moment. "Hello?"

"I've been told it's what people say to each other when they first meet."

"Oh. Well, hello." This smile was playfully mocking, and warmer. "Not the usual first thing I hear from a guy."

"My friend Dave told me hello works for him."

"Tell him to try tripping." I acknowledged her with a stupid grin and dopey head duck.

A few minutes earlier, Dave and I had been sitting at a table in the high-traffic path between the Town Club's entrance and the bar. The guys in the band tended to hang out in the farthest reaches of the room, but by midnight tonight even those booths and tables were packed. While the cool breeze from the open door was nice, we'd been bumped and knocked into repeatedly by patrons clawing through the crowd. At one rough moment my foot slid into the busy aisle by accident, and I felt someone trip. A girl with light caramel skin set off by a just-above-the-knees yellow print dress recovered her balance and stared back for a moment. I followed her progress to the bar until Dave poked me.

"Okay, there she is. Go talk to her."

"What do you mean?"

"You said you wanted to meet a girl like Helen. I think she's pretty close, don't you?"

"Oh, right. Guess I could go talk to her." I hesitated. "I don't know what to say. I haven't tried to meet a girl in a bar for—oh, let's see—ever." I hadn't been out on a date with anyone other than Pat since I was fifteen.

"Doesn't matter what, just say something."

"My mind is a blank."

"Listen buddy, it's like we've been introduced to everyone in here just by singing up there. Say hello, see what happens. If she doesn't want to talk, you'll know. If she does, she'll give you an opening. Never seen you miss an opening to talk, I'm sure you'll be fine."

Marie did want to talk, and soon conversation came easy for us. At the end of the night, Dave slapped me on the shoulder. "Man, must be going good; you've had that girl in an ear-lock every break. Ask her to breakfast with Helen and me. Maybe she'll want to come back to the apartment."

Though I was twenty-three my only sexual experience outside of teenage groping, had been with my wife—no, wait—ex-wife now. Pat and I had been lovers since adolescence, we knew everything about one other. We shared every secret, we were two parts of a single organism. Once we'd finally realized we'd been physically made to fit together, the floodgates opened. Unable to hold back the urges, we relished sex together, taking wild and crazy chances of exposure in satisfying our youthful libidos. We were thorough in our curiosity and examination of what created pleasure for each other, but there had always been a special sense of reverence and respect in our affections. That spontaneity had suffered as we became parents though, when our stifled moans of fervor were hidden behind closed doors. I might have wondered with casual curiosity what sex with someone else might be like but I'd never felt the compulsion to wander.

So, I was nervous when Marie agreed to come home with me that night. At least I was wearing my new, slim-fitting JC Penney snap-top boxer shorts. I hadn't realized how juvenile my tight white Jockeys looked until I noticed what my roommate wore. I'd blown some of my hard-earned cash on undershorts, but Marie didn't give me long to model them.

Our first night together began in a frenzied hunger that tore off clothes and drove us together for hours. Marie's sensual, carnal, and athletic passion was eye-opening and breathtaking. When something somewhere deep inside finally let go, I relaxed in some indefinable way for the first time in far too long. After, I gazed at Marie, eyes closed, spread-eagled across my bed without a trace of inhibition, a contented smile on her face. I tried to sort out how I felt about the urgent animalistic appetites I'd given in to. *Too late to be embarrassed now*, I thought.

After a moment, I curled over toward her. She murmured and rolled into me, and we lay, touching and cooling, in slanted bands of morning sun. Early traffic sounds from Monument Boulevard rumbled through the open window.

"We might have scared the squirrels," I said, probing. "We got a little loud for a while. At least you did."

"I should hope so. Mmm, it was very exciting." She was turned away from me, but I heard the expression on her face in the tone of her voice; she purred like a cat.

I managed, "Glad you came in last night," before, soothed and satiated, I fell off a cliff into death-like sleep, the girl close beside me.

"Thought you were never getting out of the rack," Dave said as I stumbled out into afternoon daylight, foraging for coffee. "Big news you're not going to believe, man. Mickey went to see Les Silvey's trio last night; he says Les wants to join the band."

"What?" That woke me up. Getting our fourth voice back, not to mention guitarist and musical arranger, would be huge. "You think he's serious?"

"Find out soon. He wants to talk to me and Mac before work tonight.

We'll have to leave a little early." He smiled and glanced toward my bedroom door. "Guess Marie will be riding in to Hayward with us tonight."

"Yeah, she will," I said, embarrassed by a smugness I couldn't hide. "But why does Les want to meet with just you two?"

"Don't know for sure. He might think we had a problem with how things worked out when we first got out here. Mac and I always understood he came here to play with his friend Jerry, though. He didn't let us down, we knew we were on our own. Might just need to reassure him."

That night, Mac and Dave were a couple of minutes late to the stage for the first set. Between songs, I asked Dave about his conversation with Les.

"Tell you at the break man. More to his deal than we thought."

Once we were off the stage, Dave steered me to a table away from everyone. He got some beer down before he spoke. "Les wants more than just to be in the band. He wants us to take his drummer and bass player, too."

I was startled. "To replace Carlos and Reno? We'd have to let them go? Damn, man."

"Yeah, it's fucked up, but what choice do we have?" Dave shifted his weight, disconcerted. "I mean we're talking about Les. With his voice, our vocals get better immediately and we can learn better songs. And the way he plays guitar for vocalists fits us much better than, well . . . Mickey. Tough, I know, but we gotta do it."

"Yeah, I get all that, and you're right but we need to talk about this . . ." I checked around to see where Carlos and Reno were. I didn't see Carlos, but I wouldn't be surprised if Reno was outside getting stoned, "…in private."

"Mac's going to stop by our apartment on the way home. We can talk it out then."

"Mac," I said, in the early morning hours after we'd gotten settled. "Dave, Mickey, and I discussed this to death driving home. Only thing we could come up with is, maybe he's bluffing. Maybe his trio doesn't have enough work. If so, Les needs a way to earn money or end up back in Indianapolis, same as us. And we've got work for several months, now. So you think Les might be bluffing about insisting we take these other guys—if so, do we dare call him on it?"

Mac stretched out on the couch. This wouldn't be a long meeting;

it was close to three. He was worn out, a little hung-over, and still had another ten miles to get home.

"So you willin to take the chance that the Bear ain't that set on bringing his boys with him? You thinkin if we push him to the wall, that stubborn sonofabitch would still come play with us?"

"When you put it that way," Dave said, "probably not."

"Mickey, what are the guys playing with Les like?" I asked.

He rubbed his chin. "They're pretty good. Bass player plays with a pick, heavy attack, does a lot of the vocals with Les. Drummer is very technical, doesn't sing. Les does most of the singing, and you already know he's a hell of a guitar player."

"What do you think about all this?" I asked him.

"I'm up for it. Hard keeping up with the vocals you guys sing, my voice isn't the best for it either—and then running the musicians and all. Doesn't mean I wouldn't keep doing it, 'cause I'm sure I'll get better. But with Les, I could concentrate on just playing and learning more."

Mac had another issue. "Les's guys ain't the problem for me. I been talkin with Joan about her and little Dani coming out here. Got to get us a place, get a car. We ain't making much money as is. How we gonna manage, when we got seven guys tryin to make do on six hundred dollars?"

Dave went into the kitchen. "Anybody want a Coke or something?"

"A beer, you got one," said Mac.

"Look, maybe you guys gotta put me out the door," Mickey said, saying what I'd been thinking. "You could get by easy enough without a second guitar."

"Naw man, can't, even if we would. Les already nixed that. Says you got to stay. He's not gonna put you outta work over this. He's got a lotta damn conditions on this deal." Mac noticed Mickey's face. "I don't mean 'cause of you, Mickey. Just sayin, he's acting pretty damn sure of himself."

Dave spoke over the sound of an ice tray cracking in the kitchen. "Les thinks we'll be a lot better with his guys. Says his bass player sings better than Carlos. With two guitars the music will be fuller, and he can take off his guitar sometimes so we can focus on big vocal tunes." Dave brought Mac his brew, and turned his eyes to me.

"Since we'll be a much better band, he thinks we should try to get paid more from the Town Club."

"Oh shit. You want me to go to Bob for more money, don't you? He won't do it, you know." I'd been blindsided. Somehow this was ending up on my plate.

"You don't know that," Mac said, "'less you go ask the man. You can at least ask."

I stood up, thinking out loud in desperation. "So I go to Bob, tell him we have to break our new long-term contract, because that's what we'll be doing when we fire Carlos, the guy who signed it. Here Bob, just sign this different contract. Don't worry that we're replacing half the band, we'll still be really good, in fact, probably fantastic, you can trust me on this. And oh, by the way, we want more money, too." I looked at them in bewilderment. "Are you guys nuts?"

"That's why you the leader, Larry. You know how to say that shit so Bob don't see it that way." Dave nodded in agreement, Mickey looked relieved.

"And, as an extra bonus, I suppose I get to let Carlos and Reno go, too."
How in hell did I get roped into this? Oh, that's right, I'm the bandleader.

10
CHANGING CHECKMATES

If you're not failing every now and again, it's a sign you're not doing anything very innovative.

— Woody Allen

June 1, 1965
Hayward, California

AFTER THE FIRST set Tuesday night, I pulled myself up onto the red leather barstool next to Bob.

"Boy, good things come in bunches, Bob."

"What good things might that be?"

"Turns out, our original guitar player wants to come back into the band. Always was our best musician, has a great voice. We'll be way better instantly. We're really stoked."

"All except Mickey, I'd guess." Bob shot me a toothy, shit-eating grin.

"No, we're planning to keep Mickey, so not only will we be better musically, we can concentrate on more impressive harmony songs."

"Okay, all right." He nodded, running a finger under his watchband.

"Presents something of a problem, though."

"Uh-huh, and that would be?"

"Means six hundred dollars for seven players, the way things stand. Seeing as the group will be better, much better, maybe you'd consider kicking us up another hundred a week. That's what we'd need to make this move."

"I see." He turned to gaze down the bar. "Paid five hundred to a damn good quartet six months ago, never gone over that 'til you guys. Based on seating, general overhead, cost of everything else, seven hundred would be over my budget. Guess I'll have to pass."

We both sat and considered the paint on the wall for a few minutes. Bob sighed and turned to me. "You thinking about reneging on your contract so you can hire this guitar player?"

"We don't want to do that, Bob. You've been great to us. This is the perfect place to build a band, just like you said."

I gave him my biggest, widest, most respectful grin. He pondered again.

"Look, I like your band, Larry, and I like you, but I'm dead serious, can't go seven hundred a week. Can't even give you hope I might change my mind." He looked at me to see if I had anything further to say. When I didn't, he said, "But I got an idea. Let me see if there's another way to find a hundred bucks. Okay?"

"Well, sure. How long until you know? Don't want our guy to get away."

"Could be tonight."

At the end of the fourth set, Bob sent a waitress to get me.

"Might have a solution for you," he said with a big grin. "I know Stan and Shirley over at Soul City pretty well."

Soul City was a weekend-only afterhours club. It was a large, well-lit, windowless rectangle entered through an attached smaller room that held a few additional booths and tables. Like all afterhours, liquor of any kind was banned, and like all the afterhours I'd seen, bottles of booze in brown bags were everywhere, though most people ducked outside to step on their soft drinks.

The stage was large, standing about three feet high above a generous dance floor. Decor was nonexistent, but it was the place to go for the late-night, weekend crowd to see bands, singers, and entertainers of all kinds from around the bay showcase themselves. Soul City was also the hot place for area insiders to see and be seen. At Bob's request, we'd sat in a few times there to advertise and draw audiences to the Town Club during regular business hours. It was fun, if tiring, but it gave us a chance to see some of the other bands in the area.

"Some of us go over there to hang out before the jam sessions on Saturday and Sunday mornings," I told Bob. "It's either that or sleep in the car. Tried going to Pleasant Hill and back before the morning jam sessions, but it's just too far."

Bob nodded. "Well, see, now you can get paid for that. Stan and Shirley agreed to take you on as the house band for the C note you need."

I studied him for a moment. "Means playing music from, I dunno, let-me-figure-this-out, nine at night to ten the next morning, two nights in a row. Thirteen hours each weekend night. Gee, who wouldn't want to do that?"

He gave me a playful nudge on the shoulder. "Oh come on, you know how it works. You play a few songs, then musicians and singers set in and you take it easy for the rest of the afterhours. Nothing to it."

I sighed and started to slip off my barstool to report back.

"Oh, one more thing. Guess they remembered the shows you did. They'd like a show out on the dance floor each night."

"So anyway, there's the bad news," I told my co-conspirators, once I'd pulled them together, out of Reno and Carlos's hearing. "But at least we get the extra hundred to pay seven guys."

"Couldn't get that Benjamin Franklin no other way?"

"No Mac, I couldn't. Bob says the room isn't big enough to pay us more. I honestly believe he'd let us go if I'd insisted."

None of us were crazy about this solution, but with no better ideas, Mac promised to call Les and finalize the deal.

Marie came back into the club and made her interest in me obvious. We were inseparable for the next several days; during daylight hours she acquainted me with new foods, like avocadoes ("alligator pears" where I came from), artichokes, tortillas, burritos, and the endless variety of Mexican food made from meat, beans, and rice. She showed me around the local area and introduced me to the sunny daytime pleasures of my new California lifestyle. No matter how tiring our exhausting schedule was at night though, the other things she introduced me to, set my senses aflame.

Sunday morning's sun was high and warm, but the full heat of the day hadn't set in as we lay crashed against sweat-dampened pillows. I couldn't remember who had started it but before I'd come to full consciousness, I'd been immersed in an intense erotic dream that revealed itself as delicious reality. I was reveling in post-orgasmic lassitude with a smoke when Marie sat up and whipped the sheet from across my waist, staring in mock surprise at my nakedness.

"¡*Que la chinga!* *Gringo*, you are a ghost. You are so. Freaking. Pale." She laughed at my reaction.

Gringo. A word I recognized from two years of disinterest in high-school Spanish.

"So you're a . . . a Mexican girl, right?" Hard to overstate how stupid that obvious fact sounded. Of course she was, I'd just never thought about it. I tried to distract her, throwing back her half of the sheet. Her honey-colored skin glowed from effort and her dark thicket of pubic hair gleamed in the sunlight dappling her body.

"Holy Moses, girl. You're so. Freaking. Tan. All over." I rested a palm on her belly and smiled up at her when she giggled.

She studied me, with a quizzical smile. "You weren't kidding, were you? You really don't know much of anything about Mexicans, do you?"

"Give me some credit, I'm trying to learn—you could say, from the inside out."

She laughed her neat, throaty laugh.

"Not my fault. Mexicans are pretty exotic in Indianapolis. Must be too far north of the border."

"My mom and dad were born in Mexico, but me, I'm a California *chica*, baby. I was born here."

She pushed me back and rolled up on top to straddle me, a lewd smile on her face. She began a wanton grind against me. I didn't think I was ready for a repeat performance but I was wrong. As I rose to the occasion, she wriggled her hips and I slid up into her slippery warmth. She arched her back and welcomed my intrusion with a furious roar.

I moaned as she ground her hips to impale me deeper, looking down with a slow, lascivious smile that engorged me further.

"Surprise," she said, panting. "Something else you don' know about me, I'm also part Chiricahua Apache."

"Which part?" I gasped, hands helping her rolling hips.

"The part that's got you surrounded, paleface," she said, beginning a relentless rhythm.

Early the following week, the new version of the Checkmates met for the first time. The four of us were sitting at a table when Les came through the front door with his guitar case and our new bandmates trailing behind.

Les stood as tall as Dave, but where Dave was willowy, Les was broad shouldered and slim-hipped, appearing more athletic than he actually was. Every strand of his wavy dark hair was in meticulous order, and his dark, piercing eyes missed nothing. He was boyish, competitive, and quick witted; often very funny, but hard to read behind his slick exterior. I hadn't seen him since he'd waved from the back of Dave's car when they'd disappeared west three months ago.

Les began introductions with Jack Beam, who dropped his bass guitar case on the stage and turned to shake hands. His oval face reminded me of a grown-up Dennis the Menace with a sprinkling of Howdy Doody freckles. His short blond hair had a little wave to the left.

"Jack was from Indianapolis before his family moved here," Les said with a grin. "Makes five of us from Naptown if we include Mac as an honorary Hoosier."

Les turned to a fair, slender guy with sandy-colored, thinning hair. "Our lone Californian, Don Hunt." Don displayed a cool-cat smile, and dipped a hand with drumsticks at us in acknowledgment.

I was forced to admit that when our new players got going, they sounded terrific. Don was rock steady, though he didn't have a big backbeat like Reno. Listening to Les reminded me again of what an excellent guitarist he was, especially for us, the way he created a frame for vocals rather than competing with them. The best thing to me was his taste, his skill to make his playing accessible to an average ear. He didn't play just to show off his chops, which seemed prevalent with guitar players around here. Sometimes, when we'd go see local bands, a guitarist would turn to hide his hand on the fretboard, afraid some watching guitar-junkie would steal his lick.

Mickey deferred to Les without question, dropping into a smooth rhythm with Jack and Don. Les told me he'd begun playing guitar only four years earlier, after he'd picked up a ukulele and played the first song he tried perfectly. A few weeks later, he'd gotten a real guitar and started singing and playing—without a single lesson—anywhere people would let him.

"Hey," Les said, "let's try some vocals, one of our old songs like *Denise* or something." It was wonderful to have Les's voice to sing with again. We got a nice four-part harmony going that gave me goose bumps. Despite Les's ultimatums, it seemed the change would be worth it. After rehearsal we sat near the stage with soft drinks from the bar dispensers.

"So, who's the leader here?" Don asked.

Mickey answered. "I'll sign the contracts 'cause I'm the union guy, but Larry speaks for us."

My de facto leadership role had required me to put Reno and Carlos on two-weeks notice last Sunday night. Reno asked me why we were letting him go and then nodded when I explained. Carlos, disconsolate, looked away without a word. *Reno had been doing more drugs than he'd let on*, I'd told myself, *and he'd let it affect his playing too often, but Carlos had never been anything but dependable.* I liked them both and resented having to fire them. Their disappointment had tugged at me every night since, and would even after their notice ended.

Don appraised me. "So what do we need to know, leader?"

I shrugged. "We play here five nights, Tuesday through Saturday, with two jam sessions, six to ten AM Saturday and Sunday mornings. And, soon as you guys start, we'll be the new host band at the Soul City afterhours Friday and Saturday nights."

"Afterhours?" Don said, like he'd bitten into a lemon. "Did you know about that, Les?"

"Yeah, they told me last week. Have to do it to get enough money to pay seven people."

Don's expression was inscrutable.

"So how's the pay thing work?" Jack said, staring at Mickey, who turned his gaze to me. We were getting down to brass tacks.

"Get cash in an envelope every Saturday night." I shrugged. "Then I divvy it up."

"Divvy it up how?"

The question surprised me. "We always split it evenly."

Jack's eyes went to Les, and Les glanced at Mac, who wouldn't meet his gaze. The silence got loud until Les cleared his throat. "Didn't you tell anyone about what we discussed for the married guys, Mac?"

"Didn't quite get it all finalized, man." He turned to me, though he spoke to all of us. "See, Jack's married, got his wife and boy with him. Can't make a go of it on a hundred dollars."

"You didn't tell us that," I said. "Did you have some plan the rest of us don't know about?" I wasn't mad, at least not yet, but as the leader, it was embarrassing that Mac had made some backroom bargain I hadn't known about.

Mac wandered around behind his chair. Maybe he wanted a clear path to the door in case he had to run for it. "You guys know I want my wife and kid out here with me, too. You heard me sayin the other night money was a problem."

"Saying, isn't the same as making some deal about how the money's paid out," Dave said.

"What'd you agree to, Mac?" I needed to know what was going on.

Les answered. "Mac told us you could get more money from the club owner, otherwise the single guys would kick in ten dollars a week so the married guys would get a little more."

"I told Les," Jack said, frowning at the floor. "Even a hundred and twenty is cutting it close. But no way can I do this for a hundred bucks a week." He shook his head. "No way."

Oh crap!

11
THE PHARMACIST AND THE NURSE

*Basically, I'm for anything that gets you through the night—
be it prayer, tranquilizers or a bottle of Jack Daniels.*

— Frank Sinatra

*July 13, 1965
Hayward, California*

HOSTING SOUL CITY every weekend night was a horrendous struggle. Those of us who lived behind the San Leandro Hills left for work early Friday evening and didn't see our beds until noon Saturday. At best, we got six hours sleep before grabbing something to eat, showering, and hustling back for the next hellish thirteen hours that wouldn't get us home until noon on Sunday, our voices and nerve endings ragged and raw.

One night in the Town Club, soon after the torturous schedule began, Mac pulled out a chair where the rest of us in the over-the-hill gang slumped, lifeless, between sets. "These all-night motherfuckers liken to kill me, man, but I got an idea. Benny Carducci's in here tonight. You remember Benny?"

"Short, dark-haired guy. Wears sunglasses even at night?" I said. "Talks about forty miles an hour? Sure, I remember him. He gave you those little red pills that were supposed to keep you awake for our trip to the beach on July 4th weekend."

Several of our club friends had decided to extend the long holiday weekend into a Monday morning beach party and took us along for our first look at the ocean. I stood in the sand gazing across an infinity of ocean, feeling the tidal pull of the Pacific within me, as I have ever since.

"We ended up dragging your sorry butt around Half Moon Bay like a corpse all day," I said.

"And you bastards left me out in the sun to fry. Woke up on the way home, bright red one side, pale as a fish belly on the other."

"I remember looking over at you, singing backup on *My Girl* with Les and Larry at Soul City," Dave said to Mac. "All of a sudden you started to disappear off the far end of the stage."

I chuckled, remembering how I instinctively reached for him as he started to tip away from me. "Got a grip on his tie and pulled him back on stage where Les and I held him upright. He kept right on singing like he never knew what happened." The audience on our side had shrieked with laughter, sure it was part of the act.

"Don't remember none of that shit," Mac muttered, "though you guys go on about it often enough."

"Man, you must remember sliding down into the splits during your dance solo," I said. "How a bunch of those pills exploded out of your shirt pocket." The little red capsules had bounced and skittered all over the dance floor. What was particularly strange was how everyone in the crowd instantly knew what they were.

"Place went nuts," Dave said. "Whooping and laughing. Guys, and girls too, all of 'em scrambling around on the floor scooping them up."

"People brought 'em back to me all night, probably got back more'n I lost. But look now, that was me who screwed up, not Benny. I just got mixed up, thought they was speed. Took one to stay awake so I wouldn't miss the beach, when I started gettin sleepier, I thought, shit—I need another one and crashed instead. Wasn't Benny's fault, though."

Mac pulled his chair in closer. "Benny's like some kind of renegade pharmacist or somethin. From over in the city. Really into bands and shit. Loves us, man. Helped me make it through last weekend. Says he'll help us all breeze through if we want him to. He's tellin me won't cost us nothin, either. Man's in the house tonight, if you up for talkin to him."

Benny was alone when Mac brought him back to our table. He'd left his rock-star entourage of nurses and young medical professionals at another table.

"Benny, these guys"—Mac's gesture included Mickey, Dave, and me—"live over Concord way, same as me. You been keeping me from wrapping my Mustang round a tree. They need the same as me."

With Joan and their young daughter Danielle now in Oakland with Mac, he needed a car. Somehow, he'd convinced Stan, one of the Soul City owners, to co-sign on a loan for a shiny new black 1965 Mustang, which he coveted above all other worldly possessions. Mac Brown seemed to find friends wherever we went in the world.

Benny's knowing smile beamed from an intense face dominated by thick black-framed shades and a matching heavy mustache. The shirt-sleeves of a two-buttons-open-at-the-neck dress shirt, covered with big blue and yellow flowers, had been turned back at the wrist over his candy-pink, sport coat's sleeves. He put an elbow on the table and raised an index finger to draw our attention.

"Guys, I have got access to some very far-out prescription-quality shit." He waved his fingers side to side. "Got some outlaw stuff, too. But what's bitchin' is, I'm hip to the pharmacology that makes 'em work the right way."

A waitress weaved toward our table, but Benny semaphored her away. He lifted his hand to us in benediction.

"I dig you are in a tough spot, my brothers, I do—crazy hours and all that—but I can assist. Lemme give you an example of how the proper use of drugs, can change everything.

"You cats probably don't think of coffee as a drug but caffeine, baby, caffeine changed the world, and it's a flat-out upper. But check this, when java hit Europe in the seventeenth century, the shit turned on the whole fucking economy. This is kinda heavy, I know, but coming to why it's important to you. Peeps who got into coffee back then could work longer and harder behind caffeine; gave 'em an edge over the other dumb moth-erfuckers. So they got the cherry jobs, more bread, and all the good shit that came with it."

He swept his hand in front of him as though sweeping away the vision of a Renaissance-bohemian coffee house. "Times change, now we got some new *molto bene* shit, can manage your engine way better than coffee. And that's the kinda edge you guys need in your scene right now."

I stared at Benny with fresh respect. "You are Doctor Feelgood, aren't you?"

"Just knowing the pharma, man, knowing the pharma." He shrugged, with a self-deprecating grin. "I dig how homo sapiens operate behind this shit, and I'm hip to your deal. Checkmates wigged me out first time I heard you cats. And since you changed players, you guys are just too fucking wicked good. Happens I'm a big fan and got the goods to help."

"So, you're saying you have drugs that can get us through the two all-nighters we have to play every weekend?" I had to ask.

Benny rocked his head, like, *now you're getting it*. "And most important, I got the know-how to use 'em. You cats need a specific regimen—which pharma, when, at what dose. Ain't just uppers and downers like most pill poppers think; these prescript drugs have their own personalities, characteristics. Each of you will react a little different to 'em."

Mac grinned and emphasized, "Benny says he don't want no money for this either, 'less it costs him outta pocket. Man just wants to help the band."

"But listen up now." Benny snapped his fingers and pointed his index finger at each of us, this time in warning. "This is some powerful, serious shit, dangerous to fuck around with. We do this, you got to follow my prescript, be true to your school. Use the way I say and nobody gets hurt, okay? We all down with that?" Despite my first misgivings, I had to admit I was impressed.

"Hell yes, I'm in," I agreed. "Last Sunday morning driving back to Pleasant Hill, I hung my head out the window hoping the breeze would keep me awake. When we got near home I said, 'Man, that was one trippy ride. Especially when those big white rabbits started running alongside the car through Crow Canyon.' Dave and Mickey looked at me like I was nuts until they figured out I was so fucked-up tired, I'd hallucinated the white mailboxes we'd passed along the road into galloping rabbits." I rubbed a hand up my arm to smooth down the prickles. "Damn glad I wasn't driving."

"Mean you weren't?" Dave said, pretending to be surprised.

"Primo," Benny said, and turned to wave a pretty Rubenesque girl from his table to ours. "Before we start next Friday night, want you cats fully revved up. This is Nurse Tedesco. She's going into your dressing room with you to take your pants down, one by one."

"Damn," Mac said. "Me first."

"Teddie, babe, shoot these cat's butts full of B-12, dig? And you have my specific permission to smack that little skinny fucker if he gets outta line." Benny gave Mac a crooked grin.

Trouble brewed on a different horizon. I'd started out admiring Don as a meticulous drummer and a serious musician. I appreciated his quick wit, though his sharp sarcasm could bite. Don's attitude toward me, though, had begun to deteriorate for no discernible reason unless he'd begun to resent my role as leader. In a skill-based environment, leadership tends to devolve to the most skillful in the group whether they're best suited to manage or not. In our business, that meant musicianship usually trumped managerial skills. I wasn't sure if me not being a player, or at least the lead vocalist, might be rubbing Don raw. Maybe he thought he or Les should be the leader. Whatever it was, I wasn't anxious to confront him about it.

At a rehearsal where we'd begun working on *Little Latin Lupe Lu*, a Righteous Brothers tune featuring Mac and Dave, the band clanked to a stop as both singers waved their hands after the first verse. *It didn't sound right to me, either.* Without thinking, I said. "Maybe the tempo's wrong."

Silence, but not for long. "What did you say, lame-ass?"

"Just thought the song felt a little slow, Don."

Don slammed his sticks down on his snare and stepped out from behind his drums scowling.

"So you think it's too slow. You, who has no what-so-fucking-ever sense of time. You, who can turn the time around on a whole song as a fucking backup singer with a tambourine."

To be honest, I hadn't known what turning the time around meant until I found out the hard way: it happens when a four beat measure gets cut in half by starting either two beats early or two beats late. The two and four get reversed.

"Hey man, take it easy. Nobody died and made you king of time."

My reply, not surprisingly, failed to calm him down. His face twisted into a mean grimace as he started to flick his thumb against his index finger in a spastic motion, mimicking how someone would snap their fingers in time, but instead doing it in an uncoordinated, jerky way, like he was flicking boogers off his thumbnail with his finger.

"Maybe we should use your time, Dunlap. Yeah, 'Dunlap Shuffle' time, goes about like this." He continued awkwardly flicking his fingers within inches of my face.

A couple of guys laughed and my face went red; I blush easily. Don had instantly dialed our difference in opinion up to nuclear; no warm-up needed. I turned to slink away.

"Play it however you want. Just saying what I thought."

He shouted at my back as I jumped down from the stage.

"Go play with your briefcase, briefcase boy. That's the only thing you're good at, carrying a little fucking cardboard fucking toy fucking briefcase, you numb-nutted idiot. And don't ever talk to me about music again, because you can't even spell it. That's who you are to me from now on—Briefcase Boy."

Don was referring to a cheap, black plastic-handled case I'd picked up to dump the band's contracts, song lists, receipts, and other details into. I wasn't what you'd call an organized guy by nature, but I'd had enough business experience to know that we, or sometimes just me, were agreeing to things we needed to keep copies of to avoid trouble. I brought it with me every night and even to rehearsals because I had a habit of misplacing things. Somehow, this simple case had become a derisive symbol of band leadership.

I didn't respond to Don's venomous attack with my own sarcastic cracks, as I might in normal circumstances. His rage meter going from 0 to 100 in seconds troubled more than angered me. He seemed ready to boil over into physical violence at any moment. I was sensitive about my lack of musicianship, though, in reality, I'd had as much training in vocal music theory in high school as any of us. Don had sniffed out my insecurity and gone right for the exposed nerve.

I sat cloaked in a black, sullen cloud reading a paperback in a back booth until rehearsal ended. Don and Jack lived close enough to go home for dinner, while the rest of us found a local fast-food restaurant. Don's tirade still seethed in the back of my mind.

Dave opened his sandwich to swathe the burger in catsup. "Man, Don lit into you today. What was that all about?"

I tried to laugh the subject away, but Les started flicking his finger like Don had. "The Dunlap Shuffle. Funny stuff. Have to remember that."

Les's insensitivity overwhelmed me at times. Didn't any of them recognize the level of contempt I'd felt from Don? Why wasn't anybody outraged on my behalf? Why hadn't anyone spoken up for me? Occasional disagreements in the band happened; we'd get mad and over it in an hour, or a day or so. Don's attack felt more personal and vitriolic than those between the members of any of my groups.

"He got some kinda hard-on for you," was Mac's considered opinion.

"Not surprising." Les concluded, picking up an onion ring. "You are such a wise-ass sometimes." *The pot calling the kettle black*, I thought. I couldn't stay silent any longer.

"And you're not?" Knowing he'd gotten under my skin, Les just grinned.

"Anyway, I wasn't being a smartass. I just questioned the tempo, a simple musical opinion. I don't think we should scream at each other for having an opinion. Besides, you set the time when you started the song. If anybody was going to be offended, should have been you, Bear."

"Something about you pisses him off." Les downed another crispy onion ring. "Maybe if you just stay cool around him for a while, it'll wear off or something."

I wasn't going to get any sympathy from Les.

12
A MESSAGE IN THE DESERT

> *Drugs are the religion of the twenty-first century.*
> *Pursuing the religious life today without using*
> *psychedelic drugs is like studying astronomy with the*
> *Naked eye because that's how they did it in the first*
> *century A.D., and besides telescopes are unnatural.*
>
> — Timothy Leary

July 19, 1965
Hayward, California

FRIDAY NIGHT BEFORE midnight, Les and the four of us from Pleasant Hill and Concord gathered at a back booth where Benny opened up his office, a black leather pharmaceutical case. Its contents were arranged into compartments filled with pills, capsules, lozenges, and caplets of several sizes, shapes, and colors. A partition snapped into the top came down to make a little table inside the case. Benny told us he used the set of tools held in place by elastic straps behind the partition to alter dosages as needed. Hard not to be impressed.

"Now, long as you guys heard the sermon and skipped the booze, we'll start with 10 megs of Dex. That'll get you through closing, equipment break down, and setup at Soul City. I'll check you around three AM, but unless something hairy happens, we'll go with Black Beauties next. These babies come on strong and will keep you grooving for four good hours. Bummer is, for most people, you come down then for about an hour before they turn back on at half-strength for a couple more.

So at seven tomorrow morning, we've got to go with a small dose of Benzedrine to get you through the low, and then the two together should get you home safe to your pads."

"This isn't costing us anything at all, Benny?" Dave was still surprised. "You're really doing this for us out of the kindness of your heart?"

"Dave," Benny said with a smile. "Like I said, big fan."

He got our attention while he dumped little yellow pills out into our palms. "Very little booze after you scarf these down now. Liquor jacks up the dose, screws the monitoring so, *mortale*, dangerous." I didn't say anything, but telling Mac booze made the drugs more potent wouldn't dissuade him from drinking, more likely the opposite.

"Just the four of you? Other guys not into it?" Benny asked. Les had disappeared when Benny started handing out the pills.

Mac shrugged. "They thinkin they don't need 'em since they don't go over the hill, but I think some of them leavin the option open."

I got Benny's attention. "Benny, Dave and I have girlfriends who'd like to stay on the same schedule with us. Would you help us with that?"

Doctor Feelgood beamed his benevolent smile. "Right on brother, bring 'em over."

By the time the midnight set got going, I felt great, burning to perform. Mac, Dave, and Mickey seemed like they were, too. The music pulsed through me, energizing me. I hated for each song to end, and the set was over too fast. I wanted us to keep cooking right up 'til closing.

At our regular booth, Marie and Helen jabbered at each other face-to-face, like long lost friends. I found a spot to break in. "Man, I am so stoked. Dexedrine may be my new best friend. Would've never guessed pills could make a person feel this good."

"You've got to get more of them," Marie said.

"Oh yeah? Why?"

"Word is, sex behind Dexies is great. You can last forever." She and Helen giggled. I made a mental note.

The girls drove to the afterhours with Benny's troupe while we packed up our gear. I didn't know whether Les or anyone else had talked to Don, but I avoided him, and though he wasn't friendly, at least he hadn't freaked out on me. I wasn't sure what Don and Jack, or Les for that matter, thought about the rest of us doing this pill thing, but they had to like the enthusiastic way we helped load up their equipment.

About the time the edges of my exuberance began wearing thin at Soul City, our personal pharmacist popped up in front of me. "You okay?" I felt an insanely wide smile crack across my face.

"Solid. Black Beauty time."

Benny palmed and slipped a thick black capsule to me. "All you cats are fixed." He checked his watch. "Suck this down in the next fifteen for max effectiveness."

Mac was amped up, and he pulled me to the dance floor to hear a singer named Roger Parker singing his tune *She's Lookin' Good*. He wore an odd-looking, short-sleeved suit, but the song was infectious and had just begun hitting the local charts. Mac wanted to learn it—sounded good to me.

The Black Beauty didn't have quite the same effect as the Dexie when it kicked in. It was harsher, grittier, but I still wanted to sing, and talk to everybody around me, though the pent-up energy made my teeth grind.

The hot topic of conversation that night was the government's recent expansion of the draft to send more soldiers to somewhere in Asia called Vietnam. Nobody here expected to be impacted by it, but several had family members or people they knew who might be vulnerable. Dave pointed out that he'd seen it coming and joined the reserves so he wouldn't get called up. He'd gone away for four months of active duty last year and was required to attend a summer camp every year to avoid getting drafted. If fact, he was due to report in a few weeks, but he'd written a letter to the army to get out of it, he'd told me. Good thing, because we'd have a hell of a time keeping our gig without him.

"Johnson's drafting 'em so they can get rid of all those college dropouts in Haight-Ashbury," one of Benny's friends said. I enthusiastically leaped into the heated discussion that erupted with lots of opinion and little knowledge about who would or wouldn't get drafted and why.

We usually hoped other bands would get up and play so we could rest, but though it would pull me away from the conversation, I couldn't wait to get back on the stage. The morning flew by, and before we knew it, it was 6 AM and we were back at the Town Club, along with Benny and his case. The guy was our White Rabbit. One pill took me higher, another brought me down. Maybe we actually could survive these weekend gauntlets after all.

One afternoon, my mother phoned. After I'd caught her up on our adventures in California, at least the ones that wouldn't give her a heart attack, and she'd brought me up to date on Cheryl's love life and how well she was doing in school, she put Dad on the phone.

"Larry, your mother's never gotten comfortable with the Ford Falcon's stick shift, so we've bought her a new car. The Falcon is yours if you can work out how to get it to California."

I jumped up and looked at the receiver in astonishment. I told Dave and Mickey the news while we were getting ready for work. Having another vehicle would take a lot of pressure off Dave.

Mickey pulled a towel off his wet hair. "I might be able to help. I'm trying to figure out how to get to my sister's wedding in Indianapolis. Half my problem would be solved if I drove your car back here Sunday after next, but I still haven't worked out how to get back there yet."

A couple of nights later, Mickey found me at a back booth with Marie.

"My folks got me on a flight home leaving next Saturday at midnight. Someone will drop me at your parents' house Sunday after the wedding, so I can get your car for you." He spread his hands.

"But I'll have to miss most of Saturday night. Les says he can cover for me if it's okay with you. He thought you should be the one to let the other guys know, though." If Les approved, everyone else would be fine, including Don. Cool of him to protect my authority.

As usual, I slept through most of Sunday, recovering from the long weekend. Before it got too late in Indiana, I called home. "Mickey came by and picked up the car this afternoon," Dad said. "Told your mother and me he was leaving for California right from here. We gave him plenty of money for gas, so I'm certain he's on the way."

When Dave had first driven out here from Indianapolis, they told me they'd driven straight through in about thirty-five hours. But they'd traded off driving and only stopped for gas and food. Mickey would need rest stops along the way so at the earliest, I estimated he wouldn't get here until late Tuesday. *Man, he'd probably be dead for the gig, even if he got here in time. I better call Les if Mickey can't play or isn't back in time.*

When I woke Tuesday, Mickey's bed was still made, and his room untouched. Leaving Marie to sleep in, I stepped onto the block of concrete landing outside our second floor apartment. A rare coastal fog had drifted inland overnight and was burning off now; it would be a beautiful afternoon, I thought, as I leaned on the rail breathing in the ocean air from the sea channel to the north. A white Ford Falcon, identical to the one I expected, sat parked on the street below. The car was locked when I went down to check. It'd be a hell of a coincidence if it wasn't mine. But if so, where was Mickey?

When I decided to consider the mystery over coffee and toast, I found a note next to the Falcon's keys on the kitchen table.

> Dear Larry,
> Your car's downstairs. Your folks are really cool. They gave me gas money for the trip plus extra for food.
> I drove straight through from Indianapolis, which wasn't a problem since Benny gave me plenty of bennies (ha ha) to keep me awake. Something happened coming across Arizona though. It's hard to talk write about. I got this feeling to stop the car when I was driving through the desert. It was getting late and the sunset was yellow and orange in front of me, quiet and beautiful. I walked out beyond the cactuses so far I couldn't see the car until the feeling told me to stop. I sat on the ground and it got dark and the stars came out. I sat there longer and a voice I knew was God told me I couldn't stay in California, not even one night. It told me I had to leave right away. I packed my stuff and by now I'm on my way back to Indiana on the bus. Tell the guys I'm sorry for bailing on them and I'm sorry about sticking you and Dave with extra rent. I know this has to sound really weird to you, but when God tells you to do something there just isn't any choice. Tell everyone I will miss them and think about them often.

Your friend,

Mickey Smith

13
BEAR ANXIETY

*Just because nobody complains doesn't
mean all parachutes are perfect.*

— Benny Hill

*July 28, 1965
Hayward, California*

WE ADAPTED QUICKLY to Mickey's absence, and getting a little more money each week helped, but not enough for us to quit Soul City. In the last few weeks, we'd gotten comfortable with each other, at least musically. We'd added several new tunes, and we were sounding better than we ever had. If our immersion in music, playing, singing, and listening to other bands and singers every waking moment didn't kill us, I could see us coming out of this a pretty damn good band.

One evening, sitting at a table with Dave on an early break, I said. "What's surprising to me is how you ever got to be our lead singer in the first place. I couldn't figure how you got so good, considering your audition. I mean, not at first anyway. Of course, that was before I realized you sang all the time, no matter what else you were doing. I remember coming over after school and you were sitting in your bathroom on the crapper, singing at the top of your lungs, with extra emphasis at certain points. Somehow, in spite of how weird that was, we still became friends."

Dave nodded. "Best friends." Conversation and nightclub noise surrounded us, cigarette smoke from the ashtray in front of him circled his head.

"It was just lucky you got into the Aristocats." My phony condescension was transparent. "Hadn't been for Hasty and Chuck insisting we take you, it wouldn't have happened."

"I remember. Told me you wanted somebody more like Frankie Valli, or the falsetto tenor from the Del Vikings."

"Right. Somebody with some real talent."

Dave rubbed an eyebrow, hiding a grin. "Those guys must have made a compelling case for me."

"Yeah, they kept telling me if we didn't take you, we couldn't sing as a quartet anymore—nobody else with a falsetto wanted to sing with us."

"Persuasive argument." Dave tipped his beer for another swallow.

Jack came up to the table, wearing a worried frown. "Larry, think we've got a problem. Les and I were just rapping, and bam, right in the middle of a sentence, he got up, said he had to leave, and walked out the door. I followed him out to the car. He's sitting out there now, and even though it's almost time to go back to work he won't come in, won't even talk about it."

Jack had assigned himself the responsibility of timekeeper, getting us on and off stage at breaks. Considering my relationship with punctuality was more of a passing acquaintance than a commitment, I was happy to have him do it. He checked his wristwatch.

"We should be up on the stage right now."

I got to my feet, wondering what this was all about. "Don't rush getting guys up there, Jack. Give me some time, maybe he'll tell me what's eating him."

The few stars able to shine through a light cloud cover and a distant streetlight did little to illuminate the parking lot blacktop, cooled after a hot day, but still warm. The humid air carried the club chatter out to where Les stared through the windshield of the driver's side of Jack's car. I had no idea what to expect when I slid in next to him. His hands gripped the steering wheel at ten and two, the way it's taught in driver's ed. All the windows were closed. He didn't acknowledge my presence.

"Hey, Bear. How ya doing?" He focused slowly, as if his consciousness had returned from somewhere distant and he'd just noticed me beside him. His glare turned accusatory.

"What are you doing here?"

"Came to remind you we need to start the next set. We have to go in now." He returned his frozen gaze to the windshield.

"I won't be able to go. You'll have to play without me."

What?

"Actually, we can't play music without our guitar picker, and that'd be you." I spoke lightly, with a nonchalance I didn't feel.

He angled his head toward me, his eyebrows beetled. "You'll have to try. Figure out something. I can't go in."

What's going on here?

"Why, Les? What's stopping you from getting out of the car?"

No response.

"Are you sick? You need a doctor?"

"Nobody can help me. Just leave me the fuck alone. My problem, not yours, not anyone else's. Go away."

"Can't do that, man. Got to help you, or you got to come in and play." I hesitated, not sure what to say or do. "Look, if you tell me what's going on, I'll try to find some way to help."

"Do you think I care what you do?" he exploded at me, hysteria flaming from his eyes. "Can't you see I'm goddamned dying here? What can you do about that? Are you a fucking cardiologist?" His furious voice thundered in the car's interior.

I drew back against the passenger door, stunned, though I tried to hide it. His panicked fury scared me, but I couldn't help responding to his fear with sympathy. *Do people having a heart attack get angry?* In those pressure-packed weeks back in Indiana when Les had become our guitar player, and almost immediately our fourth singer, I hadn't had the opportunity to get to know him well. I'd been pretty distracted with my own problems just about then, too. He came across as funny and smart, charismatic, but always under a tight rein, always maintaining a certain distance from the rest of us, which I'd attributed to being a couple of years younger than the rest of us.

"I can drive you to emergency if you need me to. Just tell me, I'll take you, swear to God, right now. We'll figure out the rest later."

"I told you, you can't do anything. Emergency won't help. They don't know what the fuck they're doing anyway. Just leave me alone. I'll either die or I won't."

His vehemence betrayed how much he hated me seeing his vulnerability, and his pained eyes told me he'd rather die alone out here than be pitied. After a few tense minutes, I tried a different tack.

"Tell you what. I'll go back in the club for ten minutes. We'll find some way to fill the time. But if you haven't come in by then, I'm coming back out here to get you. Okay?"

Les's knuckles had gone white where he gripped the steering wheel as he stared into some internal terror. Certain he'd heard me, I took his silence for a yes and hopped out.

I was out here trying to deal with this crisis because I thought that was my job as the band's leader, but I had no idea how to deal with what Les was experiencing. I'd never had any indication of Les having any serious medical problems before now. I was concerned for him, felt responsible for helping him as a brother band member, but I also worried about what would happen to the band without this job. No clues popped up to help me figure out what to say or do if he didn't come in, or worse, if something happened to him.

"Look," I said, back with the guys. "He's having some kind of problem. I don't know what exactly, but he thinks it's got something to do with his heart."

"We can take him to a hospital," Jack said. I eyed Bob on his barstool. He wasn't watching the stage, and so far, he hadn't said a word or called me over.

"Tried, he won't go. Think he might have already been to emergency, whatever they did, it didn't help."

Don started to get out from behind his drums. "I'll talk to him."

I stopped him. "Don, I've been talking to him already, and you can at the next break, but right now we've got to get some music going, and you've got to play drums."

"You trying to tell me what to do, Dunlap?"

"I'm trying not to lose our job while we figure out how to help Les." I turned to Jack before Don could reply.

"I thought I saw you talking with the guitar player from the Vagabonds, is he still here? Think he'd sit in with you guys so we can play a couple of songs? Maybe Les can work this thing out by then."

Jack returned in a couple of minutes with a long-haired guy in a buckskin shirt and stone-washed jeans who jumped on stage with a grin. "Thanks for helping out," I said, shaking hands.

He slipped Les's guitar on, fiddled with the knobs, and strummed the strings a couple of times. Les was very sensitive about anyone playing his guitar, but he'd have to go along with it this time. I couldn't help hoping they wouldn't play *Kansas City—man, every guitar player who sat in with us played that chestnut.* Sure enough, though, the chords to *Kansas City* soon clanged out into the club.

It didn't look like Les had moved a muscle when I got back to Jack's car. "I hear a guitar in there," he said, still gripping the wheel as if he was in a death race. "But he could play a guitar, just like ringing a bell. Go Johnny go . . ." The lyrics from Johnny B. Goode rang out through the club's open door, audible even inside the car.

"Yeah, yours. Got a guy sitting in for a couple of songs."

He nodded. "Give me just a couple of minutes and I think I can play."

"Great."

"You're going to sit there and watch me?"

"Sure."

He didn't say anything, but after a minute or two he sighed and popped his hands off the steering wheel as if breaking a magnetic connection. He seemed to check something deep inside before dropping his arms to his sides. After a moment, he spoke softly and reached for the door handle. "Let's go."

We got through the rest of the night without discussing the incident. In the car, on the way home, Dave and I wondered about what had happened to Les, but we came up with nothing. We would have to let the thing go and hope that Les's heart would beat the way it was meant to from now on.

14
A CALL FROM INDIANA

A lot of people refuse to do things because they don't want to go Naked, don't want to go without guarantee. But that's what's got to happen. You go Naked until you die.

— Nikki Giovanni, US poet.

July 29, 1965
Pleasant Hill, California

THE HARSH RING of our new telephone woke me the next morning before I was ready to get up.

"Hello," I said, groggy. *Must be Wednesday*, I thought, trying to clear my brain until the voice on the phone drove out everything else.

"Larry?" a sweet, tentative voice asked.

"Yeah." My mind reeled. "Pat, is that you?"

"Yes."

Oh my God.

"Do you have a minute?" The familiar sound of her voice came as a cherished shock that ran through me.

"Of course." I was glad I was alone. *Dave had stayed at Helen's last night and, thank heaven, Marie wasn't here.* I hadn't told her about Pat yet. I didn't think of it as being secretive, they just lived in different compartments of my life.

My heart stopped for a second. "Is everything okay? Are you and the boys okay, Pat?"

"Yes, we're fine. My family's helping us. We're all fine, even Georgie." *Georgie-boy, our pet Sheltie.* My eyes moistened. "Are you okay?"

"Yeah sure, sure. Everything's okay here." *I should have added more, but what?*

I hadn't talked to Pat since the Phone Call in St. Louis. The memory of getting ready to perform that evening four months ago was as fresh as if it had been last night.

After surviving two weeks in Birmingham—where we'd nearly starved before experiencing a mix of civil rights unrest, bomb threats, nightly booings, and scattered death threats from patrons who didn't appreciate us, or our music—we managed to make it to St. Louis. We never seemed able to get warm enough there, in the high-ceiling hotel rooms with smoke- and age-darkened crown molding, walls covered in ancient blue patterned wallpaper. Abe Lincoln might have asked for extra blankets in one of those drafty, chilly rooms. A giant, half-constructed, arch-like structure near the Mississippi River was just in view from one of our frost-encrusted windows.

I was excited to talk to Pat when one of the guys called me to the room phone, but I could sense something wrong, even before she spoke.

"Larry," she'd said, her voice scratchy with emotion. "You've got to come home. I mean right now, tonight." She hiccupped. "You've been gone for more than three weeks. I've barely talked to you. I don't know if you're okay or not. Everything's more important to you than your family. We can't live like this. I can't live like this."

"What?" I said. *She was ordering me home like a disobedient child*, I realized in shock. Three floors below, visible through the tall, heat-leaking windows, people walked heads-down along the snow-covered sidewalk, hunched into themselves in the approaching twilight. The view was real and how I knew this wasn't a nightmare.

"If you don't, my mother is going to help me get a divorce."

We never threatened each other like this. She knew not being good with ultimatums was one of my most defining character flaws. Mary Lou, Pat's mother, my implacable and unconquerable enemy, must have seen her opportunity and struck.

"A divorce?" The word felt so strange in my mouth that my lips struggled to shape it. *Inconceivable. We'd been connected at our souls since we were young teenagers.*

"What?" I said again, stalling, fighting the instinctive response to be heard, searching with desperation for the right thing to say . . . and failing.

"I've been thinking about things, about us, all of us." Pat's voice brought me back to the present. She hesitated. "I wondered if we should get together, face to face, discuss what's happened, you know. I mean, I thought I knew what I wanted, what you wanted. I'm not so certain anymore . . . Are you?"

"I don't know how to answer. Everything got away from me so fast . . ."

"That's what I mean. That's exactly what I mean. Everything happened so fast."

"I wish it was possible, but how?"

"I was going to suggest that I come out there to you. I've checked flight schedules and I can buy the ticket—if you want me to, that is."

"You want to come here?" I was shocked, and I tried to weigh the implications of Pat here in California, with me. In a way, I wanted to see her again more than anything, but what would happen? I was torn, unable to answer a question I never imagined I'd be asked. I dropped into a chair and stared at the linoleum kitchen floor.

"Yes, I do. I want to come out there," Pat said. "Actually, I think I need to, to see you. Only if you want me to, though."

"Yeah, yeah, sure. That would be fantastic." *So much for weighing implications.* "When would you come?"

"I can get the best fare starting a week from this coming Monday. I thought that might be good for you, too. If it's not, I can change the date."

"I'm sure that's fine. I can't think of any reason why it wouldn't be fine." I sounded like an idiot, but the realization of how little we'd thought this out was just dawning on me. *Jesus, Larry, stop it. Try to be gracious, you oaf.*

"Can't wait for you to get here, Pat. Maybe I can show you San Francisco, even though I haven't been across the bay yet, myself. A lot to see here, though. The band plays some crazy hours, so we'll have to figure it out."

"I don't want to be in the way, but I'd like to see everything I can.

What you're doing, I mean." She sounded more confident, more assured. "I'd better go now. I'll make the reservations and mail you the details. The boys send their love. We all send our love."

I choked my way through, "Love you guys, too, Pat." *God, hearing her voice was so amazing.*

I hung up the phone, processing our conversation. Pat, who I feared I might never hear from again, would be here—*here*—in a few days. *She'd said she loved me.* Of course we loved each other, but we were also divorced. I should have said something, but again, what? I wished I could see the boys. Impossible of course, but it would be so great to hug them. Too late, I wished I'd asked to talk to them.

I watched Les's next anxiety attack strike Friday night. As we ended a late set, Les almost threw his guitar in the direction of his amp before jumping awkwardly from the stage and rushing out the door without a glance left or right.

"On me this time, Dunlap. Anyway, I know him better than you do. I can fix this." I shrugged. *Be my guest, Don.*

Les's problem seemed to be psychological. There had to be some way we could help him, but he refused to talk to any of us about it. A sign of how serious everyone took this was that no one teased him.

An attitude change had migrated into the band when we changed players. The new normal had become poking at each other's weak points. Little was held sacred, and comments were often scathing. Les was one of the bigger distributors of jabbing digs, but no one mocked him about this new problem.

The rest of us sat together, waiting for Don, lost in our own thoughts.

I thought about Pat and I after last January's New Year's Eve party. I remembered the lush, sweet harmony of *This I Swear* from her favorite album, *Best of the Skyliners*, still whispering in the smoke-hazed air. We lay slumped together on the couch, listening, and still a little tipsy, undecided about whether to straighten up or go to bed and worry about it tomorrow. A slight trace of color on the pale skin beneath her eyes hinted at the late hour.

For a few months during our years at Murray State, Pat had sung with me and Dave and another couple for school functions. When we'd sung this song, everyone swore her soaring soprano made us sound just like the Skyliners. Those were the only few times we'd officially sung together. I would never hear this song without thinking of her.

Before we rang in the new year last night, Mac had suggested we create a stage act like his old band, the Casinos.

"Mac wants you guys to sing in nightclubs?" Pat's face swiveled toward me, like a meerkat lookout when I told her. "You mean, like as a job?"

"More like local clubs, weekends, but it's just the booze talking anyway, honey. We're a vocal group, not a band. We sing in the bathrooms at North Methodist, not to real audiences. We don't even know the right songs." I put my arms around her and pulled her close. "Isn't realistic, could never happen."

"Yeah, you're right." She curved her slender body snugly into mine and held her lips up for me with a sleepy smile. Our mouths found each other in an arousing, rum-sweetened, cigarette-tinged reminder of how attracted we'd always been to each other.

Perfectly molded together in sweet moments like these, I felt whole.

"God, what am I going to say to her?" I blurted out, as the unexpected phone conversation I'd had with my wife, no, ex-wife, burned through my memory.

"Whassat?" Mac said.

"Sorry, didn't realize I'd said that out loud."

"Only one person in the band allowed to go crazy at a time, bubba."

Don came back into the club, while Jack waited at the side of the stage, hopping from one foot to the other as if he had to pee. "Is he coming?" Jack asked.

Tight-lipped, Don wagged his head and hopped onto the stage. Jack glanced at me. I shrugged and stepped out into the night. When I got to the car, it was like last time—Les's hands crushed the wheel, and he was deep into a thousand-yard stare.

"How's things, Bear?" Nothing.

"Set's starting, gotta come play."

"Can't."

"C'mon man, you know you gotta come in."

He gave me a stony glance before turning his brooding gaze back to never-never land.

"Just tell me what you're feeling, man. Give me a chance to understand."

"I feel like I'm dying. Will that shut you up? I feel like my heart is going to stop beating. I'm listening for the next heartbeat to not come. I know I'm going to die, I'm just waiting for it to happen."

I pondered his words. "Les, you're not going to die sitting here in this car."

His eyes blazed up again. "And how the fuck do you know that, Larry? Does your heart stop and you wait, wondering if it'll ever beat again? And then it doesn't, and you're sure that's it, the end, and then it suddenly does?"

"Will it help if I sit here with you until you feel better?"

"Doesn't make any difference what you do." He sighed from his depths.

I sat without disturbing Les for a few minutes. "Not to be a smartass, but have you considered that if you're going to die, you could do it just as well in the club?"

"You are such a prick. You really don't give a fuck about me at all, do you? All you care about is getting me back on the stage."

"Both, man. I'm certain you feel like you're going to die, I get that it's completely real to you. On the other hand, you have failed to die previously, so I think the odds are you're not going to die this time, either. I'm trying to keep us from getting fired. What happens to you, to our band, if we lose our gig? Will being broke help you with this problem? All I can tell you, Bear, is you've got to give us some guitar music."

Les turned to me, eyes smoldering. "I'm going to get out of this car and make myself walk into the club. I'll probably keel over before I even get to the door. If not, I'll probably die on stage in front of everyone. And my death will be on you, you sonofabitch. You hear me? You'll be the one who killed me."

"Listen, man, I'll be with you, every step. Like I said, whatever you need, I'll try to find, or get, or say, or do. But I think you gotta do this."

With a quick rush, like he didn't want time to think, he dropped his grip on the steering wheel, got out of the car, and walked toward the club. I hurried around to the driver-side and closed the door he'd left open and then ran up next to him. His gaze accused me of betrayal, but his legs kept moving.

He strode to the stage, and the crowd noticed him coming in. I hoped Les wouldn't take the little ripple of applause following his progress the wrong way as he strapped on his guitar. He was a very private guy. Don counted out a song, and we began the set. Other than Les's impassive expression, no one would've guessed there'd been an issue.

As we struggled with our horrendous schedule, Les had a few more of these episodes, especially in the jam-session hours. One lasted half an hour past a break in a morning jam session. We struggled, got bass players to play guitar, sang a cappella, whatever we had to do to get through. I was thankful Bob's patience wasn't exceeded. And to keep things in perspective, we ran into times in those late mornings when not one of the singers was able to crawl onto the stage, when we were passed out sound asleep or too woozy from exhaustion. Les always was the last one standing, the iron man, playing right to the end, even when Jack and Don were at their final gasp.

15

PAT

Live to the point of tears.

— Albert Camus

August 9, 1965
Oakland, California

I PEERED INTO THE same sun-shattered sky I'd fallen through a few months ago. Pat arriving here was surreal. What had it cost her, I wondered, to call and ask to see me? What must it have cost her to confront her mother?

My last visual memory of Pat and our boys was waving goodbye to them on the porch of our duplex as Dave and I drove away. I could barely grasp the divergence of our lives since then.

The jet's giant engines whistled down, and passengers emerged to descend the wheeled metal steps. Anxious as I was to see her, I struggled to keep my eyes on the door as it revolved open. *Was there any way this could work out for us?*

Then she was there, on the stairs, her slim figure in a yellow sundress, and her corn-silk blond hair up in a ponytail made her still look like a teenager; she was a golden girl standing out from the other passengers. She came to me at the edge of the tarmac, and my stomach tightened. We embraced in the awkward way strangers do.

She looked around at everything but me.

"I'm finally here, aren't I? California. So sunny and bright. Palm trees.

And the air . . ." She turned into the terminal, and I followed. "It's hot and sticky in Indianapolis."

She made an abrupt turn to gaze into my eyes. She stared from one to the other trying to tell if I was still the same person she had known. I understood, because I searched her face for the same answer.

We kept conversation to a minimum as we got her luggage out and into the Falcon. I held the door for her, slid behind the wheel, and pulled onto the MacArthur Freeway.

"Dave and I have an apartment behind those hills on the right. We've a ways to go." Monday afternoon traffic flowed smoothly outside, but inside the car, time stood still.

Pat nodded. Her hands worked a thin cotton handkerchief in her lap. "How is Dave?"

"He's fine. He's staying somewhere else, so we can have some time alone."

"We need that." She turned toward me, staring in a wary, horrified way. "Oh God Larry, how did this happen to us?"

A thousand things flashed through my mind before I had to shake my head and simply say, "I don't know."

The sparsely furnished apartment Dave and I shared felt tawdry and insubstantial as I wrestled her suitcase upstairs. I pointed out the simple floor plan; open kitchen, living and dining room, three small bedrooms down a short hallway with a bathroom off the hall to the right.

Pat chose to perch on a kitchen chair in a corner where windows spilled sunshine onto the chipped, imitation wood table.

"Do you want a Coke, or something?" I spoke gently; she seemed so wound up that the slightest thing might set her off like old dynamite.

"Something, a Coke, water; doesn't matter."

I poured Coca Cola from a can I'd found on a bare refrigerator shelf into a cobalt-blue aluminum glass that had once held cottage cheese. I smiled uncomfortably, setting it in front of her with my left hand.

"Dave and I are not the best housekeepers."

Her eyes fell to my ring finger, where no sign of a wedding ring remained. I jerked my hand out of view. Her taut expression softened, as she turned to me and tears pooled in the corner of one eye, and then the other, before trickling down her cheeks. She didn't blink or brush them away. I moved my chair nearer, and her eyes were intent as she followed me but held no invitation to touch or hold and comfort her. My eyes stung and neither of us spoke.

"I didn't want a divorce," she whispered. "I got scared. I just wanted you to come home."

I put my hand on the table and then so did she. A pale line showed where her wedding band had been. I covered her hand with mine and she wept openly. My control melted into hot tears. For long minutes we cried, our grief inconsolable. We mourned the innocence of our childhood love; we grieved as parents of our own children. We agonized in the unfairness of the haphazard and tumultuous world we'd been pushed out into through our mothers' flesh. We wept for the first time, one among many firsts we'd shared, for the sheer emotional pain of bedrock loss.

Pat leaned into me, and I took her onto my shoulder in a clumsy embrace across the chairs.

"Your hair is shaggy. Don't you get haircuts here?" She smiled through her tears.

I shrugged and tried to grin. "Well, I am in a rock band, you know."

I led her to the couch where we sat pressed together, exhausted. Her body felt thinner than I remembered.

"So much has changed so fast." Pat looked around for a tissue. I brought her a wad of toilet paper from the bathroom. Her red and swollen eyes held a question for me.

"Before anything, Larry, I have to ask. Do you still love me? After all that's happened?"

"There will never be a day in this life when I won't love you," I said looking into her apprehensive eyes, knowing it to be as true as anything in life can be. But with a sinking feeling I tried to hide, I doubted it would be enough.

"That's what I hoped—I love you, too. It's why I'm here. And for David and Danny—they love and need their daddy."

All the air was sucked out of the room as I heard myself make annoying strangling noises. I jumped to my feet to circle the couch taking deep breaths until I could speak again.

"Do you think they remember me, Pat?"

"David does, I know he does. Sometimes he asks where you are, and when I tell him you can't come home right now, I know it makes him sad. He even tried to write you a letter. Danny isn't old enough to do anything like that, but I'm sure he remembers, too," she finished fiercely. "He must."

"I'm a bundle of nerve endings, can't think straight. It's not simple." I was drained from trying to control my whirlwind thoughts and emotions.

"How do you think I feel, Larry?" Pat's eyes blazed for a moment and then dulled. "I didn't want to jump into everything this way."

She leaned back, shoulders slumping. "I'm really, really tired. Is there somewhere I could lay down? It was a long flight, and it's three hours later for me."

I lifted her suitcase onto the bed in the vacant bedroom that had been Mickey's.

"Go wash your face. You can rest here; I'm just outside if you need anything."

As she turned to the suitcase, I slipped out and found a blanket for her. I took an opened Coke to the beach chair out on our tiny concrete landing, hoping to calm my stormy emotions.

Seeing Pat again unleashed my first memory of her. I was sixteen and she fourteen when Hastings Smith Jr. introduced us. Only seven years ago, but it felt much longer. We were so young then.

Hastings had been the catalyst for everything important, and by that I mean good, that happened to me in my last year at Shortridge. His influence continued to echo down through the years, even here in California. Besides introducing me to my future wife, my vocal group might never have existed if it hadn't been for Hasty. Compelled by an urge to sing a song called *Silhouettes* on the radio one night, I recruited two neighborhood brothers who didn't have the first idea how to sing, either. Fortunately, one of them knew Hasty, who did. He joined us and became our mentor. His first observation was a practical suggestion for me.

"Larry, if you want to sing these harmonies, it would help if you actually knew how to sing." He was a year and a half younger than me, but for reasons like this, I was soon looking up to him.

Though the semester had started, he convinced our nationally acclaimed choir director, Don Martin, to accept me late into Shortridge High's Acapella Choir. After Christmas break, Mr. Martin elevated me into the elite Madrigal Singers along with Hasty, and Chuck Tunnah, who'd become a new member in my group—and enrolled me in my first music theory class. I was learning fast, and the Aristocats, as the group was now named, were improving, but not fast enough. I wanted more, so Hasty volunteered me into the church choir at North Methodist where both of our families attended.

Several of the singers who straggled into my first choir practice were high schoolers as young as Hasty and me. My eyes widened at one achingly beautiful, blue-eyed, fair-haired girl in a fluffy sweater before I looked away in confusion.

In the echoing church corridors after rehearsal, Hasty casually asked what I thought of the choir, and then grinned.

"You liked that blond girl, didn't you? Patricia. She's in my class at Shortridge. She's also on the freshman cheerleader squad." His grin widened. "Lucky for you, she's my friend."

He walked backward through the metal door in front of me, eyeing me with a knowing grin as we pushed out into unseasonably bright February sunshine and the traffic noises from the busy intersection at Meridian and Thirty-Eighth Street.

"I could get her phone number for you, you know."

"No. I mean . . . listen." I took a breath. "She is really, really pretty, Hasty. Why would she want to talk to me?"

He nagged me until I agreed, but I only knuckled under because even if he did get her number, I wouldn't call her anyway. What would be the point? Hasty didn't seem to understand—cheerleaders and beauty queens were unobtainable to geeky guys like me.

I studied Patricia from the corner of my eye at the next couple of church choir rehearsals. She was small and slender, about five two, I guessed. Her flawless skin looked carved from some soft, porcelain-smooth material, her hair a pale confection of golden waves and curls. I listened to her gentle laugh, at ease with her friends. *She was perfect, like she'd just walked out of heaven.* I decided not to think about her anymore. It wasn't difficult; she was way out of my league.

A few weeks later, Hasty pulled me aside. "I talked to Patricia about you calling her." I'd hoped he'd forgotten. "She said it would be okay." My chest tightened.

"Don't be nervous, just talk to her. Give her a chance. She's a really sweet kid. She'll like you when she gets to know you, and I know you'll like her."

Easy for him to say; girls hung around him all the time. He was completely at ease with them. To me, girls remained an alien species: attractive, exotic, painfully tantalizing—and totally incomprehensible.

It didn't hurt that Hasty had everything going for him. He was darkly handsome, he fell out of bed in the morning with a perfect flattop that he never had to gunk up to keep in place. His family was wealthy—he and his parents played golf and lunched together at the Meridian Hills Country Club every weekend. He was going to letter in golf in his freshman year, the next best thing to the basketball team. He even had a cool, sophisticated name. And oh—did I mention he was funny, humble, and brilliant?

After dinner, a few evenings later, I sneaked off to my parents' bedroom and picked up the extension, determined to get the torture over with. The interminable stomach-clenching wait for the cheerleader to come to the phone felt the way I imagined falling off the Circle Monument downtown might feel. Saliva rose in the back of my throat. Swallowing, I thought, *I could slam the phone down right now. No one would ever have to know . . .*

"Hello?"

"Uh, hi. Patricia? I'm Larry Dunlap. I'm sure you don't remember me. Why would you? Don't worry about it, though, it's okay. I'm in the North Methodist Church choir with you. Hasty said it was okay if I called. I mean he talked to you. About me phoning . . ."

Yikes. Larry—shut up!

"Oh. Hi." Her tone sounded disappointed, or worse, disinterested. "I can't talk long. We just finished dinner and I have to wash the dishes." I nodded, understanding already—*she was going along with me calling just for Hasty.* I shouldn't have been surprised.

". . . but if you'd like to call back after eight thirty, I could talk longer. I should have my homework finished by then."

"Okay, well goodbye . . . what? What did you say?"

"I said, about eight thirty, I could talk for a few minutes, before it's time for bed, if you'd like to call back."

"Oh. Sure, that would be great. Perfect, actually. I have homework, too." *It sounded as if this angel was asking me to phone her later tonight. No harm in making sure.* "So you do want me to, to call you back at eight thirty, right?"

"Okay," she said while I was still puzzling it out. "Talk to you then. And Larry?"

"Yeah."

"Please call me Pat."

When I called her, we talked for half an hour. She told me about her day at school, and her friends, who I'd never heard of, cheerleading practice, and some of her classes. I told her about singing with my group, some classes I was bored in, and asked why she wasn't in the school choir. She had too many activities, she told me, but she'd tried out for a lead part in *Carousel*, the musical the school's Thespians Club was going to put on. We'd talked together like two normal people.

16

DELTA MOONLIGHT

To make love to the one true person who deserves that love is one of the few absolute rewards of being a human being, balancing all of the pain, loss, awkwardness, loneliness, idiocy, compromise, and clumsiness that go with the human condition. To make love to the right person makes up for a lot of mistakes.

— Dan Simmons, The Rise of Endymion

August 9, 1965
Pleasant Hill, California

I LEAPED TO ANSWER the apartment phone before its ringing disturbed Pat's nap.

"Hey man, how are things going with you and Pat?"

"I don't know, Dave. We're both so ripped up it's hard to talk to each other. There was a point when we talked about the boys that I thought I was having a heart attack."

"Sorry. Say hi and tell her I'm looking forward to seeing her. Maybe you'll have some things worked out by then. Wanted you to know I talked to Helen about getting Marie to stay away from the club the way you asked. Helen told her if she didn't want to blow it with you, she needed to get hold of herself and give you room to work this out."

Dave cleared his throat. "Not so sure it took, though. Marie's hot-blooded, and I'm pretty sure Helen's sympathies are with her."

I heard the shower stop running as I hung up and tried to remember if I'd left out clean towels and soap for Pat.

She stepped out onto the second floor landing in a white summer dress piped with blue, the same color as her eyes, and a pale sweater swung over her shoulders. A light breeze had picked up, the way it always seemed to at sundown. Lurid streaks of neon pink and lavender began to fall behind the hills to the west.

"The sunsets are spectacular here."

I took her arm. "You've got to be starving. Let's get something to eat."

The night was full dark when we pulled away from the drive-in taco stand onto Contra Costa Boulevard. "Have you decided if you like tacos?" I asked.

"Um, yum, crunchy, spicy. Yes, I like them."

She sat with a leg folded beneath her, facing me in the darkened car. Posed that way, she reminded me of high school, cruising the TeePee, Knobby's, and the Ron-de-Vu drive-in restaurants on Indianapolis's north side. I never imagined I'd have the chance to feel this way again.

I began to suggest a movie, but Pat had another idea.

"Would it be okay if we just rode around? The air is so soft and warm. I like the feel of it blowing through the window. Anyway, I shouldn't stay up late; I want to be on California time when I get up tomorrow."

Near Walnut Creek, I turned north on Ygnacio Valley Road into the desert night. Pat leaned back in the seat, her eyes closed, while the breeze, hinting of night-blooming jasmine, chased her hair. The moon and stars in the clear sky silvered everything inside and out as we drove along the country road. At Highway 4, I pulled right and then onto Leland Road until we came to lights on the left. I slowed the car.

"That's where we played when I first got here." She turned to gaze at the well-lit, isolated Hilltopper as we passed by.

"You play tomorrow night, don't you?"

"Yes." Headlights swept across her face; she seemed more relaxed. "Way over toward the bay, but I figured you'd want to come with me."

"I'm looking forward to it. But please, for now, can we keep going?" She sighed. "I could ride like this forever."

We drove though the night on country roads that ran through little Contra Costa delta towns. I knew the area just well enough not to get too lost. Outside of the tires humming on the pavement and the air flowing through the windows, silence surrounded us.

"Can't help remembering a song you sang in high school when you were in *The King and I*."

"That was in my sophomore year, after you'd transferred to North Central." In a passing light, I saw a smile glimmer on Pat's face. "You hate musicals."

"Yeah, well . . . I came as your dutiful boyfriend. That huge auditorium at Shortridge was packed. I was nervous for you. Something special happened when you stepped out to sing your solo. You seemed so small and alone in the single spotlight.

"And then you looked out right at me and sang *I Have Dreamed* just to me, your voice filling me, and the whole theater. It's stupid, I know; Caleb Mills Hall must hold twelve hundred or more people, and the place was packed. You couldn't have seen me, especially not with the stage lights in your eyes."

Pat leaned back into the seat, listening to me.

I shrugged. "Sounds goofy, but I got a little queasy. I knew right then I would ask you to marry me someday. I'd always been in love with you, but in a schoolboy crush kind of way. In that moment, I understood you were really my girl, and I couldn't imagine a day in my life without you in it to take care of."

My left little finger and thumb searched my ring finger and came away empty. The wind swept across the open windows, but it remained quiet inside.

"I almost died when you went off to North Central," she said, "and then when I had to go to Warren Central and you were in college at Butler, we were torn even farther apart . . . I got so afraid something would happen to us; I always wanted to be with you, too."

I felt her eyes on me. I thought I heard her say, "Now look at us." I glanced over to see that her head was down, pale strands of hair floating in the desert breeze, surrounding her as though she were underwater.

"The day we got married, Dave Dunn was holding my tux coat for me when I told him, 'I don't want to go to the church. I don't want to get married. Something's wrong with this.'

"And he said, 'The way I see it, if you love Pat, you've got to go down to North Methodist and marry her. But if you don't, then I'll drive you anywhere you want and stay there with you.'

"He wasn't just my best man that day; he was a good friend."

Pat fell so silent I thought she might not say anything. But then she spoke, her voice faint.

"I would have been devastated."

"There was never any chance I wouldn't show up. The important thing is, even back then I knew, gut deep, something was wrong, but I didn't understand what. Now I do. I don't think we ever had a chance, honey."

That was the first time I'd used a sweet nickname with her. It just slipped out. It would only make things worse.

"I can barely follow what you're saying. Maybe I'm not all the way here in California yet."

"I know, let's just drive."

Several minutes later, when I caught a stifled yawn from the passenger seat, without a word, I turned toward Pleasant Hill.

Outside of her bedroom, I intended to give Pat a chaste hug and say good night, but when I breathed the scent of her hair, my body trembled, remembering hers.

Like finding a dog-eared page in a well-read book, my senses filled with the thick, aromatic warmth of us entwined in the front seat of my '55 Ford—our enchanted carriage, dimly lit by streetlights diffused through windows steamed by our inner furnaces. The intimacy of kissing had been heaven, and the slow and gentle progression of breathtaking discovery and fondling more than enough to satisfy us in our mobile sanctuary through the summer nights before my senior year.

And then one fall evening, in a tactile and emotional ascent that overwhelmed all else, our young bodies joined, and we discovered how perfectly we fit together—as though we'd been shaped for each other. First times only take place once; we wanted it for ourselves, and we believed the innocent joy of that connection would last us forever.

She was my lover, my best friend, and a stranger, all at the same time, I thought, caught in a warped moment of time. I struggled with an overwhelming desire to drop my hand to cup her bottom and pull her into a familiar embrace. I remembered how she felt naked, spooned into me, and how the two of us would drift as one, satiated and safe into sleep. I hesitated.

I wasn't certain how she'd respond—nothing she'd said or done invited me into intimacy, but even if she did, it would be a betrayal.

While I yearned for those feelings of safety and home with her, it would be dishonest—we weren't safe, and we weren't home.

Thank God I held back. She turned at the door.

"Tomorrow, could we find some quiet place to talk, somewhere away from your apartment? Please don't be offended, but I feel a little strange here, in a place where you live and I don't." She paused before speaking.

"It's disorienting."

17
STAR CROSSED

A man is given the choice between loving
women and understanding them.

— Ninon de L'Enclos

August 10, 1965
Pleasant Hill, California

AT A LATE breakfast over Denny's coffee, Pat pointed out that we couldn't afford to eat out during her entire visit, as Dave and I usually did. She wanted to buy some groceries to make meals for us when we had time. We stopped at a Safeway, sharing the expense, and made a few other stops to pick up personal items she needed. The warm afternoon was well along when we lugged sub-shop sandwiches and soft drinks into a deserted little pocket park slivered between Monument Boulevard and the freeway. Trees and bushes, thick with greenery and peppered with impatiens and geraniums, offered us a narrow island of privacy, though highway traffic murmured and growled behind them.

"Where do we start?" Pat asked after we'd sat across from each other at a shaded picnic table.

"I want to say one thing first, Pat." I tore at the clear plastic wrap on my sandwich. "I'd never considered the possibility of us splitting up. Even though I seemed to fail at everything I tried to do, couldn't find the right job, or dreamed up crazy, impractical schemes—when even I had begun to believe your mother's opinions of me—even then, in the face of all that, your faith in me seemed unshakeable. Every day, you gave me the strength to face a world I seemed unable to solve. I never even imagined the possibility of us not being together, not until . . ." My mouth fell shut.

"Until I called you in St. Louis," she finished, barely audible. "Larry, I wanted you to come home. I needed you, I would have said anything."

Her voice had sounded like a stranger's when she called me that night. She been so distant; I couldn't touch her or read the expression on her face.

"I'm sorry I got so steamed, Pat. I never meant to swear at you. I didn't mean it when I told you to go ahead and get a divorce," I said. "All I could hear was that your mother was promising to put you back in school if you'd leave me. Buying you away from me with something I couldn't give you." Pat's personal goal had always been to get her diploma. It was instilled in each member of her family that to be a success, the minimum they needed to achieve was a Bachelor's degree. So far her older brother, near completing medical school, and sister, studying for a master's in nursing, had met and exceeded that standard. No doubt her younger brother would, too.

After I slammed down the phone I'd stared at it in shock, isolated in a quiet eye of a storm of movement as Dave, Mac, and Les rushed around joking, getting ready for the show. I'd lashed out at her in frustration; racked by conflicting emotions of betrayal, failure, and guilt. I'd never spoken to my wife, my love, my closest friend the way I had that night.

After an eternity, I walked unnoticed into the hotel room's bathroom and turned on the shower; the only place I could think of to be alone, to try and grasp the reality of what had happened between us. The stream of water made a hard splat as it hit the ancient tub and echoed throughout the room. The water was too hot, but the burn felt good, distracting me from the shock. After a few minutes I began to tolerate the heat, and the enormity of the disaster began to seep back in, and I felt like I'd been hit by a train. I turned the hot water faucet up until I gasped, hardly able to stand it. I kept turning down the cold and turning up the hot until the faucets wouldn't turn any further. I burned and hurt and gulped as the water fell around me, surrounded in the rising steam. I had no concept of time passing; no thought of anything but regret that I couldn't turn the water hotter.

Maybe things could have gone a different, better way that night, but then again, maybe not. I've wondered, at times, what would have happened if they had. But I've come to believe that moments like these are not singular events but tipping points, a culmination of many forces, most of them undetectable. After that phone call, the rising tide of change crested and began to flood our futures. Change rippled in ways large and small to drive us far apart—until now, here, pulled together—where we sat lost in our own thoughts.

Pat twisted at the plastic wrap around her sandwich but failed to open it. "Do you remember the night we got arrested when we went to see the band that was going to play with you guys? Just a couple of days before you left for Birmingham?"

"Not something I could ever forget." My eyes followed a misguided dragonfly swooping across the table to perch on the far edge, beating its wings in slow cadence.

"It was horrible in that jail, Larry. I was petrified all night. Sunday morning, when my mom and dad came to get me—what they said about you—was very difficult to hear. They scared me." She gazed into a patch of dappled sunlight between the trees.

"I never got the chance to tell you about that. You didn't get home until late Monday afternoon, and when you did, you were exhausted. You slept for hours and hours. We barely talked that night."

I remembered. She was right. "We spent Tuesday morning getting you ready for Birmingham. The boys and I got a quick hug before you left with Dave. We didn't have time to talk then, either. I felt as though you didn't have time for us anymore."

My heart sank: *this is the way she remembers our last moments together.* I hadn't realized how different things had looked to her. *I'd failed her and the boys again.*

"I never meant to give you that impression, Pat. Nothing has ever been more important than you guys. I thought we'd only be gone for two weeks. We were just going to break in the band, and then the booking agent wanted two more . . ."

I searched for some way to make her understand. "Everything got so screwed up. I never planned to play out of town. The guys all agreed, we were only doing this to make a little extra money in nightclubs around Indianapolis."

Her eyes accused me. "Did you tell me that? Did you call and reassure me of that?"

Did I? I wasn't sure, I couldn't remember. I crumpled the paper bag our sandwiches had come in, and launched it toward the trash can in self-disgust. Startled, the dragonfly lifted to spin beyond the hedge in search of a more peaceful pool or pond.

"If we could've just . . . If you'd only . . . Who knows." Her head dropped, and we both stared at the ground searching for answers in the neatly mown grass. I shook a couple of cigarettes partway out of my pack and offered them to her. She took one and I took the other and lit them before she went on.

"You'd only been back in Indianapolis for a few weeks, when I heard you'd suddenly left for California. You hadn't even called me. How would that make me feel important to you? What my mom and dad said about you when they picked me up at the jail made me mad, but then you were gone, and what they'd said seemed to be true."

"You never called me, either," I said, as if such a lame excuse meant anything. My stomach churned. This was the moment I dreaded. I hadn't decided for sure whether I'd tell her until now.

My voice faltered on the next words. "I realized there was a way out . . ."

Her brow furrowed, her expression puzzled.

"I didn't want to see it, Pat, but it was right there in front of me. You wanted a divorce, something I could never have imagined on my own. And then I started to consider it . . ."

She drew a startled breath. "Larry, that's horrible."

"I know, I know, I thought so, too. I tried to resist even letting the thought into my mind, but like a light in the corner of your eye, you try to blink, to glance away, you know—but sooner or later you have to look. The only person who'd always believed in me was you; once you didn't, there was no one left who did, including me. All I had to do to stop the constant blame was to let go—do nothing. Accept the inevitable. Give everyone the final failure they'd always expected from me."

Pat stared at me, mouth dropped into an O shape.

"Splitting up has been unbearable Pat, but we were never going to be able to stop her. Your mother was always going to get you away from me and ruin me with the boys sooner or later." My gaze slid away. "The way she hates me runs bone deep, she'll never change."

Pat didn't say anything.

"You know, I thought when *In The Still of the Night* started to break, things might change. I got a taste of being looked up to and appreciated in Chicago: the free meals, signing autographs, cars and drivers to take us places, the way we were treated like rock stars up there. I thought for a minute I'd be able to show everyone I wasn't just a shiftless dreamer."

"You didn't have to prove anything to me."

Did she really believe that?

"Of course I did—to you, to me, and sooner or later to David and Danny. And to our families, especially yours." I felt my lips twist into a bitter grin. That was before I understood that even if I found a cure for cancer, her family would never see me as anything but a harebrained loser.

"You thought us being apart would somehow make things better?"

I crushed my cigarette out on the table's concrete foundation.

"Pat, they're your family. I knew they'd welcome you back and keep the boys safe, something I seemed incapable of doing. The future seemed like an abyss I was never going to be able to get us across. I knew your mother would make sure things worked out for you, especially in ways I couldn't." My words tasted bitter. "Like how she'd pay to send you back to college with me out of the way.

"Don't you see?" Here was the crux of what Pat had to understand. "Your mother planned the end of us, the same way she planned our marriage. Get those sex-crazed kids to the altar, cover up their filthy sin. Later we'll pry her away from the juvenile delinquent who corrupted her, make sure those children are raised properly, and put our daughter back on track."

Pat's eyes went wide. "That's crazy," she whispered.

"You think so?" I held out my palms. "Really? Look at the pattern. Your mother took over our lives the moment she found out you were pregnant, and she's run them ever since. She called my mom and set our future in stone before I even knew I was a father." I caught her eyes.

"First, they announced a big, phony June wedding, as though it was planned, never mind that you were *sixteen* and still a junior in high school. It was never *our* wedding ceremony, Pat. It was your mother's big hypocritical staged production to hide your pregnancy. I think she convinced my family that your father's career and her family's good name would be destroyed if anyone knew the truth."

"But she asked me who I wanted to invite. I chose my own bridesmaids."

"I bet she had to approve them." She didn't answer.

"I was allowed to pick a best man and a couple of the ushers. Window dressing. An elaborate play. We were actors reading lines. Meanwhile, backstage, my parents agreed to go along with Mary Lou's plans. I think my dad worried about being embarrassed by your mother's threats." This was the wedge that had been driven between my parents and me.

"But does how we got married make so much difference? We loved each other anyway, didn't we?"

I sighed. "Of course we did, but pregnant or not, Pat, I never got to propose to you. You never had a chance to look into my eyes, and see that I chose you, and you alone, above all others. So you could look into mine, and freely accept me without any reservations. Those are powerful bonds."

I moved on.

"Did you tell your mom you wanted to go to Murray State? Did you tell her you wanted to skip your senior year of high school so you could spend your pregnancy studying for a high-school equivalency test? So you could go to some country college in a wide spot in the road in Kentucky? For Christ's sake, Pat, after you transferred to Warren Central for your junior year, you were one of the most successful kids in your school; junior prom queen, straight-A student, cheerleader, in all the choirs, top of the social ladder. Did you get an opportunity to make your own decisions about any of this? I'm asking because I sure didn't."

Pat thought for a long minute. "Maybe not, but I remember Mom saying Murray State was the only school that would accept my GED; and my sister Katie was only an hour away at Austin Peay if we needed any help with David. The way she explained it, things made sense. We didn't have many options."

"That is such bullshit. So completely not true. We didn't need to disappear into hillbilly country to go to college."

I saw doubt in her face—*at least she was listening*.

"There were plenty of options to go to a college at home in Indianapolis, where our friends and family would've been able to help us when we needed them the most. Why wouldn't there be?"

I jumped up and begun stalking back and forth across the green grass.

"Why couldn't we have found a way for you to complete your senior year of high school? We could still have gotten married, I could've gone back to Butler, or even spent a year working until you'd graduated." I hated battering at Pat this way, but I couldn't stop these pent-up feelings from exploding out of me.

"As soon as possible after the wedding, our families split the cost of a ninety-nine dollar piece-of-shit car that used more oil than gas to rush us out of town before you started showing too badly. What did they expect us to do if that old fucking Pontiac had broken down? Which, by all rights, it should have. We were teenagers, and you were five months pregnant—were we expected to get out and hitchhike or just walk along the highway? Who sends their children off to college like that?"

I felt like screaming. It sounded even worse when I heard myself say it out loud.

"They gave us a two hundred dollars a month allowance to live on," I bit off the words, "two hundred for everything, except tuition and books."

"They sent us the deposit for our first apartment. I remember that."

"Enough for a one-room kitchenette in the back of an old lady's house, Pat. Do you remember we lived on Kraft dinners and the cheapest baby formula we could find for David?"

My sandwich lay unwrapped and abandoned next to an ashed-out cigarette. Pat sat still as a statue, prey-eyes following my every move.

"How about the freezing December morning when you went into labor with David? How scared we were when that miserable excuse for a car wouldn't start? We had to borrow our landlady's phone to call a cab to the hospital and used every spare cent we could find on the fare." I blew out my breath, grinding my teeth in frustration and anger.

"And why Pat, outside of one Christmas, weren't we invited back to Indianapolis for birthdays, holidays, vacations for almost two years? Why didn't our mothers or fathers ever come to visit us? What kind of grandparents would be willing to miss their grandson's irretrievable first two years just to teach us a hard lesson?

"Kentucky was your mother's end game. At first I thought our parents had just wanted to get us out of sight—two dumb, hormonally driven teenagers who'd shamed their families. Maybe that was part of it, but I think your mother wanted to punish and break us. She wanted things to be so bad for you, you'd think, 'This sonofabitch I'm married to got me pregnant, and now my life's hell. I'm living on the edge of poverty, my child is suffering, and it's this idiot's fault.' She wanted you to dump me, Pat. Then they would rescue you, their prodigal daughter, and bring you back, chastened, into their family fold."

I sat, quivering, almost spitting with intensity. I put out my palms, hands down, trying to slow my breath, to calm down. We'd been so naïve, too much in love to even get it. We'd trusted our parents, simply accepting hardship as the price for being together. They, on the other hand, had been convinced we were too young to understand what being in love meant. They were sure we wouldn't last. Perhaps, in their cynicism, they'd forgotten what being in love was like, or maybe they never knew.

I jumped up to burn off nervous energy by stalking around the table.

"Sane parents, the loving, Christian parents they wanted the world to see them as, would have wanted us to stay together, would have kept us close, nurtured us, and helped us care for our children." I fell onto the picnic table's bench seat and leaned toward her.

"But you didn't break, did you, Pat? We were under such pressure, each of us carrying a full load of classes, even through the summers. For two years we did our best to care for our baby son on a pittance. But no, you wouldn't break—it was me. I broke. I dropped out, came home." I shook my head at the wonder of it. "And still, you wouldn't give up on me."

I ran down, wrung out. Pat's head drooped but I could tell the gears were turning, though the heavens alone knew in which direction.

"Must have been a big disappointment to your mother when you came home to me at my parents' house instead of to your family, at the end of the semester after I'd dropped out. Didn't change how badly you wanted to graduate, though. As each day, each year passed, the likelihood of you ever getting back to school and earning your degree slipped farther and farther away. Eventually, inevitably, with my hopeless daydreams and stupidity, I gave your mother an opening. She saw her chance and struck. Now she's gotten her wish, and you'll get yours, but as for our little family, it's cost us everything."

Pat sat quietly, eyes downcast; the hiss of tires from the boulevard beyond the hedge suddenly seemed loud and intrusive.

"I need to think. You make it sound as though our parents, our own families, were working against us." Her gaze wandered over the serene manicured garden around us, searching for some answer in the hot afternoon sun.

"I thought you would tell me that the group, the music, going to California, something else, was more important than me and David and Danny."

I wondered if the deep sadness in my heart showed on my face. Once outside the bubble of our dilemma, I'd begun to put two and two together. I couldn't tell her that now the trap had been sprung, I would never willingly crawl back into it. There was still more I needed to say, but not now. It would have to wait.

I brushed dust from the table and drew a deep breath.

"The guys left for California without me. They wanted me to come with them, but I didn't like being in a band: too little money; bad food; cheap, uncomfortable hotel rooms; and worst of all, being away from home. I admit, it was exciting at first, until we got out there on the road. But I didn't like dancing around like an idiot in front of people. You know doing that kind of stuff isn't me. I don't know what I was thinking when I agreed to do that.

"Just ten days after we talked, the band crashed and burned in Fort Wayne, and I came back to my mom and dad's house and found a job at RCA. I'd decided to give up everything and start over trying to figure out how to be a normal guy." She bit her lip, her head bowed.

"Then Dave called. They had an opportunity out here in California, he said—they couldn't do it without me. I kept saying no." I swung a leg to straddle the bench facing her. "I didn't want to go. But my parents, Pat—Mom and Dad, sat me down at the kitchen table and asked if I would ever regret not going.

"And here's the kicker." I tilted my head thinking about that evening, still surprised. "Mom told me they regretted the decisions they'd made for us over the last few years, and how this might be the best thing for me. Dad sat there next to her and didn't say a word.

"It was a confession, you know, most I'll ever get from them, probably. I think they finally realized how your mother's plan was going to end. I think they wanted to make up for their part in what had happened in some way—at least to me." I shrugged. "Anyway, I hadn't heard from you, and no, I didn't call. I knew you'd have to go through with the divorce—your mom wouldn't let you out of that."

Pat turned her eyes to me, transfixed.

I told her how we'd decided that Dave and Mac would have to get me a first-class airplane ticket for me to go. Somehow, I told her, fate reached down and handed it to them. How that changed everything. "I barely had time to pack."

"I didn't call you, Pat, like I said. But I didn't choose California and the group over my family, either. Wasn't like that at all."

18
I'M LATE, I'M LATE

"Oh no, is it Naked time?"

— Ilona Andrews, Magic Bleeds

August 11, 1965
Hayward, California

OUR MOOD WAS SUBDUED when we returned to the apartment, but Pat perked up when she saw Dave and gave him an affectionate hug. We sat catching up for a few minutes in the living room.

"Look, you guys have to get ready to go to the nightclub, so why don't you start now. We picked up some groceries. I can whip up a quick dinner for us."

"Okay, sounds good." Dave glanced my way for guidance. "But I thought you'd planned to come see the band in Hayward tonight?"

"I am. Leave me some hot water and enough time to change clothes."

I had a chance to talk to Dave alone, while Pat showered. "So has Helen talked to Marie again? God, tell me everything's going to be okay."

"Like I said, Helen told her she shouldn't come in, she needed to let you work this thing out, but she says Marie is definitely not happy." He shrugged. We still heard the sound of running water from the bathroom.

"So how are you guys doing? Pat seemed a little quiet, but okay."

"I love her Dave, you know that, but this is all so weird, a lot of shit coming out. Probably good we're clearing the air, but I'm worried sick for her."

Dave turned the sound down on the TV a little. "You thinking of going back?"

I could tell this had been weighing on him.

"Don't misunderstand," he said. "I love both you guys. I've known Pat as long as I've known you, but what's most important is for you guys to be happy. Question is, can that happen back in Indiana?"

"I don't see how, but we're still talking." My confusion must have been written all over my face. "It's not only Pat and me, there's the boys . . ."

"You'll figure things out. My only advice, don't get caught up in some guilt trip, or anything else that won't work out best for everybody."

At the Town Club that night, I seated Pat at a table near the back, well apart from the other wives and girlfriends. Her eyes glistened as she gazed at everything around her.

"It's kind of exciting, isn't it?"

I agreed it was, and told her how stunning she looked. An understatement—Pat in this joint was like the Hope Diamond in a dime store setting. She'd seemed so scrubbed and bright and blond when I walked her in, she almost glowed. Everyone in the band came by to say hi. Even Bob made a rare trip from his barstool to meet Pat and personally order her a cocktail. She had no idea what an honor that was. She beamed with the attention, and tuned into everything around her.

In building our playlist, we tried to play our newest, and favorite songs, first, so we could play them again later in the night if we had to repeat songs. It made for a strong first set, and I was anxious to hear what Pat thought of the band at the break.

"You guys sound fantastic." I heard pride and surprise in her tone. "Dave's voice is so powerful now." *That's true*, I thought. *Vocal cords must get stronger with a lot of use.* "It's amazing listening to you guys, you sound so professional, but isn't this place kind of seedy?"

"You think it's rough now, wait 'til you see it in the daytime. Oh, I guess you will." I grinned. "At rehearsal tomorrow."

As the night wore on, I introduced her to some of the characters who peopled our nights at the club, including Benny and some of his friends. I didn't explain why we'd nicknamed him Doctor Feelgood.

There was an uncomfortable moment when Helen came in.

"Who's the lovely girl with Dave?"

"That's his girlfriend. He's been staying with her the last few days."

She turned her attention back to me. "I like sitting here with you, but I have to admit, I can't wait to hear more of you guys singing."

On the drive home, she struggled to keep her eyes open until we turned off Crow Canyon in San Ramon. Familiar little snores emanated from the passenger seat the rest of the way. Upstairs, she sleepwalked to the bathroom for minimum nighttime preparation, and slipped into her room without a word a few minutes later.

The next afternoon, when I walked from sunshine into the nightclub's shadows for rehearsal, Les was leaning against the stage, legs crossed at the ankles, fingers flying across his unamplified guitar. He didn't look up. Other guys broke off from casual conversation. Jack's eyes flared at me, while Don's cheesy smile followed me as I walked.

"Look everybody! Briefcase Boy's arrived. The leader is here, guess we can start. Why don't you play us a tune on your briefcase, Larry?" He began his irritating, booger thumb-flick as he parodied keeping time.

"Oh, I forgot, you can't keep time. Not only are you never in time, you're never on time, either. Get it? You're half an hour late."

I knew I was late, but I hadn't realized how much. *Wasn't my fault*, I thought, but I had no excuse, either.

Mac stood and walked across the floor toward the stage. "Well shit, let's go. We wantin to do *California Girls* on stage tonight, we gotta get rehearsin."

Pat and I had left Pleasant Hill in plenty of time. She'd been quiet, taking in scenery unseen in the dark last night as we had driven to Hayward. We'd twisted through tunnels of live oak, pine, and acacia—it was fascinating how many tree varieties lived together here. Descending out of the canyons into Castro Valley, I pointed out a red-tailed hawk piloting the summer sky.

"Winding through these valleys and canyons, filled with such beautiful flowers and ferns, is so beautiful," Pat said. "Guess I won't be seeing them for much longer." Her voice trailed off. I didn't know how to respond, so I said nothing and we rode in silence until I pulled into the club's parking lot. Curious how this ratty bay area town outside my window looked so glorious deluged in California sunshine. How would it feel to not see it anymore?

I thought of Pat's whispered question before I turned onto Mission Boulevard. "What happens to us if you don't come back, Larry? What do we do?"

She'd been looking inward, I supposed, questioning her love for me in ways she never had before. The thought made me sick to my stomach. I'd leaned back against the car's sun-heated doorframe feeling heavy.

"Pat, look. If I don't go back to Indianapolis, your mother wins, which she already has anyway. She'll lecture you on how you've wasted your youth with me, but you've heard that like a broken record. The boys will be safe, though, that's what's important." I turned to her.

"But think about what would happen to me back there, and in the end, how that would affect you and the kids. Nothing's changed. I still don't see a way to daylight."

We talked in quiet intensity, not arguing but not able to agree, either.

When I opened the car door to go in to rehearsal, Pat asked for a few minutes alone. By the time she came in, the band had finally gotten started on the Beach Boys anthem to the girls of California.

Learning the song should have been easy. *California Girls* was one of the first ten songs the Checkmates had learned back in Indianapolis, but I could feel everybody blaming me for being late, and the swirling animosity made it hard for us to concentrate. It was six o'clock before we got around to performing the tune on stage with full instrumentation. The harmony was far from tight, but Les wrote it into the playlist anyway.

I pulled up a chair. Pat had dozed off a couple of times. Listening to a band learn a song is about as much fun as listening to a rusty screen door swing open over and over again.

"Sorry, couldn't spend much time with you. Guys wanted to string me up for being late."

"I'm sorry about the bad timing, Larry. It was my fault."

Dinner in an Italian restaurant on Mission before going back to begin the night was a relief. Les and Mac's gentle banter about home eased Pat's mood and theirs. They were warm and charming with Pat, and it felt good for us to be together around a dinner table.

We had a decent turnout to begin the night, and I think the band liked performing for Pat. *California Girls* came up third in the first set, and I think even the Beach Boys would've approved of the vocal blend. It wasn't altogether unusual that we'd learn a song and not get it completely down at rehearsal, but we'd hit the stage, and somehow, in the flow, we'd manage to pull it off. We did *California Girls* twice more during the night, and it pleased the crowd each time.

During an early break, Mac came to the table where Pat and I sat. "Sorry to bother you, man." He shrugged. "Les got his thing goin again. I been with Jack trying to talk him in, but he ain't havin any. You wanna try?"

I frowned and answered Pat's unasked question. "Les thinks he's dying sometimes, feels like he's having a heart attack or something. Scared the crap out of me at first; still pretty scary, but we think it's more of a mental thing now."

"Specially since he ain't died," Mac confirmed.

Les's weird-as-ever attack came with a new twist this time. I'd left him in the car after failing to persuade him to come in, when he suddenly brushed by me as I opened the club's front door, acting as though nothing had happened. It was a bizarre combination of an anxiety attack and Les's penchant for practical jokes.

On the drive home, Pat wondered again why Dave hadn't introduced her to his girlfriend.

"Maybe they're having some trouble or something," I suggested.

"They looked pretty happy together to me. She kissed him several times. Anyway, the band sounded great tonight, though you guys play pretty loud. My ears are still ringing."

"Hey. It's rock and roll."

19

PAT AND MARIE

There was no secret I didn't tell him, there was no moment I didn't share —and we didn't grow up, we grew in, like ivy wrapping, molding each other into perfect yings and yangs.

— Sarah Kay, Private Parts, spoken word poetry

August 12, 1965
Hayward, California

AFTER A FEW run-throughs with Don and Jack on stage before downbeat, the moment we began a set, we were ready to perform the new song we'd learned this afternoon. Mac had found a winner for Dave, a production rock ballad by Jay and the Americans. *Cara Mia* was an Italian love song set to three basic chord changes played at a sexy bossa nova tempo; perfect for his range. Dave owned the high, operatic notes, and his powerful falsetto rode up and over the chorus. The background harmony wasn't difficult, but with Dave taking the falsetto lead, I had to sing at the tiptop of my full voice range in the harmony. My throat burned when rehearsal ended, and it was still a little sore as the night began.

We opened with the tune while it was fresh in our minds, and though we were a bit hesitant performing it for the first time, the nine o'clock crowd gave us nice applause—but when we closed the third set with it, the place went wild, and the whole band got excited. We sang it again at the end of the fourth set and it was obvious: *Cara Mia* was going to be a signature song for us. But by then, other things were on my mind.

I slid into the booth on our final break of the night with a satisfied smile. "Wish we had a dozen of those—" I came to an abrupt stop. Pat was not smiling. "Is something wrong?"

She shook her head, looking down at the table, her lips pressed tight in concentration. Her headshake might've meant no, but I couldn't be sure. I sat still, alert for trouble.

"I went to the ladies' room a few minutes ago, though I'm not sure that pig sty can be dignified by the term." I nodded in solemn agreement. If the ladies' restroom was as nasty as the men's, I understood her complaint.

"Dave's girlfriend was in there. Helen, you told me her name was Helen." Pat fell silent, and I waited. "Another girl was with her." My heart began to hammer at its boney cage.

"She glared at me, Larry, as if she hated me. I've been trying to think why anybody here would be angry with me." She shook her head again, fitting puzzle pieces together as she spoke. "Helen didn't look friendly, either. Knowing what close friends we are with Dave, that was strange. Only one way this makes sense . . ." Her gaze held a twinge already in place.

"Do you have a girlfriend here? Is that girl with Helen your girlfriend?"

I cared and respected Pat too much to lie to her, but it felt like pulling fingers off to get the words out.

"I've had a few dates with a girl here, Pat. I don't have a girlfriend, though. No, no, nothing like that."

I watched her try to pull herself together after my admission. Wasn't difficult to guess what her next question would be, though I hoped to heaven she wouldn't ask it. As she turned to take a sip of whatever was in her glass, I thought for a moment maybe someone in heaven had heard me. I was wrong.

She peered into the ice cubes and amber liquid as if something important was melting away in there.

"Are you sleeping with her?"

There it was. Even though I'd anticipated the blow, the air still left my body.

I winced away from her accusing stare. "We were having a tough time when I first got here, you know. I slept on a bare mattress in the corner of someone's living room, alone with terrible thoughts. Every night, I'd fall asleep exhausted from trying so hard, and all I took to sleep with me was remembering all I'd lost—you, my home, my family."

I made zero sense to her, I'm certain, but I understood what I meant. Wouldn't make much difference anyway, this conversation wasn't going to go well. "Then we got the apartment. Dave started seeing Helen. And, well, I was alone . . . it just happened."

Pat's gaze at me was bleak, until her eyes fell away.

"What do you think my nights have been like?"

I wasn't often first to the stage, but this time, I even beat Jack to begin the last set. I collared Dave.

"Jesus, man. Marie's here somewhere, with Helen I guess. Pat saw them in the bathroom. Marie started looking daggers at her, and I guess Helen, too."

"I know." He shrugged in frustration. "What the hell you want me to do? Slavery went out with Lincoln, you know. I don't own the woman. She told me she thought Pat might have seen them, that Marie even stood up and cursed her from across the room last set. She said she's doing all she can to keep Marie away from her." He tilted his head. "Marie's been drinking pretty heavily; probably started before she came in."

"We've got to keep them apart. Pat knows the truth. She knows about Marie."

"You do remember she's the one who wanted the divorce, don't you?"

"She doesn't deserve this."

"Who deserves most of the shit that happens to them? I'll try again with Helen, but who knows what good it'll do?"

Pat didn't ask any questions on the way home. I noticed she'd had a lot to drink during our final set. With the exception of her slow and careful walk and a teeny stumble leaving the club, no one would've known.

Pat had disappeared into her room by the time I'd locked the car and come upstairs. What a land mine I'd stepped on. I found myself wondering why I'd agreed to her coming here. Every time we turned around, I was reminded of how I'd let her down.

As I lay in the dark, hovering in that twilight between sleep and reality, ghost fingers seemed to stroke my hair and an open palm drifted down to my cheek. I opened my eyes to see a shadow above me, leaning down, unclothed and beautiful. I sensed eyes looking into mine—though

I couldn't be certain. I pulled back the sheet and she slid in beside me, warm and supple.

My body remembered Pat in ways my mind had been unable to. Without words, she kissed me, at first with tenderness, then more fiercely, and then savagely, her teeth hard against my lips as she clung to me. A trembling hand moved like a wraith, fingers light across my chest, out to my waist, down until I felt a palm placed against my hip as if to gauge my body. Fingers brushed across my stomach, running through my pubic hair until she found and caught me with hands that knew me as well as mine knew her. I reached, longing to touch the satin sweetness of her, but she lifted a thigh to push me aside. She massaged me until, with urgent strength, she pushed me back and moved to mount me in a single motion. I was grasped in a warm, familiar intimacy I'd never expected to feel again. As she settled more fully onto me, she gasped, and we froze in a moment of intense sensation. Without warning, Pat pulled her legs tight against my sides, dipped her head, and raised her hips to drive herself onto me over and over, her breath rasping, escaping in spurts like a steam engine. I tried to mold my movements to hers, but she wasn't leading, she was taking.

Still no words, only blasting movement, and just as I thought I'd found her rhythm, she leaped from me and thrust me deep into her lips. With the same angry energy, she mouthed me over and over. Without consent or control, I thrashed upward, and she held me tight with hand and mouth until I fell back, drained. At last, unhurried, she released me and raised her head to gaze down at me. I stared into the darkness, wide-eyed and speechless. I lay unmoving, more like devoured prey than a sated lover.

It wasn't the sex. As teenagers, we'd discovered the erotic power of making each other feel wonderful. We'd been greedy and reckless beyond reason back then. Though it hadn't been easy to find romantic moments of spontaneous fervor as we grew into our role as parents, our lovemaking always remained strenuous, joyful, often untidy, and hugely satisfying. No matter how consumed we were, though, our actions had always been consensual, respectful, and caring. Something different had just happened here.

Pat's quiet tears dampened my body. I reached to bring her to me, but when I moved she slid away and out of the room as though she'd never been.

I believed I would never be able to clear my soul of my wife's searing rebuke; this memory would haunt me forever. I didn't cry, but I was certain this was the saddest I would ever be in my whole life.

But, of course, I was still young.

Well before Pat awoke, I sat at the table with coffee and a cigarette going, thinking black thoughts, wondering what would go wrong next. What a stupid fuck I'd been to agree to Pat's visit. Had I let her come here just so I could justify myself to her? And then what—I'd just ship her back to the Midwest? Had I been so selfish I couldn't bear missing a chance to see her one last time? Did I harbor some romantic notion of goodbye sex? What was I doing?

"Is every single morning here sunny?" Pat walked to the kitchen counter and picked up the Rocky the Flying Squirrel mug she'd adopted.

"Most of the time. Haven't gotten used to the weather here, either." Were we going to talk about last night? I wouldn't be the one to bring it up.

"You said we'd need to make some adjustments for the weekend because of your schedule." She pulled up a chair next to me. No reference to the sexual Armageddon of last night; no indication, discounting the puffy, dark circles bruising the fair skin under her eyes.

I explained the crazy hours ahead. How we did our normal night at the Town Club, four more hours as host band at the Soul City afterhours, and then four more hosting the morning jam session back at the Town Club.

"You're going to play and sing all night long? Until ten o'clock the next morning? You told me the band worked extra hours to make enough money, but two nights in a row like that sounds impossible."

Might as well complete the picture of what our lives are like here. "We've been doing these weekends for a few weeks now, and we've got months more to go." I dragged a hand down across my mouth and chin. "Realistically, more like fifteen to sixteen hours each weekend night, counting drive time and all. Truth is, we can't actually do it. I mean, who could?"

"But it's obvious you do." She looked puzzled. "How?"

"You met Benny on Tuesday night. Mac calls him Doctor Feelgood, or sometimes we call him the Pharmacist. He helps us."

"I remember him, the one you said always comes in with a flock of nurses."

I nodded. "One of the nurses gives us a B-12 shot in the butt every couple of weeks to keep our energy up."

Pat laughed. That loosened things up, and I felt a little easier.

"He has this case full of pills he doles out to us Friday night through to Sunday morning."

"You take drugs to stay awake?"

"Prescription drugs, most of 'em. Dexedrine diet pills, 'uppers'; give you a lot of energy, but you can feel jumpy, 'wired.' Other pills bring you down, so-called 'downers,' so you can sleep."

"Guess I'll see how that works tonight." She went back to the kitchen counter for more coffee and a cereal bowl.

"You'll never make it through the whole night. I've worked it out so I can get away from the Town Club a little early to bring you home and then race back in time for Soul City." I didn't tell her how much Don had bitched about me missing some of the last set including helping to pack and move the equipment. Well, screw him.

"Wait. What are you saying?" Pat stopped pouring cereal to turn. "I want to go to this Soul City place. I didn't travel eighteen hundred miles to stay in this crummy apartment."

Her expression showed how much she wished she could take what she'd said back. The apartment was cheap and kind of crummy, but we'd damned well earned it, so I was happy enough with the place.

"We're both worn out when we get back after a normal night. Be reasonable. What am I going to do with you if you get too tired?"

"I could sleep in the car or something. Or, maybe I should take some of those pills?"

"No, absolutely not," I said, shocked. I hadn't been concerned about me, but the thought of Pat taking them made me cringe.

"I wouldn't use them myself if they weren't necessary." *At least probably not. I had to admit they did make things kind of exciting sometimes.*

She smiled. "Okay, I didn't actually want to anyway." She looked secretly pleased. "But you can't leave me here when the band is playing. I want to go."

I thought for a moment. "If I can get the guys to agree, I'll drive you back after Soul City and then go back to the Town Club for the jam session. Would you be okay with that?"

"Better. Maybe I've got more stamina than you think; maybe I'll be able to stay awake for everything."

20
LOVE, AND OTHER CASUALTIES

And they were both Naked, the man and his wife, and were not ashamed.

—Genesis 2:25

August 13, 1965
Hayward, California

NOT SURPRISINGLY, IT had been a restless and troubled night before I'd rolled out of bed too early. I needed a nap, or at least some rest, before the weekend ordeal began. After breakfast Pat asked to take the car for a little shopping and exploration while I tried to nap. A good idea, as we'd been in each other's pocket since she arrived. I hit the couch with a new John D. MacDonald book. I had a lot of things to consider, and sometimes reading let me come at a problem sideways.

This time Travis McGee had no answers for me, and I fell into a restless doze. When Pat came through the door, the open book dropped from my chest to the floor. I heard her rustling around in the kitchen, but I felt heavy, unable to fully rouse myself until she came into the living room and spoke.

"Are you awake enough to talk?"

I swung my feet to the floor and nodded, hoping sitting up would bring me around.

"It's difficult to find a good time to discuss things with you. It's okay, though, if you don't want to right now."

"No. I know we've got stuff to figure out." I stretched and stood to go into the kitchen. "I need some ice water. Can I get you something?"

"Maybe I shouldn't, but I have to ask you about the girl from last night," Pat said, stopping me. Her lips were pursed, her expression pained.

Should I have been the one to bring this up? I wondered.

"It's not complicated: Dave was going out with Helen, and this girl, well . . . we just bumped into each other."

"You make it sound like a traffic accident."

"Please, Pat, I met her before I knew you had any interest in getting back together. I thought everything was over between us."

"You said you were sleeping with her." Pat stared at me, injured resentment clear on her face. "Is she why you don't want us to get back together?"

"That happened before you told me you wanted to come here, not since."

She turned away. I put a hand on her shoulder.

"Listen to me. Marie has nothing to do with anything I decide. I swear."

"Marie." Pat turned to me, eyes wet. "I wish it didn't make any difference to me, but it does."

We sat in silence. I felt exhausted. Not the way to start off a long weekend. I didn't have any answers Pat wanted to hear. Hell, I didn't have any I wanted to hear.

"I've got to get ready," I said. But I didn't leave the room.

"Have you already decided not to come back to us?"

We'd come to the heart of the problem.

"Pat, listen, your family is never going to accept me; your mother is determined to get the boys away from me. The deck will always be stacked in her favor, especially now." I didn't add—*since you've accepted your mother's reward for divorcing me.*

I leaned forward, searching her gaze with my eyes. "You have to understand, I can't fit in back there."

Could I make this clear enough for her to understand?

"Back in Indianapolis, I was on a hamster wheel. The harder I tried, the lower I sank, getting more confused all the time. I couldn't seem to find a way to provide for us, and not hate going to work every day.

"Here, I'm not out of step. Hundreds—no, thousands—of people are playing music or involved in some kind of creative work. Nobody looks down on them. Dreamers here are just individuals thinking new thoughts, people building or doing new things, not worthless losers. Dreams can become real in a place where people believe anything's possible. I've worked harder at being the leader of the Checkmates, making decisions, and keeping us together, than anything else I've ever done. People have paid money, as much as five dollars each, to hear us sing and play." I still marveled at that.

"There's an even more compelling reason why I can't go back to Indianapolis." I sat down beside her, reached for her hands, and searched her eyes, looking for some brilliant way to pull back the curtain between us.

"Pat, I also don't want to die. It's self-preservation. Going back to the way things were would crush me in every way that counts, and I would still lose the three of you. As much as I love you—my first love, my first lover, the mother of our precious sons—you can't keep me alive in the toxic environment back there."

She seemed to realize the truth of what I was saying, or at least my perception of it.

"Maybe we . . ." She hesitated, seeming to check her resolve before she spoke. "Maybe there's another way. Suppose we came here. What if we just left my family in Indiana, and the boys and I came to you in California? Let school go for now?"

An option I'd never considered. The ultimate temptation—a fresh start for us here, together in California. Could I have it all—everything I wanted?

"You're thinking about it, though, aren't you?" Pat examined my face.

"Sure. Of course I am. I'd love for us to be together here."

Then I thought of Jack, his wife and little boy, their pale faces behind motel room doors, never quite sure if they'd have enough money each week. And Mac, who wanted to bring his family out here. I thought for the first time about how things must look through their eyes. *How do they make it work?* I wondered. *What about school? How do they afford to have their families with them? How could we make it? I don't make enough to support us. Pat couldn't take a job, with me in a band, not when we can't be sure where, or even if, we would be working from week to week? How do you keep a family together when you're in a new, struggling band?*

"There are problems I don't have answers for, though."

"We have to find a way," she said.

I nodded, uncertain. How I could make Pat's suggestion work was all I could think of as I got ready for the coming night. I yawned until my ears popped before turning the car onto Monument to begin the drive to the East Bay.

The club filled fast; by eleven, the room was beyond capacity, with people still piling in. I found Benny when we arrived and asked if Pat could sit with him and his companions.

"Please keep her safe, Benny. Feels like the natives are restless in here tonight." I caught his eye. "But no pills. None. Not for her, okay?"

On stage, Dave waved me over. "Helen just told me Marie's outside and wants you to come out and talk to her."

"I'm not going to do that."

"She says she's coming in if you don't."

The moonlight seemed liquid, flowing in cool streams through the towering palms along Mission, as an onshore breeze moved soft salt air across the small bay city. Marie stood on the sidewalk near the club's brick wall, as laughing people brushed past us into the club. I walked the dozen steps to her.

"Why are you here? I asked you to stay away and yet you keep showing up." I didn't hide my anger from her.

"I came to apologize—for last night. It was stupid, I know. I'd been sitting at home drinking and thinking—getting crazier and crazier, I guess." Her gaze drifted down to the pavement.

"You really fucked things up, and I'm really upset about it. I don't want you in here tonight."

The fire in her brown eyes blazed. "Who are you to tell me where I can go and where I can't? You don't own me. I am not your girlfriend, as you were so quick to point out when you heard from your wife. What wife, you say? Oh, the one you didn't tell me about."

"I told you, I didn't think something like that from the past was important. Besides, she's my ex-wife. I thought our marriage was over, and she lives in a different state. And I already told you, I'm not looking for anything permanent."

After a moment, her anger receded into sorrow, and she looked away. "I won't make any more trouble. I just wanted to see you and say I'm sorry. I wasn't going to come inside, but this is where I come, you know?"

"Don't go to Soul City, either. This will all be over in a week or so. But if you come around again while my wife is here, Marie, I promise I'll never talk to you again."

"Okay, okay, don't go all ape; I said all I had to say. I'm going now. I just hope . . . Never mind, whatever's best for you." She turned to walk away.

Damn. I wanted to be firm, but I wasn't trying to hurt her.

"Look, Marie, just give me some space. I told you I still care about my wife, and there are two little boys back in Indiana whose lives will be affected by how this turns out."

She turned back to listen.

"I need to—I want to give this every chance. You've got to back off and let things go the way they go, okay?"

As usual, I was late to the stage. *Too goddamn much drama in my life*, I thought. And Don's glares weren't helping.

Trouble, always just around the corner in this club, arrived when someone cut a swath from the front door through the dancers toward the tables. He was followed closely by someone else bent on mayhem. Warfare ignited, as men and boys rushed to the dance floor from every part of the room. The perpetrators disappeared beneath a pile of squirming, pounding bodies.

"*Land of a Thousand Dances*, let's go," Jack shouted, though Don had already begun the jungle beat. I slipped over the stage edge without a word to anyone. Grunting combatants careened against me as I made a broken-field run toward the ringside tables. While guys had jumped into the scrum on the dance floor, women and girls, who'd retreated hastily to stop and stare, blocked the path I was trying to maneuver through. The band sounded strange down here. On stage, it seemed like we were playing loud as hell, but from here, it sounded muffled and thick. A high-pitched wail cut off in mid-yell. The sights and sounds of battle lifted my hackles. If anything happened to Pat, I'd never forgive myself.

I clawed my way to her, relieved to spot Benny out in front of his table where Pat and his friends were seated. Though Pat seemed horrified and fascinated, she tried to peer around him. With everyone standing, it was hard to see much of the turmoil—unless you were a participant or on the stage, where I usually was.

Within a few minutes that seemed much longer than that, the brawl subsided, as Bob's bouncers damped out trouble spots. They made no judgments, just grabbed someone in the center of a fight, victim or aggressor, and dumped them in unceremonious heaps outside on the sidewalk. Soon after the floor cleared, two girls began dancing together near the stage, then a couple. One of the bouncers began dry mopping blood spots off the floor.

I nodded thanks at Benny and glanced Pat's way. "You okay? Did anyone touch you? Anything happen?"

She was shaky, but she shook her head. "Wow, that was pretty scary."

Benny checked his overturned black case to make sure the contents were okay. "Bumkick, man, super bummer. Some asshole bikers flipped out. I was righteously amped though, ready to get my badass self on."

I put ten dollars down in front of Benny. "Would you get Pat a drink? Looks like she needs one. Something for you, too. Maybe an Irish coffee for her; she wants to go to the afterhours."

"I could give her a Dexie?" Benny, ever an evangelist for his drugs.

"No, Benny. Don't think so."

"Dexedrine. Caffeine." He shrugged, raising his palms as scales, illustrating how they balanced out.

Dave rattled a tambourine and Mac smacked a wood block in rhythm as the guys continued to punch out music when I climbed back on stage. The audience was dancing again as if nothing had happened but the band kept playing through it all, as we'd been told to.

Don, of course, smirked at me as I clambered onto the stage.

When Les signaled the song's end, Mac announced a break and the stage lights went down. Dave stood, shaking his head. "I'm never going to get used to these battles. They get started and I start feeling like a junkyard dog ready to bite somebody's head off."

Don decided he had something to say.

"Way to go, Dunlap, leaving the stage like that. Where'd you go? Piss your pants or something?"

"God damn it Don, leave me the fuck alone, will you? Or if you want to settle this thing between us right now, let's go, right here." He looked kind of spindly to me. Fearless or not, I figured I could take him. Apparently, the testosterone hadn't entirely left the room.

Jack glanced at Don. "Leave off, man. Larry's wife is here. He went to check on her. I woulda done the same."

Don glared at me before stalking off.

At his table, Benny handed out little paper packets to each of the three of us who lived over the hill. "Mac, chill out on the booze, man, or I can't lay no more goodies on you, dig? Not my bag, getting you guys dead."

Pat's expression was unreadable. She was still a little pale and her eyes glittered as she took everything in.

"Some fight out there on the dance floor," Mac said to her. "We've had worse, though. One night they had to close the club so they could sand the blood out of the dance floor. Couple guys got hurt bad."

Pat's face went paler.

"You okay?" he asked.

"This week is the wildest ride I've ever been on. Not what I expected." She thought for a moment. "Not at all what I'd expected."

"Larry says you're coming to Soul City to hang with us."

"I'm going to try. Benny is feeding me coffee laced with something. I hope I can make it. Seems really late already, though. I guess it will be a long night."

Dave sipped his Coke. "You've got no idea. I do not know how we keep doing this every weekend. I dread Fridays, knowing what's coming."

"I'll drink to that," said Mac.

"No you won't." Benny stared at Mac. "Don't go bumming me out, man, not if you want anything from the pharmacy."

At five in the morning, few souls shared the road with me, so the drive back to our apartment in Pleasant Hill was relatively quick, but the little muscles in my eyes spasmed every once in a while, making my vision jitter. I was dead tired, but I'd been doing this for a few weeks now, so it was nothing new except the precious cargo sleeping in my passenger seat. I tried to stay focused on the right edge of the road and shied away from oncoming headlights.

Pat had been fascinated with Soul City and tried hard to stay awake, but by three thirty she couldn't hide her yawns, and dozed on and off, pressed up against my side. Mac came up to the booth, in the outside room near the entrance, where most of the band slouched. "Ain't nobody wants to play right now. Got a girl singer and a guitar player, but they ain't quite ready yet, so I guess we're doing this set."

When I stood to go to the stage, Pat slumped over onto the booth seat. I gazed down at her in concern.

"Don't sweat it," Benny said. "Let her crash a while. We'll keep everything copacetic."

Not being able to watch out for her drove me crazy. It was a responsibility I'd devoted myself to from the moment she'd become my girl. She seemed small and vulnerable, curled up between two of Benny's nurses, her head on one of their jackets.

With our final set at Soul City over, I waved at Jack and Les to let them know I was leaving.

"How you making it, Larry?" Benny asked, squinting through his sunglasses at me. I hadn't taken my next pill, I didn't want to chance being too over-amped when I drove Pat back. My crash was coming on pretty harsh, but I said, "Pushing through, man, best I can."

Benny helped me get Pat onto her feet and made sure I had my Black Beauty, a long, dark oblong capsule, stashed in my pocket.

"Wait as long as you can to take that, man. Remember, you only get four hours behind that before the big downer."

As I struggled to stay alert, driving without drug enhancement, Pat's sleeping form beside me resurrected a memory of us driving to Chicago for breakfast as part of my up-all-night senior prom tradition. I was so tripped out and lost in time, I almost missed the Contra Costa off ramp, looking instead for an exit where the highway tunneled through the enormous post office building in Chicago.

Pat's grip on my arm tightened as I unlocked the apartment door and led her in. She leaned against me when she spoke, her eyes closed.

"Don't go back, Larry. Don't go back to that girl and leave me in this place all alone. I couldn't stand it." I was startled. I brought her into her bedroom and sat next to her on the bed.

"I'm just going back to work, honey," I said, helping her kick her shoes off. "That's all. Not going to see anyone, I promise. I'll be back just as soon as I can."

I felt strange undressing her, rolling her limp body back and forth to get her blouse off. I left her panties and bra on, and pulled the covers over her. Her sky-blue eyes blinked open for a moment and found mine.

"You didn't say anything to me after I came into your room." Uh-oh, where was this going? "I wanted to show you, you don't need anyone else.

There's nothing she can do for you that I can't." Her eyes fell closed again, and she rolled to her side with a sigh so deep, it was almost a moan.

Weak-kneed, I sat on the bed for a minute trying to get my bearings. What I'd taken as reproach, the night she'd come to me hadn't been that at all. She'd been competing for me. I placed a gentle palm on her hip where she lay turned away from me under the cover. Emotion roiled inside me: horror, self-disgust, and guilt rising to the top. How had I gotten us to a place where my sweet wife felt compelled to do things in bed she worried some other girl might do for me?

"Jesus Christ, Pat, this is not good. No matter what I try, everything comes out wrong. I've got to figure out what to do. What's least terrible, anyway."

I was wobbly by the time I pulled into the Town Club parking lot. A harsh sun was up, scratchy against my skin. I could feel the fabric of my shirt, and my pants rubbed against my legs as I stumbled into the club, immersed in the stench of stale sweat, alcohol, and dank hormones. The noise from the stage clattered against my ears, loud and grating. Jack and Don were up there with a couple of sit-in guitarists and a sax player, who bleated and splatted as he mangled his way through *Yakkety Sax*. Maybe twenty-five or thirty people in the club, most of them musicians.

"Pat okay?" Dave asked as I collapsed down next to him and Les at a back booth.

"Yeah, crashed out, but she's all right." I searched my pocket for the Black Beauty. Time to gear up. "This has been so goddamned stressful for her."

Les craned his neck around. "Stressful for you, too, I bet. You dealing with it all okay?"

No, Bear, I wanted to say. *I'm outta my goddamned mind with fear every moment for what's going to happen next. I'm torn apart.* I said, "Probably not, but I'm trying to keep moving, so no one gets a clear shot at me."

He nodded. I grabbed somebody's glass from the table and slammed down the silky-skinned Black Beauty hoping the high it would bring would kick in soon, and make me feel better than I felt now, like the bottom of a garbage can.

21
NIGHT FALLS

How did it get so late so soon?

— Dr. Seuss

August 13, 1965
Hayward, California

THE GRUNGY AFTERMATH of the Black Beauty's high left me sitting, inanimate, at the kitchen table already bathed in hot morning sun. I was too wrecked to move and unable to sleep. I got up the resolve to pour a cold glass of milk. My mind cycled through my problems without effect, my mushy brain too abused and numb to do more.

I crashed onto my bed, managing to kick off my shoes, certain I would lay there dazed. But I fell into a restless, dreamless sleep of exhaustion. Somewhere along the line I stripped down to underwear and crawled halfway under the covers.

Yellow beams of late-afternoon warmth poured into the room when I woke. Time to get up and do last night all over again. I shuffled barefoot out of the bedroom in jeans and a tee shirt. Pat sat at the table while the television murmured from the living room.

"Ugh." I grunted in a scratchy baritone. I waved in Pat's general direction and lumbered on toward the kitchen.

She waited until I'd loaded a mug with Maxwell House, had milk and sugar standing by and set the water to boil.

I heard her say, "This is, this is—I don't know what this is." I tried to focus my blurry eyes on her. *She isn't making any sense*, I thought, but I wasn't comprehending much of anything anyway. Had to be near time to leave; I thought about the drive to Hayward, and cringed.

"Where's Dave?" Maybe we could ride with him.

"He's gone," Pat said. "He wanted me to wake you, but I didn't. You seemed so worn out." I gazed at her, disoriented, hearing her words but not their meaning.

"What you're doing, it's part exciting and thrilling, and part long, dirty, and boring, and then there are the dangerous and scary parts."

I tried to smile. She probably thought I understood what she'd said and went on.

"I can see how you're drawn to this nightlife, I guess. It can be exciting, but what I don't understand is why you'd prefer it over your family. I've been sitting here thinking about it for hours." Her puzzled expression begged me for an explanation.

I fluttered a hand like a white flag. "Don't. I can't, Pat. Got to get ready. You have to get ready." The water began to boil, and I went to it like a dog to dinner.

I slopped hot water into my mug. *Well look at me, I'd taken the Dudley Do-Right one again.* I spooned in two healthy spoons of sugar and enough milk to cool the coffee so I could slurp it a few times. The hot liquid brought me around a little. What had Pat just said?

"Did you say you weren't sure you wanted to go?" I wondered out loud.

"Yes, but I'm going anyway."

"And, something about the girl . . . ?"

She nodded.

"Pat, you're fixated on that. She's got nothing to do with this. I don't know how many ways I can tell you. And this is a terrible time for this conversation." I gulped down more coffee, trying to wet my brain so it felt less like a soap-dried washcloth.

"There's never a good time, Larry, but we have to talk. That's why I came here, to figure things out."

"I know, I know, but not now," I said, my tongue slow in making syllables. "Maybe your trip here wasn't such a good idea after all."

Shock rippled across Pat's face as her hands dropped to the table. "What do you mean?"

What did I mean? That hadn't come out right. If it should've come out at all.

"All I meant was, maybe I shouldn't have agreed to your trip out here, not right now. I didn't mean you shouldn't have come. I'm trying to say this is my fault, not yours."

"Oh God, Larry, you can't mean that."

"Look, I'm having trouble thinking straight. I'm wrung out, and everything's a hundred times harder with you here." I got up and struggled to the sink to rinse out Dudley.

"I worry about you every minute. I feel like I can't protect you. So much stuff is going on, I can't begin to explain it all. There's tension in the band. This schedule is killing us—killing me, anyway. And then on top of everything else, all this from our old life . . ."

I heard Pat gasp, and I realized I'd screwed up again. Why wouldn't she understand we shouldn't discuss this now? What time, what time . . . Was I late? I tried to bludgeon my brain into some kind of working order while I looked at my watch. *Damn, I should already be on the road.*

"From our old life? Is that how you see me, as part of your old life? God, I wish I'd realized that's how you thought about us." Pat's face had turned ashen.

I walked into the living room and slumped down into the easy chair. *It's all coming apart, everything is disintegrating.* I hadn't fathomed what a screwed-up mess I'd left behind in Indianapolis. I hadn't faced the situation then, and now, with Pat here, it was imploding, like a concrete building falling in on itself in slow motion. I put my head in my hands and wished everything would stop for a minute and give me a chance to catch up.

"This was all for nothing, wasn't it?" I didn't need to look up to know Pat had followed me and stood staring down at me. "There was never a chance you'd come back, was there?"

"I don't know," I croaked out. I flashed to the moment I'd stepped off the plane in Oakland and known California was where I belonged. I loved my parents, my sister. I appreciated the way I'd been raised. I cherished Pat and our children more than anything. I still had a soft spot for Indianapolis, but this was my home now.

"Maybe not. I don't know. I hoped if we saw each other, the way we care for each other, we could figure something out. Like we always used to do. But I've told you all the reasons I can't go back to how it used to be in Indianapolis, and nothing we've said has changed that. I only see me diminishing in your eyes, and disaster there."

"What about what I suggested? Us coming here . . ."

I put up my hands, waggling them at her to stop.

"Wait. Think about how crazy that is. I'm hanging on by my fingernails here. Everything's so fragile. There's no guarantee that any of this will hold together. They like us at this scruffy dive where we are now, but what's next? We'll be looking for work in a few months, if we can keep the band together. What if we can't find a new job?"

"But . . ."

"No, no. Try to picture what our life would be like, Pat. Living like nomads in crappy apartments or motels. Different schools all the time. Even if the band can catch on, possibly weeks with no money. Is this the way you want the boys to live? They're so bright, so smart. We'd be ruining their chance at a future.

"And you . . ." I cocked my head at her in amazement. "Think about you, what would happen to you. You're so intelligent. You're close to getting your degree, something you might never get, following me around in a band. You need a more challenging life than that. You've already realized that."

I looked at her in desperation. "Every night in a club can be dangerous. I didn't think about that until you got here. Every night, where we play right now, somebody could die. Someone almost did one night. You're not the kind of person who should ever be in these places." I stood as it all poured out of me. "And the pills, the things we're doing to keep going.

"You said it was exhilarating. Well, sometimes it is, you're right. But more often I feel as though I'm teetering on the edge of a cliff. You want to bring our children into the middle of this? Can't you see? Isn't it obvious? I wouldn't be able to take care of you here, either. Not right now."

Pat sank onto the couch. The room stood silent except for roadway noises outside. She sighed.

"You want me to leave, don't you?" She probed, uncertain, but pushing for an answer. All at once I realized what I should have known all along. Both of us had been trying to hold on to a past that had already gotten away.

"Yes, Pat. I guess I do. It's killing me to see you—the best, most fantastic thing that has ever happened to me—slip further and further away, realizing that this is going to end with you lost to me forever. I hoped we could figure something out. It kills me to say this—but we're not going to."

I laid my head back into the chair, staring at the ceiling. I couldn't look at her anymore. I loved her more than anyone in the world, but she was lost to me now. I scrunched up my eyes, grimacing, despising myself for the arrogant fool I'd been. I recognized the inevitability of everything: from the beginning to when she'd called me in St. Louis, to now. The realization of how little control we'd had over the trajectory of our married lives was crystal clear. I'd been unable to change anything. In our desperate efforts, we'd been no more than rats scrabbling around in a maze with no way out.

I felt Pat stand. I heard her say, "I didn't want to believe how much you've changed, but you're a different person here. You live at night here, your friends are night people and you're becoming one, too. You hardly see daylight on weekends. Here it is, nearly dusk, and you're leaving to play music all night again to entertain your new friends—your new girlfriend—all the new people in your new life.

"Well I've got things I have to do, too. I have an airplane reservation to make. All I ask is for you take me to the airport when it's time."

I opened my eyes, but she'd already turned away. She'd struck out at me in her frustration and pain. I didn't blame her. She needed to steel herself to deal with the disappointment, but it still stung. We would both feel the pain for a long time.

I took a quick shower and dressed to leave. When I came out of the bedroom, the apartment was empty. I knocked on Pat's door, but she wasn't there. I assumed she'd gone out walking off her frustration. I wanted to find her, to tell her how sorry and horrible I felt. How she deserved so much more. I hated leaving her here alone tonight. But I couldn't make anything better.

I was no longer the one who could comfort her.

As I pulled onto Monument Boulevard and turned toward the freeway, tears welled in my eyes. The band had been on stage for a half an hour already, and even lead-footing it, I was at least forty minutes away.

Pat's expression was glacial when I pulled to the curb at the American Airlines terminal Sunday morning.

"I don't want you to stay. Just let me out and go," she said.

I was wrecked, my throat dry from the drug hangover and the long, long hours of running on pills and nerve endings. But that wasn't the problem. I was shattered, knowing I'd put us on an irreversible path that had already begun changing lives forever. I tried to steal some hint from her face—some indication of whether she wanted to end everything between us so disastrously—but her blue eyes were frozen cold as an Indiana winter. The icy hostility behind them was the last gift I could give her, if hating me was what she needed.

I started to get out of the car, but she warded me off.

"I can handle my own luggage. Please, just leave."

With an awkward tumble, the suitcase fell out of the backseat, and in a moment a skycap came for it. Without a backward glance, she walked away into the terminal. She was angry and hurt, but I hadn't envisioned this "salted earth" kind of ending. I had the eerie feeling I would never see her again, maybe never again hear her voice.

Following some masochistic imperative, I parked and hurried to the giant windows on the upper level. My eyes followed the receding silver speck rising higher and higher. I searched for a final glimpse in the sky, as around me, others, in their own momentous comings and goings, bustled and swirled around my silent cocoon. Inside, a dark and empty void expanded, chilling me. The greatest thing that had ever happened to me had begun when I met Pat. The girl and woman I loved, who'd loved and stood beside me at the core of my life, was gone.

22
LOSING THE BRIEFCASE

Intelligence is the ability to adapt to change.
— Stephen Hawking

August 19, 1965
Hayward, California

I NOTICED MARIE IN the club Wednesday night. I ignored her, purposely avoiding the table where she sat with Helen, to disappear into the dressing room and a paperback book. After a couple of breaks, Dave brought me a message. "Marie's here. She wants to know, would you talk to her?"

Reluctantly, I agreed, though I wanted to say no. I didn't want to put this on Dave. Even buried in my own introspection, I thought I could tell that he and Helen might be having problems. She'd seemed despondent to me, but I could have been projecting my own feelings.

Marie didn't say anything when I slipped into the booth beside her. "I just came to tell you I need time alone, Marie." She started to speak and I stopped her. "Please, I don't want to talk about anything right now. Just give me some time, okay?"

"How long?"

"Damn it, stop. I don't know. My head is spinning right now."

"How will . . ."

Though I'd heard her, I'd already slithered out and was walking away, to bury myself in Fort Lauderdale with Travis McGee on his yacht, *The Busted Flush*.

I was so blasted after Pat's departure that I came close to sleeping the clock around. Memories of my last conversation with Pat haunted me, and I fell into bed again before midnight. By Tuesday, I still hadn't had enough downtime. Dave got me to the club by nagging me along and driving us in. I staggered through the night, deflecting conversations, and in some cases, confrontation. When bandmates demanded to know why I'd missed more than a whole set Saturday night, "Sorry, personal emergency," was my only reply, and I'd refused to answer further questions.

The rest of the week sailed by in a blur. Rehearsals came and went. I avoided everyone, especially Don. I drew myself into a vacuum, reading in the dressing room between sets, trying to distract myself from cycling through all that had happened, over and over, wondering how I could have managed things better. I didn't defend myself against the spoken and unspoken resentment and criticism of the other band members. Down deep, I wanted to explain, but I was unable to muster the energy.

Mac learned to wail Junior Walker and the All Stars', *Shotgun*, while Jack picked up a new tune. It seemed stupid for me to have to drive to Hayward to learn songs I only played a tambourine on. But I came and curled up in a back booth to read until someone needed me. I ripped through the next three Travis McGee books I'd found used at the bookstore up the street. I fell asleep at one rehearsal with Ian Fleming's *The Spy Who Loved Me* open in front of me, which fried Don's berries, even though I had nothing to learn. I sleepwalked through the weekend's usual horrific night and morning hours, taking proffered uppers and downers, driving one night while Dave drove the other. I was grateful to Dave for leaving me alone behind my wall to try to process things on my own.

On Tuesday of the following week, Marie came in again. Though I found a furtive pleasure in seeing her, I didn't want her to know. Not yet anyway. Though the excruciating ordeal of Pat's leaving was still fresh, I'd begun to view it with some perspective: Pat and I were already divorced. We'd done our best at the eleventh hour to try to find a way to stay together. We couldn't. Maybe a gut-wrenching ending had been necessary to bring acceptance and closure.

Thursday afternoon, driving into Hayward, I was shocked to detect a guilty sense of physical need, wanting someone to hold onto, someone in my bed. I had to move past what had happened, I rationalized. Maybe screwing Marie's brains out would help. I hoped, in shameful lust, that she would come in tonight. I felt a wicked rise, visualizing us together as I strolled into the dim nightclub. The guys around the stage stopped talking when they saw me.

Jack gestured me toward a nearby table. Dave and Mac avoided looking at me as I walked up.

"Sorry I'm late," I said.

Don Hunt's face held a crazy-looking smile, like a mad scientist anticipating a vivisection of some small defenseless animal. "You're sorry. You're always sorry. Who gives a fuck? Sorry don't cut it anymore."

Jack cleared his throat and looked at everyone but me. "Come on, gather round here. Let's get this done." Some of them moved closer, and a couple others sat at a nearby table where Les fiddled with his guitar. The room had gone quiet enough to hear the little metallic plinking noises his strings made over the light traffic from Mission Boulevard.

This wasn't good. Something was up.

As everyone sat or slouched around the table, Jack got around to looking at me. "Here's the problem, Larry. You're goddamn late all the time. And it's a big problem. Come on over here and sit down. We need to have a meeting about you."

"Yeah, we're going to decide whether to fire your ass, Dunlap. Me, my vote's already in." Don gave me an evil grin and wiggled his fingers at me. "Bye-bye."

"Nah, that ain't so," Mac said. "You ain't fired—yet. But your ass is in trouble man. You're fuckin up somethin terrible."

Jack held up his hand. "I ain't saying he's fired, but I sure ain't saying he's not, either. We need to have a vote on it."

I couldn't have been more shocked. I couldn't believe my ears. In my worldview, already knocked sideways, I'd been sent for from Indiana because I was integral to the band. The core of the Checkmates was my vocal group. Mac and Dave had told me the band wouldn't even have existed if I hadn't come. I couldn't get fired just like that!

"Wait. What the hell?" I spit out. "Do I get to say anything?" I shook my head in disbelief as I stalked out in front of them. "This is fucking weird. I'm the leader, but I'm supposed to sit here while you guys count noses and tell me whether I'm in or out of the group—um, band? I'm not even going to get a 'damn Larry, you're messing up, better get your act together'? You really think that's the way you should treat me?"

Jack looked as if he'd bitten into a lemon and wanted to spit the bite out but couldn't figure out where.

Dave slid his feet around and spoke. "Man, just sit the fuck down over here for a minute and talk to us. I'm worried about you. Wondering if you're gonna pull outta this funk you're in."

"Screw that bullshit. Dunlap's been late since I've been in this band." Don tugged on an ear. "Besides, Briefcase Boy, you're not the leader anymore, anyway. Jack is."

Everybody except me, who stood paralyzed, started to talk until Jack overrode them. "Hold on. Hold on." He turned to me. "We've already decided, we have to have a different leader. You're late to everything—meetings, rehearsals, even the gig. Week before last, you missed a set on Friday, and you missed the first, and most of the second set on a Saturday night, for Christ's sake. Leader can't be doing that kind of shit."

"There were extenuating circumstances," I murmured. I didn't care so much about not being the leader. I'd do what I did anyway: protect and keep us together any way I could. But I cared a whole hell of a lot about being tossed aside like a dirty rag. I'd lost too much already, I couldn't lose this.

"Extenuating circumstances, my ass," Don said just loud enough for everyone to hear as he turned away. I didn't feel a lot of sympathy in the room.

"Okay, so I get you're upset with me. I'm not good with time, I know that. But you can't just throw me out of the band."

My adrenaline was cranked up, my voice high and shaky. I hated revealing my emotions this way, having my anxiety betrayed. I needed to stay calm, be cool and detached, like Travis McGee, Matt Helm, or James Bond. I paced around, tugging at my shirt and running a hand through my hair.

"Listen, you guys, I didn't mean to be disrespectful. Some personal things went really bad, and I've been trying to deal with them. That's all. I couldn't help what happened."

Jack stuck out his chin. "You act like you can do whatever the fuck you want and you don't even have to explain. Like you're fucking special in some way and don't have to follow the rules, like be on time to the gig or rehearsal or whatever."

"Well, let's talk about that," I said, trying to sound reasonable. "I'm sorry I got you all so pissed off. Give me a chance to explain."

Les spoke for the first time. "Nothing to explain. You've got to get here on time. End of story. I'm not voting to fire you, but this is a serious warning."

I remembered the times we'd been late to the stage because of Les's anxiety attacks. *We never threatened to fire him. Much harder to find a great guitar player than a half-assed background singer, I guess.* In fairness, I remembered how irritated we'd been when he was too busy dying to come play guitar, and how much I resented having to try and reason with the ticking bomb he became during an attack. The comparison got through—I could see they resented me in the same way right now.

"Well, I want a vote anyway. That's what we said we were going to do." Don got up and paced a step or two. "None of you are willing to say this, but I am: We don't really need him. We'd be a better band without him. Jack could sing his parts, and we'd be five instead of six. Nobody would notice and there'd be more money for everybody."

"Don, now you're crappin where you eatin," Mac said. "We're a different kind of band 'cause of our vocals, 'cause of the harmony, kinds of songs we can sing. This ain't about changing what kind of band we are. You gotta get off that kinda talk."

Dave spoke up. "No disrespect to Jack, but no fucking way could he sing Larry's parts. Larry sings second tenor, out of Jack's range. And Jack's tone wouldn't blend with the other voices, anyway."

I quivered inside with anger and fear, hearing my fate discussed as if I wasn't even here, having to listen to Don say things that I worried might be true. I wanted to walk out right then, to just quit—anything to shut out hearing this heap of steaming crap. But where would I go? Back to assembling record players, and my old bedroom in Indianapolis? My band was all in the world I had left. I had to stand here and take it. Not only that, I had to be smart enough to swallow it and ask for more, in order to survive.

Jack raised his voice. "Shut up, you guys. We said we'd take a goddamned vote, so let's just get on with it."

Les and Dave and Mac all tried to talk, but Les got through. "Forget it, Jack. We're not going to vote. That's stupid. We don't want to fire Larry, we want him to be on time. That's what this is about." He turned and looked at me with a gleam in his eye. "But you know now, Larry, we can fire you, and we will if you don't show up on time."

Instead of giving way to the burning anger of humiliation, I reached inside to find a humility I didn't feel. I forced every groveling word out of my mouth.

"Guess you guys are right. No, I know you're right. I really apologize. I realize I've wasted a lot of your time waiting for me." Did I sound mealy-mouthed enough? "I'll do better. Nothing's more important to me than being in this band. Truth is, being in the Checkmates has cost me everything that's ever meant anything to me." The resentment seething within me began to recede as I realized the truth I'd uttered in those last few statements.

Jack didn't like the way things had turned out. Forced to save face, he said, "Pretty clear Les and Dave and Mac won't vote to fire Larry, so no sense in voting, I guess. That'd be three out of five votes right there."

I studied my accuser's faces and found myself hyperaware of everyone's thoughts, as though I could read their minds. I sensed Dave's concern for the band and for me. Mac was concerned, too, but it was overlaid with worry about the singers losing influence in the band. Les seemed content to demonstrate to me, and everyone else, that no matter who was leader, his opinion held the most sway. Oddly, Don's sly smile told me he wasn't that disappointed in the outcome. Though it was certain he would have voted against me, seeing me humiliated seemed to be what he'd really wanted.

I understood now: It was Jack who really opposed me. Maybe he did think he could sing my parts. Maybe he wanted more money. Maybe he wanted my authority. Whatever the reason, if he and Don had influenced just one other guy this afternoon, I'd be out on the street right now. I wouldn't forget. I'd gotten the message. I'd squeaked by this time, but I was vulnerable.

"You got the briefcase with you?" Jack said.

"In the car."

"Bring it to me before rehearsal's over. Okay?"

"Sure. I'll get it now." Still Mr. Humble.

Jack turned back and said, "Let's get rehearsal going. We've wasted enough time on this crap."

Sensing as much as seeing Marie walk in the club had made the night electric. I'd been frantic for the last note to end so I could get her home with me.

"Whoosh," I said, rolling over, our sticky sweat-slicked bodies resisting separation. I gasped, my body trying to recover from oxygen debt. "Screwing your brains out turns out to be therapeutic after all. God help me, I think I'm going to die from a heart attack before I get to appreciate it, though."

"Have to admit, my brains do feel a little scrambled," she said, panting. She pretended to concentrate. "As I think back, you did seem to respond to the deep therapy I gave you." She giggled. "I know I did."

"Your fault, you know. I was just trying to get a little sleep until you decided to start things up."

"Hah." She wiggled around and pointed to the trail of clothes leading to the bedroom door. "You started ripping clothes off me the minute we got in the apartment. I was worried Dave might stumble over us humping in the hallway."

I reveled in how I'd let go the way I had. I hadn't gotten sex-crazed until the moment I realized Marie had arrived in the club. The few drinks that followed weren't enough to affect my performance, but Marie insisted on driving us back to the apartment anyway. From there, all I could remember was tactile sensations of naked flesh, and plunging and thrusting.

As I hovered in the numbing space between drunk and not drunk, the demons that tore at me seemed locked behind triple-paned glass. I knew they were there, I could see them if I chose, but they couldn't get to me. They'd be back to torment me later, I knew, but not right now.

"I'm glad you came in last night," I said with heartfelt gratitude. "Things got very fucked up yesterday."

"Me, too. Not sure you'd have gotten home in one piece if you'd had to drive yourself." She leaned over to fish cigarettes out of the jeans she'd abandoned on the floor, revealing some enticing parts.

"You were kind of a son of a bitch there, for a while."

"You're not without blame in this," I responded. "You caused me a whole lot of trouble."

She gave me a lewd gaze from over her shoulder and arched her back so her naked bottom pushed against me. "I was afraid you'd take that puny thing back to Indianapolis. Couldn't have that. Ooh, not so puny after all."

The incitement was too much. All I wanted to do was bury myself in girl flesh and forget everything outside this room. Afterward, we both lay entangled in sheets, smoking. An ashtray rested on my naked chest.

"So, what's so fucked up?"

I came drifting back from my space-out. "What? Oh, you mean yesterday?" She nodded.

"Good, because I don't want to talk about . . . you know." I took a long drag, leaking smoke out through my nose before inhaling. "We had a rehearsal yesterday afternoon, only the band decided to talk about firing me first. That's pretty fucked up."

"What? Fire you—why?"

"Ostensibly, because I've been late a lot recently, especially . . . well, very recently."

"I love when you use words like ostensen-whatever. What's it mean?"

I rolled my head toward her. "Means, I think more is going on than what's being said. The band is divided. On one side are those of us from the old vocal group: me, Dave, and Mac, and sometimes Les. On the other side are Jack and Don, the two guys Les brought into the group, and sometimes Les, too. For a while, I thought the problem was just between me and Don—we're like polar opposites in the band."

"Polar . . . bears? Don't get it."

"I mean we're the extremes. If I say something's green, Don will swear it's purple with blue and yellow polka dots. Don thinks I attacked his musicianship in some way. I didn't—I wouldn't—but he thinks so, and he's been picking away at me ever since. Could also be about me being in charge, I don't think he's good with authority. But I'm not sure he's the guy I really need to worry about anyway.

"See, here's the thing: Les has a foot in each camp. Since we're a democratic band, we decide things as a group, and majorities rule." I turned to her and said with intensity, "Yesterday at rehearsal, I was one-guy-having-a-bad-day away from being kicked out of my own band."

I sat up in bed, holding the ashtray in my left hand, my back against the wall.

I stared straight ahead. "Can't let that happen again. Just can't. What would I do? Where would I go?"

Marie twisted around until her head rested on my thigh and gazed at me, puzzled. "But you're the band's leader. How can anyone fire you?"

I frowned, ground out my cigarette, and swung my legs off the side of the bed.

"That changed yesterday. I'm not the leader anymore."

PART TWO

*Clothes make the man. Naked people have
little or no influence on society.*

— Mark Twain

23
THE NAME GAME

*...there is no Nakedness that compares to being
Naked in front of someone for the first time.*

— John Irving

September 6, 1965
Oakland, California

"COULDN'T BELEIVE THIS nasty chick frownin at me and yellin—'your band was a lot better when the black guys was in it!'." Mac ground out a cigarette in disgust at a table near the stage. "That shit pisses me off."

It wasn't the first time we'd heard comments about those other Checkmates. Who were these guys, I wondered, still haunting us all the way back to Fort Wayne, Indiana?

Les sat on the edge of the stage habitually fingering his unplugged guitar. "Well, let's change our name then. Opening a new club, perfect time."

We were at the new Casuals on the Square for an afternoon sound check before we played there Monday, our off-night from the Town Club. Somehow, a popular local band named the Casuals had managed to buy and open the self-referentially named nightclub. Some of the guys in the Casuals, liking what they'd seen of us at Soul City, had asked us to play a "soft opening" the night before their official debut. The room was large and impressive, originally an ornate theater before its rebirth as a nightclub—and located in Jack London Square, a famous themed destination of tourist shops and restaurants on the Oakland waterfront. We hoped appearing at such a new high-profile venue would showcase us to buyers interested in hiring us after the Town Club. We'd been promised the next few Mondays if things went well at the soft opening, which would mean enough money to quit the backbreaking Soul City afterhours gig.

"Changing our name is probably a good idea." I agreed. "But names are important. If we change our name, we've got to think it through. We need a unique name, and one we won't lose.

"Even though *In the Still of the Night* turned into a disaster when the master tape disappeared, we'd gotten great name recognition as the Reflections with the deejays. They'd loved our version and predicted we'd become a national recording group. If we could've gotten another record out fast enough, I'm sure the radio programmers would've given us another chance."

"So, why didn't you record another one?" Jack asked.

"They did," Les said. "It bombed."

"Figures." Don never let up.

"We tried. Our producer found us a song, and we learned and recorded it in the same night. But before he could get *In the Beginning* released, another group had snagged our name."

"Group from Detroit," Dave said with disgust, "calling themselves the Reflections, put out *Just Like Romeo and* fucking *Juliet*. It was a big hit. So now they were the Reflections and we were nobody."

"So, in the rush to get our next record out, our producer tried to rename us at the last minute; he chose the Illusions. The record was DOA. I doubt anybody heard it."

"Illusions?" Mac said. "That was a serious fuck up. Buncha groups with that name already. Probably why no one paid it any attention."

"Point is, we got really lucky as the Reflections with our first record, but that kind of luck doesn't usually strike twice. Gotta get the right name and protect it. Be ready for that luck when and if it comes."

"Well, fine." Jack smacked a rolled-up Casuals flyer against his palm. "But if we're going to make a change, let's do it before we play here Monday. Anybody got any ideas?"

"Maybe we should name ourselves after some kind of insect or something, like the Beatles," Dave said. Dave, Les, and I had gone to see the Beatles at the Cow Palace two nights ago over in San Francisco. "I read in the paper that John Lennon came up with their name because of Buddy Holly and the Crickets."

Though Les thought they were fantastic, Dave and I still shared mixed feelings about the Beatles. We'd missed them on purpose when they'd played at the fairgrounds in Indianapolis last year.

I hadn't thought their sound was anything special when I first heard them. I couldn't understand why people liked the rough, though enthusiastic, harmony of these shaggy-haired English guys, or why the girls were going so crazy for them. So when we broke onto the charts with *In the Still of the Night* in early January, a year and a half ago, I was excited to see us at number twenty-seven, while *I Want to Hold Your Hand*, barely made it into the top forty in Chicago. The next week we still outranked them, and we held on another week at seventeen. But as we were sucked back into obscurity in our final week, *I Want to Hold Your Hand* rocketed to number one.

A few days later, my disappointment was complete when I sat in puzzled astonishment at the insane audience response the Beatles received on the *Ed Sullivan Show*. From then on, those shaggy-headed bastards led an invasion of British bands that began to dominate American music, devouring opportunities for deserving American groups. Like us, for instance.

Our seats at the Cow Palace, a big, drafty barn of a place, were high in the back of an odd-shaped balcony. The atmosphere was electric, and the crowd rude and noisy while opening acts performed. They were only here for the Beatles.

The shrieking and screaming began before the Beatles even made it to the stage. We couldn't even hear them being announced. The racket spread like a gas fire into the grandstand seats and up to where we were perched as the four of them strolled out. Everyone stood, so we were forced to as well. I looked at my friends and tried to say something, but the pandemonium was so loud, it was as if the whole building had been stuffed with transparent cotton. We rolled our eyes at each other. Every once in a while, I'd catch a snatch of guitar or voice and be able to guess what song they were playing, but otherwise, it was a solid wall of roaring noise. The clamor set my teeth on edge. It was a relief when it was over.

"Can't say I'm sorry I went to see them," I said. "They're a phenomenon, no doubt. Disappointed I never heard a thing they played or sang, though. Don't understand why these girls buy tickets to their concerts and then scream so loud they can't even hear them."

"Would liked to have heard them better, myself," Les said, "but I loved it. Someday I want us to be as big as the Beatles."

Don spoke up. "Maybe we should call ourselves Dunlap and the Roaches." There were a couple of snickers, but Don's act was wearing thin. I didn't say anything.

"What about the Outsiders," Mac said. "Bein as we're from outside—bein from back East and all."

"Pretty sure that's not unique," Jack said. "The . . . the . . . ah, crap. I don't know. Something." Jack peered up at the ceiling. "The Chandeliers."

Somebody made a gagging noise.

Dave wrinkled up his face in concentration. "Maybe if we think of nouns, we can come up with a name."

"What we should do, man, is our damned sound check," Don said.

Mac began to list nearby items. "Uh, chairs, tables, glasses, drumsticks, ashtrays . . ."

"Carpet," Dave said. "Magic Carpet?"

"Nah." Mac rolled his eyes. "Sounds like some pussy band from over in the Haight."

Jack got a little flustered. "Come on, Les, you started this. Don't you have any ideas?"

"Nope. Just 'cause I know we should change our name, doesn't mean I have to know what the new name should be." He continued picking at the strings on his Stratocaster. He glanced up at us with a mocking grin. "I will know if it's wrong, though."

"How about calling ourselves Stark Naked and the Car Thieves?" I said, casually flinging the suggestion into the conversation. Everybody thought that was funny; even Don tried to hide a smile.

"That's hilarious." Jack left off his barking laugh to rub his chin, puzzled. "But what's it mean? Who's Stark Naked and how do car thieves come into it?"

"Doesn't mean anything, Jack. It's just a name," Dave told him. "We were promoting *In the Still of the Night* in Chicago when we met some guys who joked around telling us that was their group's name. We laughed so hard we almost pissed ourselves."

"Hold on now. Maybe that ain't so bad," mused Mac. "I sure seen worse. Larry's right about names bein important, though. I know bands in Cincinnati who'd fist-fight each other over a name. Heard of a group down south called Thirteen Screaming Niggers. Everybody says they're great and nobody, for damn sure, forgets their name. Stark Naked and the Car Thieves is kinda catchy, and ain't no one likely to steal it."

"Who the hell would want to?" Don said, smacking his snare as he tightened the drumhead.

Jack frowned. "We can't use Stark Naked. Unique and crazy name all right, but it's too far out. Nobody'd ever book us with a name like that. We gotta come up with something else."

Someone suggested Free Beer, so we'd be guaranteed a full house every night, which elicited a round of jeers. We went another twenty minutes with the suggestions degenerating into sillier and sillier names. When we'd run dry of ideas that cracked us up, we finally got back to the business of checking the acoustics in the club's high-ceilinged showroom.

We ran through *You've Lost That Lovin' Feeling*, *The Harlem Shuffle*, and a few other songs, trying out the PA system at various levels to get an idea of how to play the room. As our last tune, we sang *Cara Mia* to hear if the room's rich natural echo would enhance big vocal numbers. After we finished, clapping and hooting came from a few people silhouetted in the back of the room.

A voice shouted, "Hey, who are you guys?"

Realizing we didn't want to be known as the Checkmates anymore, but mostly just being a wiseass, I hollered, "Stark Naked and the Car Thieves." Laughter rolled back.

"Cool. You're going to rip this place up."

Except for an occasional yawn, Mac and I slouched quietly in the car as Dave drove us into Oakland Monday evening. I'd tried, but failed, to work up any enthusiasm for opening at Casuals. We'd hosted what we hoped would be our final Soul City afterhours over the weekend. Despite reaching that incredible milestone, neither mind nor body had been able to recover from our final Sunday morning jam session by Monday night. As Dave turned into streets illuminated by replica 1880s gaslights, Jack London Square seemed transformed. Even on a chilly October evening, many people were out bundled up in sweaters and jackets, visiting the eateries and shops. The renovated theater marquee at Casuals dominated the square as we turned into it. Dave whistled at the lighted sign above.

"I'll be damned," he said.

"No doubt."

"Larry, would'ja just look the fuck up at the sign? The gigantic sign that's hanging out over the street in front of the club?"

Mac scooted to the back window, behind Dave, and peered up. He breathed out reverently. "Sonofabitch, Stark fucking Naked and the fucking Car Thieves."

I watched the letters slide by above us in awe. *Oh crap, I'm probably going to catch the blame for this.*

Dave went around again before parking, none of us able to take our eyes off the sign.

My fears eased once we got inside. Les laughed. "You guys check out our new name outside?" He loved a practical joke; playing one on the city of Oakland apparently appealed to him.

Jack didn't seem sure what to think. Don peered at him in puzzlement, "Whose idea is that? Is Stark Naked actually going to be our name?"

"Aw, hell no, got to be a mistake." Jack gave me a sideways glance, and I didn't say a thing. "Somebody must of heard us screwing around with the name at the sound check."

At least it gave us something to laugh about and helped energize us as we started setting up our equipment.

"Hey, is that Stark Naked guy back here somewhere? I bought him some threads so he don't freeze his cogliones off." Benny Carducci's troupe thought the name change hilarious.

"You guys get a load of this yet?" He held out a thin newsprint magazine entitled *The Spot-lite*, a widely published handout freely distributed around the Bay, listing all the entertainment options. Most of the cover was dedicated to our picture with the caption "STARK NAKED AND THE CAR THIEVES—Now playing at CASUALS ON THE SQUARE." Seeing the name in print, the concept of us being actually advertised, was strange but cool.

Other fans from Hayward who'd followed us to Oakland gathered around the stage, wondering about the name on the marquee. A pretty dark-haired girl said, "I didn't think you guys were here at first. I wasn't going to stay but they told me I could come in and see if you were the real deal. What's that name on the sign mean?"

Les told her. She decided it was her duty to stand at the door and tell people the band inside was really the Checkmates, no matter what the sign said.

"Well nobody's upset anyway." Jack said returning from the front door. "Club manager thinks it's funny, says they'll just change the name next week if we play here again. Guess we might as well have some fun being Stark Naked and the Car Thieves for now."

So instead of being worn down and lethargic, we began the first set relaxed and loose. We kicked off with *I Thank You* to get the blood moving and then moved on to *Dawn*, a Four Seasons song with very cool harmony. We picked up energy from the crowd's response and added it to the natural excitement of playing in a new venue. The joke name provided fodder for Mac's quips and one-liners all night long. From the high and roomy stage, we could easily see over the dancers and perform for the crowd beyond. The Casuals had done a fantastic job of getting the word out about their club, and we were near capacity all night. I thought we'd given the Casuals' new club a pretty great beginning.

Too bad it wouldn't be us performing here after the Town Club.

24

HERB CAEN SAYS NAKED'S HOT

Being Naked approaches being revolutionary;
going barefoot is mere populism.

— John Updike

September 7, 1965
Oakland, California

THE NEXT NIGHT at the Town Club, I pulled up a chair next to Marie at our usual table. She had a tentative expression on her face. "I want to take you out to dinner."

"Doesn't the guy usually ask the girl?" I responded.

Her slim, cinnamon-brown hand played along a bracelet of bangles on her right wrist. I'd never seen her bashful before; usually she was anything but.

"I want us to go into the City, to one of the nice restaurants on Fisherman's Wharf."

I studied her, wondering what brought this on.

"I've never been to San Francisco, but I can guess what you're suggesting is expensive. I don't think I can afford that."

"Actually, I can."

"You found a job or something? Are we celebrating?" I tipped ash off my cigarette. Marie's smoldered in one of the ashtray's little grooves.

With a slight toss of her head, she reached across her forehead to brush her hair behind an ear. "No, no, I didn't get a job. I got something else." She hesitated.

"I told you I'd been married before. You remember, don't you?"

I nodded.

The usual sounds of conversation and clinking glasses blended into comfortable bar background noise. A haze of cigarette smoke blued the air around us. She looked down at her hands as they plucked at each other.

"What I didn't tell you is, we weren't actually divorced." A tight little laugh at my expression. "No, not what you think. Definitely not what you're thinking." She dug into her pack and lit another cigarette from the table's candle before realizing she already had one going.

"We'd split up and were going to get a divorce, and then he got killed, *muerto*." She paused to exhale a plume of smoke while stamping out the other cigarette. "He must've had a small life-insurance policy through his work or something. I didn't know about it until a check for five thousand dollars came in the mail a couple of weeks ago."

"Wow," I said, treading carefully. "Not sure whether to congratulate you or to commiserate. How do you feel about it?"

"Me? I'm thinking this is money from heaven." She chuckled self-consciously. "Literally, I guess. I'd already filed for divorce, you know. He wasn't an easy guy. He got rough with me a few times. So please, congratulate me." She looked up to catch my eye. "I want you to help me enjoy the money, otherwise I won't be able to."

"Marie, I don't know. You should use this money for yourself, you know. Be smart about this."

She shook her head determinedly. "You don't understand. I don't want a goddamned thing from the guy. If I don't do something like this, I want to throw the check down a storm drain. If we spend this money together, maybe I'll be able to enjoy it. If you won't let me do this my way, I'll think you don't know me at all."

"Okay, okay. Dinner in San Francisco sounds exciting. We could go Sunday night since the band's not doing Soul City anymore. But if you come to your senses before then, that'll be fine, too. Okay?"

Marie's disclosure was still on my mind when Jack waved me onto the stage before the next set. Mac, following close behind, popped his head into the huddle and said, "What the hell's goin on in this here circle jerk?"

"You will not fucking believe this." Jack held up a folded newspaper and flicked open his lighter to illuminate it. "This is from today's

San Francisco Chronicle, Herb Caen's column." He noticed the puzzled faces of the Midwesterners. "He's a famous society columnist, people read his column all over the world. Listen to what he wrote about us, 'There's a hot, new band in town called Stark Naked and the Car Thieves. They're currently playing at the new Casuals on the Square nightclub in Oakland.'"

"We're in the paper?" I said. *Stark Naked and the Car Thieves, in the paper? Us?* I waited for someone else to realize what that meant.

"Does this thing in the paper mean Stark Naked is our new name?" Don asked.

"Well," I pointed out. "We got more publicity in one night as Stark Naked and the Car Thieves than we've ever had as the Checkmates."

Our animated discussion was reluctantly postponed, as the dancers on the floor insisted we get back to playing music. All week we wrestled with what to do about our unexpected name change without resolution.

Marie decided to skip the club Saturday night and meet us at around ten o'clock Sunday morning at the jam session so she could return with me to the apartment. That way we could be together all day before our dinner date. Completely wiped out as usual, Dave and I were happy to see her so we could beg her to drive us back to Pleasant Hill.

At home, she crawled under the covers next to me and, in the best possible way, helped me relax and fall asleep. When I woke hours later, she'd left a note; she was shopping for a new outfit to wear tonight. I smiled, enjoying the thought of her excitement about our big date.

A momentary twinge flashed through me as I thought of Pat. Before I could veer my mind away from the painful memories, I thought about how much we had to work out, especially about the boys. Maybe in a few weeks things would cool down enough for us to talk.

I'd only been out of the shower a few minutes when Marie walked in with packages and news. "I've got us reservations at Alioto's on Fisherman's Wharf for an early dinner at five."

"Terrific. What kind of restaurant is Alioto's?"

"Expensive." She gave me a coquettish glance.

"Yeah, sure." I grinned at her. "But what kind of food?"

"Extravagant." She laughed. "Okay, okay, it's a seafood restaurant. You can have lobster if you want. Have you ever had lobster before?"

"Not a lot of lobsters in Indiana. My parents always took me to all-you-can-eat shrimp dinners on my birthday as a teenager, though. Lobster's just an overgrown shrimp, right?"

Our table on the second level of Alioto's overlooked a weathered fleet of fishing boats, nestling together as the floating restaurant rocked gently beneath us. Gulls wheeled and cried above the distant sound of creaking boats and murmuring diners. Across the water, the Golden Gate Bridge stretched away into a fog bank, as if linked to heaven and not just Sausalito.

I leaned toward Marie. "Isn't this incredible? Picture perfect, like a living postcard. And all these delicious, roasty smells, with"—I checked the aroma for a moment—"well maybe a little fishy smell, too, but exactly right."

The menu confirmed Marie's description: expensive. I glanced at her. She smiled and spoke to the waiter. "He's going to have the biggest lobster you've got." She ordered a smaller version of my dinner that included a filet mignon for herself. The waiter asked if we had a wine order. "Why don't you bring us whatever you think would go best with what we ordered," she said.

We'd demolished the giant prawns in the shrimp cocktail we were sharing when the waiter returned to extend a sweating green bottle of Wente Brothers Riesling for my approval. He splashed a little into my glass and made it clear that we weren't getting any more until I tasted the pale wine. After a sip, I glanced up in wonder. I'd never realized what real wine tasted like before. Its dry sweetness was fruity and delicious. The waiter smiled and signaled for our plates to be placed while he filled our glasses. The first bite, forked from the lightly-browned white meat of the huge lobster tail, dipped in drawn butter, took my breath away. The second bite, this time accompanied by the sweet, clean Riesling, shocked me. I gazed up at Marie.

"I've never tasted anything like this lobster before. The wine is amazing. Food for the gods. Together, they're like a religious experience. This is the best meal I've ever had, like something out of an Ian Fleming novel. I'll never forget it. Thank you so much, sweetheart." I would never taste Riesling again without thinking of Marie and my first wine pairing in San Francisco.

Her eyes sparkled with pride as she beamed at me, while I ravenously devoured chunks of buttered lobster tail and grinned greasily back at her. Finally, I'd winkled out every crumb from the lobster shell and poured the last drop from the bottle. Full to bursting, we drove home in a contented blur.

When we arrived at Casuals the next night, Stark Naked and the Car Thieves still dominated the marquee, and no one seemed eager to change it. We were more comfortable and enthusiastic entertaining on our second Monday night; mostly from getting more rest.

The punishing schedule we'd endured had been a crucible, forcing us to learn how to rely on one another, to develop discipline and set an expectation that each of us would do our best under the most difficult conditions. Like anyone else with a job, some nights were better than others. Playing so often made it difficult to maintain a consistently high level of enthusiasm, but we never quit trying. Though my tendencies were not perfect, I'd become much more sensitive to time, especially at performances. Somewhere along the way, I realized with pride, we'd transformed ourselves into professionals.

After a standing ovation for *Cara Mia* at the end of the fourth set, a waitress brought a message to the stage for the bandleader. Jack grimaced, but still asked me to come with him to a table halfway back in the club, where an older man in a sharp-looking suit and open-collared dress shirt maintained a half-full highball glass. He introduced himself as Dave Rapken, owner of the Galaxie nightclub in San Francisco.

"I read about you guys in the *Chronicle*. Herb Caen says you're good, and I like your name. I like the way you sound, too, though I'm not crazy about your look." His voice was raspy and direct; not arrogant, but clearly he was someone used to having things his own way.

"If I bring you into the Galaxie, you'll have to make some changes. Think you can do that?"

"Mr. Rapken, I'm sure we can do whatever you want, but I think we need to know more about what you're asking." Way to go, Jack; that seemed like exactly the right tone to me.

He considered us for a moment. "Do you guys have an agent?"

When Jack said no, he nodded. "Good. I'd work with one if I had to, but I don't like 'em much. If you're serious about wanting to play in my club, you two come to the Galaxie Thursday afternoon, one o'clock, and we'll see if we can work something out to suit us both."

"Man," Jack said, glancing over his shoulder as we walked back toward the stage. "That's one serious guy."

"No shit?" Don said, when Jack related the news. "The Galaxie? High-class topless joint, over in the city, on Broadway, or one of those North Beach streets."

"Topless?" I said. "A strip club?"

"Nah, not like that, Dunlap. You've never heard of Carol Doda and the Condor Club?" I shook my head, and he went on. "Where have you been living, under a rock?" I chose not to respond.

"About a year ago, this waitress with big knockers starts dancing topless in a bikini bottom, on a suspended grand piano, while it's coming down out of the ceiling. People from all over began lining up at the Condor in North Beach to check her out. Everything got so crazy the cops came and arrested her and a bunch of other topless waitresses. Was on TV news every night. You sure you don't remember any of this?"

"Still back in Indianapolis, Don."

"Thought everybody in the world heard about the North Beach 'topless trials.' Well, you're in San Francisco now, buddy; those clubs are the city's answer to Paris, France's Can Can dancers. The Left Bank, fancy nightclubs, it's all mixed in with intellectuals in bookstores and coffee shops. North Beach used to be famous for the beatnik thing in the fifties. Topless has made the place popular again. Everybody's making money on it. Figure that's why the city fathers decided Carol Doda dancing topless is exercising her God-given constitutional right to express herself. All the clubs over there have topless dancers now. I know two places where topless girls work with snakes. Even heard of a topless ice-cream shop." That thought gave him pause for a moment.

"Wonder what cold does to a girl's nipples?"

25
NAKED ON BROADWAY

*The moment that you feel that just possibly you
are walking down the street Naked . . . that's the
moment you may be starting to get it right.*

— Neil Gaiman

September 23, 1965
San Francisco, North Beach, California

MAC, DAVE, AND I parked in front of a three-story brick building with a twenty-foot-high vertical neon Galaxie sign hanging over the corner of Broadway and Kearney Streets. A banner plastered on the Kearney Street side announced, "The Galaxie Revue featuring Topless Teri." Scattered up and down Broadway in both directions, nightclubs advertised entertainers and topless shows. A block west, the Condor Club reminded everyone that Carol Doda danced there, as Don had told us, but he'd failed to mention that Bobby Freeman showed off dance steps to the Swim there, too. Joey Dee and the Starlighters demonstrated the Peppermint Twist at the Peppermint Lounge in the other direction, while Chubby Checker kept the original Twist alive across the street. I was awestruck. These were all big-time recording artists. We might have to invent a dance to compete here.

Between the buildings across Broadway peeked stretches of the Golden Gate Bridge below, gray in the cool, overcast afternoon. Glimpses deep into the bay revealed infamous Alcatraz Island, often lost in the mist.

Jack and Les waited near the door. All of us, except Don, who was a no-show, walked on each other's heels into a glamorous but cozy showroom steeped in deep crimson and trimmed in gold. A runway ran out into audience tables from a comfortably sized half-circle stage with ornate curtains, which were currently drawn.

"So, you brought the whole gang." Dave Rapken's expression didn't give away whether that bothered him or not. "You boys want something to drink?"

Dave and Mac accepted Heinekens, while the rest of us served ourselves soft drinks out of the bar's gun dispenser. We pulled up chairs around Dave Rapken's table near the step-down service bar.

The Galaxie's owner scrutinized each of us as we went through introductions.

"I wanted you to see the place, get a feel for it," he said, tilting his head toward the stage. "You're right out in front of everybody up there, no dance floor. As you can imagine, the girls have no problem keeping the audience's attention. Obviously, you won't have the same advantage. You'll have to put on a good show to keep the audience in their seats."

Mac nodded. "We started off as singers doin shows, Mr. Rapken. We can do this."

"Just call me Dave." Dave Rapken rubbed his chin. "I think you can, too. But if you used to be a show band, you're not one now. I've got some ideas about how we can deal with that, but at least you understand the challenge.

"I can offer you a year's employment at a thousand dollars a week with certain conditions. First, you sign with me as your personal manager and I collect ten percent of what you make. You won't have a way to know this, but I'll be spending this money on your behalf, and I want to be clear about this." He paused to make his point. "It will be spent at my discretion."

Even though we'd still make a hundred dollars more a week than we had at the Town Club, the radical idea of a commission needed some explanation.

"I'm sure you've got a good reason for handling this commission money the way you want," I said. "Maybe you could tell us more about that."

A corner of Jack's mouth began to wrinkle into a frown at my question, but he glanced away when Dave Rapken eyeballed him.

"I understand," Rapken acknowledged me. "So, let me illustrate. Assuming we make this deal, you'll take your band to a tailor where you will be fitted for custom suits with all the accessories. By the way, you've got to be fitted no later than a week from Wednesday for them to be ready opening night. Now, I'm going to get a terrific deal on these two sets of suits, but you'll pay me back with the money I'm getting from you. They'll be yours, and I'll have saved you a hell of a lot of dough." He picked up his glass and munched some ice. "Get how that works?"

Jack nodded. "Sure. I get it."

"Another thing, I'm sure you want to do some recording, try to get a record deal. I've got some connections, we'll see about that down the road."

That gave me goose bumps. I glanced at those of us from the Midwest to see a similar reaction on their faces. We were desperate for another chance to record.

"Now, about the girl performers. You'll be working with them in various forms of nudity. Don't let that give you the wrong idea. You're all adults, so what you do outside the club isn't for me to say. But when you're here, nothing goes on between you and these girls, or the waitresses either for that matter. *Capisce?*"

After some sheepish grins, Dave Rapken continued. "If you agree, I'll get contracts sent to you tomorrow. One for the musicians' union, an agreement for the club, and a personal management one with me. Three documents. You get them signed and back to me, and I'll give you the tailor's address. Any questions?"

"Havin suits, guess we'll have a dressing room, too," Mac said. "Mind if we take a look?"

Dave Rapken stood and shook hands all around. "Dressing rooms are downstairs through there." He pointed to a door in a small alcove behind us. "The ladies go down to the right, you guys to the left." He gave us the first smile we'd seen from him.

"Let's not get 'em mixed up."

On our drive into Hayward, a couple of weeks before we were due to close our long engagement at the Town Club, Dave and I were companionably quiet and a little beat. Ending Soul City had helped, but the jam session mornings were still draining. Dave gazed into the gathering dusk beyond the windshield as he broke the silence.

"I'm not going to see Helen anymore."

"Whoa. Didn't see that coming. Thought you guys had something special happening."

"Last night she talked about us moving in together. I had to say no, and we ended up breaking it off. We had a great run, and she's a super lady, but I'm not ready to be tied down."

I had some idle thoughts about the smoothly rounded hills I watched go by on my side of the car. "I'm sorry, man. I liked her for you. She seems so classy and cool."

"She is. My problem, not hers. I'm just not a one-woman guy, and I don't want to pretend differently." He paused and glanced at me before looking back at the road. "This came up because she started talking about Marie and you. She said Marie thinks you're going to ask her to move in with you. She's pretty damn serious about you." He glanced again. "Are you thinking about asking her to move in?"

"No way. I really like her, but that's all. I'm still dealing with splitting up with Pat."

"You might want to say something. I'm pretty sure she's got you lined up."

I thought about what Dave told me all the way to Hayward. She'd be in tonight, and instead of deliciously anticipating an exciting sexual romp after work, I'd have to talk to her about this. *Crap.*

Marie was in early, but I couldn't find the right time until the end of the night in the nearly deserted bar. *How do I start?* I wondered. Marie, sensing something was on my mind, fidgeted next to me.

"I'm sorry Helen and Dave are breaking up," I said. She nodded. Actually, we'd already talked this to death. "Marie, I need to talk to you about something."

Her eyes widened. She breathed out, "Omigod. I knew it. You're going to do it, aren't you? You're breaking up with me."

"What? Oh, no." I pulled up, disconcerted for a moment. "Sorry. I just meant we might need to clear up some things."

"Okay. I can start breathing again."

"Here's the thing, it's fantastic being with you, Marie. I like you a lot and I hope you feel the same way."

"Yeah. Sure. We're having a great time." She looked around in panic. "Too bad you can't order a cup of coffee in this place."

"I have to make it clear, though, it isn't more than that." *Damn, that sounded kind of brutal.*

I took another breath and kept going. "You know I just got divorced. You told me you'd have gotten divorced too, if . . ." I hesitated, trying to be delicate. "What I mean is, you told me why you were going to split up with your ex—uh, deceased husband."

I leaned forward, trying to find the right words to make her understand. "It's not like that for me, Marie. I'm not married anymore, I know that, but it hasn't changed the way I feel about her. I can't imagine caring about anyone that way ever again. Even if I could, I wouldn't want to. I don't ever want to risk destroying anyone's happiness that way again, including my own. Just couldn't do it."

Marie stared down into the ashtray at her smoldering cigarette, as if her future could be read in the rising, eddying sliver of smoke. She spoke in a monotone. "You never told me why you got divorced."

"My wife's family, her mother especially, despises me to put it mildly. Now I'm here, she's there, and the logistics don't work. I'm pretty sure she hates me now, and you're part of the reason why." I pushed those thoughts aside. "Anyway, not the point. I'm talking about us now."

"That wouldn't happen with my family," she whispered.

"I can't let you spend any more of your money on me, either. I had a terrific night with you in San Francisco last week, but I'd be taking advantage if you want something from me I can't give you."

She resolutely ground out her cigarette, picked up her purse, and stood staring down at me wordlessly. She turned on a dime, and I watched her walk away and out of the club without a word or backward glance.

I hadn't meant for her to leave. I consoled myself with believing I'd done the right thing by telling her the truth. Small comfort if I never saw or felt her again. Had I told her for her sake or mine? *Maybe the truth is over-rated,* I thought, gloomily.

Six weeks later, a new banner was raised to join "Topless Teri's Review" on the Galaxie wall: "Opening Tonight, Stark Naked and the Car Thieves." The tedious drive from Pleasant Hill into San Francisco on opening night would have been unendurable on a regular basis, but we wouldn't be making that trip much longer. Dave and I had rented a modest two-bedroom apartment across the Bay Bridge on Solano Avenue in Berkeley—and Marie had helped us pick it out.

I'd been pretty low closing night at the Town Club a few weeks ago when Marie didn't come in, at least to say goodbye during the party the club had thrown for us. I hadn't seen her since the night she'd walked away from me. Bob let us skip the Sunday morning jam as a parting gift, said we'd be too drunk anyway. So much had happened to us at this scruffy little dive. I felt a searing vulnerability in saying goodbye to all the highs and lows I'd experienced here. The hours had been tough, but Bob had been as good as his word and given us a secure place to grow. We finished packing up our equipment for the move across the bay to the Embers, a nightclub in Redwood City, where we'd play a few weeks before starting in San Francisco. As I trudged across the moonless early morning parking lot, a shadowy figure near my car materialized into a dark-haired girl with veiled eyes and a tentative smile.

"Could I interest you in make-up sex?" Marie said. I pulled her into my arms, and we comforted each other's loneliness and fears.

There were few customers in the Galaxie showroom when Dave and I walked in, but busy sounds of tinkling glasses, quiet laughter, and casual banter between the staff reached us from the service bar. The curtain was up, our equipment hidden behind a black drape at the back of the stage. When Dave and I tramped down the narrow stairs to our dressing room, the guys had already begun pulling on new suits that had been carefully hung there for us. Moments later, noisy female chatter and the click of stiletto heels on the steps alerted us that the girl performers next door were on their way upstairs to begin the night with their show.

Later, as we stood poised for our first show, I sensed how unnerved the band was. Appearing at the Galaxie, at the top tier of San Francisco's nightlife, was a gigantic leap from playing at the wild Hayward dive bar we'd called home across the bay. I often got butterflies before sets, but tonight jumping beans filled my stomach. It was odd having to avoid the distraction of near-naked girls brushing past me as they hurried from the stage.

I set a plastic smile in place hoping it would still be there when the bright lights hit us. One cool thing: I thought we looked fantastic in our new black suits, gleaming white dress shirts, and dark ties. I could smell the Brut cologne I wore, freshened in the heat of my anxiety.

The curtain lifted before my stomach was ready. Mac rolled us out with Junior Walker's *Shotgun*, and we segued into Robert Parker's toe-tapper, *Barefootin'*. I'd worried there might be a bunch of drooling men in raincoats sitting ringside or along the runway, only tolerating us until the topless girls brought their bared breasts back out for ogling. Instead, most occupied tables held hip, upscale couples, men in coats and ties, and ladies decked out in fashionable dresses. Dave followed *Barefootin'* with *Marlena*, a smooth Four Seasons tune the crowd appreciated. At Mac's insistence, we tried to recreate our moves from the show sets we used to do. We were rusty, but the audience responded to our enthusiasm, and it helped loosen us up.

We got more comfortable with the sound system as the set progressed. After a few adjustments to the vocal monitors our performance continued to improve. We closed with a song we'd learned specifically for the Galaxie: Bobby Hatfield, from the Righteous Brothers', version of the *Unchained Melody*, a dramatic blockbuster Dave blew away. His neck veins popped on the last note, until he pulled the mic away just as he ran out of breath and dipped his head. Several people stood as applause filled the room.

Les leaned back to hit a palm-sized button on the stage's back wall, and as the curtain lowered, we took our bows. Dave Rapken wanted continuous entertainment, so the stage change didn't allow time for conversation, but I thought some of the girls regarded us a little differently than they had earlier as they slipped past us. A slim redhead called Little Patti pulled a huge wad of gum out of her mouth, grinned, and parked it on the movable drum stand before we pushed it behind the back curtain.

Don had barely thrown the black drape over the drum set when one of the dancers hammered the curtain-opening button with an outstretched fist. She jumped to her spot as the recorded bass-driven dance music for their act began to thump. Dave Rapken nodded at Jack as we filed down the stairs to our dressing room. A good omen, I thought, a memorable beginning to our adventures at the Galaxie.

26
GALAXIANS

*There was just this amazing individuality. It's just
a whole different world of optimism and fearlessness,
women taking off their bras and dancing around Naked,
and a political hopefulness and involvement.*

— Jill Clayburgh

November, 1966
San Francisco, North Beach, California

IN THE EARLY sixties, a new generation of beatniks, disdainfully referred to as "hippies", since the original beats didn't consider them hip enough to be cool—began relocating their burgeoning counterculture from North Beach to a down-at-the-heels area settled originally by Russian immigrants near San Francisco's Golden Gate Park. As this hippie community, the name now popularized by Herb Caen, accreted various kinds of radicals, teenage runaways, and the disenchanted or dropped-out, this loose community swarmed into a full-blown, patched jean, tie-dyed circus around the intersection of Haight and Ashbury Streets. Fueled by newly invented and readily available hallucinogens seasoned with older, meaner opiates, the hippies mounted a free-wheeling experiment in social mores expressed in an idealized concept of peace and innocent love, and gave birth to epic upheaval in the neighborhood now known by its primary cross streets, Haight-Ashbury, or simply as the Haight.

The music erupting from the Haight, heavily influenced by folk and country, attempted to express the inexpressible. The chaotic mass of musicians, singers, and poets swirling in this kaleidoscopic stew of the senses churned out bands like the Grateful Dead; Big Brother and the Holding Company, focused by Janis Joplin's agonized voice; the Jefferson Airplane, enhanced by Grace Slick; Country Joe and the Fish; and the Electric Flag—while countless others burned like moths in the fierce, self-destructive bonfires of drugs, excess, and mental instability. The Summer of Love, in 1967, is consensually considered the height of the Peace and Love movement in San Francisco. But by the summer of 1966, while we entertained the sophisticated clientele at the Galaxie a little more than four miles north of Haight-Ashbury, Charles Manson-style predators had already begun gathering like wolves to sheep. The place was fast becoming more horror show than hippie heaven.

The Sexual Revolution was also in full swing, and Stark Naked and the Car Thieves, appearing at the Galaxie, where Broadway overlooked the Golden Gate along the cliffs of the old Barbary Coast in North Beach, were happily paid foot soldiers in the locally infamous, mammary-baring Topless Insurrection, a splinter manifestation of the bra-burning movement for women's freedom.

While the Peace and Love movement and the Topless Revolution expressed themselves in vastly different ways, both cultural eruptions had many common roots. Both emerged amid a growing thirst for individual freedom, a desire to escape from an ever-darkening shadow of war, and a national hangover following the public murder of a young and popular president.

The underlying circumstance that allowed these uprisings to take place, however, grew from an innovation in biological sciences spearheaded in the 1950s by Margaret Sanger—committed to freeing women from their reproductive cycle to enjoy sex with whomever they liked, whenever they liked—and enabled by infamous biologist and Harvard outcast, Gregory Pincus, a leading expert in human reproduction at the time.

Armed with the tiny little pill they dreamed into life as the sixties opened, women could change conception from a matter of chance to a matter of choice, as easily as taking a daily aspirin. AIDS was unheard of; sexually transmitted diseases weren't the untreatable nightmares they'd once been; and the new FDA-approved birth control pills were inexpensive and available at the corner drug store. All of this added up to the sixties briefly welcoming a more innocent, Garden of Eden-like, attitude toward sex. It could be safe and limitless.

By unchaining women from their biological roles, the years of youthfulness had been extended and the average age of marriage significantly delayed. The female half of the species was freed to join their male counterparts in the pursuit of erotic pleasure. Sexually aware women, with a newfound sense of control over their own bodies and a new social equality with men, burned their bras, went topless, and demanded more equality in all parts of society. The sixties introduced a rock and roll term never known before, *groupie*, a role that couldn't have existed previously. Without the pill, groupies would have rapidly been transformed into mommies before the label could have had time to stick. The flimsy social structure of the Peace and Love movement would have been crushed under its own weight, with babies and children, had its women been unable to control motherhood.

A year ago, before I'd fallen into this sea of erupting change, I'd been a young husband and father of two small sons struggling to sell newspaper advertising in Indianapolis. Now, I found myself divorced and singing professionally in a San Francisco topless club—eighteen hundred miles away, at one of the epicenters of the greatest seismic culture shift of the twentieth century. Instead of sharing a life with the woman I'd expected to be married to forever, I shared a dressing room, divided by thin wallboard, with a covey of topless showgirls and dancers. When I focused too hard on the magnitude of unimaginable change I'd experienced in the intervening months, my grasp on reality teetered. When we began this amazing year at the Galaxie, I couldn't imagine what to expect next from being exposed to these young women in such intimate surroundings.

Topless Teri, the headliner, provided my first hint. To her, the only reason our band existed was to give her a break between shows. Her apparent disdain, I came to realize, was an expression of her single-minded obsession with her career. She bounded her life by the intense competition she believed existed between her and the other top-billed, bare-breasted headliners around town. Chief among them, I'm certain, were Carol Doda, the original topless girl at the Condor, and Yvonne D'Angiers, the Iranian bombshell at the Off Broadway who, as a newspaper noted at the time, "owned two of San Francisco's three most famous landmarks." Yvonne gained worldwide notoriety when her work visa ran out and she chained herself to the Golden Gate Bridge to avoid deportation; a maneuver that Teri considered a cheap publicity stunt. I was certain that even Mrs. Gaye "Mommy" Spiegelman, a topless-dancer mother of eight with a body that made it hard to believe that she'd ever given birth, appearing nightly at El Cid, gave Teri sleepless nights.

At first, the girl performers tended to ignore us; they were the main attraction as far as they were concerned. At various times, the girls could be raucous, bold, and loud, or quiet and feminine, and occasionally, thoughtful and perceptive. They each had their own histories, and lived their unique lives like girls anywhere. The exception was Teri, who wasn't really like anybody I'd ever known.

Teri decided she needed to improve her already sizeable breasts with silicone implants soon after our contract began. Breast enhancement being a relatively new procedure, the other girls looked forward to seeing the result. After her scheduled days off for the surgery, Teri returned to the stage—not quite as expected.

"Man—you guys catch Teri up on stage yet?" Mac said, popping into the dressing room to change for the first show. We hadn't. "Well, that is something you gotta experience for yourselves. Never seen nothin like it."

When I slipped out of the dressing room and got upstairs, Teri came into view, dancing to the recorded music at the far end of the stage. With a grind, she bumped her bikini-covered bottom in the direction of the crowd, before rotating to dance back across the stage. Before the turn, she'd looked like the Teri we knew; but when she faced the other way, her left breast, now prominent, protruded, round and unyielding. At center stage, she swung to the front and pranced out onto the runway. I blinked. Shoulders back, she proudly presented one generously-sized, naturally plumped breast, next to the other, a bloated, pink-tipped bobbing sphere. Shocked titters and murmurs rose from the audience.

Downstairs, one of the other showgirls explained, through gales of laughter. "Teri told me she had to pay a traffic ticket or lose her license. She didn't have enough left to get them both done. I guess she did what she could afford."

It was ludicrous and hilarious, but Teri reveled, unabashed, in the notoriety. Weeks later, on a Saturday night after a few more days off,

Teri proudly exhibited her new, evenly balanced, gravity-defying, outrageously expanded spherical frontage.

The two topless beauties who flanked Teri during their show, Dorrie and Bambi, were showgirls with very distinct personalities. Dorrie, fair, sweet, and lightly freckled, had recently arrived from some small Iowa or Kansas town and was the first of the girls I became friends with. I think we found common ground because both of us were still a little dewy behind the ears. We spent a couple of awkward nights together before agreeing to remain just friends. She danced in a cowboy-themed outfit with a top she removed to unleash what Dave considered the most perfect pair of breasts in captivity. But it was Bambi, a quick-witted, petite, dark-haired stunner, who captured Dave's affection at the Galaxie early on.

Not all the girls appeared on stage topless. Delilah's soulful renditions of R&B classics, rather than her trim, dark, athletic body in a bikini, were her main contributions to the show. She told us the all-girl backstage scene on her side of the wall was usually pretty entertaining, but sometimes the girls got petty and pathetic. Easy to understand—sometimes we did, too.

A pair of scantily clad, bikini-topped go-go dancers completed the cast. These lean, taut-skinned girls were Savannah—tall, smooth, and elegant; and Little Patti—the tiniest and most energetic of them all.

The fantasy life we were experiencing intensified, as celebrities became common in our audiences. Mac came to the mic wide-eyed one night to welcome a huge contingent of the San Francisco Forty-Niners football team sitting off to our left. Local television and political celebrities were often present, and many of the artists performing nearby came in. I'd never met nor even seen anyone famous in Indiana, let alone performed for them. I was in constant awe of their presence in our audience.

When an important celebrity was in the house, an electric thrill flickered through the crowd. The most obvious celebrity was Wilt Chamberlain. He towered from his aisle seat, and when he met us after the show. I stuck my hand straight up so that he could engulf it in his giant paw. He came back several more times to see us—or maybe to see the girls—but he always made sure to compliment us. Lee Majors, from the *Big Valley* TV series, was the first television star I remember coming to the Galaxie. Soon after, Farrah Fawcett, with enormous blond curls cascading to her shoulders, dazzled our showroom. I held her hand, dumbfounded, when I met her.

Playing on Broadway within walking distance of celebrity entertainers made every night an adventure. We saw Johnny Rivers in his own show, and in our audience; the Ramsey Lewis trio, performing their hit record *The In Crowd*, starred at the Off Broadway; and jazz great Cal Tjader held court a few doors down the street.

Two blocks south, the Purple Onion and the Hungry i featured everyone from the Kingston Trio, to Barbra Streisand, Woody Allen, and the hilarious Steve Martin. Walking along foggy North Beach streets between our shows—where the sounds of lonely foghorns from the harbor were interspersed with seal barks—added to the surreal experience of seeing, and often being acknowledged by, other artists. Meanwhile, Herb Caen continued to find ways to write about Stark Naked and the Car Thieves in his column, and most of the local papers carried ads to see us at the Galaxie.

How do you get used to living such an unbelievable life? I wondered.

27

LEONARD

*Most truths are so Naked that people feel sorry for
them and cover them up, at least a little bit.*

— Edward R. Murrow

*November 25, 1965
San Francisco, North Beach, California*

"SOMETHING'S GOT TO be done about Don," I said, even before everyone had filed into the dressing room. As usual, Don was out the door first after rehearsal, which gave me a chance to gather the rest of the band before they left. I was nervous, dreading the confrontation to come.

After a short ceasefire during our first few weeks here, Don's sharp digs, complaints, and sarcasm had returned. Feet shuffled, cigarette lighters clicked, someone coughed, but there was none of the usual banter, as we sat or stood along the narrow bench in front of our individual closet spaces.

"We've got to get this situation resolved." I pressed the point as everyone seemed to look away. With no fans running during the afternoon, the air in the basement room was close and stuffy.

"What do you want us to do, Larry, fire him?" Les said, a slow burn already beginning.

"If it comes to it, yeah, I do. He's really unhappy in this band."

"He's really unhappy with you, you mean."

"I can't help that, Les. I was here when he got in the band, and I'm still here now."

"Come on now," Mac said. "This thing's been buildin up for awhile. We got to get it out in the open, get this rabbit-ass crap figured out."

Dave sipped coffee and cleared his throat. "I like Don a lot, Les, but he's unhappy. Doesn't matter why. Drags us down when someone's griping and threatening to leave the band all the time. Can you talk to him? Try to calm him down?"

Les turned away to stalk along his side of the room, chin out, frowning, but not at anyone in particular. "I've talked to him. Says this band's not musically challenging enough for him, and he despises Larry. Says he's a no-talent—"

"Yeah, yeah, I've heard enough from him and I think I've tolerated his abuse pretty goddamned well, considering."

"Not that fucking well. You go out of your way to piss him off."

"Hard not to. He's pissed off we breathe the same air. Look, he's in the band because you wanted him in. Our focus is on vocals, and he wants to be in something more instrumental, not backing up singers. So let's stop making Don's problems all about me."

There was more to this than Don and me feuding. We'd been split into two factions since Les had forced us to bring Don and Jack with him into the band. Belonging to both sides made Les the wildcard. He wasn't going to be in my corner about this. There would be hard feelings no matter how things turned out.

"Are you saying, asshole, this is somehow my fault? You're putting this on me? You fucking coward cocksucker, you've got no idea what you're talking about." Les's face thundered up, dark and menacing. His voice got harsh and aggressive as he stoked himself into a towering rage. I'd expected the discussion to be tough, but crap, would this be more than I bargained for? Dave and Mac didn't want to get between Les and me, but to give them credit, they kind of sidled toward us.

Les glared at me over a hunched and threatening shoulder. *Not a Daddy Bear right now, no.* I'd seen, and been the focus of, his intimidating anger before, but this was the most worked up I'd ever seen him. *I might be quivering inside, but I'd rather risk being broken in half than let him see me cringe.*

Jack hadn't said anything up until now. "Hold on now, hold on goddammit. If anybody's firing anybody, I'll be the one to do it, so hold your damn horses."

Mac turned to Jack. "So how you gonna solve this, Mr. Leader?"

Jack tipped ash off his smoke and thought for a moment. "We can't go on a lot longer with these two at each other. I agree on that much."

"Well, I reckon I'm the one got this ruckus started." Grim resolve pinched Mac's face as he dragged a hand through his hair to rub the back of his neck. "I did mention to Larry about not likin the way Don drums on my tunes." His defiant gaze bounced around the four of us, daring anyone to contradict him.

"I like the guy well enough, and if you say he's the best musician, Les, maybe even better than you, who am I to say he ain't? But I liked when Reno's drummin kicked me in the ass on my R&B tunes. Least when he was straight, which, I admit, wasn't all the time. Just not gettin that kick from Don, my brothers." He shook his head with a final fiery glare.

Mac gave quite a speech; I had always thought of him as more of our "go along to get along" guy. I silently applauded him for his eloquence.

"I think Don drums okay, but I agree with Mac," Dave said. "I think he probably likes jazz more than rock. I'm not sure he's the right drummer for our band, especially since he seems so unhappy."

"Well shit." Jack had a twisted frown on his face. "Played with Don for quite a while now. I admire him. I'm a better musician 'cause of him, and I wanta keep playing with him. Never seen this side of him before, he's like a crazy man about Larry. And I guess Don's on Larry's ass more than vice versa, though I think Larry coulda, whadyacallit . . . defused the situation lots of times, instead of egging him on the way he does." Jack took a deep breath before going on.

"I say one of them's got to go. Larry's been with you guys since the beginning and he's a decent singer, but we'd do okay without him, and I'd rather keep Don." Jack wouldn't look at me. I'd expected him to come down on the side of his trio buddy, but it made my guts hurt anyway. It got the adrenaline shakes going, and I couldn't hold back any longer.

"Fuck you, Jack. This is not about which of us goes, it's about whether Don goes. He's the problem, not me. If he stays, goes, gets fired, sets his hair on fire, or lights up like a goddamned Roman candle, I'm still in this band. I'm not quitting, and I'm not getting fired. Anyone who thinks so better plan on bodily picking my ass up and throwing me out of here.

Don goes because, and you can believe me on this or not, it's what's best for the band. He's been way outta line with me, but even more important, we need a different drummer."

Les turned on me again, indignation burning hot in his eyes. "You dumbass, who are you to say we need a new drummer? You're not a musician, you've got no idea what you're talking about." Les clenched and unclenched his fists. We stood faced off against each other, eyes locked, tension ratcheting to fever pitch.

I said nothing, but I mustered up the hardest sullen glare I had, not backing down, hoping he wouldn't hit me. Dave, Mac, and I always assumed a special, geographical bond existed between the four of us from the Midwest. Les had become our fourth singer when we'd formed the Checkmates in Indiana. But in reality, we'd only performed together for four weeks plus half a night. Les had actually played longer with his trio than he'd sung with us. Jack and Don could quite possibly mean more to him than we did. Hard to tell, though. Les was secretive by nature and hid his deeper feelings. Somebody might be driving me to an emergency room if I had this figured wrong.

He raised his right shoulder and fist as if to strike, but I wouldn't cower. His jaw tightened as he launched his punch. His fist flew toward and then past my face as he pivoted at the last moment, purposefully ramming it into the wallboard separating our side of the dressing room from the dancers. The blow drove his arm through the wallboard up past his elbow. Under different circumstances, we might have laughed ourselves silly watching him struggle to get his trapped arm out of the wall.

Without thinking, I stepped forward, reaching out tentatively. "Les, you okay, man? Are you hurt?" We'd be without a guitar player for a while if his hand had hit a stud.

"Stay the fuck away from me, Larry," He hissed at me through clenched teeth. With a final twist, bits of drywall and chalk dust followed his arm and hand out of the hole. They were dusted ghostly pale but apparently undamaged.

"I don't give a shit about this son of a bitch's opinion, but go ahead and fire Don. That's the way I vote. He deserves to be in a better band than this one," he said. "Maybe I do, too." With a final baleful glare, Les stalked out of the dressing room, taking a lot of the air with him. I knew my relationship with Les was badly damaged, perhaps irreparably. I hoped not, but Les was not a forgiving guy.

I don't think Les had realized what sacrificing Reno and Carlos had meant to us when he'd insisted Don and Jack be brought into our band. We'd wanted him back and agreed our band would be much better because of him, so we accepted his ultimatum. But now Don had to go, for the betterment of the band, on several levels.

"Well I ain't firin' him," Jack said, in the emotional void Les left behind. "Somebody else gonna have to do it, 'cause I'm not going to." He stamped his cigarette out on the floor.

"Shit, Jack." Mac glowered at Jack, as if he were a bug crawling along the floor. "You're the goddamned leader; ain't an option, part of the job."

I spoke quietly to Dave and Mac. "Give me the briefcase, just for the night. I'll let him go."

Jack scowled at me. "You do want your revenge, don't you?"

"Not about revenge, Jack. We just can't waste any more time on this."

Firing Don didn't turn out to be difficult. I was a little uncomfortable when I asked him to sit with me at the end of the following night. Whether or not Les or Jack had told him already, he knew what was coming.

"So, you finally got up on your back legs and made something happen." He wore his patented superior smirk when he sat down at a back table with me.

"You're sacking me tonight, aren't you, Dunlap? Funny, I'd 'a thought Jack would've been the one. Kind of insulting, if you ask me."

"You should consider it a compliment. I always hoped I'd earn your respect. I didn't, and that's my failure." I shrugged and took a sip of the ice water in front of me. "I actually hate to let you go, but I care about the survival of my band. You're disruptive and unhappy; we both need to move on."

"Well, I can respect that." He nodded thoughtfully. "Didn't picture things ending this way, but maybe it's not so surprising. Glad you saved me the trouble of giving notice. Jack and Les wouldn't let me quit when I told them weeks ago I wanted to."

"You should've asked me." I grinned at him. "I'd have let you."

Don grinned back. In some other time continuum, we might have been friends. A cocktail waitress with a tray full of empties pushed past us in a hurry to finish her night.

"You should take a look at the guy at Big Al's," Don said.

"Who's at Big Al's?"

"Rock drummer. Plays solo for a topless dancer with a snake. You'd probably be happy together. And no, I don't mean with the snake," he said with a genuine smile. "Used to see the guy play in San Leandro, where I came up. Can't remember his name, but he's a good drummer and a good guy."

Mac told me after Leonard Souza had come over from Big Al's to audition, he'd kicked his bass drum so hard, Mac's pants moved.

He liked that.

On the first Tuesday after Don Hunt's two weeks notice ended, Leonard lifted his sticks for the first time as a Naked Car Thief. We'd been able to get new suits made for him in time. He preened behind his drums.

"Okay," Les said, looking back at him. "Until you're familiar with our songs, I'll be counting off the tunes. Watch me for downbeats. You okay?" Leonard's sad, hound-dog eyes made it difficult to tell what he was thinking. He gave Les a solemn nod, and then his sallow Portuguese face split into a rictus grin we would become very familiar with.

"Okay, here we go." Les dropped his guitar head on the downbeat of the *Harlem Shuffle*. Leonard smacked his snare with one of his thick sticks, and a rim shot ripped around the stage as Les slapped the button to send the curtain into motion.

Jack fumbled with the volume on his bass to match Leonard's drums as the curtain rose, and when that wasn't enough, he jumped back to his amp and gave its volume knob a twist. He duck-walked back to the front of the stage, still working the knobs, before the curtain was all the way open.

Dave and Mac stepped forward dancing the hitchhike and sang: "move it to the right . . ." Any doubt about Leonard as a rock drummer disappeared. Leonard played up on top of the beat, hammering at us, pushing us, adding excitement, though the vocals became harder to hear. I smacked my tambourine on the two and four, and I dropped back stage right, near the drums. I watched as the front skin of the bass drum rippled each time he kicked it. He stared at me, thick, straight black hair slicked back, the tip of his tongue just peeking out between his heavy lips on the right side. Couldn't tell from his expression, but I was pretty sure he was having a good time.

He came to a fill, did a tasty little run across his top toms, did a kick, then a rim shot, and leaned back into the rhythm. He stared at me, expressionless, all the way through. I nodded along and moved to the beat.

We were sweaty and excited at the end of the set. Not only did we sound a lot more like a rock band, Leonard didn't begrudge me the ground I walked on. We gathered around him for quick congratulations as the curtain came down and the girls rushed around us onto the stage. We hurried through our stage change chores under Teri's narrowed eyes until we tumbled down the steps and off the stage where she loved to perform and considered her own. She shrugged, plastered on a smile, and began to dance the pony to the pounding recorded music, her bare breasts wobbling and bobbing as she reached center stage.

Mac was first to grab Leonard's arm. "Man, you was rippin it up. That was so cool."

Leonard smiled bashfully and kind of giggled. "I messed up the end of the Shuffle song, but Les got me out okay. This is so much frickin' fun. I was playing for a snake last night, now here I am in this amazing band. Been waiting a long time for this."

Yeah, Leonard, I thought, *me, too.*

28

ADOPTION

*My ideal is to wake up in the morning and
run around the meadow Naked.*

— Daryl Hannah

December 17, 1965
San Francisco, North Beach, California

A FEW DAYS AFTER my birthday, I lounged around the apartment in sock feet, tee shirt, and jeans. Dave's bedroom door was still closed, and I wasn't sure he was alone. I'd started reading Frank Herbert's *Dune*, intrigued since it had won a Nebula award. I'd been put off reading the book for a while though, by a couple of unfavorable reviews. I was happily finding they were unfounded. The concept of melange, a spice that provided immortality as the currency of a star-spanning civilization was intriguing, and I was falling into the story. Science fiction epics set in star-spanning empires were my favorites. I was settling in for the afternoon with Paul Atreides when the phone rang.

Cheryl's voice said, "Hello brother. Did you get the gift?"

"Who knew you could get White Castle hamburgers shipped here from Indianapolis? We held an Indiana pig-out on our night off. They didn't last long, must've scarfed down a dozen myself."

"Well, happy twenty-fourth. I told Mom that's what you'd like. Anyway, I have another reason to call; hope that's okay."

I got a little more comfortable in the worn easy chair. "Always love hearing from home, especially you. Everything okay with the family? Your dancing going good?"

"I'm doing great. I'm at the top of my dance classes, even kind of outgrowing them. We've gotten a little troupe together, including a band. We go around to hospitals and retirement homes, different places, where we sing and do dance numbers for the holidays. I better be careful or I'm going to end up in a band like you.

"As for the family thing, this is more about yours, about Pat, about the boys."

I sat up straight, but tried to speak calmly. "About Pat and the boys?" I looked over at the coffee table toward my smokes, but the cord wasn't long enough to reach them.

"Mom asked me to call, to ask you to call her. You know how she is, she hates to pick up a phone to dial anyone locally, but California, she's not sure long distance reaches that far. Anyway, she'd like to talk to you and hear how you're doing, so you should call."

"I will, but can't you tell me what this is all about?" I stood and paced as far as the cord would let me.

"I think Mom wants to tell you herself, so I better not. She's got something to ask you about. So, will you call?"

"I'll call now. Good to talk to you, sis, love you."

"Love you, big brother. Sorry to sound so mysterious. Not anything too bad, they're all okay, so don't get worried."

I went back to the refrigerator for more orange juice, wondering what this was all about. I looked down at the phone as I lit a cigarette, hoping it might give up some answers before I picked it up. When it didn't, I blew out a big exhale and dialed.

"Larry, is that you?"

"Hi, Mom. Just got off the phone with Cheryl. She said you wanted to ask me something about Pat and the kids. Can you talk for a minute?"

"Of course. You got our gift and the cards out there in California okay?" She made it sound like California was just south of Timbuktu.

"The White Castles were perfect, Mom, a tremendous hit. Your wintery Christmas card reminded me of how enlightened we are about snow here—we visit it up in the mountains, and then leave it there and come home." I waited expectantly.

"Well, happy birthday, Larry." I sensed my mother's hesitation. "Pat has come by to see us, several times. She brings the children, you know, so we can visit with them. They're healthy and well—just beautiful boys. So blond. So like their mother. She loves them so much."

I dropped into my chair, my memories filled with their little faces, and Pat's, too. "They are beautiful, Mom. I love them, too. Pat's probably still mad at me, but I was hoping I could talk to them. I don't know where to call on their birthdays. I've already missed David's, as it is."

"I know, Larry." I waited expectantly again. *Come on, Mom, what's going on?*

"It might not be the best time for you to call them." Her breath caught. "The last time Pat was here, she came alone, without the boys. She says she's found another man. Someone she's fallen in love with and intends to marry. From what she's told me, he sounds like an excellent gentleman. I hope this doesn't come as too much of a . . . of a shock to you?"

My heart clenched, making breathing extra hard. After a moment, I spoke softly into the receiver. "You know I want her to be happy, Mom. I can't explain, but I still love her. I couldn't—we couldn't work out how to be together, but I do love her." I considered for a moment. "I guess this had to happen, but so soon . . ."

"He's a captain in the Air Force, a steady, stable man, and Larry, he loves the boys. That's important, you know—with you so far away, and traveling around so much, they're going to need a father figure."

"Pat really loves him? She really wants to marry this person?"

"Yes, she says so."

I waited. "Mom, that's not everything, is it?"

"She has something she wants me to talk to you about. She says this man won't consider marriage unless he's able to adopt the boys. He wants to raise them as his own. She wants you to let him do that." I was floored and speechless.

"She says she understands, after being out there in California with you, that you don't make enough money to send her child support. This way, you wouldn't have to bear the responsibility of that, she said. And she's confident this man will be very, very good to them and take excellent care of them."

"Mom. They're my kids, my boys. Your grandsons."

"Yes, and they always will be. Blood is blood, and that can't be changed with a piece of paper. This is just a legal thing, really. So Pat can get on with her life, the way you're getting on with yours."

"Do you think I should do this?"

"I find this hard to say, but I think I do. Under the circumstances, it's probably best for everybody. But you'll have to decide."

"I'm not sure what to think. Hearing this . . . I can't say anything right now. I hope you don't mind, Mom, but I need to get off the phone. I love you, but I have to get off the phone right now."

"I understand, son. Remember, I love you, and this doesn't reflect on you. It's just how things turned out. You think the matter over. Pat wanted an answer as soon as possible, but you take as much time as you need, sweetheart."

I tried to read, or find some football or basketball game on TV—something to distract me from what was being asked of me. My mind chewed on the conversation with my mother as I gave in to watching mindless television. It was still front and center in my mind when Dave and I got into the Falcon that night.

"Got a problem, Dave. Talked with my mom and sister today. Pat asked them to call me." I glanced over at Dave. "She's found some guy she wants to marry and she wants me to let him adopt Dave and Danny when they're married."

"Damn. What did you say?"

"Nothing yet. I told my mom I'd have to think about it."

"Your mom's okay with this? Seems weird to me."

"Well, she says Pat told her we don't make much money doing music and I can't support them. And Mom says it would make Pat happy, and you know I want that. Kills me to think of her with somebody else, but Christ Almighty, what was I expecting—she would stay single?"

"Do you think she's so pissed off she's just trying to get back at you? Doesn't sound like the Pat I know, but did you consider that?"

"I just can't see it. I've never known her to have a mean bone in her body. No, I take what my mother told me at face value, but what kind of guy would demand I give up my children? I want Pat to be happy and I'd do almost anything for her, but this is asking too much. Guess it's true I can't pay much support yet, but we're getting to be a better band. Maybe we're going to make more money."

"I know you love those boys and Dave's named after me, almost like my godson. My opinion only, but I hope you don't give them up." I pulled onto the Bay Bridge ramp to take us up, over, and into the City.

One night, Dave Rapken flagged me down.

"Hey, Larry."

"'Yeah?"

"Ever hear of Judy Davis?" I thought for a moment.

"Can't say I have."

"How 'bout Barbra Streisand?"

"Well, sure. Of course."

"Well, when Barbra Streisand's here in San Francisco, say at the Purple Onion or whatever, she goes to see this Judy Davis. She's a hot vocal teacher or something. I know a guy who can set Dave up with her if he wants to go."

"Just Dave?"

"You think some of the other guys would want to go?"

"I would." Ever since it had been made clear I was expendable, I wanted to improve in any way I could.

"Okay, so ask your guys. I'll pick up the tab for the first week for anyone who wants to go, after that you got to pay your own way, but it will be at a discount rate. Okay?"

"I'm not sure how you two got past the front door. Who are you?" Judy Davis perched like a bird at a huge grand piano in her studio in Oakland. We'd been led into her presence by a receptionist. The room was spare; holding only a couple of director's chairs, a floor-standing ashtray, and another made of heavy glass that sat on the glistening full-grand piano top. Her studio had a window wall overlooking a grass-covered slope that descended down to a small street that intersected College Avenue.

I felt so cowed I could've been back in Don Martin's choir room in high school. Dave said, "We're singers at the Galaxie in North Beach. Dave Rapken said he arranged vocal lessons with you."

"Ah, now we're getting somewhere. You do realize you have to pass an audition for me to work with you? Let's start there."

We ran vocal scales and Judy checked our ranges. I was fascinated to learn there were as many as seven falsetto ranges, two of them in the lower registers. I couldn't entirely access the first falsetto range above normal voice. Dave's power and tone she judged, of course, to be stellar.

"You, Dave, I can help. You've got an instrument. You," she said, swiveling to me. "I don't know how much good I can do for you. Singers are singers. I can't work miracles, but at least I can give you good technique and habits, show you how to protect your voice, how to work with what you have."

Good enough for me. While I'd never been driven to sing lead, sometimes I felt my biggest weakness was confidence. Judy Davis certainly wasn't going to improve that—additional technique would have to do instead.

"Okay then, off to the doctor," she said, dismissing us. "I don't start with anyone until they get a full ENT checkup. You'd be surprised how a thorough medical exam by the right doctor can clear up voices. Once I get his report, I'll set up a schedule for you."

Within a few weeks, Judy Davis's techniques were helping us enormously. I'd been apprehensive when the ear, nose, and throat doctor dove into my ear with a hooked needle tool that looked more suited to a dentist's office. But there was no discomfort when he pulled out a splendid round sphere of earwax from each ear so big he had to squeeze it into the prescription bottle he'd given me when I said I'd like to keep the things as souvenirs. I wondered how I'd ever been able to hear anything at all with so much gunk in my ears.

Judy taught us warm-up exercises for the beginning of the night. They involved stretching our mouths into wide clown smiles with our teeth clenched, while we "buzzed" scales, higher and higher. The other guys made fun of our warm-up buzzes, then got a little irritated with them, and finally just accepted our routine. Vocal cords, like any other muscle, she told us, need calisthenics to warm them up and stretch them so they wouldn't strain on the first note we sang. Though the hours weren't as long at the Galaxie as they had been across the bay, most of the songs we did now called for high-powered vocals; the wear and tear on our voices was far greater without dance tunes to give us breaks to rest them.

Before Judy, when Dave's voice began to tire, he'd drink boiling hot coffee or tea with lemon to help revive his voice. She told him that tea, well-warmed, not boiling, would help, but the acid from the lemons was a big no-no: it would strip the natural lubricant from his vocal cords. She recommended honey as the closest substitute to the organ's natural lubricant. If we felt like we had to pour hard liquor over our money-makers, she said, at least make our drinks mixed. While she also recommended giving up smoking and spicy food, those first two lessons were the most valuable. I always thought it was unfortunate we couldn't get these lessons with Judy for Mac. I think it would've helped him, but supporting his family had to be his priority.

29

THE DIME BAG

In order to swim one takes off all one's clothes—in order to aspire to the truth one must undress in a far more inward sense, divest oneself of all one's inward clothes, of thoughts, conceptions, selfishness etc. before one is sufficiently Naked.

— Soren Kierkegaard

January 17, 1966
Berkeley, California

AT THE NEXT exhale, everything around me changed in some fundamental way. Or, I observed, it could be I'd changed, altering my perception of everything else. A space had opened in my head, some added dimension, previously hidden around a corner I'd never been aware of before.

"Wait, wait, wait. Hold on, everyone. Stop everything. Seriously. Something is happening. I think I might be getting high right now. Whew. Actually I am high, right now." I laughed and noticed how the muscles in my cheeks rolled up. *Damn! This is the most amazing, most intense, interesting, grooviest feeling, ever.*

"Sooo cool, foxy lady . . ." I definitely hadn't felt like this when Mac offered me hits of marijuana in Indianapolis when we first met.

"You're stoned," Marie said, at the dining room table, rolling again.

"Yup, that's true, I am." I meditated for a moment in somber appreciation. "My folks would not approve of this, you know. But if feeling this good is wrong, I don't wanna be right."

"Sounds like a country song," Dave said.

"You guys are tripping." Marie's tricky fingers kept rolling.

"Tripping?" Dave said, "Really? Can't argue, though, too fucked up to tell."

I laughed at him, inhaled another sizeable toke, and dropped the hot nub-end into the ashtray. Dave was shaking his fingers to cool them off, too.

"These ends are too small to smoke anymore," he said. "Got more joints over on the table?"

"Those 'ends' are called roaches," Marie said. "Don't waste 'em. Bring them over here, and oh, bring my purse."

A few hours earlier, before the nice dinner Marie had planned, I'd shuffled out of my bedroom holding up a baggie for Dave and Marie's inspection and a suggestion for the night's entertainment.

"How about smoking some of this, guys? Mac's never gonna give me back the money I spent on it. Dave and I have been talking about trying again. Seems like tonight's a good night for it."

"Where'd you get that?" Marie glanced at me from the couch, where a framed velvet bullfighter stared down at her. She wore a burgundy ribbed knit sweater over beige, jean-cut corduroys, and white, pointy-toed sneakers. It was becoming our routine for her to travel up to Berkeley from Union City on nights off so we could spend time together.

"About a month ago at rehearsal, some guy came to the club to deliver this to Mac. Mac was gone, but I told him I'd make sure he got it. He sorta sized me up and said, 'Sure man, got him this fine dime bag, but you gotta pay up first.' So I figure no big deal, right, and handed him a dime. The guy stared at me suspiciously and said, 'What's this ten cents for, fool? You got to give me ten dollars.' I felt pretty dumb, so I laughed like I was joking around, and gave him the ten bucks."

Marie held her hand out, so I walked the baggie over to her.

"Mac never seems to have ten he can spare, so it's been living in my sock drawer for weeks. Figure it's mine now."

Marie examined the cuttings through the clear plastic. "Mainly flowers and buds, hardly any stems or seeds. Righteous three-finger lid." She rested her cigarette in the ashtray, unsealed the baggie, and sniffed inside. "Not skunky, either. Pretty impressive for ten dollars."

"So we going to smoke that shit, or just talk about it?" Dave asked.

She resealed and dropped the baggie on the coffee table. "I'm not sure this is such a great idea." Her reluctance puzzled me.

"Dave and I already decided we're going to try this loco weed again sooner or later. We've got some, so why not tonight?"

Dave grinned in enthusiastic support from across the room.

"You did tell me you knew how to roll cigarettes out of this stuff. We'll probably make a big mess of it if you won't help."

Seeing I was determined, Marie's resolve wavered. "First off, *chico*, don't call them cigarettes. Joints, doobies, blunts, whatever, but never cigarettes." She rubbed the middle of her forehead. "Neither of you guys ever rolled a joint? You don't have any idea how to do this? Separate the good grass from the junk? None of that?"

"No," I said with a shrug. Dave shook his head and added. "Sounds like you do, though."

"I grew up in the barrio, Dave." She lifted her chin with a touch of defiance. "Weed's entertainment, employment, and, a lotta times, unemployment in my neighborhood." Resigned, she stood and gazed down at me with a wry grin.

"Okay, since you're going to do it anyway. I'll do the rolling and keep an eye on you guys, but"—she waggled her hand at me—"I'm not smoking."

We eagerly agreed.

After chili verde, beans, rice, and tortillas, Dave and I cleared and washed dishes, while Marie went out. By the time we were finished, Marie was back and dumping the mummified contents of the baggie onto the dining room table next to a little packet of Zig Zag rolling papers and a bottle of Chardonnay.

The wine was for her, she told us. There was juice in the refrigerator for us. She deftly separated out the small seeds and thin stems from the clumped buds and desiccated flowers with a playing card as we sat next to her. The cuttings smelled sharp, and stale. We lit cigarettes while she scooped stems and seeds back into the baggie.

"I was taught," she said, "don't waste nothing."

She rough-chopped the pile and carded it into a bowl. She pulled a thin, pre-folded rolling paper out of the Zig Zag pack and pinched in a little of the chopped-up weed while holding the paper's fold open with a finger. *Maybe too little*, I worried.

"You sure those are thick enough?"

Her right index finger bent the paper over the filling, then, switching a hand to each end, she snugged and rolled the paper until only a long, narrow edge was left.

"They'll be fine. This is good grass, don't want to put too much in. Burns up too fast, wasteful." She ran the tip of her tongue along the length of the exposed paper, twisted both ends tight, and popped the whole thing into her mouth, dragging it out slowly.

"Your problem is, you probably don't know how to smoke 'em right." She smiled owlishly.

Marie handed the thin, neatly rolled cylinder to Dave and noticed our attentiveness. "What? You're watching me like I'm a trained seal." Dave and I had been staring, fascinated at the clever competence of her quick fingers. We smiled.

"Stop staring at me, you weirdos. Go over and turn the TV on or something."

In our open-plan apartment, the living room was defined by the presence of a neutral-colored sofa and an easy chair, lumpy veterans of many former tenants' butts. They presided over a scarred coffee table and a nicked-up Sylvania television set.

I flicked on the TV. A *Monkees* episode coalesced on the screen; they were committing vocal havoc, so I flipped it off. As a future version of Micky Dolenz would someday admit, the Monkees really becoming a band was equivalent to Leonard Nimoy really becoming a Vulcan.

By the time I was back on the couch, Marie handed me a joint. "Give me a minute to get some snacks and stuff, and I'll show you how to smoke 'em, if you want me to."

Dave twiddled one of the thin, handmade marijuana smokes like it was Groucho's cigar.

"I don't need no stinkin' lessons," he growled in his best Bogart imitation. He stuck the joint in his mouth, flipped open his Zippo, and lit up. The end flared for a second and fitfully burned down about a third. A warm, sweet, but acrid odor I remembered from Mac's basement in Indianapolis wafted through the air. He pulled a lungful in, hard, squinting against the smoke, and suddenly began hacking as if his lungs had caught fire.

"Whew," he said, with a rasp. He wiped his flushed face and watery eyes as the hacking subsided. "Wasn't sure if I was going to shit or go blind. Remind me to get a another carton of these."

Marie sat down next to me, giggling while dumping chips, salsa, and glasses on the coffee table. She had a nice laugh, easy and rich.

"Dave Dunn, listen to me. Drag the smoke in slow and steady and try to keep it in long as you can." She demonstrated, sucking in air in short bursts.

"Take little air-sips to pull the smoke deeper into your lungs. When you can't hold your breath anymore, let it out, slow as you can."

I stuck my joint in my mouth and reached for the lighter. Marie grabbed it first.

"Wastes too much grass, lighting it like a regular smoke," she said, cupping the joint in the palm of her left hand, between thumb and forefinger, and held the tip to the lighter's flame. "Stoners light up like this." She stuck the barely lit cylinder back between my lips.

"Stoners, huh? Maybe you should be an instructor at pot school. Marijuana Smoking 101. Is there a diploma I get or something if I graduate?"

Dave choked out a laugh, trying to hold back his inhale. Marie snorted a little giggle.

"I thought you Midwest guys grew this stuff in your corn fields. Or at least learned how to smoke dope in college." She turned back to Dave. "So, next toke, take a drag, suck in steady. Sip, sip, sip . . . Yep, like that . . . Now let the smoke out slow . . . Now you've got it."

Following the instructions she'd given Dave, I'd smoked my joint better than halfway down when my mouth desperately craved a cigarette. I one-handed a smoke out of a pack and lit up.

"You still smoking those weird Lark cigarettes?" Dave said, "Thought you gave those up. They got a funny odor."

"Not as funny as the one you're smoking. Anyway, I like Larks. They taste cinnamony. This one tastes especially cinnamony." I smacked my lips, tasting the word, with the cigarette in one hand, my joint smoldering in the other.

"Cinnamony ain't a real word, man. You're making that up."

That's when I realized I must be getting high.

30
MOTHER'S MILK

I'd rather go Naked than wear fur.

— Christy Turlington

January 17, 1966
Berkeley, California

DAVE AND I worked our way over to Marie at the dining room table where she dug a hair clip out of her purse and carefully lodged my blackened joint end in the metal spring. "Need something better for this, though. Alligator clips from the drugstore make good roach holders." She lit the scrap of paper and weed, held it out to me for a final hit, and then did the same for Dave.

"And now," she said, pinching out the tiny scraps of joint left and handing them back to us, "squeeze these into little balls and swallow them."

Dave did a double take. "What? You kidding? Swallow these? They're all burnt up, they'll taste like shit."

"Don't taste them, swallow them. The resins that get you high are concentrated down into 'em."

I put my little marijuana pill on my tongue and swallowed.

"Jeez, with all the slang, techniques, and little tools, we must be members of some secret cannabis club now, with weird handshakes and rituals. And . . . and this is some kind of initiation or something."

Dave nodded and reached for another one of the paper twists loaded with weed on the table. "The fucking Far Out Club, man, is what this club is."

"You guys are about to become a pain to be around for someone who's not high, especially this motor mouth." Marie gave me a deadpan grin. "So I'll get you juice and soda for the dry throats you're gonna get, and tortilla chips and salsa for the munchies. Then I'm gonna go watch *Peyton Place* on the TV. You guys can sit here and smoke yourselves stupid without any help from me. If I haven't rolled enough, I'll come do more."

"You know, Dave"—I lit up my next joint the way Marie had shown me—"it's pretty damn cool, Marie showing us all this, taking care of everything. Mexican ladies, seems to me, take really good care of their men. And, oh my God, the sex. If Marie's any example, Mexican girls are incredibly sexy," I stage-whispered to Dave, "and inventive." My eyes widened. "And flexible."

"You do realize I'm only a few feet away, right?" Marie worked the TV, trying to hide a smile. "I can hear you."

I nodded dreamily. "I didn't have the first clue about Mexicans when we first got here, you know."

Marie shook her head at my ignorance. "I keep telling you I'm *Chicana*, darlin'. Wasn't born in Mexico any more than you were born in Ireland. I'm as American as you are." But she didn't seem offended.

"I remember when you met Helen. I thought, wow, what a beautiful girl. I want to meet a golden girl like her."

"Helen's really great," Dave grunted out. "One of those things," he said, holding the smoke in. "Just didn't work out." He exhaled.

"Growing up in Indiana, the only difference between people I was aware of was white ones and black ones." I hesitated, pulling my thoughts together before continuing, certain he'd want to hear how this disparity had come to my attention.

"See one day, think I must have been in fourth grade, soon after my family moved to Salem Street anyway, I brought a kid home after school to play basketball with me. We were shooting around in the back yard until my mom called me in for dinner. I didn't want my friend to leave so I went through the back door into the kitchen and asked, 'Mom, can Randolph stay for dinner?'"

I leaned toward Dave and said in a low voice. "'No Larry, he can't. That boy's different. He can't stay to dinner with us.' I went back to the screen door, and studied the boy shooting baskets. When I came back I said, 'I don't think there's anything different about him, Mom.' And she says, 'He's got brown skin, honey. He's a colored boy.' I told Randolph I had to go inside, so he had to go home.

"I was troubled by what had happened. Not about the skin color thing so much, I wasn't color-blind. I knew his skin color wasn't the same as mine; what I hadn't known, until Mom pointed it out, was that it made a difference. I'd wanted to hang out with my new friend, but I'd just been taught that playmates with skin too much different colored than mine were a liability. They might have to go home early when I wanted them to stay and play."

Sound reasoning, I thought, nodding.

I studied the "Hang In There, Baby" cat poster hanging across the table from me. *Secret to life*, I nodded to myself.

"My best friend," Dave said, "along with Tom Gerlach across the street, was George Pride. You'd have to say George was a colored guy, I guess. Part, anyway. Never thought he was different from anyone else, though, 'cept for a permanent suntan." Dave was pawing around on the table looking for Marie's hair clip, his second joint now a roach.

"You're making my point." I reached for another joint, got it going. "You can't protect yourself from what comes into your mind through mother's milk. You get this package of unproven beliefs and opinions and shit that seem like facts, like natural law, without even knowing you're getting it. Understandable, really. Parents show you how to eat, walk, talk, when and where to poop, and how to wipe your butt after. They're all-powerful gods when you're little. For all you know, they make the sun go up and come down. You ingest this crap into your psyche before there's a guardian at the gate to question anything. Hard to root out or even notice those things later, after you've been hard-wired to accept these opinions, old wives' tales, and prejudices as facts."

"You're into some heavy, heavy shit, man," Dave said.

"Can't blame my mother for thinking like that. She was brought up in Vermont; probably didn't know anything about black people. Might have come ingrained in her, likely from her own mother's milk. Probably have to give her credit for never making me aware of skin color sooner. In most ways she was a saint, you know, would give her last dollar to anyone who needed it. One time she saved a cardinal with a broken wing I brought home. Stayed up for nights, chopped up food for it, crazy stuff. None of us thought it would live."

"A cardinal? What?" Marie said, listening in.

"The bird. You know, the Indiana state bird, the red one with a topknot?" Dave nodded.

"Anyway, she passed this particular imprinted opinion of hers right into my brain." I frowned. "I'm truly unhappy that I'm infected with shit like that."

Something nagged at me, something else about this.

"To be fair, Odell Bradshaw drove the fear home, though," I continued.

"Who? Odell?"

"This orange juice is so sweet. Have you tasted how good this orange juice is, man?" I smacked my lips. This was the best orange juice ever. "Did you get special OJ when you went out, Marie?"

"Yeah, right. Special," she said, rolling her eyes, though she never turned from the TV.

I turned back to Dave, who chased his last roach with grape juice he seemed to be appreciating. "You remember how they were bussing colored kids into Shortridge, Dave? Began in the middle of my sophomore year, I think."

"Yup. Bussed black kids from Crispus Attucks into Broad Ripple, too. Some from Tech."

"Well, one of the bussed-in kids was a guy who looked about twenty, skin so black it had dark-purple highlights. He had this perfectly spherical head, with small, springy, wound-wire black tufts popping out of his skull," I illustrated with little finger twirls. "And white, white teeth. He would give me a shark's grin most mornings when I got to school and say, 'Hey man, lemme hold a quarter man. Lemme hold a quarter 'n I won't have to bust yore ass.' If I gave him a quarter, he'd want another one. If I didn't have one, he'd keep scaring the crap out of me. I told my folks, but they didn't have any answers. My dad said, 'You're going to have to stand up to bullies your whole life, Larry. Don't give him the money. You stand up to him—bullies are cowards. They'll always back down.' Right, Dad. The guy was six inches taller than me and rock hard. Would've been suicide."

I hit the joint. Hard.

Dave dipped a humongous load of salsa onto a tortilla chip and nodded, trying to concentrate on what I was saying. "Mmm, salsa's incredible," he murmured. "You should try some, man."

"I had health and safety class with Odell. His desk was alone in the back. I sat up a row, and over a few seats. A couple of girls sat at desks in front of his. Odell had a cock on him over a foot long, see." I stretched out my hands. "Reason I know that, he'd loose that anaconda out of his pants right in class and threaten those girls to give him money. He'd grab it like a sock puppet and shake it at them whispering, 'This here snake gonna come gobble you up, girl, you don' give me some money.'"

"He'd sit back there, stroking his thing like a pet. When he stood up, you could see that thing stretched down near the knee, inside his jeans. Those girls had to have been scarred for life. I sure as hell was. Pictures I'll never be able to get out of my head." I shuddered.

"Teacher didn't dare go anywhere near the back of the room. I tell ya, it was Odell who put the fear of the Negro in me."

I reached for the chips and poured more juice. Smoking the roach was too complicated. I just swallowed the joint-end down with more OJ.

The drama on the TV continued, and Dave was into either his third or fourth joint. He gazed in my direction and blurted, "Gazorninplat."

"Yeah? What's that?"

"Gazorninplat. Word just popped into my head," he said with satisfaction. "I like it."

The more hits I took, the more cognitions popped up.

"Speaking of things popping up," I mused, "the shape of those hills around Castro Valley fascinate me. I've never seen soft rolling hills like those before. Did you ever notice that they're shaped like female breasts? In the right frame of mind, just looking at those soft round hills can give a guy an erection. Two of those hills together, at the right angle, makes me think of a girl's naked ass. I think men must be more stimulated by pure shapes and curves than women. I once mentioned this to Marie. I think she understood, 'cause she told me God only put enough blood in men's bodies to run one of their two heads at a time, and the little one, she said, is always up for symbolism."

This time Marie did look away from her television show to grin at me, before shaking her head and turning back.

I relished the crunchy, nutty corn flavor of the chips for a moment and stacked some in front of me for easy access. Dave was drifting around somewhere, listening, I hoped. Hardly made any difference as another thought had already begun spilling out.

"Here's a good example of both those points together. When I was a freshman at Shortridge, I started to become friends with a guy in one of my classes. We walked home together from school a couple of times because my house was on his way home."

Uh, that reminded me of Shelly who I also used to walk home with sometimes that year. "Did I ever tell you about Shelly Blank? Remind me to tell you about her, next, although the ending's really sad.

"Anyway, this guy invited me . . . Damn, can't remember his name. Says I should come over on Saturday and hang out." I nodded at Dave, who was still toking and air-sipping when he wasn't crunching chips or draining the grape juice carton.

He nodded back, so I figured he was still with me.

"He lived up past Thirty-Eighth Street, on Capitol, Graceland, one of those streets near Crown Hill Cemetery. After his mom made us lunch, she left to go somewhere. He suggests we go up to his room and look at some dirty cartoon books, eight-page bibles he calls 'em, and before long, he suggests group masturbation. The erotic cartoons of Popeye and Wimpy doing Olive Oyl, though extremely shocking, had their effect on the walking stack of hormones that was my young teenage self. My little head's brain, in control at the time, thinks, well . . . okay.

"My friend decides to use his spare hand to help me masturbate, and I think, this is a weird feeling. His technique's a little rough, doesn't do it as good as me, either. But I am getting sensation without doing the work, that's worth something. But when he puts my hand on his dick, the switch instantly flips, my hand flies off him at the same time the alarm in my head starts clanging: *wrong, wrong, wrong.* I'm outta his house so fast, I'm still zipping up my jeans on the sidewalk outside. I kept rubbing my hand on my pants leg and getting these little 'yuk' shivers, all the way home."

Dave cracked up and I heard suppressed laughter from the easy chair in the living room.

"Are you laughing at the sexual landmines and perils a young man traverses on his way to manhood over there?" I asked Marie in mock concern.

The laughter was no longer suppressed. "I'm planning on getting you high and selling tickets. I'll be rich in no time. Dave hasn't had a chance to get a word in edgewise. Well, except for Gazornin-whatever."

Dave and Marie laughed uproariously while I nearly wriggled with impatience to remind them how I'd successfully referenced both "erotic symbolism," and "erections" in my last observation, as promised. I thought I could've gotten mother's milk in there, too, since we could safely conclude from my firsthand experience, no pun intended, sexual preference was genetic and unaffected by homoerotic stimulation. And I'd promised to tell them about Shelly and several other things that had since churned to the surface from my inner self.

Instead, Dave claimed he'd gotten too high and had to go to bed before he got sick. Marie professed zero interest in my "grass-fueled philosophy" and since nothing but news was on television, she opted for sleep. I was left bursting with frustrated epiphanies, as the two of them disappeared into separate bedrooms. I sat in front of the television and tried to watch, but the fury in my brain wouldn't slow down. My mind relentlessly sifted through important, world-changing observations and conclusions that I desperately wanted—needed—to tell somebody. I considered waking one or the other of them up, then thought better of it and decided to write down these lustrous pearls of self-discovery instead. While considering whether I'd be able to write fast enough to keep up with my racing consciousness, my mind flared out and I passed out in the easy chair. In the early morning chill, Marie found me curled tightly into the seat, all those mind-blowing insights lost forever, dissipated into the breaking dawn along with the gray cells that had been entrusted with them.

She led me to bed, warmth, and physical solace. I woke next to her later in the morning, contented. I smiled, wriggled closer, into a spoon position, knowing most of the baggie's magical herb was still left. I'd get high again in the future. A lot. But I would never ever again feel the intense, magical sense of being oh-so-close to grasping the meaning of the universe around me.

31

THE GOOMBA

"And if that goomba tries any rough stuff,
you tell him I ain't no bandleader."

— Jack Woltz, (Mario Puzo, The Godfather)

April 7, 1966
San Francisco, North Beach, California

ONE NIGHT BEFORE our first show, Dave Rapken left his table to talk to me where I slouched against the service bar, waiting for a Coke.

"Got a surprise for your boys." He flicked an index finger toward the bartender, who immediately started building him a drink. "Remember I mentioned we needed to work on the band's stage appearance?"

"Of course." I nodded.

"You thinkin about gettin us some more cool suits, Mr. Rapken?" Mac asked, catching the drift of the conversation as he walked up. "'Cause if you are, I got some ideas."

Dave sidled up for hot coffee to warm his vocal cords.

"Not what I meant," Rapken said, leaning into the bar and his drink. "Next Tuesday you're gonna meet a friend of mine. Making him the new club manager; he'll be in charge of the operation." His eyes gleamed with a hidden smile. "That's not the real reason he's here, though." He waited for one of us to respond.

"Something to do with us?" I took the hint.

"He's agreed to take over training you guys as entertainers. You're gonna love him. He had a Vegas act called the Satellites, played there for fifteen years. His name is Eddie Pru. You should think of him as your mentor."

"Sounds great," Mac said enthusiastically. Dave sipped his coffee, nodding.

"You're gonna want to listen to everything he says. He knows. So, you and your boys come in a half hour early next Tuesday, meet the man, press the flesh a little. Okay?"

Down in the dressing room, I spoke as I pulled my suit coat off the hanger in my locker. "So, the thing is, Rapken wants us here before show time Tuesday to meet this guy." High-pitched conversation and occasional shrieks leaked through from the girls' side; it had gotten considerably louder since Les had ventilated the wall.

"That's good, right?" Leonard, our new drummer, said. "I mean, he played Las Vegas for fifteen years. Somebody like that's got to help us, right?" He checked around to see if anybody agreed with him.

"Sure is, bub." Mac, Mister Showman, welcomed anything that could improve our stage presence. He already had his dress shirt on and was winding a single Windsor knot into his gold tie. My dad had only taught me how to tie huge double Windsor knots; I couldn't get a single Windsor or four-in-hand right to save my life.

Les and Jack had reservations, I could tell, but whatever they were thinking they held back, until Les grinned and said, "If the guy makes me do the splits, though, I'll kick his ass."

We all guffawed and kept dressing; Les was famous for ripping the crotch out of his pants during one of our shows, when he was trying to get down into the radical dance move. We hadn't talked about it, but Les seemed to have eased his way past our blowup. Fortunately, he liked Leonard, and everyone welcomed peace in the brotherhood.

My sister called on Sunday. Usually, I loved her phone calls, and listening to her tales of everyday life in Indianapolis sometimes made me nostalgic, but I'd been dreading this one. I'd tried to put the decision about the boys out of my mind, avoiding the answer I knew was going to disappoint everyone in Indiana.

"Mom wanted me to check on what you thought about Pat's proposal.

About David and Danny. I think Pat's getting anxious, Larry. Mom said to remind you, it's been six weeks."

I stalked around the room tethered to the telephone, the receiver up to my ear.

"I'm still wrestling with the right thing to do, Sis. But the truth is, I don't see any way I can give the boys up for adoption. How can they even be adopted, anyway? It doesn't make sense to me. I mean, I'm not dead. They have an actual flesh-and-blood father. How can anything make them not my sons?"

"Mom said she's sure it's just a technical thing." I heard in my sister's voice that she had some mixed feelings, too. "Necessary so Jim can take care of them if he had to, paperwork mainly, sign to put them into school, handle things if they get hurt or something."

"Yes, but saying I'm not their father . . ." I'd promised myself I would do anything to make Pat happy. I knew how badly I'd disappointed her, but this, this seemed too much. "I just don't think I should do it."

"I understand." Cheryl hesitated. "Mom will probably take your decision pretty hard, though." I heard sorrow and regret in her voice.

"Why should she? I understand she'd like to help Pat. I know she loves her, but these are her grandchildren, too." Why was it so crucial that I give them up?

"She didn't tell you? About what Pat said would happen if you wouldn't agree?"

"Pat said something would happen? Like what?"

"Pat said if you wouldn't go along with the adoption, it would be difficult for her to bring the boys to see Mom again."

I stopped pacing and lifted the receiver from my ear for a moment to stare out the window before speaking.

"I don't believe that."

"Mom says she's lost you already. She doesn't mean that in a bad way, only that you're grown up and gone away. She doesn't want to lose her grandsons. Pat promises if you do this, nothing will change between us here, and her new guy, Jim, agrees. Mom and I can see the boys whenever we want to." Cheryl paused for a moment. "She says she'll still be like a big sister to me. It's only a technicality."

I was silent.

"She really wants to marry this man, Larry. I guess she thinks you, or Mom, or me, or all of us, are keeping her from doing that. On purpose."

"What about Dad? Has he said anything?" I said, trying to buy time to think.

"My impression is he doesn't know what to think either way, but he wants Mom to be happy."

"Give me a minute, Sis." I sat in the easy chair. There wasn't any way out. I was ringed in, the outcome once again inevitable. Like everything else in this disastrous heartbreak between Pat and I, the widening ripples of loss never seemed to end. Anything salvageable always seemed just out of reach. "This guy is a good man?" I asked my sister. "Have you met him?"

"No. I don't know that Mom has met him, either, but Pat's opinion is what counts. You know how much she loves David and Danny. I believe she wants what's best for them."

After my stomach settled down, I called my mother. Our conversation wasn't long, I told her I would agree to the adoption. She had nothing to say when I told her Cheryl had filled me in on Pat's veiled threat. I could tell how bad she felt; there was no need for further discussion. It was only a technicality, she said again. Everybody knows I'm still their father, how could I not be? They were still my boys either way, weren't they? Nothing changed that. I was hundreds of miles away and couldn't be with them right now anyway. At least my mom would still have her grandsons. Maybe tensions would ease, emotions lessen; hurt feelings might have a chance to heal if I gave in on this.

Tuesday night at the Galaxie, a note on our dressing-room door reminded us to go up to the service bar after dressing for the show. A very Italian-looking guy, with thick, slicked-back dark hair, sat at the table usually reserved for Rapken. His youthful appearance and dress contradicted a closer view that revealed tiny wrinkles around the smoky, cynical eyes in his olive complexion. I guessed he was at least ten years older than us, maybe a little more. He was slender, dressed to kill in a dark sharkskin suit, wine-red tie with light checks, and a tie pin clinging to a gleaming-white, high-collared dress shirt. As each of us arrived, he motioned us to take a chair. We bantered with each other, but the most we got from him was a grim smile and an occasional slight shrug as his fingers habitually checked the distance between his heavily-linked French cuffs and his coat sleeve.

"Okay, six," he counted, as Mac slid into his chair. "That's alla youse, then." He took the time to make eye contact with each of us. "My name's Eddie Pru, and my friend Dave Rapken hired me to see if anything can be made 'a you. The rules are simple: you listen to me and do what I tell you. If you do, you'll learn something. Can't do nothin' about your talent—youse either got it or you don't—but this ain't so much about talent anyway. It's about being amazing entertainers."

He raised a finger as he continued. "If you decide not to listen, which I advise against, we'll cover that then."

Eddie sounded like he was right out of Little Italy to me. I'd been born in Brooklyn, but my family had moved upstate while I was in diapers, so I couldn't be sure. Still, his accent was thick with New York City Italian machismo.

He gestured toward the stage. "Tonight I'm gonna watch you guys perform. Won't have nothin' to say to you, though, until rehearsal tomorrow."

"Uh." I hesitated. "Should we call you Eddie or Mister Pru?"

"Eddie or Pru. Probably safest you go with Eddie for now."

"Okay, Eddie. We don't have a rehearsal scheduled for tomorrow."

"Perhaps I'm not speaking in a language you are familiar with here on the West Coast. I said we start tomorrow at rehearsal. I didn't ask you if, or for your permission, so since I told you I would talk to you at rehearsal tomorrow, you now have a rehearsal scheduled for tomorrow. Any further questions?"

It was quiet around the table until Mac said, "What time?"

We were on stage for rehearsal before 3 PM Wednesday afternoon when Eddie walked in and called us down to a couple of tables at the front of the stage near the runway. He was wearing a light, expensive-looking, black leather jacket over a high-collared, custom-made deep-purple dress shirt, two buttons open at the top. I caught a glimpse of a heavy gold chain around his neck.

Eddie glared at us. "Listen up, you *cazzos*, I watched as mucha you as I could stand last night. I turned my head a couple a times, and you sounded okay, but Holy Mother of God, youse guys look like shit-on-a-stick up there. No wonder Rapken called me."

Mac spoke for us. "Really, that bad?"

"Worse. But the good thing is you're not too bad-looking. But *che cazzo fai*, you guys don't look like you even want to be up there. Lead singer, what's your name?"

"I'm Dave."

"Well, listen Dave, you look like somebody stuck a broomstick handle up your ass. We're going to have to do surgery, get it outta you. Guitar player, you look like you're eatin' lemons. We don't eat lemons on stage. Bass player, you on some kinda long hike or somethin'? I mean, come on, where in hell you marchin' to? You, caveman guy, you ever smile? And you, other guy, what the hell do you do, anyway?"

He was looking at me. "I'm Larry. Like you said, I'm mostly the 'other guy.'"

I heard a couple of snickers.

"So you're the funnyman. Do the one-liners for the crowd? Do some standup, maybe?" But a little grin slid across his face. He was making it clear this was his "back East" shtick, and we shouldn't get too offended.

"So here's what you got to understand." Eddie stood up and hiked himself, one-handed, up onto the runway. He strutted up and down in his high-heeled, Italian-leather, dress boots like he was strolling the Avenue on the Lower East Side while he talked.

"These people spend good money to get in this joint. Ain't much free parking around here, so they pay big for valet service. We touch 'em up for a watered-down two-drink minimum, and the club's gonna start a door charge soon. Figure a party of two, with tips and all, is dropping fifty, sixty clams on a weekend night in here by the time you bastards come on stage."

He walked to the runway edge to peer down on us. "Fellas, even if you take your shirts and pants off, you ain't got nothin' to compete with what our girls got. So, what you gonna do to make these people feel like they didn't just get shafted outta all that moola?" He rubbed his thumb and forefinger in the universal money sign at us.

"Get off the stage quick so Topless Teri can get on?" Les said.

"Another crackup comedian. Anybody else?"

"Guess we could play and sing real well," Leonard tried, to his credit.

"I reckon we got to get the crowd goin." Mac dropped his smoke into an ashtray. "When I was in the Casinos, seemed like the crowd liked bein part of the show. Liked it better when we got 'em to entertain themselves, even more than us entertainin them."

Eddie beamed. "Okay Front Man, good. What's your name again?"

"Mac. Mac Brown."

"So Mac here, has got the right idea, close enough for me to tell you what you guys have to learn." He swept his right hand along the stage. "If youse just stand up here, playing and singing, you might as well be on television or a movie screen, or be a goddamned record player." He scowled back at us. "Guess what? You ain't never gonna sound as perfect live as a record." He started to pace again, staring us down, one by one.

"What you gotta do is break that barrier between you up there and the paying customers out here. You got to get out to them, seduce 'em, bring 'em into the show. We're gonna start learning how to do that.

"And another thing. You can't stand up on the goddamn stage, moving around a little, kinda grooving, thinkin' you'll pick up the chicks by being cool. You gotta show some energy; these people gotta believe you want nothing more outta life than to make this the greatest night of their lives."

He jumped down from the stage. "And it don't stop—or even start—there. You got to remember even when you're not performing, you're still in the public eye. You've got to work the club, go out to the tables, meet the people. You have to make friends and allies in this joint, you got to learn how to get 'em on your side. We're gonna do all that if you guys just listen to your *goomba* here."

Over the following nights and days, Eddie hammered at us about the many details of being a band in a showplace. He came in one night with pancake makeup, and showed us how to apply just enough that the bright lights wouldn't wash us out. Dave learned to lightly Vaseline his lips and eyebrows, so they'd gleam before each show.

We learned to make sure our audiences recognized how hard we worked. We began loosening our ties early in each set, shedding suit coat jackets, rolling up our sleeves, and dabbing our foreheads with our matching handkerchiefs as the show progressed. By the set's end, Eddie wanted the audience to see us drenched in sweat.

He showed us how to block our songs—how to move the audience's attention from one person or part of the stage to another. He insisted that Dave, shy as he was, move out onto the runway and sing to the women in the audience, even getting down on a knee to serenade them.

"Look those women in the eye, lead singer, real soft, like you're making love to them. Get 'em wet with your eyes. Then, you make 'em come with your voice."

One night, I watched Eddie stop Leonard at the service bar as he started to walk away with a Coke. I'd never yet seen Leonard order an alcoholic drink.

"Hey, Lenny, you got a dollar?" We'd all just gotten off the stage, so Eddie waved us over to the bar.

Leonard, surprised, pulled a dollar bill out his billfold. Eddie grabbed it from him and slammed the bill down on the service bar for the bartender.

"Listen, you fucks. You ever come over here and order a drink from the service bar, or from one of the girls, even if it's free, and you don't lay down at least a dollar beside the glass, you are gonna answer to me. These people are the ones who talk to the customers, everybody around the business, up and down the street. They can fucking kill your act if they don't like you. They're paid spit, tips is their living. This tip shows them you understand this is how they make their money. You let them know, you know and respect that, and they'll make you."

Leonard shrugged. "What if I don't have any extra money, not even a dollar?"

"Then you can't afford to buy this free drink, you stupid fuck." He rounded on all of us with a warning finger in our faces.

"You guys remember that."

32

TORCHIE AND THE PRU

A Naked woman in heels is a beautiful thing.
A Naked man in shoes looks like a fool.

— Christian Louboutin

May 17, 1966
San Francisco, North Beach, California

"ALL RIGHT YOUSE, get ready. I'm going to run the curtain up. Tell me when you're set." Eddie was on stage behind the curtain, amping us up before Saturday's midnight show. We had a sold-out house. He'd told us the crowds would pick up as the weather improved, but he'd also had to reluctantly admit we were already becoming a top draw on Broadway. Even with a cover charge and a two-drink minimum, the line to get in the Galaxie extended down the Kearney Street hill.

A few moments later, Les signaled for him to hit the button.

"Quick, before I run up the curtain, come over here a minute. Allayahs now, put your hands out here together, like a sports team."

Everybody crowded in to place a hand on top of his. Without warning, Eddie crushed something that tinkled like glass with his other hand and immediately forced it under each of our noses, ending with his own. An acrid smell jolted me. I thought for a moment we'd had an earthquake and I was falling. He cackled while we tried to recover from what hit us, and slammed his palm on the curtain button.

"Give 'em a terrific show, you rat bastards," he yelled.

Eddie Pru had more surprises than amyl nitrate poppers. A couple of weeks later, he called us together near the service bar before a show. Standing next to him, hips loose and brazenly hipshot, was the most incredible woman I'd ever seen in the flesh. She'd been poured into one of the Galaxie's Playboy-style waitress costumes. The skimpy outfit's high-hipped cut and fishnet stockings revealed an impossibly perfect hour-glass figure and long, elegant legs. She was simultaneously tawdry, classy, and embarrassingly alluring. Eddie pulled her to him, almost knocking her off her glittery spiked heels. She tossed her highlighted sandy-brown hair in exasperation while we stood entranced.

"I want youse guys to meet Torchie. She's my girl and the new head waitress at the Galaxie." Torchie might have been a little older than us, but the sexual challenge smoldering in her green-flecked hazel eyes seemed as old as the Garden of Eden. Eddie's girl was having a big problem with his possessive attitude.

"All right, sweet cakes, get back to work." He put his hands on her shoulders and turned her toward the bar before pushing her on her way with a slap on her nicely rounded ass. She shot back a killer glance, but he didn't seem to notice, his eyes following only her swaying backside.

"Woman means the world to me," he said to himself for us to overhear. He pulled his attention back to us with a glare. "I don't want nobody messin' with her. You got that?" He scowled like the alpha male he was. "And by that I mean, you notice anybody nosing around her, talking her up, anything like that, staff in this joint, or customers, anybody, you come get me. Immediately." He shuffled his feet like a boxer setting his stance.

"Something else you guys should know. I'm walkin' heavy." He gazed around suspiciously to be sure nobody could see into our loose huddle. He patted his coat back to reveal a pistol-shaped lump tucked into the back waistband of his slacks. "I'm always walkin' heavy, boys. Don't any a youse ever think I won't use it, 'cause I have and I will. Now go, do a great show."

This wasn't our first indication that our goomba might have another, more unsavory occupation, but it was the most concrete. We hadn't learned of Dave Rapken's affiliation with the Giancana family yet, but we'd had some strong indicators he and Pru were not just your average citizens.

"A Jewish wedding song?" I blurted out. "You're kidding me?" After the first few weeks, Eddie hadn't come to our rehearsals as often, but when he did he sometimes had some screwy ideas. This one seemed the farthest out yet.

"Nah, ain't just a wedding song. Song's about celebrating anything. Listen, you guys want to play these better clubs, maybe even Vegas someday, you gotta have some tunes for the Jews. They're big in entertainment, own a lotta clubs, and are powerful people. Besides, this kinda song is fun, easy to do, easy to learn. I'm gonna teach you *Hava Nagila* right now. Clap your hands with me, like this."

That's Eddie Pru, I thought. *Never asks if we want to do something, he just does it, and before we realize what we're doing, we're going right along with him. Of course,* I reminded myself, *he carries a gun.* He started clapping out a beat, and I halfheartedly joined in.

Eddie sang, "Hava nagila, hava nagila, hava nagila ve-nis-mecha." He started to stamp his feet and dance around in a circle as he sang the lyric again. He faced Dave and sang, "Hava neranenah, hava neranenah, hava neranenah ve-nis-mecha," grinning like an idiot. Leonard, sitting behind the drums, started to bang out a rhythm to the hand clapping. Eddie repeated the lyric, getting into each of our faces. As he started into the next section, he raised his hands in the air, singing loudly, "Ooh-ru, uru a-chim, uru a-chim be-lev a-meah" several times. Les found the right key and strummed a pattern with the beat. Jack added a basic bass line. "Ooh." Eddie pointed at us and sang, "Ru" until we were following him repeating these two nonsense syllables and grinning ourselves. He stopped everybody with an open palm, and dramatically sang, "Ooh-ru a-chim, Ooh-ru a-chim," holding out the last note. He stopped, caught Leonard's eye for a moment, and then began the song over again at double time, constantly speeding up the tempo until he was singing as fast as he could. We broke up laughing as the rhythms broke down trying to stay up with him.

"See, it's simple. I can teach Dave these lyrics in ten minutes, the music is nothing, as you can tell. The secret is in how you present it, how you change the time, get people involved singing with you. This will be a big number for youse."

"What do these words mean?" Dave asked.

"Who the hell knows? Who cares? Probably something like, Hey!

Everything's swell, wonderful, let's eat and drink and get laid. At least that's the way I always think of it. I'm gonna teach it to you the way I learned it, by how it sounds. So let's go."

We got the song down quickly. Eddie showed us how he wanted us to slow or speed the tempo, where to get the audience involved, and how to block the song on stage to feature the guitar, or Dave as the lead singer, or Mac and me with tambourines attempting a Russian kick dance out on the runway. I'd never imagined us doing folk songs, but we'd be doing one tonight.

During a short break before continuing rehearsal, Eddie motioned me over to the table where he and Rapken usually sat. He sipped what looked like a triple bourbon straight from a double rocks glass.

"Sit down here a minute, Larry, take a load off. You remember some weeks ago, how I told alla youse Torchie is my woman, how forgetting that wouldn't be good for nobody? You remember, right?"

"Of course I remember, Eddie." Anything about Torchie would be difficult to forget. As far as I knew, there was no more stunning woman than Torchie Delgado in the whole of North Beach. And Eddie had made his hands-off policy dangerously clear.

"See, along with the hot Dago blood, she's got some Spanish in her, too, and sometimes, well, sometimes we have these little moments, you know . . ." I did know. A couple of nights ago, she'd pitched a cocktail tray full of half-empty glasses at him. Probably a good thing Dave Rapken wasn't in that night. There'd been some yelling between them since then, too.

"So like any female who gets a hard-on toward her man, she might go sniffin' around, try to make him jealous." He gave me a baleful stare. "You can see how getting involved in this minor scuffle between me and Torchie wouldn't be wise. I'm not a good guy to get jealous. I can forget myself."

I stuck my hands up, palms out. "Hey, wait a minute, Eddie. If you think I would ever . . ."

"Nah, I don't think you or any of your guys would ever do me rotten." His mood turned morose, as he drained his glass. "But you should remind your boys what I'm sayin' here. I know we're friends, so I can tell you this, things have been a little tense with Torchie and me." He shook his head slowly, shoulders hunched, his gaze centered on the bottom of his empty glass. "She threatened to fuck somebody else just to get up on me."

"I'm sure you have nothing to worry about from us. Torchie's a gorgeous girl, Eddie, but we would know better. If it would make you feel easier, I'll talk to the guys."

He clapped me on the shoulder. "Yeah, you talk to them, you give 'em the word, remind 'em I wouldn't want nothing to happen to any of them." He brushed a hand across a bulge on his hip, with a bent smile.

Eddie left while we finished up rehearsal with a brush-up on James Brown's *I Got You* for Mac, which we'd pulled back into rehearsal to clean up. Afterward, before anybody got away, I pulled the band together in the dressing room. Though Jack was still officially in charge on the contract, ever since I'd been the one to fire Don Hunt, I'd become the de facto leader again. Made no difference to me. I just did what I do anyway, make sure everything keeps going, make sure we stayed together.

After Les had gone over the rehearsal schedule and song assignments, I called for everyone's attention.

"Eddie the Pru has something he wanted me to say to you, though I'm only stating the obvious. He says he and Torchie have been having some problems. What's news, he says she's threatening him with screwing somebody else."

A lot of hoots, whistles, and rude suggestions followed.

"Now hold on, hold on. I get the woman is pure walking sex, but this can be a dangerous situation. The guy carries a gun, and he was drinking pretty heavy down at the bar earlier. I, for one, don't doubt he's used it before. He asked me to emphasize how unhappy he'd be if anything happened, so this is a simple, probably unnecessary, reminder to stay the hell away from Torchie. Probably shouldn't even say hello until the storm passes, okay? Wouldn't be smart to get Eddie's imagination going."

"Larry," Dave said, his expression deadpan.

"What."

"Too late, man." A slow, lazy smile crept over his face. "Sorry, but the opportunity came up, and I couldn't let it go by."

"Goddamn it Dave, you're my roommate. How in hell did you do that without me knowing?" I said, trying to get my head around the enormity of what Dave was saying. "I'm not sure whether I'm totally jealous or scared shitless. Probably both."

"Met her after rehearsal last Thursday. Remember when Eddie said he had to go out of town for a couple of days? You have to remember I didn't come home that night, stayed here in the city?"

"Last Thursday." Mac spoke up, picking at his teeth with a toothpick. "Well my brother, got there a week afore you then."

"Omigod. You guys do know Pru's a soldier, maybe even a made man for some mob, don't you? What were you guys thinking?"

Dave considered me for a moment before answering. "Well I can't speak for Mac, but Lord Almighty, you've seen the woman. What I was thinking was, I'd do it again if she gave me the chance. She is, was—pardon my French—fucking amazing. Though I guess I should apologize in advance if I've gotten any of you guys killed."

Mac's nod and dreamy smile was enough, but he said anyway, "Yeah, me, too."

"Man, I can't believe you slept with Torchie. God in heaven. If Eddie ever finds out . . ." The lights on the Bay Bridge whizzed by as we rode into the late-afternoon leaden skies over the bay toward Treasure Island, leapfrogging over to Berkeley. Dave flicked ash through the small triangular window of the passenger seat of the Falcon.

"I'm going to tell you something, man. I've never had anything like the experience of seeing and touching a woman like Torchie; I doubt I ever will again. Had to do her or regret it forever."

"But Eddie . . ." I said, shaking my head. "The guy could shoot you."

"Believe this or not, Larry, but if she was lying in front of you naked and willing, even if you knew you were going to die for it, you'd have to jump on anyway and go to heaven happy." He seemed to drift off in a vision for a moment.

"You've seen how amazing she looks with her clothes on? Without 'em she's so incredible she almost hurt my eyes. I was with her all night and believe me, I saw every bit of her."

The interior in the old Falcon was loud from the heavy bay breezes whistling through its cracks and crannies. Dave and I sat lost in our own thoughts as the Bay Bridge swooped us up to carry us the rest of the way home.

33

TWIN PEAKS

*Well, for me, gratuitous abstinence is
just as bad as gratuitous sex.*

— Bianca Sommerland

June 16, 1966
San Francisco, North Beach, California

WE WERE HEALTHY young adults in the prime of our lives. It shouldn't be surprising that a certain amount of fraternization and friendship sprung up between the opposite sexes working in such close contact over the many months of our contract. Though my casual intimacy with Marie continued in the form of visits from her a night or two in Berkeley most weeks, she never showed interest in the glittery nightlife in North Beach. Our relationship stayed on the east side of the bay.

While I became friends with several of the girls who worked at the Galaxie and had a little fling with Dorrie, I didn't develop an attraction to any of them until I met Maria, who joined the topless show several months after we started. Her specialty was flame dancing. Tassels, hanging from the pasties that barely covered her areolae, were doused in lighter fluid and lit behind the curtain. She'd enter, from backstage, dancing and twirling them to the recorded rock music without missing a beat. Then she'd reverse the direction of the whirling tassels, and, for the finale, spin them in opposing directions.

What I liked best about her, besides her beauty, her breathtaking deep-brown eyes, and dark hair, was how perfectly proportioned she was, and she was just the right height for me at about five foot four.

I tried to engage her in conversation, and she even agreed to join me for coffee in a diner one night after the club closed. She was bright and articulate, and I enjoyed being with her. I made it clear I liked her, and I thought she liked me, too, but that seemed to be where it ended.

As far as I could tell, she didn't order or accept anything but soft drinks from the bar, and I never noticed anyone waiting for her at the end of the night. She was polite to everyone but kept her distance from customers, the other dancers, club employees, and the band (including me). Until one evening, deep into the summer of 1966, when Maria found a moment to slip up behind me and whisper in my ear.

"What are you doing later tonight?" I pulled away to look at her. Her eyes sparkled, bright and playful, her expression was focused, her smile a little nervous.

"Nothing planned; just going back to Berkeley unless you've got a better idea." I smiled, hoping she might want to go for coffee again.

The next time she whispered, her lips brushed against my ear. "Would you like to come home with me? Tonight?" She leaned back, and our eyes locked, my breath caught.

"More than anything."

After the last show, she drove us straight to her apartment in Twin Peaks, not even stopping for breakfast. The distance Maria had maintained disintegrated into an escalating sexual hunger as we rode up the winding road into the San Francisco night sky. We were going to make love without any pretense of seduction. Each step toward her bedroom was direct but unhurried, natural, as though we'd been intimate before.

Despite our eagerness for one another, we savored the sweetness of delayed gratification. Our lovemaking, languorous with certain frenzied moments, instilled in me a sense of intense sharing on so many levels that my soul felt hugged. Afterward, lying in the darkened room, replete, full of thoughts and contemplation, I realized I didn't even know her last name.

"I know," she replied. "I never told it to you. Doesn't matter, Maria's not my real name anyway." She turned on her side and leaned on an arm. "You know I like you, and I know you like me, but I want you to understand, this is only temporary. I didn't even mean for things to get this far but, well, we both wanted this so . . ."

"Temporary," I said, turning the word over in my mind. I rolled onto my side and ran a palm along her shoulder and arm. "What does that mean? Don't you enjoy us being together like this?"

"That's not the point. Of course I like this. I went back on birth control because I knew I was going to bring you home with me. And making love with you is every bit as wonderful as I'd hoped, but it doesn't make any difference." The sheets rustled as she moved away from me searching for a cigarette.

"I'm dancing at the Galaxie to pay for college. That's my real life, and I keep it separate from work. I'm going to graduate soon, and I've saved enough for grad school. When college is over, the dancer side of my life will disappear. I've been following this plan for a long time." She rested a hand on my chest.

"You're on the dancer side of my life, Larry, that's just how things are with me. You have to accept that, or we can't do this again."

I tried to sort out my emotions. We seemed so comfortable together as people, and now in bed, too. Didn't that mean we shared something deeper? My first instinct was to feel a sense of rejection tempered with confusion. We'd just had amazing sex, she'd implied she wanted to sleep with me again. *Temporary?* I thought again. I couldn't reconcile the two signals.

"Besides, the last thing I want to do is get involved with a musician."

"What's that supposed to mean?" My increased bewilderment made me sound more truculent than I'd meant.

"It means . . . Larry, how many women have you had sex with?"

I stared at her, speechless. What an odd and embarrassing thing to ask. Wasn't I experienced enough for her?

"Come on. Don't be shy, tell me."

"Well, I married the first girl I made love to in high school. We divorced last year so . . ."

She swept her dark hair back from her eyes with one hand. "Okay, let's get real. I already know you and Dorrie had a thing."

"That was not a *thing*, just a couple of people trying something out. And it wasn't a secret, happened way before you started working at the Galaxie, anyway."

"You're telling me you've slept with two girls, only two girls, until now, tonight with me?"

"Well, there's another . . ." I wondered if I would have to explain my complicated relationship with Marie.

"Three, then. I'm supposed to believe I'm the fourth girl you've ever been in bed with?" She flounced around until her cynical grin faced me, her eyes searching mine as she spoke. "I'm not from the city, but you shouldn't assume I just fell off the avocado truck in the middle of Market Street or something."

"I don't expect you to believe anything. You started this, and I don't know why." *Damn it, I sound so sullen. Control yourself, Larry.*

"Even if what you're saying is true." I opened my mouth to defend myself, but she put the tips of her fingers to my lips. "And no, I don't want to discuss it because it's not the point. There's going to be a whole lot more women who'll want to sleep with you where you're headed. Even if I were tempted, being a camp follower isn't the kind of life I want."

She must have noticed my perplexed frown in the dim light of the bedroom. She leaned into me and pulled herself under my arm.

"Listen, if anything changes later, if I wanted to find you, your band's name is Stark Naked and the Car Thieves. How hard would you be to find? That's all I can promise you, sweetie, nothing more."

In the morning, her side of the bed lay empty. I dressed, washed up, and walked into the diminutive living area of her little jewel box of an apartment. A note on the small table, flanked by two chairs in the dining nook, read: *Have breakfast, take your time. Off to school. See you tonight.*

Over coffee and toast, I gazed out the little bay window at a beheaded Coit Tower drifting over low cloud cover. Through a break in the cloud, sunshine showered the distant span of the Bay Bridge, hop-scotching to the other side of the bay. On a clearer day, I might have been able to see all the way to Berkeley.

I dialed Dave to tell him the obvious, deflecting his eager questions, promising to tell him more after I'd found a bus or trolley down to North Beach in time for rehearsal. After I locked the door to this tiny little place in the clouds I turned to walk down a narrow path to the street. The dramatic hillside vistas of the city and the bay below drifted in and out of view, reminding me again of how far, and in how many ways, I'd distanced myself from my previous life in Indiana.

I was uncomfortable with how I was brooding about the limitations Maria had set for us, as I walked down toward a main street. I hiked along, trying to think it through. This was what I said I wanted, wasn't it? No long-term commitments. Maybe the real problem was with me, my pride; I wasn't in control. Getting us together had been Maria's decision, and I was lucky to be the recipient of her affection. Why wasn't I able to just live in the moment, why couldn't I just accept someone falling into my life, even for a short time, without demanding more from it?

A few nights later as we lay side by side in her quiet bedroom, arms and legs entangled, I realized a bookcase covering one of her walls and a bookshelf above the bed were stacked with books in haphazard order, a sign of recent use.

"You read," I said before thinking.

"You say that like you're surprised," she said, amused.

"No, I . . . I just meant, I read, too."

"So you want me to be surprised?" She had a knack of always being a step ahead of me.

"No." I hesitated. "What do you like to read?"

"Poetry mostly, and high fantasy: Tolkien, Baum, T. H. White. Some literary horror—Lovecraft, Poe. How about you?"

I told her the truth. "Science fiction, all kinds. Adventures I guess, spy thrillers, some mysteries. What's high fantasy?"

"Fantasy worlds, barely connected to our world. Like the Arthurian Cycle, Ursula LeGuin's stories. Some friends at school turned me onto J. R. R. Tolkien. I love his writing. Have you heard of him? *The Hobbit* or *The Lord of the Rings*?"

"No." I rolled onto an elbow. "What are they like?"

"I don't think they're like anything. The world he's created seems like a real place in some lost historical time even though there are elves and sorcerers and little hobbits and different kinds of people other than humans all through it."

I gazed down at her eyes, alight, as she described the books, dark hair mussed against the white pillow.

"I might have read about hobbits or hobbes," I said, "Something like them in the Grimm's fairy tales. I read tons of those when I was a kid. Are they mischievous, dangerous gnomes?"

"Don't think those are Tolkien's hobbits. But there's some seriously dark philosophy in these books. Think you'd like to read one?"

"Yeah, I think I would." She nodded, and it seemed I'd passed some kind of test.

"You should start with *The Hobbit*. *The Lord of the Rings* is a long trilogy. You don't want to begin with that."

She rose to her knees and turned, naked, to search the books on the shelf above her bed. The view of her back tapering to a narrow waist and widening into perfectly sculpted hips, revealed a thrilling tuft of brunette peeking from between her thighs that caused my interest in books to wane. She turned to hold out *The Hobbit* for me.

I hefted it for a moment. "Guess this means I'll see you again, at least." I leaned across her to place the book on the nightstand.

She glanced down in surprise at my ascending reaction to the view she'd given me when her back was turned and smiled in encouragement. I reached for her, and with a lewd glance over her left shoulder, she turned away from me again.

Our last night in Maria's eyrie high above the city, our physical enjoyment of each other was deeper, more powerful than ever. The bitter spice of knowing our time together was nearing the end fueled our passion. I'd returned her book and told her how much I'd enjoyed Gandalf the wizard and Bilbo's adventure with the dwarves and Gollum and Smaug the dragon in the roots of Lonely Mountain. At the end of the night, just as we were falling asleep, she curled up close behind me and stretched her arms around me.

"I wanted to lend you the first book in the Tolkien trilogy," she whispered. "But now it's too late." I didn't have to ask what she meant. One night she wasn't at the club anymore. She hadn't said goodbye, and that was okay. She'd told me she wouldn't and I understood. She wasn't really a part of my life, and I was just a footnote in hers.

And now that role was over.

34

THE GALAXIE GIRLS

"Girls do not dress for boys. They dress for themselves and, of course, each other. If girls dressed for boys they'd just walk around Naked at all times."

— *Betsey Johnson*

August 6, 1966
San Francisco, North Beach, California

I HAD ONE FINAL encounter with a Galaxie girl in the fall near the end of our year there. I'd stayed around for a coffee nightcap at the service bar before driving home when Savannah, one of the featured dancers, slipped onto the stool next to me and smiled.

"Come on you, you're going home with me."

Savannah, mysterious, beautiful, slim, tall, and athletic, with long raven hair and dark smoldering eyes, had shown no interest in me whatsoever before now. I'd gotten the impression I wasn't her type, maybe even a step or two below her standard. This night, she turned her sloe-eyed seductive power on me, and me alone, surprising and flattering me. I felt sophisticated and urbane as I considered the possibility of a night of remarkable sex with no emotional complications.

Savannah drove us to a quietly luxurious apartment building on the back side of Russian Hill, not far inland from North Beach. The apartment we stepped into had no impressive view but was large and filled with rich furnishings. She'd kissed and fondled me in the elevator, previewing the physical pleasures I anticipated ahead as we moved through the door. Inside, she swayed toward a cabinet bar and made us drinks. She handed me a slug of what was probably premium bourbon over ice in a heavy rocks glass, but it was wasted on me. I didn't care for whiskey, especially straight.

"I love Ella Fitzgerald. Do you mind if I put her on?" she said, pulling a turntable out of a full-sized stereo player. "This is one of my favorites, show tunes."

"Sure, that's fine." I hated musicals. I sipped my drink with both palms gripping the glass, hoping their warmth would melt the ice and dilute the booze.

"Why don't you make yourself comfortable while I go change. I'll be back for you in a moment, cutie." Then she turned her back to me and added over her shoulder, "But you could help me get this zipper in back started. It's sooo hard to reach . . ."

I pulled the zipper down until the cleavage of her ass showed, and she turned to me for another long kiss. "When I come back, I'll help you with your zipper."

She sent me a slow, sidelong glance as she pulled away into a dramatic stroll reminiscent of the ancient Loretta Young TV show, exiting through a door at the far end of the living room. I cocked my head for a moment; I felt like I was on a movie set. I wanted to look around to check if cameras were rolling. *Well, whatever she wanted—the girl sure could kiss.*

She left me alone for a long and restless fifteen minutes. Ella had crooned into the fifth or sixth cut, something about somebody from somewhere appearing somehow, when Savannah made her entrance draped in a dark, full-length, hooded robe. She glided across the room then slowed to allow the robe to drop dramatically to the floor while she stood with naked pride in front of me.

Once again, the scene felt staged, right up until the moment I didn't care what it seemed like anymore.

Her scalp was stubbled; she was bald, had no hair. That beautiful dark mane had been a wig, expensive, I guessed, since I'd never suspected. Her breasts, where had they gone? I'd felt them up against me earlier. What I had imagined as bountiful flesh had melted away into puckered-up, pink-tipped bumps. With shaved bare eyebrows, eyelashes invisible without mascara, no makeup to enlarge her eyes, no pancake or blush to give her skin color, Savannah's face was as unremarkable as a mannequin's. Her dancer's body was whip slim and lithe, but she had no waist between her torso and boyish hips, her ass flat as a dinner plate. And where her legs met, an uncarpeted pubic bone poked from beneath the flesh.

I stepped back as I took her in, and all the horror and shock on my face must have registered with her. I will admit I considered for a moment what a good kisser she'd been, wondering if I could somehow put this horrifying vision out of my mind, once we were in a completely dark room. But I couldn't unsee what I'd just seen. I grabbed my jacket and tried not to break an ankle in a rush for the door as I spoke without looking at her too closely.

"Can't do this, Savannah, sorry. Parts of you look like you might be my little brother and other parts look like a plastic doll. Just can't do it. Gotta go."

I guess she wasn't much fazed. I heard her laughter follow me as I retreated down the hall in misery, not looking forward to figuring out how to get back to my car in North Beach this late at night.

"I'm telling you, man," I told Dave the next morning. "I thought the next thing she might do was pop out a glass eye or something." He laughed and laughed, until he spilled his coffee. I shivered at the memory.

During our last month in San Francisco, we recorded for the first time since Indianapolis, at Columbus Recorders, where we were told the Kingston Trio recorded, in an odd-shaped triangular room with no sweetening. All a sham—Dave Rapken's idea of keeping his promise to record us, I suppose. We recorded *Cara Mia*, *Stay*, *Shout*, *Back to Summer Place*, and *Peanuts*, a song featuring Dave's falsetto, direct to acetate. All copy tunes. The whole process made no sense, though the acetate recordings would turn out to have some value later.

As Eddie continued to work with us on stage, break poppers into our noses that we'd mostly learned to deflect, and school us on professionalism, the fall drew to a close. Many times we battled Eddie tooth and nail to retain our rock and roll roots, but Dave Rapken had been right—we were leaving as a much better band. Though we weren't the reincarnation of Eddie's old band the Satellites, as he must've hoped, we learned a lot about stagecraft and how to combine it in creative ways with our own choice of music. The long, grueling six months at the Town Club across the bay, followed by a year of high-pressure performances had burnished us into confident, professional entertainers.

We had one other thing to be grateful for—looked like we'd be long gone before anyone outside of the six of us discovered what Mac and Dave had done with Torchie.

35
HOLLYWOOD AFTER HOURS

Acting is standing up Naked and turning around slowly.
—Rosalind Russell

September 6, 1966
Downey, California

THE PINK CAROUSEL looked like a single layer of a giant pink, rectangular wedding cake somebody had set on stilts over a huge parking lot. Three smaller covered staircase landings stair-stepped up to the entrance. On the building's side, a marquee announced, "Now Playing: Stark Naked and the Car Thieves." The high-ceilinged club felt larger inside than it appeared from outside, and it seemed well maintained. A sizeable stage against the farthest wall looked over a dance floor. Opposite the entrance, a long and well-stocked bar harbored a line of comfortable barstools.

Another adventure, I'd thought when I heard we were going to Los Angeles to work for a club owner Rapken knew. *We'll play a few weeks, visit Disneyland, check out Hollywood, go to the beach, and then we'll come back home.* A seven-hour drive south, two across the enormous city and through a pint-sized downtown, brought us to a town named Downey. Los Angeles seemed to be an enormous sprawl of houses and strip malls separated into little cities and connected by massive urban roadways called freeways, which were an absolute necessity to get around in this massive megatropolis. The tall palms, with little fingers wafting in the gentle breezes above the low horizon, in front of distant mountains, were a nice touch, though. I didn't know how close to the ocean we were, but the sun-warmed October air under powder-blue skies toasted our skins and felt fantastic.

The club drew large, enthusiastic crowds who made us comfortable from our first note. Our harmony-heavy song list and recent show experience gave us confidence, but we were short on dance tunes, and the nights seemed long at first. We'd had no reason to update our dance list for over a year, but the crowd seemed to like our production numbers, and accepted our resuscitated dance tunes well enough while we took on the task of adding new ones. The only negative was that once the dance floor filled up, we could no longer see our audience from the low stage. We'd become used to performing for, and playing off, the audience's reaction.

"Look," Mark Anthony, one of the bartenders, told a couple of us hanging out at the bar during the first few nights, "Downey is in the sticks. A lot of the cool stuff you guys do won't be appreciated here."

Mark had a thatch of dark, unruly hair, a witty, enthusiastic attitude, and was a relentless chain smoker. He hailed from Phoenix and said he tended bar at the Carousel while waiting to catch his big break as a standup comic. He'd taken an instant liking to the band.

"You want to dig what's happening in the heart of show business, you gotta go into Hollywood. Even better, you guys need to play Hollywood. Hell yes, that's it. That's what you gotta do. Stark Naked and the Car Thieves needs to play at the Hullabaloo."

"What's a hullabaloo," asked Leonard. "Some kind of African animal?"

"A fantastic afterhours nightclub right on Sunset Boulevard, Leonard, with a gigantic rotating stage you've got to see to believe. I'm sure George can get you a slot this weekend." George Simone, the owner of the Pink Carousel, was turning out to be a great guy to work for. "Leave everything to me. You're going to see some stuff you never dreamed you'd see." Mark had worked himself into a lather, and that got us excited, too.

George knew a good showing at the Hullabaloo might attract people to his club in Downey, so he let us finish the last set early on Saturday night. We were in the thick of the 101 Freeway traffic, speeding west into Hollywood by 2 AM. A half an hour later, the elegant theaters, restaurants, and still bustling sidewalks filled our eyes as we cruised Hollywood Boulevard to Vine Street, then south, and west again down Sunset Boulevard. A few blocks ahead, a circus seemed to be in full swing as revolving spotlights filled the skies. We crawled ahead in the traffic jam toward streams of people filing into the cavernous, psychedelically painted Aquarius Theater. Tall, elegant date palms and short, bushy royal palms waving in front cast dramatic shadows in the roaming spotlights illuminating the building's entrance. We pulled into a lane where we could drop off our equipment while Mark, our self-appointed guide and roadie, went off to find someone who might be expecting us. It looked like we'd arrived at a major movie premier. We stared big-eyed at each other. The smell of get-high herb, now a familiar scent, emanated from everywhere.

Marie and I had gotten teary-eyed our last night together in Berkeley, but we expected I'd be back in a few weeks. Meanwhile, I'd met a sweet girl at the Carousel named Penny who had come to the Hullabaloo with me. At least I hoped she was Penny. I'd met her opening night along with her gorgeous, absolutely identical twin. One of their favorite tricks was pretending to be each other. It was interesting to consider just how far they might take this impersonation thing. This twin wore white go-go boots with black-and-white-striped tights under an A-line skirt sporting giant red polka dots. She'd teased her lustrous dark hair into a towering beehive that might attract nesting hummingbirds. Several people who had followed us from the Carousel waved as we strolled in.

The huge building had once been a live theater, until it was converted for use as a live television game show set. Now, the gigantic room was the biggest, most glamorous afterhours club in the western United States.

"Everybody seems so young," I said. The huge crowd seemed to be half teenagers. Even without a dance floor, people danced all the new dances up and down the aisles. A girl did the jerk so hard buttons popped off the back of her blouse like tiny missiles.

"Yeah," Penny said, brushing loose wisps of hair off her face. "You only have to be sixteen to get in and eighteen after midnight. My friends and I came to Hullabaloo a few times last year before I turned twenty-one—now it makes me feel kind of old."

You feel old, I thought. *I'm twenty-four and feel ancient.* But the youthfulness added a special energy to the event.

Mark found a corner in the massive back stage for our equipment. Close by, an eighty-foot expanse held an embedded sixty-foot turntable stage.

A curtain bisected the stage's rotatable center muffling music leaking through from a band playing to the audience on the opposite side. On this side, a band called Dick Dale and the Del-Tones finished setting up their equipment. The spectacle kicked up king-sized butterflies in my belly.

Mark rushed up to us. "Okay, here's the scoop. You guys are on in about an hour. That's a good time slot. Group called Hourglass will go on first, followed by Pat and Lolly Vegas, then you." He turned to point farther off into the gloom.

"Oh, dressing rooms are back that-a-way." He grinned at me. "Gotta get back out front. Met a real honey out there, but she's only got one tooth." He ran his comic patter. "Says it's a tooth, but the dang thing's in a different place every time she smiles. I'm gonna go French kiss her, see if it's not really a Chiclet."

Mac and I checked out the dressing rooms, which turned out to be huge, with mirrors and makeup tables along one wall and individual private rooms lining the opposite side. A strong feral odor accompanied by ferocious growls and hisses emerging from one of the closed rooms was drawing a lot of attention. Somebody identified it as Dick Dale's dressing room, containing his white cheetah, unhappy about being alone while he was onstage. We agreed it would be better to bring our suits next time instead of wearing them, but I was glad we wouldn't need a dressing room tonight.

A roar of laughter met me as I joined Penny and the rest of our friends out in front. They'd found enough folding chairs so we could sit together. On the end of a ramp extended from the stage, a skinny black comedian kept slipping something dark in and out of his pocket, sniffing at it as though it was getting him stoned.

"What? You wondering if I'm up here on this stage getting high man? Now what kinda fool do you think I am? You do realize cops's all over this place looking for dope, don't you?" He shook his head, checking all around before speaking to some imaginary narcs.

"I ain't got nothin' illegal, nope, not me. I do my own kinda thing, and it ain't against the law, least not yet." He pulled the black cloth object out of his jacket pocket again. "See here, now?" He shook out a narrow swatch of cloth. "This be a dirty sock. Whew! Gets me so fucked up I can hardly read my wristwatch."

The audience broke up laughing, and so did we. We whispered between ourselves, "Who is this guy? He's incredible." Somebody whispered back, "Richard Pryor."

I'd never heard of him before, but his edgy humor, soft voice, and self-deprecating jokes kept the place booming with laughs. In his next bit, he lay down on stage in a fetal position, all twisted up, with the mic sandwiched in by his mouth. Now he'd become one of a pair of twins just about to be born. I laughed so hard my butterflies flew away, at least until his act ended. Mark and I agreed his show was hilarious, though he added, "Speaking as an out-of-work comic, though, it's a little depressing for me."

Hourglass played down and dirty R&B, swamp-water blues, and Otis Redding tunes. Mac loved them, while I had my doubts. He was still teaching me to appreciate James Brown and introducing me to Otis.

Pat and Lolly Vegas were great, though muffled, through the curtain as we began our setup on the back half of the turntable stage. Their version of the Stones' *Satisfaction* sounded good, and now they sounded terrific on *La Bamba*.

Leonard looked a little tired when he'd finished setting up his drum set on the high drum platform. I asked him if he was okay. "Yeah, I'm okay. Drummer out there is rocking, though." He seemed to be deflecting away my concern.

"You know Pat and Lolly Vegas were in the Shindogs?" Les kneeled down to pull his guitar from its case. That got my attention. I hoped I'd get to meet them. The backup musicians for the *Shindig!* television show had been called the Shindogs.

In Indianapolis, long before we could have imagined where we'd be now, the Aristocats recorded several songs to send to Jimmy O'Neill, a popular LA deejay who'd been announced as host of *Shindig!*, a new music television show. We'd found an ad in the back of a music magazine requesting open auditions for male vocal backup groups several months prior to the show's premier. It was naive to believe anyone from where we lived would be considered. But up until the last moment, we'd held out hope that our audition tape was good enough that we'd hear from Jimmy or somebody. When *Shindig!* finally aired, a group called the Wellingtons had snagged the vocal group spot we'd coveted.

"Who I want to hear," Les said, slinging his guitar over his shoulder, "is Larry Carlton. His trio's on after us. He's supposed to be one hot-shit guitar player."

My butterflies returned to do backflips. We were about to perform for the largest, youngest, and hippest audience we'd ever played to before. And the featured groups, singers, and musicians were the best around, or at least the most popular. The atmosphere in this massive arena had the feel of a major concert. The apprehension I sometimes got of being an imposter during big moments lifted its ugly head. I would have to pretend as though I belonged here and get through the performance. That's what worked before.

We'd been told to start playing before the big stage started to turn, to cover the rumble of the turntable wheel. We were opening with the Four Seasons' *Sherry*, so Les told Jack and Leonard to repeat the opening chord progression without voices until the stage had rotated all the way to the front, in case the mic stands wobbled and tried to knock our front teeth out. So instead of beginning to sing, the singers clapped to the beat as the floor beneath us began to move. The turntable stage was so huge, it seemed as though it was the world around us that was moving instead of the band during our thirty-second trip to the front. Pat and Lolly's music faded, as their half of the stage rumbled behind the curtain while for us, the applauding audience came into view. Les had it right; the turntable jiggled as the massive wheel stopped, we could have looked really stupid.

At the next entry point, the singers stepped into the mics, singing, "Shar-reee, Sherry baby," and rolled on into the song. Our vocals resonated throughout the room, thunderous and powerful, over the best PA system I'd ever heard our voices on. We used all the stagecraft we'd learned to give our best performance and, as usual, once I realized how good we sounded, my butterflies flew away and my confidence returned. We'd chosen just four songs and closed with *Cara Mia*, which brought the house down, of course. After we'd bowed and soaked up the audience's long, standing ovation, Leonard's sticks counted out *Cara Mia* again, and we repeated the ending chorus as the stage began to move.

"What an amazing ride," one of us shouted as we revolved behind the curtain. "Better than anything at Disneyland." It had been exhilarating. We'd come to LA, to Hollywood, to another fantastic challenge and we'd rocked. I thought we'd proven ourselves as performers equal to anyone we'd seen tonight. I felt incredible, I loved the way we pulled together when we were pushed to do our best. I loved being in my band.

The Larry Carlton Trio was live now, so Les rushed out front to hear them. Another band, the Yellow Payges, waited for access to the turntable, so we quickly moved our equipment and went out into the crowd to catch compliments from the audience.

The magical scene was so intoxicating, it was difficult to leave, but Leonard complained of a bad headache and looked haggard. I had to get Penny home anyway, so we left with him. Dave decided he'd stay, heavily influenced by a cage-dancer named Tammy who flaunted fluorescent lipstick and blond hair piled a foot high. He told us he'd catch a ride with Mark or one of the other guys—he grinned—depending upon how things worked out with Tammy.

36
PIANO PLAYER

I had a dream about you. I was running barefoot on the beach, and you were chasing me because you were a cop, and I was Naked. I couldn't believe you tried to arrest me. What, is it a crime to run with no shoes?

— Jarod Kintz, I had a dream about you 2

September 11, 1966
Downey, California

I LAZED AROUND IN bed late Sunday morning, attention split between wishing Penny could have stayed overnight and where bacon and eggs with a stack of pancakes could be found, when someone banged on the door. Les, Jack, and Leonard's wife Paula pushed into my room.

"It's Leonard," Jack said, leading the charge.

"He's sick." Paula followed Jack, still in her bathrobe, random pale-blond spikes of hair sticking out of a roughly bound ponytail, her face wearing a worried expression. "Really sick." I glanced at Les, who shrugged.

"Leonard's sick? Is it something serious?"

She looked embarrassed for a moment. "Sounds silly, I know, but the doctor says he has to stay inside, away from people for two weeks." She glanced away. "He's got the mumps. His neck is all swollen up."

I wanted to laugh, but Les and Jack's expression stopped me.

"The mumps. That's contagious, isn't it?" Maybe this was more serious than a simple childhood disease. "I remember having mumps when

I was a kid. My mom had to keep me quiet and out of sunlight for some reason. And, I'm pretty sure it's catchy."

Paula's gaze was glum, she nodded.

"Jeez. What're we gonna do without Leonard for two weeks?" I rubbed my sleep-matted hair, trying to get myself together. "What about tonight?"

"Already got somebody lined up," Jack said. "He's supposed to be good, and he'll play as long as we need him. Be rough on Leonard, though, since we'll have to use his money to pay the guy."

Paula shook her head. "That's okay. Leonard told me to tell you he loves playing in this band, and nothing else is more important. He just wants me to ask you guys to give him two weeks to get better, then he'll be right back drumming."

After such a strong start at the Carousel, a temporary drummer might have set us back, but Leonard's replacement turned out to be a good player, a good guy, and a fast learner. With a little extra effort, we'd be fine while Leonard was out of commission.

One afternoon, lazily watching daytime television, I noticed an ad offering piano rentals for fifteen dollars a month. I got a crazy idea I knew no one in the band would go for, but I still wanted to try. Now that we played in a dance club again, where almost no one could see us when people got up to dance, I didn't have much to do when I wasn't singing. Though nothing had come of it yet, I still felt Jack harbored hopes of eliminating me. I needed to make myself more valuable to the band.

Along with ballroom dancing, etiquette, and other social training forced on me as a young savage, my mother insisted I take piano lessons. Though I avoided practicing as much as possible so I could ruin my knees running on cement basketball courts, I was certain I remembered enough to make basic chords on the keyboard. Maybe that would be enough.

I planned on keeping the rental piano in my room to practice in secret, but when I called, the music store declined to deliver it there, but agreed to take it to the Pink Carousel. The next afternoon, the delivery men dragged the upright piano up the outside staircase, tuning it on the stage before they left. I tinkled the keys for a while before I gave up, dismayed at my awkward lack of skill. But if I could convince Les to give me some chords to play, I still wanted to give my idea a try.

That night, no one said anything about the piano, and I didn't offer any explanation. I think they assumed it belonged to the club and someone had dragged it on stage and left there for some reason. During a couple of songs, *Louie Louie* and *Knock on Wood*, I meandered to the back of the stage to bang on the keys as the dance floor filled. I tried to find notes that sounded right, but I couldn't hear much of anything in the clatter of the band. I liked pounding away on the keys a whole lot better than standing on stage like somebody's drunk uncle, though. Outside of the slightly annoyed looks Les gave me over his shoulder, nobody commented.

We planned to learn *When a Man Loves a Woman*, a Percy Sledge song rising up the charts. With no backup vocals and a prominent keyboard part, it would be the perfect song to begin my career as a keyboard player. Dave came to rehearsal ready with the words he'd learned from the record, and Les with the chord changes that he taught to Jack, while our replacement easily picked up the simple drum part. We'd gotten the tune down pat within an hour. When we took a break for a few minutes, I caught Les's attention.

"Hey, Bear, I'd like to learn the changes for this song."

"Why, you planning on tuning the tambourine?" He grinned at his own joke.

"I learned to play piano when I was a kid. Thought I'd find out how much I remembered with a tune like this. Sounds like straight changes, nothing too fancy."

"True, the chords do change right on the beat, but the chords themselves aren't so simple." He thought for a moment and then noticed my pad and pencil. "You're serious." When I nodded, he studied me for a moment.

"Okay, song starts in C, but the second change isn't an A minor like a standard ballad. Goes to G for a beat and then to B before an A minor seventh . . ." He fingered the chords on the guitar, which meant less than nothing to me, but I continued writing down the chord changes as he said them. I thought I could figure out the ones he'd mentioned on the piano so far.

"There's one spot where . . ." He stopped and handed me a handwritten sheet of lyrics and chords. "Here, think you can follow these?"

"Sure." I wasn't at all sure, but I'd try.

"Copy it and give the original back to me."

After rehearsal, I stayed behind. One of the best things about working at the Pink Carousel was that we each lived in our own efficiency apartments in a building George Simone owned, a short walking distance from the club. A small refrigerator and a hot plate completed the kitchen area, but the sitting room and bedroom were separate from each other. Dave and I had been great roommates for a year and a half, but having my own privacy was a nice change. No one would notice I was still at the club.

I doodled around with the chords. I was something like twelve the last time I'd tried to play anything more than *Heart and Soul* on a piano. This time when I touched the keys more came back than I expected. I couldn't make the changes on time, my fingering was awful, and I wasn't sure how to form some of the chords, but I was heartened. After an hour or so, I had a rough idea of how the song went. I promised myself I'd keep working at it.

Friday night I tried to play along with *When a Man Loves a Woman*. I waited until Dave stepped to the mic before I slipped back to the piano. After the song was well started, I began to bash away at the keys, still unable to hear much but trying to match the timing of Les's chord changes. I wasn't altogether sure, but I might have gotten half the chords right, though I'd missed the timing altogether.

Afterward, Dave asked, "Were you playing the piano on my new song just now?"

"Yeah, trying to anyway."

"I couldn't hear it very well."

"Sounds best that way for now."

"Didn't know you played the piano, bro," Mac said, walking up on us.

"Had piano lessons as a kid. Never followed through, though."

They both nodded, and we went on to talk about something else.

37
MATTRESS DIVING

Naked is the best disguise.

— Jeanette Winterson.

September 21, 1966
Downey, California

"GEORGE SAYS SOME booking agent named Bob Leonard is in here and wants to talk to us." Jack had spoken with the club owner at the bar during our break. "George says he wishes he could keep us on, but he's got a contract with some group called the Mojo Men. Says we need to talk to agents like this guy about getting another gig, but he wants to book us back soon as he can."

"I thought we were going back to San Francisco or somewhere in the Bay Area," I said.

"Who should we contact for that?" Jack said. "Do we call Rapken?"

I didn't know. We'd let this get ahead of us, we hadn't had to think about finding new jobs since our first audition at the Town Club. They just seemed to appear when we needed them.

"I like playing here at the Carousel," I said. "Wouldn't mind if we stayed a few more weeks, but if we can't, we better figure out something else quick."

Everyone nodded in agreement.

Mac and Dave trailed along with me after Jack to a table near the door where a blondish balding man sat talking with the owner. After introductions, George excused himself.

"Hey, you guys are outta sight. Dig your band a lot. Lucky break I dropped in here to talk to George. He says you're here two more weeks and then you don't know where you're goin'. Think I can get you into a fantastic nightclub in Vegas. How's about that for luck? You interested?" The guy talked a million miles a minute.

Jack nodded. "What kind of money would that be?"

"Have to check it out. Didn't realize I'd be seeing a band tonight good enough to send over to Bob Hirsch, sight unseen. Wouldn't be less than you're making here, though."

Jack glanced at us. This was coming at us fast but so was the end of our contract. I didn't know what to think. Las Vegas meant nothing special to me, or to Dave or Mac as far as I knew. Mac's subtle shrug signaled Jack to go ahead.

"Guess we'd be interested if we got an offer, Mr. Leonard."

"You're Jack, right? Call me Bob. Tell you what, I'll get on the horn first thing tomorrow and try to get this nailed down. But if I get you an offer, I'll be expecting you to take it. Long as it ain't less money than here, okay? I don't want to get Bob all stirred up and end up with squat in my hand." He frowned at us one by one, as if accusing of us cancelling out on his contract right there and then.

"Guess we can agree to that," Jack said.

When we finished our first set Tuesday, I was shocked to see Leonard sitting at the bar talking with our bartender friend Mark.

"What are you doing here? Aren't you contagious?" I kept my distance. "Shouldn't you be home getting better?"

Leonard slid his 7Up around on the bar. "All the swelling's gone down, doctor says I'm not infected anymore. Little weak maybe, but I can't give it to anybody. Would never take a chance on getting you guys sick. I heard we might play in Vegas?"

"Yeah, maybe. Who told you?"

"Mac." He shook his head, his mournful eyes on me. "I wouldn't want to miss that, Larry. I want to play Vegas more than anywhere."

"Why would you miss it? You'll be back next week, right?"

Leonard looked at me with a question in his eyes. "Sure. I want to. Been listening, though, this other drummer's good."

I talked to Jack before we began the next set. "Leonard's here, at the bar. Says he's okay, but he's worried we'll replace him." We sat with Leonard on our break and reassured him he'd be back playing with us next week. He left before we finished the last set, and I didn't see him again for a couple of days.

When I did, I was sitting at a table with Penny on a break between sets when, out of the corner of my eye I caught movement out at the edge of the dance floor, darkened during our breaks. Leonard was wrestling around with an old mattress he'd found somewhere in backstage storage. He awkwardly manhandled it out to the middle of the floor.

"Hey, what's Leonard doing?" Dave had noticed him from a nearby table. I shrugged.

We watched him, chin in hand, study the mattress from one angle, then another, before bending down to pull the corner an inch or two this way and that, then examining it again. He tried nudging the mattress with his foot, but it wouldn't move. He tried again, this time shoving with his foot, but got the same result. In frustration he pulled his leg back and aimed an ineffective kick at the mattress, which caused him to lose his balance and fall onto it. Quick as a wink, he popped up as if he'd never fallen, eyeing an invisible audience who might have seen him embarrass himself.

Those of us close by grinned, exchanging glances as we watched. Titters rose from around the room, causing more people to turn to see what was going on. The recorded music playing through breaks provided a perfect soundtrack for his one-man show.

Leonard circled the mattress, as if taking stock of an enemy combatant. He took an abrupt step back in feigned surprise, and then stepped closer to whatever he'd spotted, bending down for a closer look until, in slow-motion, he toppled onto the mattress and, as before, sprang to an upright position as if bounced from a trampoline.

Pretending he hadn't fallen at all, he strode around the mattress, composure regained. He stopped to note a bit of dust or a feather on the mattress, which he stooped to remove. He raised his fingers and blew the mote away, but, realizing he hadn't blown hard enough, he reached to brush the modicum of dust away from its intended landfall back onto the mattress. But he overreached until, tilted at a precarious angle, he seemed caught between leaning and falling. He flailed his arms, trying to avoid falling until, helpless, he slow-motion dropped to the mattress again. This time, instead of rebounding, he tucked his shoulder and rolled into a somersault whose momentum took him to the opposite side of the mattress and back to his feet and vertical again. Peter Sellers's Inspector Clouseau had nothing on our drummer. A quiet round of golf applause followed, peppered by gales of laughter.

He looked surprised to find himself on his feet and reversed his roll back the other way, once again coming up to his feet. Peering around as though he'd hatched some sort of idea he suspected someone would steal, he grabbed up a corner of the mattress and stealthily dragged it back behind the stage. A round of applause and a couple of whistles broke out from the crowd.

"What the hell was that?" Jack wanted to know as we gathered on the stage. We all grinned and shook our heads, but we couldn't ask Leonard—he was nowhere to be found. Leonard's mysterious and dramatic comings and goings were coming as a complete surprise, showing a side of him I'd never guessed existed. We didn't see him again until midway through the next night.

Once again, Leonard appeared on the darkened dance floor during a break, dragging his trusty mattress behind him. He positioned, adjusted, and brushed as before but without pratfalls before striding away. A moment or two later, screeching and scraping noises emerged from the back of the stage, loud enough to be heard over the recorded music. At first, on a busy weekend night like tonight, not many people might have noticed Leonard's activity on the dim dance floor. But the growing racket attracted attention before Leonard appeared, pulling a clattering twelve-foot stepladder behind him onto the dance floor.

Leonard took a while placing the ladder in the precise spot where he thought it should go. Finally satisfied, he climbed to the top to sit, dangling his feet out over the mattress. *Did he intend to jump onto the mattress?* He leaned forward, bit by bit, until, as he began to fall, he tucked and did a perfect one-and-a-half gainer, landing on his back and bounding to his feet the way he had before, followed by another suspicious glance around the room.

Leonard didn't acknowledge the applause, continuing on as if there was no one there. The crowd loved it. He climbed the ladder again, slipping a couple of times on purpose, until he stood on the top, looking around with a hand to his brow. He put a foot out as though testing the water and then pulled it back. I was getting worried he could kill himself if he wasn't careful. *What possessed him to start doing this stuff?* He turned around as though he'd changed his mind, teetered, and slid partway down the steps until pushing off into a backflip onto the mattress, landing on his back, popping up again and glancing around in surprise. We were all on our feet, applauding, but I turned to Jack.

"I don't know what he's doing, but you've got to stop him. What he's doing is dangerous. He could get really hurt." By then, Leonard had begun returning his props behind the stage. He was still moving them as we passed him on our way to start playing.

"What are you doing, Leonard?" I whispered to him. "That was some very funny stuff, but too dangerous—what's going on?" He didn't say anything until the mattress and stepladder were back in place. He came to the front of the stage with his hangdog face and shrugged with a shy smile.

"Didn't want you guys forgetting about me. I'm still your drummer, right?"

"You're worried about that?" I couldn't believe this guy. I knelt down, so only he could hear me. "Your replacement is good, sure, but Leonard, you are our drummer." He smiled a little.

"Wasn't all that dangerous really; I was on the Navy high dive team in Hawaii for two years." He shook his head. "I had to do something, my nerves were getting to me. Had to do something."

I was coming to realize he was a bundle of insecurities. Maybe he needed the band to help him find his place in the world, the way I did, that is, if I could manage to keep myself in the band.

"Keep the funny part, Leonard. You're a natural, but don't do any more dangerous stuff. Band can't afford to lose you, man." I thought it was important we didn't squelch this playful nature he was showing us. He had a deft, unteachable sense of comedic timing.

A note was waiting for us at the bar when we got off stage at the end of the night. Bob Leonard had called and left a number. We gathered around the pay phone near the front door while Jack called. Leaning close, I could make out a tinny voice over the receiver's speaker.

"Okay, you guys are on for Vegas. Figured you wouldn't want any downtime so you gotta be there Monday, the next night after you close the Carousel. What? I'm not hearing any breathing on this line. You guys still there?"

"Yeah," Jack said. "Still here. So you're saying you want us to open Monday night right after we close here on Sunday night, next week?"

"That's what I'm sayin', boyo. Had to pull every known string in the book to get you guys in without Jack Turner seeing you. But I told Bob, he's the owner—'Hey, call George Simone at the Pink Carousel, you don't believe me how good these guys are.' So he does, and George tells him you guys are the best band he's ever had at his place, so Bob told me just tonight to make the booking. I can count on you guys now, can't I? You're on, right?"

"You got a contract for us to sign?"

"Well, of course I do. Las Vegas union paper. Club owner's got it all filled out and signed, waiting for you when you get there."

"You're not bringing it to us, or sending it to us?" *Good boy, Jack.*

"Nah, ain't enough time. I can't get there, and you'd never get it back in time if I mailed it. What, you got another offer in Vegas or something? What are you thinking? Just go up there, sign the fucking paper, and start playing. What's the problem?"

Jack held his hand over the receiver and looked at us. The guy'd talked so loud we'd all heard him. "Guess he's right," I said. "Wouldn't make much difference since we don't have any options, anyway." Jack's intense glance at the rest of us asked for opinions, but nobody had anything to say.

"I want to go to Vegas, man," Leonard said, and the scale was tipped.

"Okay, where we playing?"

"Write this down somewheres. You'll look for the Pussycat A' Go Go, right on the Las Vegas Strip near the Sands. Owner's name is Bob Hirsch, but find Jack Turner, the club manager, when you get there." He gave us the phone number and address. "Way it works, they got two bands, play on two different stages. One band starts early, plays a couple a sets, and the bands alternate for a few sets, then the late band does the final two sets. You catch a little break 'cause your first set doesn't start 'til ten. Get to the joint early as you can, though, okay?"

"Yeah, sure."

"One other piece of advice: You're crossing the high desert to get to Vegas so you should travel together. It's fall, so it won't be too hot, but that stretch of road is tough on cars any time of year. Leave early and stick together. All right. Have a good gig. I'll talk to you after you get there."

An older, perspiring balding gentleman came up to the stage after our ten o'clock set during our final week at the Pink Carousel and asked to talk to us. A few of us, including Jack, followed him to a table where he passed out business cards identifying himself as Howard King, Artist Bookings and Representation.

"Heard about you guys, Stark Naked and the Car Thieves, from a nightclub owner who caught your show at the Hullabaloo in Hollywood. Asked me to check you out," he said, voice full of gravel. "What a name." He shook his head. "You working with an agent?"

When we said no, he went on.

"Good. I like your band. There's a lotta rooms around town I can book you in. Have a place in mind right now, when can you go?"

Jack mentioned our Las Vegas gig starting next week.

Howard King tried not to, but his face scrunched up like he smelled dog shit on somebody's shoe.

"Next week? The Pussycat A' Go Go? How'd you get that job?" he said, in an accusatory tone.

The moment Jack mentioned Bob Leonard's name, a slow burn started on Howard King's face and neck. "That guy, he's a bad one. I don't like to talk down other agents, but him I would worry about. You sure everything's on the up and up with this job?"

Jack said he thought so, but he would double-check, of course.

"Well, I had an opening for you at a top club in the San Fernando Valley, but if your Las Vegas job is on the level, your schedule won't match up. Use the number on my card, call me as soon as you know when you're going to be available after that, okay?"

After Howard King left, I said, "Jack, I think we better find out more about this Las Vegas gig, don't you?"

"Yeah, we should. How the hell do we do that?"

"Let's start with talking to George. Bob Leonard said the owner of the Las Vegas nightclub called him for a reference."

George was glad to help. "Yeah, guy called, name of Bob something, said he owned the Pusssycat A' Go Go, over in Vegas. Told him you guys were the best. What else would I say?"

Jack shrugged. "Another agent, Howard King, came in tonight who said Bob Leonard might not be a straight arrow. We'd like to make sure everything's on the up and up."

George nodded his head thinking. "Guy left me his number. Want me to give him a quick call, make sure he's expecting you guys—what, Monday?"

George proved again he was a great guy to work for.

When we came off the stage, George confirmed Bob Hirsch, the owner, had a contract for the Pussycat and was expecting us next Monday so we breathed a little easier.

Closing night ended with a wild party in the club from the minute the doors opened, hosted by Mark as much as anyone, with George standing by, playing godfather. George even agreed to arrange for my rental piano to be picked up.

We loaded up the equipment after closing, prepared to hit the road as soon as everybody was out of bed the next morning. Back at our apartment building, I walked along the outside corridor on the second level, still getting accustomed to apartment doors opening to the outside world. Mac's room overflowed with people out on the walkway between rooms. I peered in, surprised to see Mark Anthony weaving some odd mixture of his stand-up routine with strange fantasy storytelling to a rapt audience of girls and guys who I thought I'd seen at the club earlier. He was as fucked up as I'd ever seen him, eyes lit by a manic sparkle as he raved on.

Mac sat nearby, pulling on a joint, enjoying the scene. Joan had stayed in Concord, assuming, as we all had, we'd be back home soon. He was planning to bring her and Dani to Las Vegas once we got settled, but he also planned to keep his apartment in Oakland for now. *She'd rein him in.* I grinned at Mark's fanciful tale, waved, and walked on two doors to my room, where I looked forward to getting high and reading myself to sleep.

Smoking grass seemed to drop me right into whatever book I was reading, immersing me into the story more than television or a movie. I'd finally begun *The Fellowship of the Ring*, the first book in Tolkien's *Lord of the Rings* trilogy—the book Maria, the flame dancer from the Galaxie, had recommended to me. I'd bought the books in a hardbound set in

Berkeley weeks ago, but I'd been reading spy or science-fiction novels since. I wasn't sure if I'd put off reading them to avoid thinking of her or not.

Now I found myself entombed deep in the ancient underground dwarf city of Moria with Frodo and his fellowship of friends, surrounded by orcs. I was fascinated by the depth and detail of Middle Earth. I looked forward to falling back into the adventure. Books were the cheapest, and to me, my favorite entertainment; they were my most prized possessions and dominated my luggage. When I was too poor to buy a book, I never minded visiting old friends, rereading old favorites.

I especially turned to them whenever the distance between what was going on in my life now, and everything I'd known before, grew too uncomfortably wide.

38
CITY OF ILLUSIONS

> *In a city of illusion, where change is what the city does, it's no wonder Las Vegas is the court of last resort, the last place to start over, to reinvent yourself in the same way that the city does, time after time.*
>
> —Hal Rothman, Neon Metropolis

October 3, 1966
Interstate 15, Mojave Desert, California

FOR THE LAST forty-five minutes, we'd been descending down a gentle slope at about seventy-five to eighty miles an hour. Petrified rivers of rock and gravel flowed across ancient basalt and stone meadows outside our windows. Thin, brilliant afternoon sunlight cast the mirage of a flat lake sparkling off to the south as the road bottomed out.

"This place looks like Mars," I said, gazing at the desolation of the Mojave Desert. The gradient out of the valley began to increase just enough to force constant shifting between third and fourth gears. The slow uphill grind was exacting a toll on our little caravan's vehicles.

"How far to Nevada, you think?"

Mac checked the map. He rode with me because he'd left his red Mustang in the Bay Area for Joan.

"Ain't far," he said. "Been thinkin, you know, rollin along like we are. Never coulda imagined you and me ridin cross these badlands on the way to Las Vegas when I got together with you guys. Damn long way from the bars in OTR."

"OTR? What's that? "

"Over the Rhine, ass end of Cincinnati, mainly bars, whores, and gangs, as I recall it. My whole world when I was a kid. I was about ten when I got into the music business. Played some harmonica, so me and my best buddy Ray, who picked some guitar, thought we'd be good enough to earn a bit a money singin and playin to people outside the Vine Street bars. My little brother Frank held out a cup to collect tips, and he was damn good at it."

"You never told me about this before." I glanced sideways at him.

"What about you? How'd you come to singin?"

"I was kind of lost in my school years. Didn't really fit in anywhere. Kinda geeky, into reading science fiction, invented a four-player chess board, stuff like that, but kind of a jock, too, hooked on playing basketball whenever I could." Mac nodded.

I'd had high hopes for high school after taking driver's ed and typing in summer school before freshman classes started. Getting my driver's license when I turned fifteen and a half was super cool, and something about typing appealed to my obsessive nature; I found myself finger-typing on everything around me. But when regular classes began at Shortridge, I'd become instantly lost in the thousands of kids there.

"So you bein like sixteen, and you ain't even listenin to music yet?" Mac asked.

"That's not what I said. I went to parties and stuff. There were some songs I thought were cool, *Teardrops*, Lee . . ."

"Lee Andrews and the Hearts."

"Right. *Why Do Fools Fall in Love, Earth Angel, I Only Have Eyes for You*, to name a few."

Mac nodded. "Yup, Frankie Lymon, the Penguins, and man—loved the Flamingos's arrangement of *I Only Have Eyes for You*."

"Yeah. So one night, I was up on my mom and dad's bed with the radio on, supposedly doing homework, I got to thinking about girls instead—did a lot of that." I glanced at Mac. "Then something happened."

"You mean besides you whackin off?"

"No, you idiot." I gave him a pained smile. "You must have gotten that station out of Nashville late at night in Cincinnati? You remember Randy's Record Shop?"

"Sure. 'Brought to y'all by White Rose Petroleum Jelly from Gallatin,

Tennessee.' Couldn't get it 'til after eight, nine o'clock. Had a lotta good ole R&B on that show."

"I'd never listened to the radio much before that night. All of a sudden the station came in clear as could be and I heard . . . 'Took a walk and passed your house, late last night . . .,'" I sang.

"Hell, yeah. *Silhouettes*, the Rays. Loved that tune."

"Me, too. Damn song hypnotized me, possessed me. Remember that cool key change before the last verse?"

Mac nodded.

"That just got me. Had to learn how to sing those harmonies. Made up my mind to find some guys and figure out how to sing *Silhouettes*. As I'm sure you noticed, I've never let not knowing how to do something stand in my way of doing it anyway." I grinned and took a hand from the wheel to gesture toward Mac. "Perry Baldwin, guy you replaced, was one of those first guys."

We were silent for a couple of miles.

"I come up a lot different way than what you and Dave did. Went to an all-black junior high. Most days, those black boys wanted to kick my white ass, 'til one day I filled in for a singer in one of the neighborhood groups. Then I was cool. Met Joan there, think she mighta been the only other white kid in the school. We promised ourselves we'd get outta OTR together."

"Never understood why you wanted to join the Reflections," I prompted Mac, curious to hear more. "You were in a money-making nightclub band, and we sang in our living rooms. Even though I came to find you, I was pretty sure you'd turn us down and go home to Cincinnati, probably rejoin the Casinos."

"Guess I liked how your group had a record good enough to get on WLS in Chicago. Gettin in the studio was big for me, hoped we'd keep recordin if I came on board. Liked the way you guys was with each other, too, like brothers, singing together, just your voices. Made me think of the Legends, my old group in Washington Park before I got with the Casinos. Went with them to make some money, ain't no money in street singin. Problem was, always some kinda hassle going on in the Casinos. Knew I'd have to quit 'em one day. Just didn't know it'd be in Indianapolis."

He glanced my way with a wide grin on his face. He must have noticed me wondering what the big smile was about.

"Just rememberin the day you come to the door at Bunny and Phylis's house tryin to find me. Scared them girls half to death, you in your suit and tie, carryin a damn notebook." I grinned too, remembering how I'd slipped away from cold-calling advertisers for the *Indianapolis Times* that day.

I'd driven to the Rat Fink to see if anyone had any idea how to find Mac Brown who'd played in the band there. The place looked even more scruffy and rundown in daylight. A cute young coat check girl, who seemed to have little better to do on a warm afternoon in the vacant club than work on her nails, thought she could help me.

"Bunny's friend, Mac? Maybe. Have to see. Wait here." She retired her nail file long enough to make a telephone call from somewhere deep in her empty closet. She turned back to me and shouted, "Who wants to see him?"

"Larry, my name is Larry. Want to talk to him about singing." I'd begun to feel kind of foolish, stalking somebody this way.

After she returned, she pulled a bar napkin to her and scribbled an address a few blocks north on Meridian.

"Okay. Ring the bell, don't knock, and ask for Bunny. Got that?" I said I did and thanked her, but she'd already returned to her nails and lonely vigil at the coat check door.

She'd written an address just north of Fall Creek, a stream of water running through town dividing the decaying city center and the suburban north side. A few large homes, some of them junior mansions, remained along this stretch of Meridian. Most had been abandoned by owners escaping the urban blight of the early fifties; many had been knocked down and replaced by nondescript office buildings or overgrown vacant lots. The ones left standing looked like semi-healthy teeth in an otherwise rotted mouth.

I parked my several-years-old Ford Pinto at the curb in front of one of those still-standing homes, this one bracketed by overgrown, weed-covered lots. I got out, wondering what I was going to say. I straightened my JC Penney suit jacket and took a deep breath before walking up the long sidewalk and porch steps to a large carved front door.

Ring, don't knock, I remembered, *or was it knock, don't ring?* I took a deep breath and pushed a doorbell that chimed somewhere deep in the house. *This whole thing is stupid,* I thought as I waited. *This guy Mac is going to think I'm an idiot. Why would he want to sing with us? We've played a few sock hops, sang to our record at some high schools in Chicago before it died. We don't perform, we just sing. What am I doing here?*

I glanced at Mac across the front seat. "Must be why I got such a weird welcome. I was nervous standing outside waiting to talk to you."

I remembered a young woman in a purple terrycloth bathrobe, wearing a puffy shower cap with little wisps of dark hair poking out, no makeup on a plain face, smacking the door open against the security chain. "Yeah, and what do you want?" she said, staring darts at me through the opening.

I began to repeat my story, but before I'd finished, she'd thrown the door wide and motioned me into the house, while I continued to yammer about who knows what.

She broke in and said, "Why don't you go sit in there," indicating a sitting room off to my right. "Mac's getting out of the bathtub. He'll be down when he's dry."

I drifted into the sitting room and to an antique sofa backed against the front windows. The house had great bones with high wooden wainscoting along the walls, though it was decorated in manic fashion. Furniture that didn't look like it was quite comfortable together, or even in this house, crouched in various awkward spots around the rooms in view. Accessories seemed halfheartedly strewn about on various flat spots, and odd, uninspired pictures hung on the walls that weren't bare. An odd, sweet odor I didn't recognize then but now knew as cannabis drifted through the room. Still, the couch where I perched seemed comfortable, so I waited. And waited. Muted traffic noise murmured in from Meridian Street. At one point, a different young woman stuck her head around the corner and glared at me for a moment before disappearing.

A skinny guy about my height with damp hair jogged down the stairs and padded into the sitting room. He was barefooted, wearing a white tee shirt over beltless dress slacks. He had sharp features with mischievous, bright brown eyes. His open smile belied his puzzlement.

"I'm Mac. Hear you're looking for me." His voice was a raspy baritone. He dropped into an easy chair near the couch, letting his glowing cigarette fall into the coffee table's ashtray. "I remember you. You was in the Rat Fink the other night."

I explained why I'd come looking for him, and as we talked he didn't seem disinterested. The second girl, the one who'd stuck her head in earlier, joined us, toweling off short white-blond curls while gazing at me with suspicious curiosity. She plopped down on the arm of Mac's chair.

"This is Bunny." Shorts and a brief halter top set off a taut, athletic body. Smoldering green eyes turned an unremarkable face into dangerous beauty. I introduced myself to her. She seemed to come to a decision and nodded to Mac.

"Girls thought you mighta been vice," Mac said, devilish eyes dancing. "We know most of the detectives, so many of 'em bein clients and all, but you can't never be too sure, guy walkin up in a suit. So, Phyllis called Darlene, coat check girl at the club. She's Bunny's contact girl, and she said she'd sent you."

Phyllis must have been the dark-haired girl in the shower cap who'd answered the door. *Looks like everybody's taking baths in the middle of the afternoon here*, I thought. God help me, I was innocent then.

"Man, you don't get it, do you?" Mac said, with a laugh. "What do you think this big old house is? Larry Dunlap, my man, you have stepped into the best, most expensive fancy house in the Midwest this side of Chicago."

Something on the road up ahead caught Mac's eye. "Smoke comin' outta Leonard and Paula's car. Looks like that piece of shit Leonard's brother give him off his used car lot ain't going to get 'em cross this damn desert."

We pulled up behind Leonard, vapor steaming out from under the Plymouth's open hood where Leonard had thrown a towel over the radiator. The rest of our cars dotted the side of the highway.

"Anything we can do?" I hollered.

"Naw, just has to cool down enough for me to get the frigging radiator cap off. I brought along water in case of this. We'll be okay."

Paula stood well away from the car frowning in distrust as if expecting a Wile E. Coyote–type explosion. Their little boy jumped up and down beside her in exuberant freedom from the confines of the rear seat.

Leonard glanced over at them. "Paula, don't let Jerry run out in the desert. Probably rattlesnakes all over the place." Her worried glare deepened as she glanced in every direction for reptiles preparing to leap at her.

Leonard hopped and capered, working at the cap until it blew off and he had to jump back from the boiling spume. The knock the running engine had developed faded as he poured water from his plastic milk jugs into the radiator.

Before long, we rolled back out onto the interstate, heading east.

We crossed into Nevada at an unassuming spot called Stateline where two gas stations and a small grocery huddled in the lonely desert. We pulled into the station pumps nearest the store, so Leonard could check his radiator while the rest of us stretched our legs walking to the little market for cold drinks. I noticed customers who received change from their purchases depositing their coins into slot machines near the door on the way out.

So, I too, slid quarters, dimes, even nickels into machines that rewarded a lever pull with a chunky thunk and spinning wheels in little windows. Bells dinged, lights flashed, and machinery whirred as images of fruit and numbers clicked into place. Even though I lost, same as everybody else, the action almost seemed worth the price of playing.

"Strange," I muttered, as we rode east across blasted earth no better than the California side, though the road surface on the Nevada side seemed smoother and better cared for.

"Thought I'd won me a thousand bucks there for a minute, way the damn machine sounded," Mac said, grinning at me.

39
TWO-NIGHT STAND

It's not the city I wrote about. It's not the same place at all. You'll notice that even the —what do you call them? —milestone or trademark casinos are now gone.

— HUNTER S. THOMPSON, author

October 3, 1966
Las Vegas, Nevada

I DIDN'T KNOW WHAT to expect of Nevada, none of us had been here before, though Leonard's brother loved the place and shared his wisdom about it with him. The state had been the Old West, with nothing but cowboy towns and desert, he'd said, until Bugsy Siegel and the mob came to Las Vegas and filled the town with grand gambling palaces built with teamsters' money. That was the main thing, Leonard's brother said, gambling, "cause that paid for everything else, and everything else was anything you wanted, long as you could afford it."

I tried, and failed, to picture western saloons full of guys in trench coats armed with drum-magazine mounted Tommy guns wetting their whistles alongside cowboys dusty from the trail toting their six-shooters and Winchesters rifles.

Half an hour passed before we noticed a building—either a slightly above average motel, or possibly a seedy hotel—isolated among straggling sagebrush and stunted Yucca trees. A gigantic neon sign screamed, "Fried Chicken, all you can eat. Lobster feast, $4.99." *Lobster, out here? Could that be possible?*

Within a few miles, we began to glide down into another wide desert valley, but this one wasn't empty. As the highway leveled out and a fiery sun hung low above the western mountains, our little caravan followed a simple street sign pointing off at a shallow angle to a country road with the pretentious name of Las Vegas Boulevard. In a few minutes, we passed the Hacienda, a grand Mexican-style ranch house that declared itself a hotel and gambling hall. A glittery sign announced food plus "Easy Craps." That made me laugh. *Easy Craps.* I wondered out loud if they sold laxatives or featured comfy toilets.

"Naw, man, craps is a dice gamblin game," Mac said. "You ain't never played dice?"

"No. Used them in board games, Monopoly, Risk, whatever."

The road widened and separated, broadening into more lanes, and our excitement and anticipation mounted as larger and more interesting buildings loomed ahead. Something about the Tropicana tower reminded me of Florida, though I'd never been there. A discordant vision of a golf course's fresh green grass, glistening in sprinkler water droplets, made an abrupt appearance on the right. Next, the Aladdin, an Arabian fantasy casino with two wide wings for hotel guests. Motels, pizza restaurants, souvenir shops, and gas stations littered the dusty land between the large hotels. On a corner ahead, the Dunes' sign rose high into the air. *What a perfect name for a glamorous desert resort.* On Mac's side of the street, we spotted a tall sign ahead emblazoned with a giant pink Flamingo—even I'd heard of the Flamingo Hotel. It was the most impressive resort we'd seen yet, until I looked out my window to the left.

Rows of slim trees escorted twin driveways the length of a football field past majestic fountains, jetting arcs of water forty or fifty feet high. The driveways met in front of a columned entrance adorned with Roman statuary and urns. The other hotels had seemed huge, but in comparison, Caesars Palace's re-creation of a Roman palace was twice as big and ten times more glamorous than any of them. I slowed to rubberneck, provoking angry car horns from drivers behind me. *What does that place look like inside?* I couldn't wait to see.

Just beyond the Sands Hotel, movie-perfect in its refined elegance, a sly, silhouetted cat face winked down at us, showing us where to turn into the Pussycat A' Go Go's back parking lot.

I knew the Pussycat would be perfect for us before we finished the first set. The two stages stood high along the room's long walls, on either side of the dance floor. Almost every table had a clear view of the performers, giving us an audience to play to, no matter how many dancers filled the floor. Our blend of rock, harmony production tunes, and R&B, and our stage presentation, made us a perfect band for a Las Vegas rock club.

Mac's personality shined. As he introduced us and our songs, slipping in little anecdotes, he drew everyone in the club into an intimate party with his infectious patter. With an excellent PA system and decent vocal monitors, Dave impressed with his voice and range, and the singers gained confidence from the first song. Les inspired and pulled Leonard and Jack along with him. We put all the stagecraft and polish we'd learned at the Galaxie on display, and the crowd was quick to show us their appreciation. I loved when we performed like this. Jack Turner, the club's manager, stepped out of his office to watch with a reluctant grin. A good sign. Because there was a manic quality to our energy. We faced a desperate situation.

After our long trip across the desert, we'd begun to drag the equipment into the club when Jack stalked back from meeting Jack Turner, the manager. He cursed as much as I'd ever heard him as he climbed onto the stage.

"All right, come on around here, guys. I got some bad news and some worse news." We sidled closer, our apprehension strong as our unwashed odor.

"Well, shit. Turns out this fucking job isn't a real gig at all. More like an audition."

Leonard went white. "We're not going to get paid?"

"No, not that way. I mean the contract that Bob Leonard a-hole got us isn't for four weeks or even two weeks. It's only for two nights. If they like us, they'll sign us to a real contract."

"Whew, had me worried for a minute, bub." Mac laughed. "We'll kick this place down. Ain't no big problem."

"Wait, that was the bad news. Here's the worse. Club manager says he's not sure when the club's schedule will be open next. He's got some other bands lined up that he already wants, so he's not sure when there'd be a spot for us, even if he likes us."

The frightening specter of nowhere to play after tomorrow night brought us down to earth in a hurry.

"We've got to make sure he wants us," I said. "We've never been out of work before. We're new to this town, no one here knows who we are. Not a good place to start over. We'll have to kick ass, make something happen."

I went to the edge of the stage to jump down. I glanced back at Jack. "What time do we start tonight? You and Leonard with your wives and kids have got to check into a motel somewhere; the rest of us, too. Then let's eat and work out a plan."

We met at the Silver Slipper, a modest casino with a no-frills dining room a little north and just across the Strip, as everyone called Las Vegas Boulevard along hotel row. Exhausted from the drive and dispirited with the news, we needed time to recuperate before tonight, but first we needed dinner. The Slipper's food was good, plentiful, and as the menu promised, inexpensive. Our confidence lifted a little as we filled up and worked up the first-night sets.

The Pussycat always has two bands, the club manager had explained to Jack earlier. Headliner performs on the big stage and the second band on the smaller one. We pushed back our plates and listened as Jack went on. "Man says we play on the main stage tonight. We start at ten o'clock, after the other band plays two sets on the small stage. We alternate sets with the other band until we close the night with sets at two and three o'clock in the morning. Crowd hits its peak around midnight, tapers off from there. Tomorrow night, we're on the little stage, and we start at eight."

Outside of putting on the best show we knew how, we didn't have any great plan. We had to do what we'd done before, somehow play our way into a job. Since the crowd would be at its largest when we began, our first two sets needed to be as great as we could make them.

"Okay everybody," Jack said. "Go get some rest for a couple of hours." I wanted to go see the fancy casinos, like that Caesars Palace hotel, but Jack was right. I was beat, and we had to impress tonight.

"Don't forget now," Mac warned us as we came off the stage into the dressing room at the end of the first set to warm applause. The first chords from an electrified twelve-string guitar from the four piece folk-rock band on the small stage rang across the room. "We got to get out there and meet the bartenders and waitresses, security at the door, and don't forget the blackjack dealers in the back. Got here early myself, already been out there with 'em. Seem like good people far as I can tell." As Eddie had taught us, these people were our most potent allies. We needed to recruit them fast.

"And customers, stop and meet the people out front at the tables, too," Jack added.

Dave tried to clear his throat. "Man, I feel my voice drying out just breathing this desert air. I need more hot tea and honey."

"Good excuse to go say hi to that cute little waitress, Melanie, at the service bar, brother," Mac said, grinning at Dave. "She'll get you what you need. She did ask could she meet you."

Even though Monday was the slowest night of the week, the club was near capacity when we began the midnight show. The Pussycat wasn't a glamorous room on its own, not even that well kept up. But, as we learned, the clientele at the Cat provided the glitz and glamour. These were the people that made the town go.

The beautiful showgirls and dancers, the waitresses, bartenders, and casino dealers, the working girls, and the locals came here to mellow out after their shifts. The staff at the Cat referred to them by an old carny term—rounders. There were tourists, of course, but it was the rounders' recommendations—from cabbies, doormen, valets, bartenders, or waitresses in the hotels—that got them here.

Audiences were often star-studded with celebrity headliners fresh from their performances in the hotel main rooms and lounges, and the A-list musicians in their shows. We played to an audience full of professionals, the "in" crowd, from every level of the Las Vegas entertainment scene. There wasn't a more discerning audience of professionals in New York City or Los Angeles than the one in the Pussycat every night. Here, they could let their hair down in the best rock club in town—the only rock club on the Strip.

Before the night ended, Jack Turner began talking about bringing us back to the Cat as a headliner, which was almost unheard of. Most bands had to win an audition to begin with, and pass that before being hired to play the small stage. If they succeeded in the second slot, only then would they get invited back for a four-week slot on the main stage.

Mac worked overtime making friends with everyone, and Dave did his best to break hearts with his voice. It was a terrible contradiction to feel we'd found a home in Las Vegas even as we were being evicted from it.

We woke to cold reality the next day; only one night left, and no idea where to turn next. Jack Turner made it clear the Cat wanted us, which was good, and as a headline act, which was even better, but he hadn't committed to a date. All we could do was go to the club and do our best.

We started at eight Tuesday night to a sparse early crowd. After the big stage, the little one felt cramped, and the PA wasn't as good, either. Our gravest concern appeared at ten o'clock when the new band, Six the Hardway, opened up on the big stage across the dance floor from us. They would be the new headliner for the next four weeks, and there was no way we were going to blow them out of the Cat.

Their vocals and instrumentation were excellent, but their lead singer, Chuck Girard, sang like an angel, and played guitar and keyboard, too. His voice moved seamlessly between falsetto and full voice with impossible range and incredible tone. Joe Kelley, the other lead singer, had a terrific R&B voice. In a way, they were our doppelgangers. With the pride we took in our vocals, it was humbling to accept the fact that while we could match them vocally, musically they were better than us. Our one advantage was stagecraft. Our year at the Galaxie helped us present ourselves as more personable, more professional, and better dressed for a Las Vegas stage.

We did our best, but it was crushing to know we couldn't compete from the small stage, where we didn't sound as good, and couldn't perform as well as the previous night. But we must have done well enough. About halfway through the night Jack pulled us all together in a corner away from the bar.

"Jack Turner says he went to bat for us. Club owner is offering us four weeks following Six the Hardway. But he wants an answer no later than tomorrow."

He held up a palm as we all tried to speak at once. "I know, I know. What do we do for four weeks? Anybody got any bright ideas?"

"We gotta stay, man. I mean this is Las Vegas," Leonard said. "This is our foothold. We got to stay here somehow." His long face sagged more than usual. "Problem is I don't see how." After losing paychecks in Downey, he couldn't have much of a cushion left.

"We got to figure out a way to take this gig they're offerin, boys," Mac said. "I see the kinda talent they get in here, and I don't mean the girls, though they ain't bad, either. This is where we belong. Got the same situation as Leonard, though. Joan and Dani are stuck in northern California with no money. Don't know what I'm gonna do."

"We have to look for work anywhere, even in California," I said. "We can play somewhere else and still come back for this gig. The logistics might be tough, but we don't necessarily have to stay in Las Vegas. Let's call that Howard King agent. Anybody we can think of—except that Bob Leonard asshole."

"Okay, I'll tell Jack Turner we want the job," Jack said, "but I won't confirm until tomorrow, give us a little more time to figure things out."

At the end of the night, we sat in the Silver Slipper again digging into $1.99 breakfasts. The Pussycat had offered us their two off-nights each week until our booking started, bringing in about four hundred dollars a week. It was a start.

"We're a band, a team," I told the guys. "We all work or none of us do. We depend on each other every time we go on stage and here we are, needing to depend on each other to figure this situation out. I've got a few bucks and I hope some of you do, too. Let's take every penny we've got along with the $360 for the last two nights." That's what was left after Bob Leonard's agent percentage had been taken out by the club. "We'll put it all in the pot and tough this out somehow. We'll get whatever work we can. We'll double and triple up in the motel, whatever, but we've got to be all in on this, all of us."

After we'd shouted down Mac's alternate solution—put everything we had on the craps table in the Slipper's casino and let it ride 'til we won what we needed—we decided Dave would hold the money. Dave, Les, Mac, and I would bunk together in a single room. Jack and Leonard, with their wives and kids, would keep their rooms.

Jack signed the contract. There wasn't a decision to make. We had to take the job in hand, even if it didn't start for four long weeks. This was going to be a great club for us to play, and I was beginning to understand all the excitement about Las Vegas, though it was still as exotic as another planet to me.

Jack called Howard King, but he didn't have any openings soon enough, though he wasn't shy about reminding us that he'd told us so, and that with enough notice, he had an interested club in North Hollywood. The Pink Carousel couldn't open up a slot for us in time, nor was anything available at the Embers in Palo Alto. Dave Rapken didn't return our call; I guessed we'd been abandoned by him. Returning to the East Bay wasn't even considered.

Out of ideas, we settled into survival mode.

40
BACKSTABBED

There are few nudities so objectionable as the Naked truth.

— Agnes Repplier

October 18, 1966
Las Vegas, Nevada

THREE WEEKS LATER, I stared in dismay at the little triangle of raised floor someone had laughingly decided to call a stage.

"Leonard, we're desperate, no shit. But please tell me you're kidding." Honest John's Casino, notwithstanding the lofty label of casino, was nothing but a storefront jammed with slot machines in a strip mall half a block east of the Strip on Sahara. It shared a parking lot with a souvenir store, a bookshop, and a shared common entrance to the fried chicken restaurant next door.

"I know what you're thinking, Larry, but it's better than starving," he protested, with a mournful gaze at the tiny uncarpeted space where his drums would sit. "Listen Larry, we get free soft drinks, much as we can eat from the salad bar thing, and we each get a roll of quarters for the slots each night. We can keep whatever we win."

It was hard to believe we'd come to this. Though money seemed to flow around us everywhere in Las Vegas, we'd discovered it was a disastrous place to be broke. Our pot of money had shrunk to a thimble. It was doubtful it could sustain us, even in the hungry and miserable state we were, through another week. Leonard was driven to play here in Vegas, the pinnacle of the entertainment business to him, but I'd watched him grow ever more anxious about Paula and little Jerry as the days stretched out. He pushed himself daily to find us the cheapest buffets, sharing coupons for groceries or fast food, no savings too insignificant. Despite his concern for his family, he dumped every last penny he was able to scratch together into the communal kitty. Honest John's may not have been Leonard's best idea, but if performing here meant staying alive for the last few days before we could draw against our first paycheck—he knew we'd do it.

We didn't need encouragement to ravage the salad bar the first night, and we went back for seconds and thirds. We shared imaginative ways to turn salad makings and dinner rolls into something resembling sandwiches. Munching lettuce, hard-boiled egg, and black olive sandwiches, we played most of our quarters on breaks, desperate enough to pocket a few when we thought no one was looking, to buy smokes.

The five of us who weren't Leonard stood in a line in front of him, singing into a couple of mics hooked into an unintelligible PA. We quickly discovered the mics were actually plugged into the amplification system for table seating in the chicken restaurant next door. Someone over there would flip a switch and hijack the speaker, often right in the middle of a song, to summon "Moses, table for three," or whoever was waiting to be seated. In order to hear our own voices the rest of the time, we played at such a low volume that when jackpots hit in the banks of slot machines around us, the sirens and bells drowned us out completely.

We got it, we understood—survival for the final days of the home stretch was at stake. No one we knew would see us, or ever know we'd performed here, and maybe we'd even laugh about it between ourselves someday. But morale had sunk to an all-time low during the last three weeks, and these desperate nights capped it off. I'd read and reread every paperback I owned. This was an ignominious humbling after the string of successes we'd gotten used to over the last year and a half.

I'd hoped the imposed hardship would bond us tighter, but instead suspicions and rumors were pulling us apart. We worried that Leonard, desperate, might be considering leaving us to play with another band. Then there was an anxious moment when we thought Les might have accepted an offer. Danger and fear inflamed each day.

Most troubling to me were Jack's not-so-secret attempts to eliminate me from the band. He disputed my worth to whoever would listen, pointing out that with me gone, I'd be eliminated from sharing in the ever shrinking money pool. He argued that while we weren't working was the perfect opportunity to eliminate my parts from the vocal arrangements, and to share out my leads. I'd known since he'd tried to get me fired in Hayward and when we'd disagreed over Don Hunt at the Galaxie that Jack wanted me gone. I felt the knife-edge of despair and fear of abandonment more sharply than anyone through the last few weeks.

At the moment, though, I struggled with a dilemma. I'd noticed Jack sneaking several JC Penney shopping bags from his car into his motel room a couple of mornings ago. The packages must've contained recent purchases, an obvious breech of our agreement to share our resources. When we agreed we'd pool every penny we had or got our hands on, we'd also agreed we wouldn't spend any money for anything but absolute necessities.

My predicament wasn't whether I would call Jack on this, only how. I couldn't just outright accuse him. What if I was wrong, and he had some reasonable explanation? Too much chance of blowback with the bad blood between us so obvious. I had to prove his iniquity without risking myself. I needn't have worried.

We'd decided to maintain regular rehearsals to concentrate on songs with intricate vocals we probably wouldn't have had time to tackle when we were working. We used some of the time to finish some complex harmony work and polish the phrasing and blend on the classic Lettermen tune, *The Way You Look Tonight*, for Dave, Les, and me. The day after we started at Honest John's, the vocalists were gathering to continue work on the Four Seasons' challenging and sophisticated arrangement of *I've Got You Under My Skin*, which required every voice in the band, including Jack's. I was wrestling with how to take advantage of the miraculous opportunity to eliminate my tormentor and the danger he represented when he walked into our motel room. I couldn't take my eyes off him.

"Uh, Jack?" I said in feigned surprise, unable to believe my luck. "Nice shirt. Looks good on you. New?"

"Thanks. Cindy picked it out." What was he saying? Didn't he realize what he'd just admitted?

The room went quiet. I followed up with a casual question. "You do realize none of us are supposed to be buying anything but bare necessities until we get working, don't you?"

Jack's face began to redden. "Well, yeah, sure. Of course I know the deal. But this doesn't count. Cindy's mother sent us some money to buy clothes . . ." Jack had begun to realize how lame he sounded.

"Leonard would shit a brick were he hearin this, Jack," Mac said.

"You know we're all going hungry trying to get through until we can start at the Cat." Dave's face had gone grim.

Jack began to stammer and talk with his hands. "You have to understand, it's not like the money was mine. In a way, it's not even Cindy's, it's my mother-in-law's. Cindy's mom gave it to her, you know. It was a gift. I'm not holding out on you."

"Those khakis new too?" I said. "What else did you get?"

"Well, some shirts, slacks . . ." Jack's new shirt had begun developing sweat patches. ". . . and shoes."

"That money should have gone in the pot, Jack." Les swung his guitar off onto his lap and frowned at the floor. I knew better than to say another word. I got out a smoke and lit up. *Time to keep my trap shut and let this boulder roll downhill.*

"Hey, fuck you guys." Jack's desperate anger was only going to make this worse for him. "It wasn't my money to give up. It was my wife's money, and you can't hold me accountable for how she spends it. That's not right."

"I think we need to talk this over without you." Les carried the ball now. "Maybe you better leave while we do."

"I want to defend myself if you're going to talk about this." He'd backed himself up against the door.

"Whatever you got to say you ain't already said, bub, say it now." Mac turned away from him.

"You can't fire me. I don't care about these clothes. Burn them if you want to. It wasn't me, Cindy wanted me to get them." *He was melting down.* "Besides, if you fire me, it's too late to get another bass player before the Pussycat, anyway."

"You better leave now," Les warned him. Jack had just buried himself and patted down the sod. After Jack had gone, Mac went to find Leonard. I didn't think he'd be in the motel, his anxiety usually kept him out searching for something, anything, to help get us through, but he was in his room and came to ours.

When we told him what Jack had done, Leonard dropped onto one of the beds. "This is not good." He shifted his gaze around to each of us. "What are we going to do?"

"I say he's got to go," Dave said. I knew he felt betrayed; so did Mac, who nodded.

Les said, "I think so, too." Leonard shrugged in agreement.

I put on my crestfallen face and nodded without saying anything. But I brought up what I thought were the obvious problems, though I would find solutions no matter what it took.

"Jack's right about one thing, we don't have a lot of time to find another bass player. And what he didn't mention, he signed our contract for the Cat. The way the musicians' union will see it, Jack owns the contract. If we're going to do something about this, we need to move fast."

During our enforced time off, we hung out at the Cat and had gotten to know the guys in Six the Hardway. It was really the only place we could go since the Cat extended free soft drinks to us every night even though we only played Monday and Tuesday. Leonard and Six the Hardway's drummer, Ernie, became fast friends, while Dave, Mac, and I learned more about Chuck and Joe. Their story had certain similarities to ours.

Chuck and Joe sang together in a high-school vocal group called the Castells, who had an early hit like the Reflections did. Of course, their master hadn't gotten destroyed and everything screwed up by their penniless producer—like the Reflections. Instead, living in Southern California, Chuck knew people who knew people in the recording business in Hollywood. Opportunities unavailable to us in the barren hinterland of Indianapolis were accessible to him. Bitterness aside, I loved the Castells' two hits, *Sacred* and *So This Is Love*. Flawless, beautiful harmony. I'd listened to these songs over and over while I was in school in Kentucky; I would've sung those songs if my group had existed at the time.

Chuck had a more recent hit, *Little Honda*, with producer Gary Usher, who'd gotten the song from Brian Wilson and Mike Love of the Beach Boys. Usher put together some of Capitol Record's fabulous studio players to do the tracks, including Glen Campbell playing guitar and Hal Blaine on drums. Though they were called the Hondels they weren't a real group, just a bunch of studio guys. When the song climbed into the top ten on Billboard's singles charts, an actual Hondels traveling band had to be formed. So Joe teamed up with Chuck and some sidemen to tour, while continuing to do studio work when they were home. I was more than a little impressed. These Hondels had also included Craig Richards, Six the Hardway's bass player.

The night everyone in our band except me—to avoid inflaming the situation—met with Jack to let him go, I wasted no time in finding Craig at the Cat. Even before Jack's new clothes blunder, rumblings about the future of Six the Hardway had reached us. Despite being such a talented band, drugs and booze had gotten out of control in the band, and were doing what they can do—destroying from the inside out.

"Rumor is you guys might be splitting up after this gig. Sorry to hear it, you guys are a great band." We sat at a table in the back of the club. Craig stood six foot two or three, taller than Dave or Les, but pear shaped and far less athletic. He had a baby face and light wispy hair, and though he tended to be a name-dropper, he seemed like a good-enough guy.

"Not sure what's going to happen," Craig said. "Chuck's going through some changes, and it's shaking things up. He's been doing a lot of acid and weed, says it's helping him 'find God' and keeping him from drinking." Craig shook his head, with a twisted smile. "Says he may need to leave the band to take the next step."

"No. Chuck's one of the best singers I've ever heard." It startled me to think he might stop singing. For some reason, I felt cheated. "I love his voice. Can't believe he'd give up music. That would be a sin."

"Funny you should put it that way. Don't think Chuck means to stop playing. He and Denny Correll from Fifth Cav have gotten tight; he's a Jesus freak, too."

Fifth Cavalry was another Southern California band in regular rotation at the Cat. They wore interesting remnants of the late eighteen hundreds mounted cavalry clothing on stage. They were another good band, and were playing the small stage during Six the Hardway's run.

"I think Chuck and Ernie are planning to go back to California with Denny and get into religious music."

"Look Craig, if a spot came up to play bass in Stark Naked and the Car Thieves, would you be interested?" I crossed my fingers—a lot rode on his answer.

He studied me, obviously surprised.

"You've got an excellent band, but if this is a serious offer, I need to know more about what your plans are. Vegas is cool, but I'm ready to get back to LA. I want to record, I've got some good connections in Hollywood." He thought for a moment. "Timing is important, too. I wouldn't want to be out of work in the transition."

"No problem," I assured him. "We open here at the Cat next Tuesday. We'd want you to start within a week, two at most. Our next gig is in North Hollywood, and we'd like to get back to the studio, too. How about you stay interested while we see how things play out in the next day or two. Soon as I can make a formal offer, I will. Okay?"

Within days, Craig was on board to become the newest Car Thief.

We weren't out of the woods yet. We sat in Jack Turner's office at the Pussycat late one afternoon just a few days before we were scheduled to open. This had to be a delicate negotiation or things would go off the tracks in a hurry.

"Thanks for making time to see us, Jack. You might not remember my name but I'm Larry, one of the singers in Stark Naked and the Car Thieves, and this is Les and that's Dave."

"Of course I remember you guys. The band getting excited to start playing here next week?"

"Can't wait. Been a tough few weeks," Dave said.

"Jack," I said, "a situation's come up that doesn't affect our ability to perform but has some ramifications with the musician's union. We'd like to ask you to help us with it." In my opinion, always better to approach a problem in a way that the person you need to go along with it can feel they're helping rather than just dumping it in their lap.

"Why don't you tell me what's going on first?"

"Sure. We're replacing our bass player with Craig Richards from Six the Hardway. Seems some of the guys are leaving their band after they close here, and Craig decided he'd like to stay and play with us." Jack Turner had started nodding when I mentioned Craig's name.

"He seems to be a good musician. I'm sure he'll work out for you." He tilted his head, seeming a little perplexed. "I appreciate the heads up, but I don't have to approve a change like that."

"The fly in the ointment is our current bass player, Jack Beam, signed our contract with the Pussycat—which is why we need your help."

"Of course. Jack." He thought for a moment, bemused. "Well, I can't see any real difficulty. You plan to give him two-weeks notice, right?"

"We've discussed it with him, but the musicians' union rules don't allow sidemen, the guys in the band, to fire their bandleader." I shrugged and smiled, trying to exude confidence. "Some of the union's rules are a little archaic for partnership bands like ours. Jack thinks he owns the contract to play here. We need to work with you to make sure this isn't a problem."

"What do you want me to do?"

I could tell he was starting to get edgy about where this was headed as he realized he might have to put some effort into dealing with this. But I also knew his options were pretty limited. The Pussycat had to have a band on the main stage next Tuesday night.

"It's really pretty simple. The rest of us, who are considered sidemen in Stark Naked and the Car Thieves, will quit the band next Tuesday, opening night. Then we'll immediately reform the band around Craig Richards as our new leader. Jack doesn't own our name, and without a band, Jack can't fulfill his contract; it will be null and void. A new agreement, on union paper and signed by Craig, will be ready for your signature."

Turner mulled this over as he tapped out a nervous rhythm on his desk with a cigarette lighter shaped like a silver bullet. I added, "And we will pay Jack for two weeks."

Now came the closer. "Everything's pre-arranged and approved by Local 369, although the union rep who suggested this solution asked me not to mention his name unless necessary." I put on my best used-car salesman smile. "All you'll need to do is sign the new contract before we start playing Tuesday night. If you're at all concerned, I think we can arrange for a union rep to be here opening night, to make sure it all goes smoothly." I also believe you should try to bring a solution along with the problem when you need someone's help.

Jack looked at me with more attention. "Pretty slick. Guess you've got everything covered, but if there's any hassle over this, I'm going to come looking for you, buddy boy."

At long last, with nobody left who wanted anybody else out of the band, I could breathe a lot easier.

Clear sailing at last. Sure, that's the way it would go.

41
ACROSS THE STREET, ACROSS THE MUSICAL UNIVERSE

If you want to be a rock star or just be famous, then run down the street Naked, you'll make the news or something. But if you want music to be your livelihood, then play, play, play and play! And eventually you'll get to where you want to be.

— Eddie Van Halen

November 1, 1966
Las Vegas, Nevada

DURING THE STRESSFUL weeks we'd played the off-nights between the two stages, the Cat had become our hangout. We'd made friends, captured fans, and found allies. Now that we were the headliners, the rounders, regulars in the club, showed up in numbers and recommended us to out-of-towners they met at their jobs. We were the hot, "must-see" rock act on the Strip. Six the Hardway had generously helped us by letting us sit in with them, and they'd encouraged their followers to come see us after they closed. A quiet word-of-mouth buzz developed that led to a confidence-building full house on opening night.

Our showmanship and slick, tight harmony style served us well. Mac turned the club into a running party beginning at ten o'clock every night, and Dave's voice, now adjusted to the dry desert air, sounded as fantastic as ever. By the weekend, the bouncers enforced a waiting list for the lines at the door. In short, and at least for right now, we were heating up in Las Vegas. Not hard to understand our motivation to do our very best every night. We were excited to be back on stage, and relieved to still be together. I felt a slight twinge of regret for my part in forcing Jack out of the band, but most of the damage had been self-inflicted. If it was me on the outside looking in, I doubt he would have spared any remorse for me.

Craig worked himself into the band with relative ease, enriching our harmonies with another decent tenor voice; he was a major improvement over Jack's scratchy baritone. The sound of his Rickenbacker bass and the way he fingered and plucked the strings, unlike Jack's heavy-handed use of a guitar pick, altered our musical style. While we didn't drive as hard, the band's musicality gained more texture, more touch, with Craig's throbbing, rumbling bass lines.

After our low point of being less popular than the featured condiment at Honest John's salad bar, I was feeling we'd come full circle when Trish Turner strolled up between shows one night. Someone I didn't know shadowed her.

"Hey, Larry," she said. "Got somebody you'll wanna meet."

Trish, a talented and attractive mocha-skinned R&B singer, often sat in with us in the early morning hours. Our late-night sets had begun to attract ad hoc sit-ins by skilled, and often famous, musicians and singers. I didn't know Trish well, but she seemed like a sweet girl.

The slight, pasty-faced guy behind her, with a mustache so thin it looked painted on, introduced himself as Clyde Carson and offered to buy drinks after we shook hands.

Following small talk and complimentary comments about the band, Trish excused herself, and Clyde made me an inconceivable proposition.

"Would you guys be interested in playing across the street at Caesars Palace?" he said, after we settled in with our drinks.

As he hinted at the connections he assured me would guarantee an audition to open the rumored new lounge at the opulent hotel, my incredulity grew. Disbelief must have been written all over my face.

Though it wasn't far north and across the street from the Pussycat physically, Caesars Palace might as well have been across the musical universe for a band like Stark Naked and the Car Thieves. Only the biggest, most well-known stars in entertainment appeared there. Andy Williams, who hosted his own prime-time, top-rated television show, had opened the hotel's main showroom when it had opened its doors a few months ago. An international audience of celebrities and the wealthy had been flown in from around the world for the event.

No rock artist or group, no matter how famous or talented, had ever performed in a major Las Vegas Strip hotel, not even in a lounge. One day, rock and roll would break the barrier, but not here, not now, and not with an unknown band without hit records or a national reputation. And above all, it would not be at Jay Sarno's luxurious Caesars Palace, already legendary internationally for glamour and extravagance.

When a rock artist did break through, it would be the Beatles, or Elvis, or maybe the Four Seasons or the Beach Boys—somebody famous worldwide. It was laughable to think our transient popularity in a local rock nightclub would translate to a stage at the mammoth casino. Caesars's extravagance overshadowed every hotel on the Las Vegas Strip, maybe even the country. What Clyde proposed was like a talented Little League team being offered an opportunity to play with the New York Yankees in major league baseball.

And, as is common in fairy tales, Prince Charming added a catch. We'd have to kiss a frog—Clyde Carson, himself. He wanted to be our personal manager. Besides the sheer presumption of getting us an audition, forget about an offer, there were other issues, starting with his qualifications. He seemed surprised when I questioned his knowledge of the music business and the art of performance, his answers vague or nonexistent. He couldn't offer any contacts in the recording industry, our main objective, and outside of the alleged Caesars Palace connection, none in other major venues. Had he wanted a finder's fee, even a big one, that would have been one thing. Asking us to turn over our career to him, based on this conversation, verged on the insane.

And, of course, there was our unresolved relationship with Dave Rapken. Rapken had demanded we sign a personal management contract with him before we could play at the Galaxie in San Francisco. I'd been reluctant, petrified really, to confront him about this since I'd come to realize he was connected to a Chicago crime family.

But being young, stupid, and certain of our own immortality, we decided the potential reward so outweighed the downside, and it was so improbable anyway, we'd worry about any repercussions in the great by-and-by. We did alter Clyde's proposal in one way: just getting us an audition wouldn't be enough. We'd agree only if a multiyear, union-approved contract to play at Caesars Palace resulted from his illusory audition.

A few days later, I flopped down on my motel room bed in shock when Clyde gave me the news on the phone.

"I got your audition, Larry," he crowed. "Knew you didn't believe I could do it, but you're all set. Pack up your gear and take it to the main-room stage at Caesars by four o'clock Thursday afternoon. Audition is at five sharp."

Even though appearances suggested Clyde had gotten us an actual tryout at Caesars, I couldn't help wondering if we were on our way to a tragic, practical joke. I imagined us getting to the stage door where everyone would fall down laughing and tell us they'd never heard of anyone named Clyde Carson.

We picked six songs and changed into suits for our audition, but we were totally unprepared for the Circus Maximus showroom stage, a cavernous expanse where entire New York Broadway musicals were presented to nearly a thousand dinner guests. We felt vulnerable and insignificant, clustered together in the stage's barren center without even a drum stand to group around. A couple of stagehands helped us through a desultory sound check, but there was only one vocal monitor in front of Dave. When we asked for more monitors, the stage crew didn't know who to ask—the rest of us would have to guess at pitch and harmony.

Clyde signaled us to start after he and five nonresponsive suits seated themselves about half a football field away in one of the dinner booths on the second ring. Blinding light engulfed us as someone threw a switch. Without the energy of a live audience to feed on, especially for Mac, we felt intimidated and our little set felt stiff. No one from Clyde's entourage applauded or commented between songs. Overwhelmed by the environment, I believed we'd stunk by any reasonable standard.

After a half gesture of some kind from Clyde, his party stood to leave halfway through the last song. Might have been the one-finger salute for all I could tell. We didn't say much to each other while we broke down our equipment to schlep back to the Pussycat stage. Though we wouldn't have to confront the personal manager issue, I think down deep we realized we'd choked at the magnitude of the opportunity. It had seemed so impossible we hadn't gotten ourselves up for the audition; we hadn't been ready. Our daubers were down, but at least we'd go back to a club that loved our brand of rock music and made us feel like stars.

When Clyde dropped by the Cat later that night, I was sure he'd come to tell us how bad we'd been at the audition. Instead, he told us we'd passed. Unthinkable! What crazy parallel world had we stepped into? Clyde gave us the details: In less than six weeks, Dave Victorson, the entertainment director at Caesars, planned to open a 250-seat showroom lounge called Nero's Nook—and he wanted us in the opening night lineup. The promotion would be huge, Clyde said. There'd be worldwide coverage.

Dave Victorson would be expecting me at the Caesars Palace entertainment office Friday afternoon to close the deal.

42
NEGOTIATIONS

Las Vegas is sort of like how God would do it if he had money.

— Steve Wynn

November 11, 1966
Las Vegas, Nevada

THERE WAS AN overwhelming rush of unreality walking through what seemed like a mile and a half of plush casino and up the stairs to the Caesars Palace entertainment office—it was an experience I'd never forget. I'd visited this lavish temple of Las Vegas extravagance before, of course. I'd seen the short-skirted, toga-clad waitresses, their long ponytails pulled through some kind of cone. Had lunch in the cafe, lost twenty dollars at a blackjack table, walked the gallery. But the feeling was much different, considering we might be performing here in a few weeks.

I noticed the temporary wood barriers disguising construction on the south side of the domed casino floor when I entered. I couldn't imagine what Nero's Nook would look like when those walls came down, but it would no doubt be spectacular. I couldn't contain a goofy smile when I thought about how cool it would be when Stark Naked and the Car Thieves took that stage to open it.

Clyde waited for me in a glassed-in conference room inside the entertainment offices. I wondered for a moment why we were meeting here rather than in Dave Victorson's office.

"Larry," he said, grinning as if he'd won a thousand-dollar double-down at blackjack. He stood to usher me into a chair across a corner of the conference table.

"Like I promised, band's got the job. Contract's right here, and it's fantastic." He patted a packet of papers in front of him.

"You play four, four-week engagements a year over the next three years, guaranteed, with automatic bumps. Adds up to almost $300,000 for you guys, already approved by the musicians' union, everything's ready to go. The headliner is Xavier Cugat, and Mort Sahl, the Ritz Brothers are on the bill, and the Checkmates, Ltd.—"

"What? The Checkmates? Not those guys again . . ." I said, shaking my head in disbelief. Would these guys ever stop haunting us?

"What do you mean?"

"Both our bands are from Indiana. We called ourselves the Checkmates when we were a brand-new band, too. Before we'd heard of them." I grinned. "Before they got limited."

Clyde stared back as if I was jabbering in Tagalog. I didn't see an ashtray on the polished conference table; I wondered if I could smoke.

"They seem to pop up everywhere we go before we get there." *With tragic results,* I thought. "They're one of the main reasons we're called Stark Naked and the Car Thieves now." Clyde was not following along, I realized.

"Never mind, never mind, not important. Deal sounds good," I mumbled. I guess you'd think I'd be more impressed with the size of the contract than whether some other band would be on the bill with us, but three hundred thousand dollars was more money than I could comprehend, and three years was an eternity. I couldn't really process it.

"We'll need new stage clothes for this, Clyde. You'll set something up with a tailor for us, right?" I assumed, like Dave Rapken, he'd advance us whatever was necessary for this expense.

"Um, you don't have the money for that?" Clyde's response didn't inspire confidence.

"Despite the rumored wealth of undiscovered rock bands, we're pretty much check to check. As our manager, figured you could advance us money for expenses like that. You stand to make a pretty good cut on this contract."

"Well, I'll see what I can come up with," Clyde said, frowning. I realized he didn't have any money to loan us or a clue where to get it. "You guys cut me down to ten percent, you know, way below what personal managers are supposed to get."

I nodded. Thirty thousand dollars over the next three years when he couldn't offer anything other than this job seemed like a lot to me.

"Look, I'll go to LA, meet your regular agent, work out dates with him, and so on," he said, leaning forward across the gleaming table.

"We haven't got a regular agent, and the one who wants to be our agent is not going to be too happy when I cancel the gig he thinks we're going to show up for in LA so we can take this one," I countered.

"I'll go with you to talk to him, we'll figure something out. But first there are some items Dave V. wants me to discuss with you." Clyde squirmed around as though his underwear had begun migrating up his butt.

"Caesars has a problem with . . . Well, to be frank, putting your name on the marquee." Clyde spoke to the floor beside me instead of to me.

"Like it's too long to fit up there or something?" I feared what was coming.

"They want you to use a different name. In fact, they've picked the name for you. A hit musical is being shipped here straight from Broadway, opening in the main room on New Year's after Johnny Mathis closes. *Sweet Charity*, starring Juliet Prowse. The powers that be want to promote the hell out of the show, which means they'll be promoting the hell out of you guys, 'cause you're going to be the Big Spenders. *Hey, Big Spender*, is a popular song from the musical. See how this works? Your name will cross-promote the musical to the lounge, and the song's name will bring people to the lounge . . ."

"You've got to be kidding. The Big Spenders? Why would we want to promote a name that's not ours?" I was incredulous.

"This is a deal breaker. Gotta go with this."

"But the guys will never agree to this. Goddamit!"

"You have to make them. This is just a start. We can work on this over time with the hotel, after *Sweet Charity* closes, maybe. Another thing . . ."

"This isn't going to get better, is it?"

"No, no, this isn't so bad, kind of a compliment, really. You guys play great R&B and rock, but what you're exceptional at is big harmony stuff. The hotel decided your show should focus on—well, to be candid—all your big vocal numbers. Like the Lettermen and Beach Boys tunes you do. You know, the Association, Four Seasons, those kind of songs."

"I'm not so sure about this . . ."

"Like that *Cara Mia* people go crazy for . . . Who recorded that?"

"Jay and the Americans," I said. "Listen, we need balance, you know. We need some rock and R&B for pacing. Could we do a song like the Isley Brothers' *Shout*? It's our best audience participation number, a great set closer."

"See, here's the thing," Clyde responded, arms and legs twitching like a sprung marionette. "With the Checkmates doing almost all rhythm and blues, the hotel feels there's enough loud music in the lineup. The Checkmates' repertoire is narrower than yours, right? You're more flexible, so this time you guys are the crooners. Okay?"

"Clyde, this is not gonna work," I said, feeling the floor falling out from under me. One of the worst things about being leader is having to listen to outside demands and opinions, and relay them back to the group. All the flak rains down on—guess who?

"Larry, this is a gigantic fucking deal. You're the first real rock band to get into a Strip hotel. But everything's got to go down the way I'm telling you to start off. You get through these opening four weeks, do what they ask, and things can change. Sign this contract today, now, before your lucky break slips away," he said, eyes pleading.

I rotated my chair away so he couldn't get a look at me, my face flushing in anger, taking deep breaths, trying to keep my self-control and my eye on the big picture, the big reward. I spun toward him.

"Clyde, can you get us any wiggle room on this stuff?" I asked, swinging back to facing him. "I mean the name thing is such complete bullshit . . ."

He shook his head, "Only one final piece to the puzzle," he muttered, glancing sideways at me.

"What? More? Damn, Clyde!"

"You remember Trish Turner, the girl who introduced us, sings with you sometimes at the Pussycat? Yeah? Well, she's part of the show. Do a couple or three numbers with her each set. Okay?"

"Let me get this straight. You're putting a girl into our band? Now we're a backup band to a girl singer? We're the first rock band in a Las

Vegas Strip hotel, but we can't play any rock? You know what, forget the money, the Strip hotel, whatever. I am not doing this."

I was out of my chair and walking in circles on the plush rug, but I couldn't make my feet walk out the door. How would I explain this? We'd been so snookered.

"No, no, calm down. Won't be like that. You'll back her on a couple of classic R&B numbers from Diana Ross, or Martha and the Vandellas, the Ronettes. Like when she sings with you at the Pussycat, like you're hosting a revue, sort of. It'll be cool. I'm telling you, just get through these four weeks. Be successful and a lot of stuff is possible. Work with me."

"You're telling me to be successful and yet you're taking away what we need to be successful. Our name, which draws our people, cutting half or more of our repertoire . . . plus, making us a backup band?"

"You won't be a backup band. Trish will bring her own backup singers. And you'll be doing rock . . . well, rock ballads. Smoothing out the rock a little. Keep focused on the opportunities going forward from here. Give it a chance, Larry."

"I'm not the only one who's got to go along with this." I was whining, but I couldn't help myself. "I'm the leader, sure, I speak for the band but I don't own it. I'm just the guy who's willing to walk over here and do the deal, but we all have to agree to the terms. Nobody's expecting all this new crap you're laying on me. I can't tell them all this. Are you going to?"

"Better coming from you, I think. Let's get the contract out of the way, right now, though. I've got it right here . . ."

"Jesus Christ, you mean right this second? You're not going to give me time to talk this over with my guys?"

"Here we are," Clyde said, pulling a stack of paper from the slipcase in front of him. "Sign these where they're marked, and I'll send our copy to the union for their stamp."

I thought furiously. *Everyone in the band might hate me for agreeing to all this crap, but they'd hate me more if I turned it down.*

"Where's Dave Victorson? I thought we were meeting him?" I glanced around in desperation, hoping for some distraction to slow things down.

"He was detained, but look, he's already signed. We sign it and it's a done deal. Come on, let's get this done. Too many people miss incredible opportunities because they hesitate. Bottom line—three years, fantastic money. Take a gander at this schedule. Think of it! Ten grand a week in the last year, your band will earn a hundred and sixty thousand bucks in 1969 from just sixteen weeks at Caesars."

With apprehension in my heart, I looked over the contracts. Four copies. On each document were our names and union numbers, the Big Spenders, and sure enough, the money was on the attached schedule, as Clyde said. The figures for the third year seemed incredible.

Even if I had all the guys here in front of me, I thought, trying to imagine them here; *oh, we'd bitch and moan, but in the end, we'd all agree: after all, it was Caesars Palace, too big a deal, too much money to just walk away from.*

Clyde slipped them into their case one by one, as I signed them. He said he'd give the union their copy and register our copy with them. That's the manager's job, he said, handle the details, file the contract with the union and keep the band's copy safe.

43
THE SUNSET LA BREA TRAVELODGE

*Two or three things I know for sure, and one is that I'd rather
go Naked than wear the coat the world has made for me.*

— Dorothy Allison

*November 22, 1966
Hollywood, California*

"COME IN, COME on in. Now what's happened?" Trish held the door for us as we piled into her second-floor motel room at the TraveLodge Motel on Sunset Boulevard in Hollywood. Fortunately, we'd remembered that Trish and a couple of her girlfriends had planned to stay here until our engagement at Caesars Palace began in four weeks.

"Like I said on the phone, I think we missed our plane." If there had ever been one, as I was beginning to suspect.

After my meeting with Clyde at the Caesars entertainment office, the four-week engagement at Caesars would eclipse Howard King's long-delayed job in North Hollywood, and he was not happy when I called him to reschedule or cancel it. When he demanded to be included as agent of record on our Caesars contract in return, a huge chunk of money over three years for something he'd had no part in, I refused and he lost his temper. He swore he'd never book us again. Worse, he refused to talk to me about an opening to cover the four open weeks immediately ahead in someplace called Cucamonga. I'd learned enough about agents to understand that they'd book the devil at Easter Sunday services if they'd make a commission on it. He'd be back. But I guessed he wouldn't do anything for us until he got over his anger, which I didn't think would happen in time to fix our dilemma.

I thought I held a hole card, though. I'd gotten an offer from Bob Leonard, the agent who'd booked the two-night audition at the Pussycat we'd thought was a real gig. He'd lied to us, I knew that. I'd also come to realize the relationship between artists and agents is complicated. He pitched those precious four upcoming weeks following the Cat at a plush, four-star hotel in Mexico, when we were within days of having nothing. We'd already been through a rough four weeks out of work before the Cat, and we'd gratefully accept a job from anyone to avoid that again.

"Okay Larry, listen." Bob Leonard's voice squeaked through the motel room phone. "You guys are going to love this. Biggest club in Mexico City, inside this luxurious hotel, and once the contract is signed, you're on the plane, they pay half in escrow in US dollars into a US bank, other half when you close." Man, this guy was a fast talker.

"But you got to be on the ten o'clock plane from LA on Sunday night, son. Flight's booked for the band, deal is done, in the bank. I have the contracts right here and will meet you at the airport to sign them. *Capisce?*"

"Bob, you do know we're playing the last night of our contract at the Cat here in Las Vegas Sunday night, don't you? We aren't off the stage until four o'clock Monday morning. That plane would be taking off about the same time we start the night."

"Larry, baby," Bob pleaded. "Make this happen. Big bucks, exotic gig, beautiful señoritas, fantastic hotel rooms for you guys."

"We want to go, but be reasonable. Jack Turner's not going to let us leave a night early." I tried a bluff. "Look, Howard King's already got something for us in the same time slot, maybe not so nice as yours, but at least we could get there. We'd rather be on the plane to Mexico City, but your schedule is too tight. Can't you do something on your end?"

In the silence I could almost hear the gears grinding. "Okay. All right. We can still make this work. I'm pretty sure Aeromexico flies out of LA at one o'clock Monday afternoon, direct to Mexico City. Can you make that? I mean for sure, because you gotta open Monday night. You'd have to sleep on the plane, go right to the club from the airport."

"Means driving to LA, no sleep, but okay, sure, we'll make the flight." I dreaded what I was promising.

"Have to be here an hour before boarding, minimum. No later than noon. I'll double-check the flight and call you if anything changes. Otherwise, meet me at the Aeromexico gate at noon. Right? You gotta promise me now. My balls are hanging out on this."

I was not proud of the decision I made to work with Bob, but I was desperate. On the plus side, we had Caesars in hand, and if everything worked out we'd be sitting pretty with two high-profile, high-paying jobs in a row. I'd tried not to think about what would happen if something went wrong.

And, now it had.

After closing Sunday night at the Cat, we rushed to pack up and raced against dawn across the desert to reach LA International by noon Monday, as promised. When the LA traffic made arriving on time questionable, I stopped to call and check if our flight was on time. Aeromexico said no flights were scheduled for Mexico City until the evening. I'd called Bob Leonard's office from pay phones several times since we'd gotten into the 213 area code, but all I'd gotten was an answering service.

"Use this place as home base," Trish urged, when she heard my woeful tale, "until you figure out what's going on." I nodded a fervent thanks, but I didn't know what to do now. Our finances hadn't recovered from the lost weeks before the Cat.

"Guess I should call that son of a bitch Bob Leonard again, leave this number in case he ever calls us back, which I doubt he ever will."

Craig got up from the table in the crowded motel room and handed me a slip of paper he'd written a phone number on. "I'm going over the hill to my parents' house in Panorama City. Call me when you figure things out." He stopped, at the expression on our faces.

"What?" he said,

"You're just going to leave?" I glanced at the other guys. "Maybe you can help us figure out what to do. You live around here."

"I can't think of anything to help right now. You've got to find that idiot agent you believed and figure out what's going on. Don't know where you're going to stay, but at least I won't add to the problem. I'll call you here at Trish's room if I think of anything. Catch ya later."

"Loser," Leonard coughed into his hand as the door closed behind Craig.

I frowned but grabbed the room phone to try Bob Leonard again. "Mr. Leonard still hasn't checked in with us, but I'll give him your message when he does, Mr. Dunlap," the cool, disinterested answering service voice repeated again.

Trish joined us at a Denny's around the corner on La Brea where we gathered for dinner. When all of us, except Trish, pooled our resources, we confirmed we were even worse off than we'd been in Las Vegas a month ago.

"Look, you guys crash in my room," Trish said. "We'll have to sneak you in so they won't charge us more money. Maybe some of you can sleep in the daytime or something. We'll work it out." Trish was turning into a lifesaver.

Leonard had some money so we figured out a way get a separate room for his little family, and a couple of us could sneak in at night there, too. We couldn't think of anything better to do for tonight, so after Trish went up to her room, we snuck up one at a time over the next half an hour for a troubled sleep wherever we could find a soft spot.

"Yeah, well too bad. I found another group that could leave Monday night. Last I heard, they were having a fantastic time, too, and the club loves 'em."

"You son of a bitch," I swore into the phone.

"Next time, you think twice before you screw Bob Leonard out of a commission, buddy boy."

By Bob Leonard's calculations, since he'd booked us into the two-night audition at the Cat, he was entitled to a commission every time we played there after that. We'd never considered paying it, and if the club hadn't withheld his commission for the two nights, we would have kept that, too, just for misleading us.

"And you didn't get to take that old faker Howard King's gig, either. An added bonus I thought worked out well, too."

"There'll never be a next time, Bob," I said, a fangless threat, as I hung up on him. Even though I was stiff from the floor and tired from the trip, I felt slightly better. At least I knew what we were facing.

To stay away from the motel, Dave, Les, Mac, and I walked the neighborhood around Hollywood Boulevard, dropping into places for a Coca Cola or glass of water, or sitting on the curb. It didn't take long to realize that whatever fantasy Hollywood was supposed to offer wasn't obvious out on these streets in the daytime. It was dirty and crowded and parts of it dilapidated to the point of being condemned. But in some indefinable way, an air of expectation, anticipation, wafted over the neighborhood surrounding Hollywood's most famous, if nondescript, intersection, Sunset and Vine.

We sat at the curb gazing across Sunset Boulevard at the Cinerama Dome. Its entrance fronted what looked like a gigantic golf ball buried halfway into the ground. Les asked me if I intended to call home for money.

"No, can't, much as I wish I could. I think about it, though." I sighed and stuck my hands in my pockets. "My dad made me promise not to call for money, not unless I needed a way to get home. Not doing that."

Dave nodded. "Can't ask my mom for money. She doesn't have enough as things are."

"Yeah, that's what I thought," Les said. "I don't have anyone to call, either."

We sat gazing at the movie theater, wishing we had enough spare cash to see what a wraparound movie looked like.

Tuesday, Howard King called Trish's room. Despite knowing how angry he was with me, I'd called Howard's office to beg for help soon after I realized we were stranded in Hollywood. After listening to a lecture about Bob Leonard, which I had coming, he repeated he didn't have any jobs up to our standards on such short notice, but he said he'd try to come up with something. I didn't have a great taste in my mouth about agents, but he seemed sincere. The next day he called back.

"Larry, five nights at Gazzarri's, starting next Tuesday. Only pays a hundred bucks a night but it may help, and you'll get a little notoriety around town."

"Great Howard, we'll do anything at this point."

"All right. No commission on this, too small, so don't worry about anything for me. Call Bill Gazzarri and get your show times, okay? But remember, you're going out to the Valley to the Rag Doll right after Caesars. Don't even think about cancelling."

"A hundred dollars a night," Leonard groused. "That's not enough."

"You're missing the point. We need money. You're the one who had us play Honest John's for quarters. You do see the irony, don't you?" I asked.

Leonard said he didn't understand irony, so no, he didn't see any. "Just not much money is all I'm saying." He brooded at the thin carpet in Trish's room.

"Can't you at least try to get us more?" Les asked. Before my frustration forced me to stick my foot in my mouth, Craig spoke up. He'd showed for our little meeting.

"Nope, standard rate for Bill Gazzarri, except when the standard is zero. These Hollywood clubs pay shit. Original bands flopping out in Laurel Canyon or downtown, play in these Hollywood joints like the Troub, the Whisky, or Gazzarri's for *bubkes*. They'll do anything for exposure. Most of these clubs are way west on Sunset, near most of the record companies. A&R guys are notoriously lazy so they're more likely to walk into these local places to get drunk than drive anywhere."

One of our prowls took us past a biker bar on Hollywood Boulevard, east of La Brea, where raucous laughter and shouting rose and fell inside. Out in front, many motorcycles, gleaming in the warm winter sun, stood parked in tight rows, out to the middle of the street.

I wanted a closer look at a metallic-blue Harley with sissy bars, and I slipped stepping off the curb. When I stuck out my hand to steady myself, the bike began a glacial tumble into the next one, which teetered and toppled, until one after another they all crashed to the pavement like a domino chain. I stared at Dave and Les in panic. They turned and ran, as if they'd seen demons fresh from hell behind me. I wasn't sure what they'd seen, but I didn't look back and soon caught up and passed them. We turned on a side street and ran all the way down to Sunset and into an alley. Once we were certain no one was chasing us, I took a lot of teasing for being such a clumsy idiot.

For the next week, we continued to sneak into Trish's room and walk the streets of Hollywood. We came up with enough money to buy a couple of loaves of bread and leaned on PB&J sandwiches for survival. We could only wonder what Craig was eating, since he never came around.

There were two reasons why I felt like a clown after our eleven o'clock set on Wednesday, our second night at Gazzarri's. From one perspective, this felt like a sad little club where a bunch of loser bands played one right after another. The place was hypocritical and mean-spirited, taking advantage of struggling musicians and the doped-up high-school dropouts who came to see them alike. Here we were, clothed in our suits and ties and Las Vegas attitude, as out of place as a swing band. We must have looked like car salesmen to these people in bandana headbands, torn jeans, and rainbow tee shirts. We were as out of place as Tony Bennett opening at a Rolling Stones concert. I was embarrassed for us, and didn't think we deserved to feel that way about ourselves.

On the other hand, someone there had called us a "cover band." Though I don't think the comment was meant to be derogatory, only descriptive, I was embarrassed. We didn't have any of our own songs to play, not even an original arrangement. We played the music we liked to listen to, priding ourselves on sounding like the people who'd recorded the songs, because we respected and honored them. For the first time, I considered the concept of us as cheaters, copying other artists' hits to make our own living, unwilling or unable to risk our own musical creations to an audience. For the tiniest of moments, I questioned our musical spirit.

These two dissonant viewpoints seemed to focus my attention on how far we'd drifted from the fabulous dreams the Reflections had gotten a taste of in a way I couldn't explain, other than an uneasiness that we were somehow losing our way. The perception stayed with me the next day like a bad stomachache. When Dave and I got into the car to drive to Gazzarri's, the lights along Sunset tripped a rush of emotion in me. I made a sudden U-turn back to Highland and turned toward Hollywood Boulevard. I was surprised Dave hadn't said a thing. I pulled to the curb in front of a pizza place and idled the car. We sat in companionable, if somber, silence for a minute.

"Can't go in that place tonight, Dave." I stared at my hands on the steering wheel. "I just can't deal with it. I don't know if I can even explain why, but I can't go there tonight." I stuttered with intensity.

"Yeah," he said, his voice plaintive. "I know. Do you want to get a pizza?"

"That's exactly what I want to do." We used some of the cash we'd gotten from Gazzarri's, where they paid us every night, five twenty-dollar bills we split six ways.

We took our pizza and soft drinks up to Mulholland Drive on the crest of the Santa Monica Mountains, where a carpet of lights spread out over Hollywood and off to the ocean to the southwest. The muted rumble of the great engine driving this mammoth city, unnoticeable down below, reached us up here. By the time we'd parked, it was eight o'clock and we should have been on stage with our band brothers. We hadn't even warned them, but then we hadn't known we'd crack.

We shared pizza out of the box and drank our Cokes, watching the night deepen and the cloud cover roll in until the lights below were more like a blanket of stars fallen to earth. It was quiet, and I felt drained and empty. I pulled out a couple of tightly rolled joints, thanks again to Trish's generosity, and handed one to Dave.

We smoked until I'd distanced myself enough to try and sort out what was bugging me. I sighed. "What are we doing, man?"

"I'm eating pizza."

I tried to make sense of my confusion. I began talking in a stream of consciousness, not knowing what would come out.

"I feel like we're doing something wrong, but I don't know what. I feel like it should be obvious to me, but I still don't know what it is. It's like, well you know, the place behind your eyes, in back of you, the place you never see because whenever you turn your head, it's always behind you. Well, I think it's like that. I mean whatever's wrong is right here with us, but I can't see it, even when I turn to look for it. Figuratively speaking, of course."

"Uh-huh." Dave opened the pizza box and tilted out another pepperoni and sausage slice.

"What are we doing in Las Vegas, Dave? I mean, for real? We were so excited about recording in Indianapolis and . . . I don't know. I mean we're doing fantastic, of course, well not right at the moment so much, but I miss just singing. I miss singing our own vocal arrangements. Like when we played around with *In the Still of the Night* and came up with our own version. That was fun and exhilarating—Chuck Tunnah just riffing on a bass line, me and Perry playing with the harmony and then you throwing the melody on top . . . Even when we rushed to get *In the*

Beginning arranged to sound like a Four Seasons song, so we could get it released right away. I loved that.

"I just wish we were writing and singing our own music." I thought about that for a moment. "I hate that nightclub down there, you know, I despise the place, the whole cheesy pretend-artsy kind of atmosphere."

I ran out of steam. I tried to look at my words, but they'd already disappeared into the night. I realized what I really wanted was to be down there at Gazzarri's, but with something of our own to sing and play. Something really good, something worthwhile.

Dave, deep in thought, considered the view. "What are we going to say to the other guys?"

"I don't know. Honestly, I just don't know. The ups and downs have been brutal since we left the Bay Area. I feel stretched out like an old rubber band."

After a while, we went down the hill, but we didn't go to Gazzarri's. Instead, we went to Trish's room and waited, a little apprehensive about what Mac and Leonard and Les would say. Craig would just go back to Panorama City.

They straggled in after eleven. We needn't have worried.

"Noticed you guys played hooky," Mac said. "I get that. Want a hit?" He held out a lit joint to us. We nodded yeah and that was pretty much it. They'd played without us, no one noticing or caring how few vocals there'd been. We let them split our thirty-two dollars and change between them. All except for Craig.

By the end of the week, we'd pooled enough money to get another room at the Sunset La Brea TraveLodge so Trish could have her room and privacy back. We snuck into our own room, one by one, each night over the next two weeks. We didn't practice, we didn't learn vocals for any new songs. Leonard discovered the Pioneer Chicken fast-food restaurant on Sunset and made us go with him whenever he could. Craig got himself a brand new Mosrite bass guitar, and I quietly turned twenty-five.

Otherwise, we just survived each day until we could leave for Vegas.

44
ROCK FIGHT

*We've never played at this place before. This place is big,
and I'm kinda nervous, so we're going to make it feel
small by pretending we're in a . . . bedroom. We'll hang off
the edge of the bed, take off our shoes and get Naked!*

— Dave Matthews

January 7, 1967
Las Vegas, Nevada

I TRIED TO MAKE out the figure moving below us through the blinding lights, until . . . wait—holy crap! That's Debbie Reynolds down there pulling on Dave's leg!

"Sing it, baby, sing it!" she yelled. A broad, encouraging grin spread across her face as he stood braced, high above her, to hit the high full voice note near the end of *I've Got You Under My Skin*.

When we'd peeked through the curtain, we'd seen half the Rat Pack—Joey Bishop, Peter Lawford, and Sammy Davis Jr.; Bill Cosby; the Bobby Hatfield half of the Righteous Brothers; Sergio Franchi; Johnny Mathis, who'd closed the main room tonight; along with twenty or more other Strip headliners and major film and television luminaries. Debbie Reynolds had been seated at an aisle table a few rows from the stage with her husband.

As Dave's ringing tenor swept high, and then higher, into a dramatic falsetto run, she'd stretched on tiptoe to grasp the only part of him she could reach, his left pants leg just above a white patent leather boot.

Laughing with joyful spontaneity, she shook it back and forth, like a dog with a sock puppet.

Dave had to be as astounded as the rest of us, but he closed his eyes, pushed his mic farther up and out, and leaned back to let those golden pipes rip. Nothing would faze us tonight. It was our second Saturday on stage in the new lounge at Caesars Palace, Nero's Nook. The mini-showroom's luxurious tiers of tables and two balconies were built to hold 250 people. Tonight the place was standing room only, jammed far beyond capacity. We were on one of the hottest tickets in Las Vegas. Blazing light silhouetted everything beyond the stage except smoke-haloed cigarette lighters sparking like fireflies in an Indiana autumn evening. We basked in the exquisite connection we shared with an electrified audience.

"I've got you . . ." Dave crooned a cappella, working into the final phrasing of the song, with the movie star still hanging onto his pants leg, staring at him with a huge grin. I stole a glance at Mac, his eyes wide as beacons. I knew mine were just as big as we joined our voices with Les and Craig in building the ending harmony.

"Never win, never win . . ." The lounge erupted, peppering another standing ovation with yells and excited shouts that crackled over thundering applause. More people rushed to the front of the stage as we hit the big finish and took our bows while the frenzied uproar mounted to a pounding pressure.

I looked left toward the rest of the band, trying to take us in, all of us in a zone, the way a basketball team gets when their shots can't miss. Jackets from our dark suits lay rumpled around us. Purple-and-white polka-dotted ties hung loose or strewn across the stage or amps. Burgundy cuff links on our custom tailored white-on-white dress shirts sparkled in the brilliant light. Leonard was sopping wet behind the drums, his dress shirt translucent. At last we'd let loose and shown ourselves as the confident rock band we actually were, and the celebrity-filled audience showered us with appreciation.

Leonard clicked his drumsticks in tempo, and we jumped back into the closing refrain of *I've Got You Under My Skin*, as the descending curtain began to mute the applause. We tried twice to close the set, but the crowd refused to let us go. The curtain had lifted again and then again, each time drawing us back into the song's ending, while we reveled in an entertainer's ultimate narcotic, an audience's capricious adoration.

Finally, the thick curtain settled to the floor, muffling hoots, whistles, and impassioned clapping, as Les signaled the song's end. None of us moved, suddenly enclosed in a deafening sphere of silence on the darkened stage—stretching the transcendent moment—saying nothing, knowing a word would break the spell and return us to reality.

There'd be a price to pay for what we'd just done, though—not something I wanted to think about yet. For now, I wanted to soak in all that had just happened. We'd played to some great audiences and gotten our share of standing ovations and cheers, but tonight we'd wrung out our hearts to perform for a room packed with stars from entertainment's biggest leagues. As a common courtesy, entertainers understand and are generous to one another, but the energy that had flowed into us in response to our show had been ferocious. We'd gotten loud. We'd rocked.

We'd been right, I thought, *this was what our audiences here wanted from us*. For the first time at Caesars, we'd let it all out. We'd been in the moment, thinking of nothing but the performance. Even Trish and her two girl backup singers had caught the fever in her segment. Now, we stood consumed, depleted, panting, dripping wet. I'd never been more proud of us, never loved us so much as tonight. I was so happy to be a part of this brotherhood, even including Craig, as we gazed in amazed stupor at one other, luxuriating in the afterglow.

In that moment, Les said something I knew I'd remember for as long as I remembered this night, as he slipped out of his guitar strap.

"What?" I said, ears not recovered from the pounding they'd taken.

"I said," he repeated louder, "we've made it to the top of the bottom."

Les's nature was to relieve stress by letting all the air out of the party balloons, but he could have held off a while longer as far as I was concerned.

"Hell of a thing to say, Bear. I guess you mean we reached the top tonight—like in nightclubs, bars, casinos? Like that? To get to the top of the top, we gotta have hit records, do concert tours, be teen idols, all that? Right?"

"Exactly."

The stage crew came out to begin moving our equipment as some of Xavier Cugat's band members milled around; our fleeting moment in the sun had dissipated.

"Okay, I get that," I said with reluctance. "But, jeez, can't we enjoy what just happened out there?"

"Don't want us to lose sight of what we're really after." He turned to pick up his suit coat from the top of his amp before we left the stage.

Not everyone was happy with us. Xavier Cugat stepped out of the backstage shadows, hissing at me, "You *hijos de puta* ran fifteen minutes over on my show!" Charo glided by. I couldn't tell if her enigmatic frown was meant for me or the famous bandleader.

"Sorry," I said, and meant it, even if I couldn't bring myself to regret what had happened.

"You have not heard the last of this, *por Dios*. I am the headliner!" he spat over his shoulder as he brushed past me in fury.

Clyde Carson's face popped up in front of me before I'd recovered from Cugat's venom. "Fucker!" he blurted out. "You fuckers! What in hell did you think you were doing out there? What were you thinking? We agreed when you signed the contract. Dave V. will be super pissed. He'll chew my ass, and yours too, you son of a bitch."

I didn't try to talk to him before he stalked away. He was too upset to listen, and it wasn't as though I hadn't expected to catch hell after what we'd decided in the dressing room before coming down to do the show.

Earlier, in the upstairs dressing room before the show, Dave had been the first to voice his discontent. He'd dabbed light pancake makeup onto his face and, peering into the mirror, begun to smooth a smidgen of Vaseline over his eyebrows, the way Eddie Pru had taught us.

"Larry, we're getting screwed. The Checkmates are lighting up this place, and we can't compete with them."

"Feel like I oughta play with brushes," Leonard chipped in. "Don't mind brushes, you know, but we're not that kind of band. We play rock."

Leonard used small tree trunks for drumsticks. I was pretty sure he didn't even own brushes, but I understood his frustration. Craig shook his head in sour agreement as Leonard went on.

"I understand the early sets, they're like dinner shows, so I see why we do mellow music for them. I get that," Leonard conceded. "But we've got one really good, hot time slot at eleven, right after the Checks' set. Those guys are great entertainers, but I think we outplay 'em, and outsing 'em. But we need all our tunes to do that. You say the hotel says they're an R&B band, but they do a whole lotta rock, too. Don't understand why they can rock and we can't."

"I know guys, I know," I said. "We're at the bottom of the bill, and there's a lot of restrictions on our shows, and we play a lot of weird hours. I knew this would be tough when I signed the contract. Have to admit I didn't realize how hard it would be to stand backstage while the crowd goes nuts for Sweet Louie, Bobby, and Sonny knowing we have to follow them with a bunch of ballads." I ran a comb through my intractable hair and searched for the hairspray. "But the bottom line is, we agreed to the contract terms."

"No we didn't. You agreed to them," Craig said. "Not me. I'd rather be back at the Cat playing what we want."

"Listen man. I ain't no fool, I want to be right here," Mac said pulling his jacket off a wooden hanger. "I dig what this gig means, but I got no songs at all, man. Can't do Isley Brothers shit, no Sam & Dave, no Otis, or James Brown 'cause only the fucking Checks are allowed to do soul tunes. Freaks me out. Somebody needs to punch that pissant Clyde Carson in the face for this. I'm like Dave's emcee, way things are now."

Everybody was dead serious and the room went quiet while they stared at me. This was a gut-deep issue. After almost two weeks in the thin air of the highest level of entertainment in the world, in the most exclusive hotel in Las Vegas, we should be sky high. Instead, we were coal-mine low.

"Well, what do you guys suggest we do?" I asked, palms out. "Right or wrong, guys, the band comes first for me. So whatever you decide, I'm on board."

"We should be ourselves," said Les, hammering in the final nail. "Feels like whoring, what we're doing. I'm hating music right now, and that never happens."

"You know there'll be trouble if we break out? And you do understand we're more than likely kicking away hundreds of thousands of dollars? Right?"

"You gonna try to talk us out of it, Dunlap?" Mac said, eyes narrow. I hated it when people referred to me by my last name. Everybody looked ready to start yelling.

"I would if I thought I could." I sighed, dropping into a makeup chair. "If I didn't agree with you. Jesus, I think we stink right now. We're not the Lettermen, and we don't have enough quality songs to stretch through a whole set pretending to be. It's cool we're the first rock band to break into the Las Vegas hotels, might even mean something if we actually played rock music. Guess we might have sacrificed too much of ourselves agreeing to the hotel's demands. We don't seem very happy as the Big fucking Spenders." I stood, wanting to see into everybody's eyes.

The eyes voted: it was unanimous.

"If we really do this, maybe there's some slim hope the hotel will realize we're really good rock entertainers, see how two excellent bands performing hot back-to-back sets, playing off each other, could make Nero's Nook the most popular lounge in town. Could be they'll love the real Stark Naked and the Car Thieves when they really see us for the first time."

Little chance of that, I thought, *but if not, maybe we shouldn't be here anyway.* This wasn't a rational decision, of course. I knew that. In fact, as a business decision, it was Three Stooges stupid. But bands are emotional. We had to take our own path.

"Okay then, let's do it. Let's start pulling a new set list together right now."

"Fuck yeah," Mac yelled. Despite the sure knowledge of the flak we'd get, everybody's spirits lifted as we filled the room with black humor, tied ties, and pulled-on jackets, energized like a football team filing out of the locker room for Homecoming.

We'd packed our show with the best of everything we knew. Soul music featuring Mac and Dave, big harmony production rock numbers featuring Dave and intricate background vocals, kicking rock; there'd be no mellow songs this set. As we neared the stage, we heard the crowd going wild for the Checkmates, Ltd., but we didn't mind. We weren't bringing soft ballads to a rock fight tonight.

In the wake of Clyde's tirade following the best show we'd ever done, two maitre d's appeared backstage with requests to join patrons at their tables. One came from Sammy Davis Jr.—an incredible coincidence. I'd just finished Sammy's autobiography, *Yes I Can*, and been so inspired that I'd bought copies for the entire band, hoping it would motivate them as much as it had me. In my wildest dreams, there was no scenario I could have imagined where I'd get to meet Sammy Davis. Now, he was here, and he wanted to meet us. The other invitation was a personal request for Dave to join Debbie Reynolds and her husband at their table. I didn't know where the other guys were going, but I wanted to meet Sammy.

The house lights were up as Mac and I wedged our way through the crowded room, heady with aromas of cigarette smoke, expensive perfume, premium booze, and celebrity. Voices and light laughter crackled across the room, as we smiled and acknowledged people I'd only seen on a screen or stage before tonight.

"Hey, guys." Sammy stood, lighting up his famous megawatt smile for us. A rich red tie and stickpin, stylishly askew, fell across his high-collared white-on-brilliant-white dress shirt and low-cut brocaded vest; matching blood-red cuff links peeked out from dark velvet jacket cuffs.

"Wanted to tell you guys firsthand, you do a great show, man. I mean, love the voices, love the energy. Sexual. This is what rock music is all about, is it not?" Mac and I said thanks, as he invited us to sit.

"Sonny, here"—Sammy waved a hand with multi-ringed fingers toward an empty chair where Sonny Charles from the Checkmates had been sitting—"well, when he was here, tells me you guys' real name is Stark Naked and the Car Thieves. So cool. Love it. Heard of you, killing it at the Pussycat A' Go Go club, right? Crazy, man, crazy. Love that." His animated charisma was dazzling.

"So what's with the name change? Big Spenders? What's that all about?" He took a drag off his cigarette and answered his own question. "Oh, I see. Hotel don't like 'Stark Naked' up there in six-foot letters, right?" He nodded, exhaled, and crushed out his smoke. "Goddamn these hotel buyers, man. Sometimes they just don't get it." Mac and I nodded in agreement.

"Where's your band from, man, where's home?" He shook out a Camel filter and offered the pack to us. He tilted his head a bit to the left to keep us in his good eye. Mac took one, and a light from Sammy's lighter.

"Most of us come from the Midwest, but we live wherever we play. Guess that's LA right now," I said. So crazy, Sammy Davis wanted to know about us. These last few months had been a roller coaster ride, impossible to describe. What was I thinking? These last two years, from when I was someone else, my life in tatters, my marriage exploding, the Reflections up in smoke, building record players on an assembly line in Indianapolis, to here and now. What Pat would think, I wondered, if she knew who we'd just performed for, who I was talking with now. I wondered where she was, what she was doing, how David and Danny were.

"Good. Me, too." Sammy inhaled and let it out. "Going home to LA after we close next week. Maybe we can get together when you get back. I'd like to help you guys. Talent like yours needs to be seen and heard. Whadaya say?"

"That would be fantastic, Sammy!" Mac said. We glanced at each other's huge grins.

I told Sammy how much his book and life story had meant to me, how his biography was inspiring the band. *At least I hope so*, I amended silently. He nodded and leaned forward.

"Look, guys, got to get over to the Sands for the late show. Why don't you bring the band over Monday night. That's your dark night, right? We can fit in some hang time between shows." He snuffed out his cigarette and stood up. "Come back to my dressing room after the early show, I'll take care of the tickets. You up for that?"

We straggled back to the dressing room to shed our wet and wrinkled suits. We wouldn't be able to wear these for another set. Leonard collected the clothes, counting every matching tie, shirt, dress handkerchief, cuff link, and boot into his inventory. Just as I was the briefcase, his off-stage gig was laundry, keeping our outfits cleaned and organized for each show.

Dave threw open the dressing-room door, coat and tie draped over his arm, and dropped onto a chair with a satisfied sigh. Our dressing room was large, as you'd expect at Caesars, but outside of the deep pile carpet, there weren't a lot of frills, it was more like a locker room than a dressing room for performers. A tall row of plain lockers hunkered along one wall, and a row of mirrors, some full length, others with well-lit makeup tables, clung to another. An entryway led into showers and toilets while an eclectic mix of upholstered and folding chairs huddled along the fourth wall next to the door.

"So tell us about Debbie Reynolds and . . . what's her husband's name?" I asked Dave.

"Mr. Reynolds," Leonard quipped as he snatched up another sodden dress shirt and grabbed Dave's coat. "Get outta those pants, Dave."

"That was so crazy man, her hanging on your leg, way she did. What'd she say about that?" Mac asked.

"Her husband's name is Harry. They're both terrific. They just really liked our show, Mac." Dave's face held the wide grin of a ten-year old at Disneyland. "And she—Debbie—is really sweet. Told me I sang my ass off. Hah! Said she had to run up and grab something and push me to sing harder."

"Glad you didn't accidentally kick her," Les said. "I can see the headlines now. *Singer Kicks Movie Star in Nero's Nook.*"

"One thing was weird, though in a very cool way," Dave said as he stood to take off his pants. "When I shook hands with her, you know, while Debbie introduced me to her husband, she held onto my hand, you know, really tight, for a long time, felt like a couple of minutes. Probably wasn't that long though."

"Guys, listen up for a minute," I said, now that everyone was here. "Clyde grabbed me as we were leaving the stage. Cussed me up one side and down the other. Says Dave Victorson is going to be royally pissed." Nobody said anything. Dave Victorson was lord and emperor over all the talent at Caesars Palace.

Would he throw us to the lions?

45
A CASINO CHRISTMAS CAROL

Bigger and smaller!
— Alice (Lewis Carroll, Alice in Wonderland)

January 8, 1967
Las Vegas, Nevada

AT THE END of each week at Caesars, I picked up a chit from the hotel's entertainment office to exchange at the casino cage for a stack of twenty-seven one hundred dollar bills: three thousand dollars a week, minus three hundred skimmed off the top for Clyde Carson. After Clyde's recent reaming, I hadn't seen him again, or heard anything from the entertainment office. I began to suspect Clyde had been a go-between for somebody else—someone with enough clout to arrange for the hotel to withhold the personal manager's commission without our consent.

The routine continued as I filled seven hotel envelopes with cash, six of them with a band member's name written on them, while the seventh got three hundred for the band's fund; collected to pay for common expenses such as dry cleaning, records and music we wanted to learn, and other band needs.

After handing out the envelopes following our eleven o'clock show the Sunday of our third week, I found myself ambling through the massive casino. Everyone else had disappeared, off to the Cat or out somewhere else on the Strip. Because of our odd schedule, I was left with about three hours to kill before our final show at 3 AM. Major casinos aren't designed for casual lounging. Seating is only available at gambling tables, bars, restaurants, or other service areas where transactions are expected. Tonight, alone and introspective, I slipped onto a stool at a closed blackjack table for a moment. The noises of gambling—the sudden shouts from a craps table, distant bells from the slot machines, and murmured conversations—blended into an oddly comforting ambiance where I sat beneath the casino's lofty dome and surrounded by columned and caparisoned walls,

Scrounging peanut butter and jelly sandwiches a few short weeks ago still stuck in my mind, as did those searing, insecure weeks before achieving such unexpected acclaim at the Pussycat. Thoughts of Gazzarri's, Honest John's Casino—the velocity and amplitude of our intense emotional highs and desperate lows that had brought me to this fantastical place—were disorienting. We'd been so small, so big, and then so small, and then here, now, big again, like Alice's trip through Wonderland. There was some kind of inevitability about all we'd experienced, as though we were adrift, hanging on in some Universal flow. What were we really? Where were we going?

Christmas had loomed, then rapidly disappeared in the surreal whirlwind of our opening in this glittering desert oasis. There'd been no time for my family to receive my address to send a card or gift. I'd only been able to manage a short "touch base" phone call.

Without warning, a vision of my last Christmas with Pat and our boys burst into my thoughts. Pat and I had managed to create a huge pile of presents under a well-decorated tree for the boys. We helped little Danny open his gifts, the Christmas morning celebration still an overwhelming mystery to him. Dave tore through his packages like a ravaging Mongol, seeming to enjoy the opening more than the contents. Like me as a kid, he took more time with the odd little toys and puzzles in his stocking than the larger gifts under the tree.

The kinesthetic, physical memory of kissing Pat two years ago caused me to gasp before I wrenched my mind away. I tasted her lips, touched the warm curve of her body against mine, and remembered flashes from the night that followed.

An unsettling sense of rootlessness rolled over me. Struggling with memories like these made me question whether I was built to withstand the rigors of our nomadic lifestyle. I liked having a home, the creature comforts, and belonging to and with one special person.

In an ashtray, next to a hard pack of Parliaments, white smoke rose in gentle curls from my cigarette until a waitress in a short Caesars miniskirt shuffled a clean ashtray in front of me with quick, deft motions, swapping my cigarette into it. Deep in my morose reverie, I hadn't noticed that a dealer was opening the table and people were filling the stools next to me. Hiding my confusion, I asked for a Jack Daniels and Seven, and threw down one of my precious hundred-dollar bills in front of the dealer. She positioned the bill over a plastic slot and used a clear vinyl slab to push it into her money box. Her nimble hand selected five twenty-dollar chips, rapped them twice on her chip tray to alert the pit boss, and said, "Changing a hundred." Supple fingers manipulated them into two stacks of two and three chips as she placed them in front of me.

I began to play at the table-minimum five dollars, and before long I added a one-hundred-dollar black chip to my stack, doubling my stake. After adding another black chip to my stack, and tipping my waitress and dealer a ten-dollar chip each, I decided to risk twenty dollars a hand. My stake went up and down until I realized I had five black chips in front of me, so I turned them in for a green five-hundred-dollar chip, leaving the table and twenty dollars for the dealer, though by now, this was the third dealer. I only wanted the five-hundred-dollar chip so I could say I'd had one. The dreamy unreality I'd been feeling persisted: I'd won this money without effort, just playing on instinct.

Another thing about casinos, they don't have clocks or windows, they're kept at a consistent level of brightness, never glaring, creating a subtle avoidance of the passage of time, because the longer a gambler plays, the more the true odds will favor the house. Caesars added to the timelessness with a domed ceiling that drank the light and focused eyes on the lit gaming tables. I checked my watch, still forty-five minutes before I needed to be in the dressing room.

I browsed the blackjack pit and found a table where there was an empty seat opposite the gun, meaning to the far right of the dealer where the last card was dealt in each hand. I didn't like the hard looks other players gave me when they thought my decisions affected what cards they drew. *Also*, I thought, *being the last player to get cards gave me a better chance to figure what card might be dealt next.* In the weeks we'd been in Las Vegas, I'd learned to play some of the casino games, risked a few dollars, striking a roughly even balance between winning and losing. I liked blackjack best because I thought my love for social card and strategy games gave me a better feel for the game's principles.

As I slipped onto a stool, I ordered another free drink I didn't need from one of the ubiquitous hair-coned enablers and slid my green chip across the felt to the dealer. She rapped the chip on her tray, and when I asked for hundreds she returned five black chips in stacks of two and three.

Time to make a little history, I thought, and plunked down a black chip on my playing space. Internally, I gasped at the impudence of daring hundred dollars on the turn of the cards, but I was playing with the house's money. With no consecutive wins in ten hands, my five hundred evaporated in about fifteen minutes. *Oh well*, I thought, pulling out my original hundred-dollar stake, *just a bad run that can't keep going. I'll try another hundred.* I won but then lost again when the dealer pulled a blackjack. Angry, and a little tipsy, I pulled out another hundred-dollar bill and said, "Money plays." The dealer looked over her shoulder at the pit boss, who nodded, and let the hundred-dollar bill stay on the green surface where it lay.

I got an ace, lit another cigarette hoping for a face, but got a second ace instead. The dealer showed a seven. This was dicey. I split the aces; if I caught two blackjacks I'd recover half of my lost five hundred on one hand. I put another hundred on the table. Even hitting one blackjack would put me back in the game. The dealer nailed my first ace with a nine, a soft twenty I'd have to stay with. She kissed the second ace with an awkward five. *Six or sixteen, have to hit.* A four made my hand a natural ten, or a soft twenty. Before I could think too much, I brushed my hand on the table in front of me and caught a ten. Now both hands sat at twenty. I was the last player. The dealer turned up her under card, a six, her hand totaling thirteen. I'd hoped she'd give herself a picture or a ten so I'd have an easy win, instead she'd have to hit. *The odds are still with me, though, I should win both hands.* I held my breath—she flipped an eight. Twenty-one.

The chagrin was palpable as I checked my envelope. Nope, no mistake. I'd blown right through three of my four hundred-dollar bills along with the five hundred I'd been ahead in a matter of minutes. I was an idiot, a fool.

I went through the motions during the last show of the night, seething with indignation at a loss that would cost me for days to come. We'd had a lot of weeks without pay; I didn't have three hundred dollars to lose.

After our last show ended, everyone else left for breakfast, or to our motel down the Strip almost to the Hacienda. I should have gone with them. But I was sure I'd figured out a winning strategy. I'd seemed to win when I bet five dollars at a time at blackjack. If I played a conservative, focused strategy using my last hundred to get a little ahead, put the hundred back in my pocket, I could use the casino's money to win back some of my paycheck. If I played on my winnings and lost, well, at least I wouldn't be any worse off than I was now. I had to try.

The problem with my plan was twofold. My powers of concentration were not at their best, and worse, I lost the first hand; my immediate concern became playing to hold onto my last hundred, my back against the wall. I never got ahead to create a stake. *Soon*, I promised myself, *if I can just break even, get my hundred back, I'll stand up and leave.* I don't know if I would have or not. I never got the chance. I struggled and fought and managed my dwindling supply of chips until the last one was gone. I pushed away from the table, and without looking back, walked out the front door of the casino.

A chill in the air brought shivers I felt I deserved. If the Universe was guiding my path in some unseen way, I could obviously still make bad decisions all on my own. The sun silhouetted the western mountains; the imminent desert morning loomed lonely and dismal. I had no idea how I was going to get through the next week. I walked out to the street, my unseeing eyes gazing across at the Flamingo's lights before turning to cross Flamingo Road. Las Vegas Boulevard at the busiest corner of the Strip was deserted this early. I walked past the Dunes, south, until the sidewalk ended. I trudged through packed sand and dirt toward my motel, as the sun's early rays began to fall across my shoulders.

Later, I realized I'd been in the grip of a gambling fever. I was grateful I hadn't been tempted to dip into the band's fund envelope, or had I just forgotten it was in my coat pocket? It was the only good thing I could take away from that night. I was never able to get comfortable at a blackjack table again.

Les and especially Dave were generous in helping me through the week, and I was relieved they didn't judge or tease me. On the following Sunday night, we packed our equipment to leave Caesars Palace without ceremony. While I was proud of the way we finished out our contract, the hotel made its position clear, shunning us and removing "Trish Turner and the Big Spenders," our complete nom de plume, from the marquee, tiny as it had been, before we'd even closed. In our early sets each night, we'd performed our more melodic songs, but in the later sets we played what we thought our audience wanted, and we were rewarded with a full and responsive audience for every show.

I tried a few times to find Dave Victorson in hopes that I could reason with him, but he was always busy or away from his office. In the end, I never even met the man. The musicians' union claimed the only contract ever filed with them was for four weeks; there was no record of a three-year agreement, they said. We'd collected twelve thousand dollars, minus twelve hundred, of course, of our promised long term $300,000 contract with Caesars Palace. The copy Clyde was supposed to have been holding for us never surfaced. It was clear; we wouldn't be playing at Caesars again.

They might not even let us through the front door.

46
RAG DOLL

Nakedness reveals itself. Nudity is placed on display. The nude is condemned to never being Naked. Nudity is a form of dress.

—John Berger

January 17, 1967
North Hollywood, California

AFTER THE BRILLIANT January afternoon sunshine, it was pitch black and cool inside the North Hollywood nightclub. As our eyes adjusted, a short, stocky Italian man in a Hawaiian shirt with a shock of dark hair came to meet us.

"Okay, which one of you is Larry?" Smile wrinkles around his eyes lifted his eyebrows until his whole rugged face grinned as he welcomed us. I stuck out a hand to receive an enthusiastic handshake.

"Tony Ferra," he said. "Am I ever glad to see you guys. You're gonna love playing at the Rag Doll. Going to be my personal goal. Saw you boys at the Hullabaloo in Hollywood. Fantastic. Called Howard King, told him, 'Get me that band for the Rag Doll, Howard. They'll be perfect.' That's what I told him, and now you're here. At last. So what in hell took you so long?" He seemed to be only half-joking.

After meeting everyone, he offered a suggestion. "Unload your equipment for now, and go get settled before setting up. Check out the Mid-Valley Motel over on Workman. Farther from the club than some of the motels on Lankershim, but they've got nice little units with kitchens for about the same money. You'll be more comfortable there."

Riding down Victory gave me a chance to get oriented, always necessary for me to feel settled in a new place. North Hollywood, despite its name, was nowhere near Sunset and Vine. Instead, the Rag Doll was located at Victory and Lankershim Boulevards, two busy streets in a suburban residential neighborhood. North Hollywood and Hollywood connected through the Santa Monica Mountains along an old stagecoach route that wound through the Cahuenga Pass, better known in modern times as the Hollywood Freeway. A million people lived on this side of the mountains in the San Fernando Valley, many of them in bedroom communities where they commuted through the canyons to the city.

Our little caravan, minus Craig, who'd disappeared as soon as he'd off-loaded his amp, pulled into the Mid-Valley's long driveway in a working-class neighborhood. Nothing fancy about the rooms, but they were homey nonetheless and perfect for our needs. Each unit contained a bedroom, bath, and a sitting/living area with a small kitchen. They were inexpensive enough that each of us could afford our own. From my front window, tall palm trees waved from above a fence on the far side of the driveway in the dry Santa Ana breeze.

Tony Ferra was fiery and wore his heart on his sleeve. He wanted us to feel like family and invited us into his home for dinner with his wife and daughters. We liked that about him and made every effort to deliver on his investment in us. He hired a publicist, and soon the band's name began popping up in the entertainment columns of the *LA Times* and regional Valley papers. As our local audience grew, they seemed more like the Midwesterners I'd grown up with than anywhere else we'd been. Even if the momentous things that would happen to us here hadn't happened, I'm sure the Rag Doll would still have been our home club in California.

Leonard had shown more willingness to reveal his quirky humor since his crazy mattress-diving act at the Pink Carousel. Even at the Pussycat, his drum solos had become comedic experiments with some funny moments. Sometimes, deep into a drum solo he'd stop, like he'd lost his place in his mind. With a tentative bang on a drum or cymbal, he seemed to test them before taking off again full steam. Sometimes he experimented with just petering out and stealthily exiting the stage instead of the normal big drum solo ending. It was often weird, and audiences weren't always sure what to think or how to respond. His comedy had the quixotic humor of Victor

Borge or Peter Sellers with a touch of Jerry Lewis's self-deprecating slapstick thrown in.

I'd encouraged him to find ways to express the whimsical part of his nature when it first surfaced, and now we'd come to anticipate Leonard's next antic with enthusiasm mixed with a certain amount of dread. We began ending one set most nights by leading Leonard into his drum solo while we left the stage, so he could try out whatever spontaneous comedy he wanted, even if it wasn't always funny.

One night at the Rag Doll, he picked up a cowbell and kept the rhythm going while he stepped out from behind the drums. He played on mic stands and anything else within reach, rapping out the same rhythmic cadence. He jumped from the stage, working his way through the tables, clicking and clacking his sticks on everything he came to, even people's drinks, once making light strokes on some fellow's head. People hopped up to follow him as he pounded away on the cowbell, leading them in a line around the room. Mac joined the line, then Dave, so I did, too. Les found a guitar rhythm on stage and Craig joined in. Leonard twisted and twined us in a tight spiral on the dance floor until the lines became confused and tangled, and everybody broke up in laughter while Leonard leaped to the stage to orchestrate a rhythmic ending to his solo. Something so simple brought down the house. Leonard's conga line became a staple while we entertained at the Rag Doll.

We were lounging around after rehearsal one afternoon when Tony and Leonard began an animated conversation at the bar. They seemed to be developing a bond between them, maybe something related to their Italian and Portuguese heritages.

"What gets you going, makes you get out there like you do, with that thing you bang on, bang, bang, bang?" Tony smacked his palm on the bar, teasing Leonard.

Leonard gave Tony a sheepish grin. "I don't know, something just comes over me when it feels right, you know." He gestured around toward the rest of us. "And the guys let me do this crazy stuff."

"You should be on TV," Tony said.

"I think so, too," Leonard said, a semi-serious look on his face. "We're funnier than those Monkees, and we're a real group. We should have a series."

"Hey, I know a lotta people in television. Lots of 'em came into my old club in Panorama City over near the studios. You're right, I should get 'em in here to see Stark Naked and the Car Thieves. The guy from the big TV music show, he lived close to the club, came in all the time with his wife. Jimmy O'Neill, nice guy. I think his wife's name was Sherry, or Sharon."

I walked to the bar when I heard Tony.

"You know Jimmy O'Neill? From *Shindig!*? We recorded an audition tape to send to him, back in Indianapolis. Does he ever come in here?"

Friday night began the final weekend of our four-week stay. The club was nearly full at the end of our first set, when Tony came up to the stage with a big grin and waved us to a table near the back. I stopped in shock: sitting there in person was Jimmy O'Neill, same famous smile I remembered from my own television in another time stream. Next to him sat a slim, pretty blond girl with short hair and a crisp white short-sleeved blouse. He introduced her as Eve.

I watched from the sidelines for the entire break, not saying much, trying not to stare, thinking, *How crazy is this?* I was unable to fully connect the reality of this moment to the hours and days we'd spent making an audition tape for him—this guy—three years ago. I thought about how hard we'd worked, renting time in Jan Eden's little local studio, how good we'd tried to make that tape. How sure we'd been that it would get Jimmy O'Neill or somebody important's attention. As everybody else filtered away, Jimmy tilted his head in expectation as though he sensed my unasked question.

"We made a tape for you," I blurted out. "An audition tape for *Shindig!*—to be the show's backup vocal group. Did you ever hear it?"

"No. I don't remember hearing any audition tapes. But I wouldn't have. The producers would have been the ones to hear anything like that, I suppose." I nodded, realizing again how naive we'd been.

"I can see you're disappointed, but it was years ago."

"I know." A wan smile. "Guess I'm just feeling sorry for a stupid kid in Indianapolis who believed something in a fan music magazine."

"I understand. There was plenty of disappointment to go around when the show was canceled. *Shindig!* started off so well, much better than we expected. We were just supposed to be a half-hour summer fill-in for *Hootenanny*. You remember that show?" I nodded. "We were so successful the network wanted an hour in the fall lineup. I think that's what killed us, we just weren't able to make the transition to an hour show." He gave me his own dismal smile.

I stood, reaching to shake their hands before going back to the stage.

"Thanks so much for coming in to see us, Jimmy. Means the absolute world to us. Can't express how much it means to me personally."

"We plan to stay a while, don't we, Eve? We like listening to your band. If that's okay with you, of course." He grinned at me. "Why don't you come see us on your next break?"

I went to Jimmy's table at every opportunity, as the night wore on, hearing how he, too, had been a singer and how an imitation he'd done of Liberace had somehow gotten him to Hollywood for a screen test. He talked about growing up in Oklahoma, how he'd gotten into radio and eventually become a big-time deejay here in LA on KFWB.

"Jimmy started a nightclub for teenagers called Pandora's Box down on Sunset," Eve said, eyes proud. "He thought there should be a safe place for teens to listen to music at night."

"I'm not sure how well that turned out." He sighed. "But I met Liberace's personal manager, Seymour Heller. My partner Burt Jacobs and I are affiliated with him now. By the way, I think my assistant Eve has one of my cards." Her eyes sparkled as she handed me a business card with Jimmy O'Neill's name and "B-J Enterprises" printed on it.

"I like your band a lot, Larry. Do you think you'd be interested in having me represent you?" I was dumbstruck. "Hold on," I told him. "Don't you go anywhere. I'll bring the guys over on our next break." I danced on clouds back to the stage.

"Guys, he wants to manage us. A real manager, not some club owner. We've got to decide as a group, but for me I'm in, I think it sounds fantastic."

Everybody talked at once on the darkened stage. Craig wanted to know if Jimmy could get us equipment endorsements; can he get us a record deal? Les asked; and Dave and Mac nodded in agreement.

"Do you think he can get us on TV?" Leonard asked. "I think we need him to try and get us a television series. I mean once we get a hit record. We'd be perfect." We laughed at Leonard's proposal, and he did, too, but I didn't think he was joking. He loved drumming, but he wanted to be a personality, maybe even more than a musician. Confusing here—talking without Jimmy above and now Jimmy talking to band below

"Look fellas," Jimmy said with a grin after the set, waving helpless hands. "I understand what you want. Every band wants those things." He turned to Craig. "I know some people at Vox and Fender, and other places, too. I'm sure we can work something out once you're a Jimmy O'Neill artist." He grinned. "And Les, we're associated with a production company. I'd planned on presenting you to them as part of a package deal. Do you have anything you've recorded I can show them?"

"We have those acetates we recorded in San Francisco," I said.

"Those aren't any good." Les ran a hand across his mouth. "They're dry, no echo, nothing, just some copy tunes."

"Might be enough. When can you get them for me?"

After Les left to retrieve the recordings from his room at the Mid-Valley, Jimmy turned to Leonard. "And you want the band to be on television. Right?"

"Well, if we got famous or something, yeah, I think we'd be really great."

"You, Leonard, could definitely become famous." He glanced around to smile at the rest of us. "And who knows? Maybe the other guys, too."

When we closed at the Rag Doll to return to Las Vegas and the Cat, my mind was spinning with possibilities. We'd found a real manager, a guy like Dick Clark, who knew everybody. He had to be connected to all the artists from his show, plus all the people who booked, represented, and recorded them. He'd know everybody! And it sounded like he'd get us a recording contract, too.

Jimmy promised to contact me in Las Vegas. I crossed my fingers and hoped his promise would pan out better than Sammy Davis's promises. Dave, Mac, and I had gone to Sammy's show at the Sands a couple of nights after we'd met him at Caesars. He'd gotten us front-row seats and introduced us to his showroom audience. We'd spent most of the night hanging out with him, almost like we were part of our own private rat pack. I was sure we were going to become real friends afterward, but we never heard from him again. I couldn't help wondering if had anything to do with how we'd pissed off the powers-that-be at Caesars.

We felt lucky to have found a comfortable home in Southern California at the Rag Doll, and Tony wanted us back as soon as possible, but we looked forward to returning to the Pussycat, too. This time we would follow Gary Puckett and the Union Gap, whose huge hit, *Woman, Woman*, rode high on the charts. Not for the first time, I wished we'd had that song for Dave. Gary Puckett sounded great of course, but that song was written for Dave—he just killed on it.

47
MARTONI'S

Beware of the Naked man who offers you his shirt.

—Navjot Singh Sidhu

February 23, 1967
Las Vegas, Nevada

ON A RARE cold and overcast afternoon in mid-February, Dave was describing how Nancy Wilson had flirted with him as she glided across the Pussycat's dance floor the previous night, and Mac was swearing it was true when I arrived for rehearsal.

After our grand debut at Caesars, I wondered how we would be accepted at the Pussycat. We had a nice-sized opening crowd the first night, but nobody seemed to notice that we'd appeared as the Big Spenders at the giant hotel. The rounders, the amazing entertainers, musicians, backup singers, dancers, and the locals who made the town run, and tourists they sent continued to come and the lines outside the Cat swelled.

"Got a call from Jimmy," I said, with suppressed excitement. "He's putting management and recording contracts in the mail for us to look over. He wants to sign them as soon as we get back to LA, says Eddie Cobb wants to get us in the studio right away."

"But we're going to the Bay Area first, aren't we?" Leonard broke in. He referred to an upscale nightclub we were suppose to open in a brand-new Executive Suites resort hotel being built on the California coast, south of San Francisco. Jimmy had arranged the engagement through a friend who was an executive with the hotel. Leonard was anxious to return to northern California so he and his wife Paula could visit their families.

"Jimmy says it's all arranged. Four weeks at the Executive Suites followed by the Rag Doll or Pink Carousel. Whichever works best for recording dates—and pays the most money, of course. Important since we'll be paying an agent, and a manager, by then." I shook daydream dust bunnies out of my head and gazed at my Midwestern buddies in disbelief.

"Do you realize what's happening? All the threads that are coming together? Out of the blue, of all the people we could run into, Jimmy O'Neill from *Shindig!*—the only person the Aristocats ever made an audition tape for *ever* pops up in our lives? And he asks us, *us*, if he can be our personal manager? I mean, that's gotta be the Universe speaking, doesn't it?"

"As I always say," Les said, dropping into to a chair. "These are the good times, and we're havin 'em. So, we going to do this deal?"

"It's like it was meant to be." I glanced back and forth between the other three who'd come out here from Indianapolis. "Picture the four of us at my duplex on Winthrop New Year's Eve, two years ago. If someone had told you then, when we were hanging around the fireplace talking about how I was driving a Wonder Bread truck, Les a Coke truck, Dave a Banquet Milk truck, and Mac was . . . well, living with Bunny—even at our most outrageously inebriated—could you have imagined for a second that two years later Jimmy O'Neil from *Shindig!* would be asking to manage us? And that one of the Four Preps, a singer from one of the smoothest vocal groups ever, wanted to make records with us? And, you guys—we'd be professionals, getting paid to entertain in California?" I shook my head. "It's inconceivable, right? I mean, how could that happen?"

Leonard hovered around behind us overflowing with nervous energy. He found it difficult to stay still for long.

Craig scooted up a chair. "Jimmy says he knows some guys at Vox, thinks he can get me a new bass amp. I'm liking that a lot."

"But you already got a Vox amp," Mac said, puzzled.

"Yeah, but I paid for it. Get me a free one, I can sell that puppy."

"Wonder if he could get me a new organ?" I said. I'd only been able to afford a crappy little used Farfisa organ and desperately wanted something better.

"Vox makes an organ. If he can get me an amp, maybe he could get you one of those."

Keeps getting better and better, I thought. "So any reason why we shouldn't do this? Guess we probably should have an attorney look at these contracts, but I don't know any."

"I do." Craig shrugged. "Worked with Gary Usher on a project—met the attorney they used—but he's big time, don't think we could afford him."

Les took a big swig of Coke, crunched some ice. "I didn't notice anybody else in line waiting to sign us. I say, let the good times roll."

Six weeks later, after we'd returned to the Rag Doll, Jimmy invited us to lunch in the private dining room at Martoni's Italian restaurant on Cahuenga Boulevard in downtown Hollywood.

"Everyone in the music or film business eats here, guys. Sinatra to the Jackson 5, and it's the best Italian food in town," Jimmy told us.

Ciro Marino, the owner, welcomed us at the door and ushered us into the special room in the back. Jimmy, in his usual sweater vest over a collared dress shirt, greeted and waved at a number of people. He pointed out Phil Spector and Sonny Bono, who, he told us, had written the flip side of *I've Got You Babe* in this restaurant. He told us the Beatles had come here for meals, and rumors suggested Sam Cooke's last meal had been in one of these red leather booths. Every night, actors, agents, producers, music executives, and wannabes crowded the bar, three deep.

"Here's something you might find interesting," he said, "Wally Heider's studio is across the street. You know where we met you out in the parking lot? He needed an echo chamber and couldn't find anywhere to build it so Ciro let him build it right under where we parked."

A picture window separated our cozy room from the rest of the crowd, allowing them to peer in and wonder what famous group we were, as we seated ourselves around a huge dining table decorated with green-glass, candle-dripped Chianti bottles. Jimmy's gesture of bringing us here to sign our management and recording contracts gave me a heady feeling of rising stardom. After lunch and contract signing, he planned to give us a tour of our new manager's offices and a working meeting with Eddie Cobb, our new producer. Difficult not to be impressed; good thing, too, because my confidence in Jimmy had taken a big hit.

"I want to apologize to all of you for the Executive Suites screw-up," Jimmy said as we found our places and sat down. Four weeks ago, he'd sent us to open the new Executive Suites hotel miles from anywhere on the California coast, near Santa Cruz.

"I've known the guy who set that up for a long time. Don't know what comes over a man to steal from his own company and run off leaving his wife and daughter behind."

His girlfriend's expensive tastes and her professional degree in oral persuasion from Stanford had been the general consensus we'd heard around the worksite.

I wasn't going to mention anything to Jimmy, but I'd caught hell for the Executive Suites disaster. When we got there, the place was still under construction, no conceivable way would it be ready for many weeks. Jimmy assured me, though, if we set up our equipment in the unfinished showroom, to show our readiness to play, we'd get paid. His friend guaranteed it. For the guys, it was one blown contract too many. Despite our successes, we seemed unable to string jobs together, and Les, along with everyone else, blamed me.

"You're the leader of the group, Larry. You might think about checking things out first."

"Okay, okay," Dave said, reacting to the sullen looks between me and Les in the cheap motel room we were forced to share. "We all need showers and some food, but for my sake, let's smoke the peace pipe between you two."

More angry and frustrated than anyone else, I commandeered the shower first. When I got out, a little refreshed, I heard Les and Dave laughing uproariously in the other room. I toweled off and walked out in fresh underwear.

They were sharing a peace pipe in the form of a half-smoked joint. Les held out what was left to me.

"We were discussing who'd get the single and who'd have to share the double bed. I told Dave we'd better give you the single bed because as bad as you been fucking up lately, you might roll over and accidentally fuck one of us."

I took a big hit on the doobie, trying to decide if I was even more pissed off at what Les said, or if it was actually pretty funny. When I began to laugh, none of us could stop.

Jimmy had been able to get us a check for one week of the four we were owed, before the hotel fell into receivership. But we'd gone three weeks without paychecks again, and despite Jimmy's protestations, we would never see another penny of the money his friend had guaranteed.

Ciro hustled around the room making sure we were comfortable and found entrees we'd like. I chose the highly recommended shrimp scampi and an Italian salad hiding little leggy things called calamari in it.

"Ciro," Jimmy said, with a big grin as our server hurried off with our lunch order. "Meet Stark Naked and the Car Thieves, who are about to become big stars. We're here to continue the history of famous contract signings in your restaurant." Eve began shifting small piles of paperwork toward us for signatures.

Ciro beamed. "Listen, you boys. You ever need anything, want to use the room here, whatever you need, ask for me. I'll make sure you get the best. Friends of Jimmy's, friends of mine."

We'd seen the agreements. Just as horrible and unfair as the ones I remembered signing back in Indianapolis, normal for the business, I guessed. They promised little in return for locking up our services for five years. Within minutes, Jimmy and his partner in B-J Enterprises whom we hadn't met yet, Burt Jacobs, were officially our personal managers, while our recording future was solidly in the hands of Greengrass Productions—Eddie Cobb and his partner, Ray Harris.

Following the delicious discovery of cannoli, I was threading my way through the tables out of the restaurant with the group when a young man wearing a dark turtleneck sweater and belled jeans, with a hair style similar to Jimmy's, stopped him for a moment. When Jimmy joined us outside, he showed us a business card imprinted with Sebring International.

"That's my hair stylist, Jay Sebring. He's got this terrific haircut system he invented. You guys need to stay well groomed now that you're going to be seen by the world." He flipped the card over to show where "20% off" had been handwritten and signed by Jay Sebring, and handed it to me.

"Jay has a shop in Beverly Hills and another on Fairfax, the one I usually go to." We walked along the driveway toward the parking in back. "You can ask for Jay personally, but he's in big demand, and spends a lot of time on location doing hair for movies and television, so if he's not available ask for Joe, Jay's right-hand man. He'll give you an incredible cut."

Between Jay Sebring's in LA and Izzy Marion, who cut our hair at Isadore's, his salon at Caesars, whenever we were in Vegas, our hair would be as fashionable as anybody's in show business.

Living large.

48
WELCOME TO THE BIG TIME

> *. . . storytellers clothed the Naked body of the myth
> in their own traditions, so that listeners could
> relate more easily to its deeper meaning.*
>
> — Joan D. Vinge

April 6, 1967
Hollywood, California

WITH THE INK still drying on our new contracts and our stomachs comfortably full of Martoni's pasta, Jimmy escorted us up Sunset Boulevard to his office below the Hollywood Hills at 9220. The low-slung steel-and-glass building on the southwest corner of San Vicente looked down its nose south, toward the Troubadour and West Hollywood, back to the east to the clubs, studios, and deal-making restaurants along Sunset, and west, where the boulevard made an abrupt, elegant curve through the manicured mansions and tall palms of the Beverly Hills flats on its way to Jan and Dean's "dead man's curve" and the sparkling Pacific.

"Guys, I'm going to take you to see Eddie, but before I do, I'd like to show you off a little." Jimmy paraded us out of his office into the center of a suite of offices covering the second floor. He gestured into a small cubicle near his, occupied by an odd little man wearing gigantic round glasses that made his eyes look permanently startled and a dead groundhog on his head passing itself off as a toupee.

"First, say hi to my partner, Burt Jacobs, fellas," Jimmy said, as we passed by. Burt wriggled lips that looked like pale little worms as they struggled to form a smile. He raised a plump elfin hand in either a wave or dismissal.

"There's someone special I want you to meet," Jimmy said, ushering us into a huge office taking up the suite's farthest corner. A squat, gnome-like older gentleman popped out from behind his desk to greet us. His snowy-white sideburns swept back like wings to join alabaster nape hair in retreat from a gleaming bald dome. As Jimmy introduced us one by one to Seymour Heller, Seymour noticed where my attention had gone.

"You're admiring my desk, Larry, is it? Come, take a closer look." Seymour almost pirouetted, leading us across the room. The gleaming ebony surface had begun life as the top of a grand piano, before its legs had been hacked off to lower it to a comfortable height for the tall leather chair behind it.

Drawers had been built into the flat side where a keyboard would have been. A couple of lonesome pieces of paper and a manila folder lay on the glossy black surface, along with a few personal pictures. A frame held a family photo with Seymour and a pleasant-looking woman, two boys, and a middle girl; his wife and children, I supposed. Another displayed a signed head shot of Liberace, and the last, a snapshot of Seymour next to a black English taxicab.

"Lee gave me this desk several years ago," he said with pride, running his fingers over the inky-black, mirror-like desktop. Lee was Liberace, I assumed. "The guy is the greatest." He beamed at us, over a paternal smile.

"I'm counting on you fellows having the same sort of relationship with Jimmy I've enjoyed with Lee and the Treniers through the years." *Who are the Treniers?* I wondered, but didn't ask, not wanting to reveal my ignorance nor offend.

The floor-to-ceiling glass corner walls behind the desk overlooked a tangled green, overgrown hill to the south and west. The longest interior wall was completely carpeted with photos of all sorts of celebrities posed with, and autographed to, Seymour. His secretary fluttered around, anxious to be rid of us before her daily schedule went to hell. "Sy, phone conference with New York in ten minutes," she said.

"I became Lee's personal manager on a one-year contract in 1950,"

Seymour went on, unconcerned, "and seventeen years later we're still working on the same contract. The Treniers, whom I've managed even longer, have always worked with me on a simple handshake. That's the kind of loyalty I get and give." We tried to say all the appropriate things as we were led out, to the immense satisfaction of Seymour's guard-dog secretary.

Before reaching Eddie's office, we passed an office even more cramped than Burt Jacobs's, where a wedged-in desk, side chair, and filing cabinet jostled for room in the limited space.

In his docent voice, Jimmy announced, "Ray Harris, Eddie's partner in Greengrass Productions." We dutifully waved; Ray, a frown that looked perpetual on his downturned face, ignored us.

"Ray," Jimmy said, leaning through the doorframe. "These are your newest stars, Stark Naked and the Car Thieves."

If he glanced up, I didn't see it. "Yeah, yeah. Hey, welcome guys. Kinda busy, talk later."

Eddie Cobb's room, darkened by drawn blinds, appeared to be more warehouse than office. Records, in and out of dust jackets and covers, lay stacked high in disorganized piles. On the credenza, behind the overladen metal desk, stood hills of acetate recordings and cassette tapes. Eddie was fair, and at six foot four or five, overtopped us all as he stood to greet his new recording artists. His boyish, open face and enthusiasm buoyed me up as he talked about recording us.

"Loved the way you guys sound on those acetates of yours. Raw, no echo, live, and still good. I'm familiar with The studio where you recorded them.. I've been up to San Francisco for Kingston Trio sessions." Eddie pushed up the rolled-up cuffs of his pale, pin-striped dress shirt, and got down to business.

"I've already begun looking for songs for the group. Found some I'd like to get your opinions on. If we can pick some things today, we can get started right away."

"You were one of the Four Preps!" I burst out, my pent-up zeal unleashed. Why wouldn't I be excited about having a producer who sang such glassy-smooth harmony in the Preps, who had lots of hits I admired?

"That's right." He nodded without expanding further.

"I grew up listening to your songs," I babbled on. "We sang *26 Miles*, of course, and the one with, the ah . . . little pufferbellies all in a row' song too—*Down By the Station*, right? And *Big Man Yesterday* . . ." I was starting to fawn all over the guy, so I stopped to explain.

"The thing is, our band started off as a vocal group back in Indiana based on harmony groups like the Four Preps, we sang . . ."

"Hold on, Larry. Slow down." Jimmy laughed, holding up his hands. "Life stories later. Give the guy a break. Eddie's got songs ready for you to listen to and not a lot of time." He turned to Eddie. "I'll find some folding chairs and leave the guys with you."

We listened to, and discussed, several demos, most on cassette tape, some on acetate or reels until we came up with four we agreed to start with. In my opinion, *The Pleasure of Your Company* had pretty cheesy lyrics and a so-so melody, but Eddie seemed set on the song so we accepted it with good grace, but a couple of the others had real possibilities. We put in place the method we would use in all our production meetings with Eddie. Once he'd given us his ideas on how he heard a selection, he turned it over to Les to arrange the vocals and rhythm section.

Jimmy had a schedule worked out with Tony Ferra to accommodate our recording sessions. During the first three weeks, while at the Rag Doll, we'd work on the arrangements in our downtime. Then Tony would move us to the Red Velvet for four weeks, his other club on Sunset, not far from Producer's Workshop, where we'd be recording. He'd told us he'd wanted to see how Ike and Tina Turner, longtime regulars in his Hollywood club, would work out at the Rag Doll. Afterward, we'd switch back for another couple of weeks, before heading back to Vegas.

After our intoxicating meetings in Hollywood, I felt an urge to share the big news with someone, and Marie was my first choice. As soon as she heard we were in North Hollywood, she wanted to come down to LA. Not a good idea, I told her with regret. We had a heavy rehearsal and studio schedule planned, and I needed to avoid any distractions.

When Marie promised the graphically described distractions she had in mind for me wouldn't be distractions at all, but methods guaranteed to relax, clear the mind, and relieve tension, imagination won over celibacy. Two days later, I picked her up at the San Fernando train station and drove in a frenzy to my Mid-Valley Motel room. By the time I got to work that night, Marie had been right—my psyche felt revitalized.

Les took the challenge of arranging our vocals to heart, working alone on his vocal arrangements for the songs we were going to record at every possible minute. When they were ready, he showed us our parts, and as we built up the harmony stacks and progressions, our enthusiasm and confidence grew. The concepts he was unveiling would show anyone we were as imaginative and talented as any vocal group on Billboard's Hot 100. The harmonies might seem simple to the average ear, but a knowledgeable listener would know they held intricate, subtle changes that gave us a thick, rich sound. We didn't have a consistent vocal signature yet, nothing like the Mamas and Papas's suspended fourths, but I sensed we could get there, especially when we were working on songs written specifically for us.

I worried about our voices in the studio, though. Singers who sang such demanding vocal material as we did, five hours a night, six nights a week, always had chronic sore throats. Learning to push through discomfort while protecting your voice from further damage was key to survival. Sick or well, we had to perform every night. Though Mac's baritone R&B tunes weren't near as demanding as Dave's, he still sang the second most leads, and his voice wasn't holding up well. Whether from lack of technique, the kind Dave and I had learned from Judy Davis, or the volume of alcohol he poured through his vocal cords, Mac's voice had deteriorated from gruff to gravel, and worse, his range had shrunk to little more than an octave. We worried he might have developed nodes on this vocal cords, but it was probably just rest he needed.

When I first listened to *Contact*, one of the other songs we'd picked, I thought Mac's voice, in peak condition, would have been better suited for the lead than Dave's; I think Les and Dave agreed. But it wasn't, so he didn't get it. On stage we'd learned a lot of ways to hide deficiencies, but there was no hiding voice quality in the studio.

As Les revealed his vocal arrangements at rehearsals, I got more and more excited about singing and hearing them in a world-class recording studio. For *The Merry-Go-Round Is Slowing You Down*, he devised a memorable series of rounds in the chorus in an atmospheric minor key that set the hook of the song. Even *The Pleasure of Your Company*, despite the uninspired title and trite lyrics, might be saved by Les's imaginative vocal arrangement. On *Pleasure* he'd constructed a resolving harmony structure, with intricate internal chord changes and high ringing full-voice parts. For *Contact*, which I'd originally considered a kind of hokey psychedelic tune, Les designed a similar progressive harmony structure to *Pleasure*, except it rolled our voices down into a powerful bass major chord.

All of us believed *Maria, Love and Music* was the best song Eddie had found for us, and Les gave it his full attention. I believed the haunting background harmony framing Dave's full range and power would make this song a signature hit and take us to the "top of the top." *Look Back in Love*, our fourth song, seemed like a lollypop tune with solid rhythm that our male voices sounded good on, but something special would have to happen in the studio for it to blossom.

If our vocal style were to define us as a band, as I hoped, these could be our first steps.

Learning these arrangements reminded me of the first version of my high-school vocal group, even before we had a name, as we struggled to figure out and sing the intricate key-change harmony just before the last verse in *Silhouettes*. It took us a year to become proficient enough harmony vocalists to understand and sing those chord changes. I hoped some young group of singers listening to our records would be inspired to decipher these cascading vocals Les had created, the same way we had.

Les demanded every note be right and the timing perfect, and though he could be a martinet, I loved every minute of it. Mac caught the most flak for missing notes and timing, often receiving the "finger" lecture, where Les would point out how each of his fingers on the fret board represented one of our voices. "So watch your finger and sing that note," he'd say. Mac's usual chagrined response became, "Hey, man, that ain't the same finger I had yesterday." I worried about what these challenging parts would sound like in the studio considering the condition of Mac's voice, and to some degree, all of our voices. And I worried that Les had overestimated the top of my range in certain spots.

The second week at the Doll, our weeknight crowds, including the circuit dancers who'd made us a regular stop now, seemed as large as the weekends. In the third week, full-house audiences waited for our first set when we began each night. Friday and Saturdays, lines formed outside the club. We oozed confidence, we felt ready for the studio, songs rehearsed, ready to impress, ready to shine and become stars.

49
HOLLYWOOD SESSIONS

*I've learned that I work best when I'm entirely
Naked. The recording process was done that way.*

— Emilie Autumn

April 25, 1967
Hollywood, California

ON TUESDAY, OUR opening night, more than a few people made their disappointment known when they found a slick-suited, white vocal band on stage at the Red Velvet, instead of Ike and Tina Turner's raw rhythm and blues. We shrugged off being under-appreciated; we were here for a greater purpose.

Producer's Workshop, where we met at midmorning the next day, shared a single-story building with the Mastering Lab on Sunset Boulevard. We entered the studio's control room through a small lounge. Eddie stopped fiddling with the recording console controls long enough to introduce us to Emory Gordy, our sound engineer, and Ron Hitchcock, his second. A hint of sour-smelling vomit hung in the air. They were finishing the icky job of cleaning up the room.

"Ugh," Emory said. "Group in here with their own engineers, really crapped up the place. Wish Ray wouldn't let anyone work in here without our own staff looking out for the place." Eddie blew out his breath and muttered about having to pay the rent. He waved Ron over.

"Guys, we'll be working on the music tracks first, so Leonard, set up your drums in the booth. Les, Craig—Ron will show you where your bass and guitar amps go. The rest of you won't have much to do until we get these tracks done, so try not to get in the way. Tight schedule, let's get cracking."

The single session in San Francisco and the recording experiences Dave, Les, and I had in Indianapolis made us the most knowledgeable. Especially me and Dave, since Jan Hutchens had drafted us as slave labor to help build his studio from the wood framing out to its egg-crated walls. But in reality, we were all rookies. There wasn't much comparison between the primitive two-track studio and sound board in an Indianapolis storefront, and the long, intricate-looking recording console, sixteen-track recorder, mastering machine, huge speakers, and large recording room with an enclosed sound booth in the back. But I recognized most everything's function and tried to take it all in.

Emory and Ron, who looked like a skinny teenager, worked smoothly together. Eddie seemed to have disappeared, and Emory explained he'd returned to the office while he and Ron got things ready to record over the next few hours.

After Ron set up a single mic near the control room window for Dave to record a rough reference track of the lead vocal to keep everyone in the right place, he mic'd a small guitar amp for Les to monitor. Craig would hear his bass through headphones.

Meanwhile, Emory focused on the drums, giving long and careful attention to the snare. He suggested that Leonard consider using smaller sticks rather than his normal tree trunks, explaining the volume should come from the console, not the massive impact of a much-more-difficult-to-control, huge club struck against a drum head. Mics don't like to be overdriven, he explained.

Leonard agreed, it was his nature to try his best to please, and Emory was extremely gentle with him, but I could tell our drummer's confidence was suffering, making him self-conscious and uncomfortable. He was a physical guy, unused to the studio, and liked to lean into his licks.

Once he climbed behind the console, Emory's quiet competence made him seem like a pilot in the cockpit of a jet airplane as he focused on perfecting every sound from the studio. He was the master of every dial, slide, switch, and microphone—fully grasping every aspect of the studio under his control. He directed Ron in fine-tuning mic placements in the recording room, using a grease pencil and masking tape to mark channels and dial settings on the sound board as he went. The drums alone took hours as Emory adjusted, or directed Ron to adjust, several mics, sometimes minutely, and moved baffles, changed equalization settings, and made numerous other board adjustments, all the while trying to calm Leonard, whose anxiety continued to grow. I think he felt it was his fault that it was taking so long, but, as I later would learn, drums can seem to take forever to get just right.

We took a short dinner break for sandwiches, and by the time we were done Eddie had returned, ready to begin the lengthy job of getting basic tracks down. All of this preparation was new, yet tedious, leaching out the excitement and spontaneity we'd had entering the studio hours earlier.

By the time we left for work at the Velvet, the musicians might have laid down a decent musical track for our first track, *Contact*, but Eddie wouldn't say for sure, not until he'd heard it with fresh ears, he said. Outside of Dave's lead vocal reference track, the vocalists hadn't sung a note; still, I was worn out before the first note at the Velvet that night. The players struggled with switching back to playing live. It was all we could do to get through the night.

Eddie worked all week with us in the studio doing music tracks. On Monday, without the pressure of going to work on our off-night, Dave, Les, Mac, Craig, and I began laying down final background vocal tracks. In the studio, Dave could join the background voices, helping to thicken the harmony, but sometimes overpowering it when he unleashed the full power of his voice. Once those were finished, Dave could start on his leads.

I was already weirded-out by trying to sing this early in the morning when I pulled one side of the headphones off to whisper to Les, "This isn't sounding the way it did in rehearsal."

The control-room window was a bright rectangle on the distant wall, the studio light dim to disguise the reality of a warm California sun shining bright outside. A Sennheiser microphone, suspended in a spidery shock mount, hung between the five of us. The playback of the background harmony for *The Pleasure of Your Company* rang through my headphones.

"It's too harsh, it's like we're yelling. Pitch is awful, we're not breathing together. God, we don't *blend*!" I was shocked at how pathetic we sounded, and I wasn't excusing myself.

Les, an ear clear of his headphones, looked puzzled. "Look, it'll be okay. Some adjustment they need to make on the mics or the board or something."

"Sounds great, guys. Ready to go again?" Eddie's voice blared from the control room. I'd been excited to begin recording the harmony we'd worked so hard on, but my heart began to sink; maybe I'd let my expectations get too high. We were in a new environment; I should be more patient, trust the experts.

Les motioned for everyone to listen to him. "Look, we're standing here in a circle so we can see each other sing. Follow me, watch each other's mouths, and make sure we hit and end the notes at the same time—and make the changes crisper. Larry, keep your pitch up, you're going flat on the top notes." He glanced at Mac. "And you, don't make me get my guitar out and finger your part for you again." We all grinned, but it felt forced; we were far from loose. I didn't think any of us were pleased with what we'd heard so far.

The music track started up again, and as the opening drum fill ended, Les gestured us into the first chord. Maybe the playback track in our headphones was too high, we were still screaming the harmony instead of singing it. I couldn't hear my own voice in the mix. I hoped I wasn't going flat. I raised my eyebrows at the top of the harmony to keep my pitch up, as Judy Davis had instructed.

Hours passed, my voice used up and squeaky before we trudged into the control room to listen to what we'd sung. In the big speakers, with the music track higher, the vocals sounded fuller, the chord changes right, our timing better if not perfect, but our voices still sounded shouty and didn't blend. The different textures and tones of our voices bothered me. The Reflections, even the Aristocats, wouldn't have been satisfied with this. We'd have made sure this harmony was tighter than a gnat's ass.

"Maybe we should try again," I suggested.

"No, this will work," Eddie said, adjusting dials as Emory worked at resetting some channels on the console while Ron set up another, smaller recorder.

"You're hearing your voices dry. Once I get some echo on this puppy, double-track the voices a little, it'll be great. We have a lot more to do today. Ready to try *Contact*?"

Somewhere near dawn the next morning, I slipped into bed next to Marie, bone weary. Her body felt warm next to mine as I snuggled in, pulling the covers over us. Though exhausted, the clamor in my mind from the long night wouldn't quiet.

"What time is it?" Marie mumbled, with a sleepy peek at the clock radio. "Damn, you've been gone all day and night. How did the session go?"

I whooshed out my breath, too complicated a question for a brain squeezed dry. "Exhilarating, frustrating, tiring, boring—fantastic in every way."

"Does that mean you guys did good?"

"That's the problem. I don't know." I punched my pillow and scootched up against the headboard. "I'm not sure. Harmonies don't sound the way I hoped they would, but I heard them so often I can't remember what I expected us to sound like anymore."

My throat felt hot. I hadn't meant to smoke another cigarette tonight, but out of habit I lit up from a pack on the nightstand.

"Still have a long way to go. Dave hasn't even started on his leads yet."

"You sound kind of worried . . ." Marie grabbed my cigarette and hot-boxed it before handing it back. "You get like that sometimes, and then everything works out fine. Maybe you need to give this some space. It's not all going to happen in one night."

I waited for the cigarette to cool, wishing I could smoke a joint instead, before drawing in another lungful and nodding. "Yeah, you're right. Just one night, one session. We learned a lot, that's good anyway." She snuggled up under my arm. "Finish your cigarette and come down here with me, I know how to help you unwind."

We spent our last off-night in Hollywood at the studio. Dave battled with *Maria, Love and Music*, his frustration building. "I don't know what the hell you want me to do," he snapped back into the mic at Eddie. He was tired and running into something he'd always found difficult.

"Dave," Eddie said, ignoring the nastiness in Dave's voice. "Just be natural, this is the end of the song, going into fade out, just feel the song, let go and be spontaneous."

If he'd known Dave better, he wouldn't have asked that of him. Dave didn't have many weaknesses as a singer, but spontaneity was the biggest. Improvisation hadn't been part of our original singing group's DNA. We learned songs whole hog, with all the chops and riffs the artists who'd recorded them included. He could sing any melody or lick without flaw if he heard it first, but he struggled when he tried to express the moment with his voice.

"I'm going to let the chorus loop, take all the time you need, ad-lib any way you want to."

Maybe, if someone had coached him, sat at a piano alone with him for a few minutes, if a vocal arranger had worked on some note combinations, given him some ideas, it would have gone better. Not sure what to do, Dave fell back on his strengths, range and power. He jumped up an octave and sang the same melody line only higher, moved higher yet, holding out a long note that dipped back to the tonic. The chorus kept rolling in Dave's headset for several minutes while Dave did pretty much the same thing over and over, sometimes even resorting to screeching as he reached higher and higher, extending to a note that sounded more like a whistle than a human voice. Later he told me he thought he'd hit B flat below double high C, his highest note. I wouldn't have been surprised if a pack of dogs came scratching at the studio door.

Unperturbed after a painful hour or more of this, when I expected Dave's tonsils to be hanging out of his mouth, Eddie said, "Great, I'll take it. Thanks, Dave. Enough for tonight." He told Dave he planned to cut and edit and find ways to use what he had, and not to worry, it would be fine.

I didn't see any way Dave's performance would be fine. The entire lead recording had issues; certain phrasings in the song required Dave to slip in and out of full voice, a smooth transition that resulted in a neat, breathy tone when Dave's voice was rested. The strain of singing every night at the Red Velvet, being in every background vocal, and doing every lead had left him worn in voice and imagination. His voice had either broken, or was near breaking in those transitions tonight. His frustration at not being at his best made his intonation nasal and flat as he tried to force it to deliver.

Though we needed more studio time, especially for vocals, I believed the band was exhausted, burned-out, and couldn't have done much with it anyway. We'd had some highs and lows and struggled against our weaknesses and inexperience, but I felt we'd proved we had an immense amount of recording potential if we, or somebody, could figure out how to unlock us. Now it would be up to whatever Eddie and Emory could do in the final mix and mastering process.

50
THE B3

Now, music almost feels Naked in my mind.

— Sean Lennon

May 9, 1967
Downey, California

WE'D PLANNED TO work at the Velvet for four weeks, but as we neared the end of the third week, Tony said he needed us back in the Valley. The experiment had backfired. However mediocre things had gone for us on Sunset Boulevard, Ike and Tina were in full revolt out in the Valley, they hated playing in suburbia.

We performed like burned-out zombies during our last week at the Red Velvet. During the final few days in the studio, Les recorded guitar solos and added some rhythm tracks, while Dave spent a few hours touching up some vocals.

We were glad to get back to the Rag Doll, happy for the mental pickup our fans there gave us. We didn't talk much about it, but I sensed uncertainty with how we felt our studio experience had gone. With so much attention on recording, we'd fallen behind on new songs for the stage. I picked up the Foundations' *Baby, Now That I've Found You*, Mac wanted to do another Sam and Dave tune, *Hold On, I'm Coming*, and we finally added Gary Puckett's *Woman, Woman*, which Dave just tore up. Another nice addition was the Association's *Windy*, featuring Craig.

Explaining that Stark Naked and the Car Thieves needed to be on a better business basis, Jimmy recommended a business manager named Don Lehman to handle the band's finances and help the band establish bank credit. Mr. Lehman strongly suggested that we let him handle our individual affairs as well. As the band had continued to become more organized, Dave's offstage role had become books; he handled the band's money in the same way that I, as the briefcase, handled leadership tasks, and Leonard dealt with laundry. He met with our new business manager, and within days, the band acquired a badly needed new Ford van to move our gear with. A few days later, Dave was zipping around the Valley in a beautiful new red Cadillac with a white convertible top. When Mac saw Dave's new car, he asked Dave how he'd gotten it. The next day he made an appointment with our new business manager to turn over his personal finances, and within a week, he, too, was tooling around in the same model Cadillac, except in green with a black top. We had to be getting closer to the top of the top now.

For me, this was a near life-changing event. Don Lehman helped me acquire the instrumental love of my life, a Hammond B3 organ. Thank God for the new van, or I wouldn't have had a way to move the beautiful new Hammond organ with its two Leslie speakers I'd bought with the line of bank credit he'd arranged for me. I had to turn all my income over to him and let him put me on an allowance, but it was well worth it as this incredible instrument became my most prized possession. I polished the cabinet with Black Gold every day and loved it the way I could never love the whiny little Farfisa or the faint-hearted Vox organ I'd been playing.

Nothing compared to sitting behind my B3, starting the motor and feeling it purr to life like a giant, breathing creature. The harmonics and beefy volume came from the drawbars, called stops, the sliding levers above the keyboard—where the term "pulling out all the stops" came from. The B3 sounded so cool it made me seem like a far better player than I was; even a mistake could sound pretty damn good. Spinning up the Leslie amplifiers' horns ramped up the notes, their analog vibrato creating excitement—or slowing them down, which is when the B3 sounded so sexy—and the lazy Doppler effect that made whatever I played ooze sensuality. Setting the drawbars to a hard edge, I could add rhythm to the drums and bass when Les took off on a solo; or I could adjust them to thicken our harmonies with rich, vocal-like chords; or I could over-drive the B3, to make it sound rough and dirty, perfect for some of our R&B tunes. I never became an accomplished soloist or gained much independence with my left hand, but I achieved a meaningful role in the musicianship of the band just by owning the right instrument.

Jimmy had also been busy finding equipment endorsements, beginning with obtaining a new Vox amp for Craig. After visiting the Mosrite shop in Bakersfield, Les decided he liked their guitars; Jimmy helped negotiate a standard guitar for him, along with an odd-looking double-necked guitar, too. Soon, Les and Craig had color-matched guitars and bass on stage.

We'd be playing next at the iconic Thunderbird Hotel in Las Vegas. Jimmy told me Seymour had called in a favor; our reconciliation with the Strip hotels would start at this venerable institution. I put Marie on the train to Fremont the day before we left, both of us swearing to stay in touch, though I wondered if we would. Neither of us knew where our sporadic relationship was going. Marie didn't cry or complain, but her lovemaking expressed her desire.

Two event-packed weeks later, instead of settling in at the Thunderbird in Las Vegas for two more weeks, we were unpacking in the little apartments in Downey, California. George Simone was as surprised as we were when he welcomed us back to the Pink Carousel. I was also happy to be there—happy to be anywhere really—since we'd just gotten our asses, along with pink slips, handed to us at the Thunderbird. So much for our big comeback on the Las Vegas Strip.

During our second Friday night at the Thunderbird, Mac had yelled something over the mic at someone waving his arms wildly and screeching at the top of his lungs near the lounge's side door.

"What happened, Mac?" I asked, pulling the mic away from my mouth.

"Aw, some sonofabitch out there shoutin about us bein too loud. Heard that crap since we got here; but stompin into our room yellin at us outta the audience is too goddamn uncool." He grinned crookedly at me. "So I told 'em to shut the fuck up."

Uh-oh. Would I have to let our new Hollywood management office know our option for the next two weeks wasn't likely to be picked up?

I mulled this over as Dave and Mac began gliding across the stage, gathering steam on *Soul Man*, while I tried to find the right combination to mimic the horn hits on my new B3.

All of a sudden the keys produced no sound. Leonard's drums pounded on by themselves. Every stage light had gone out, the guitar amps and PA were silent, too. Mac and Dave looked back at me, questions on their faces.

I slid off my stool and headed backstage to find somebody to fix a blown fuse when the stage manager rushed out making a cutting motion across his throat.

"What's that mean?"

"Means you assholes are done. Pack your shit and get out."

"Hey, that's kind of rude." I thought we were okay with the stage staff at least.

"Yeah, well fuck you, bud. And if I lose my job over this, which is looking very possible, I'll call you a hell of a lot worse. I been telling you guys you played too damn loud. You're leaking into the showroom, and that's a big, expensive show over there."

"Jeez, sorry about that. We can play quieter."

He squinted at me as if he expected marbles to start rolling out of my ears. "You don't get it. You're done. Your ass is grass, and I'm the fucking lawn mower." He stared again. "Didn't you recognize who you guys just cussed out?"

"Hard to see through the lights. Just heard somebody raising a ruckus."

"Yeah, well that somebody signs my check and will sign the last check you'll ever get here. So do me a favor and get the hell off the stage as fast as you can so I can get someone else up here. I need this job, and he's already told me to see him after you're out of here."

This was a first—we'd never had the power turned off on us. The stage manager actually brought our check to me as we lugged the last of the drums off the stage, witnessed by a quiet audience who hadn't realized watching an act get fired in front of them was on the bill that night.

"Well guys, might as well get some dinner," I said, as we lugged equipment down to our new van. "Most of Friday night's left, and I bet they're not going to pick up our option." A little bitter laughter.

"Goddamn it Mac," Les said, still steaming. "You just blew off a hotel owner. What are you thinking?"

"I'm thinking some old fool comin in yellin around in the middle of our show is a fucked-up asshole with no class at all."

Les shook his head while Leonard hung his.

"I think this is my fault. I shoulda cut down on the drums. I wanted to play here, the Thunderbird is old Vegas. My brother was so excited I was playing here."

We'd been fortunate George had been able to accept us into the Carousel so fast, but that no longer occupied my mind. A couple of days after we'd settled in, Dave dropped by my little apartment. "What happened to you, man? You're white as a sheet," he said, noticing the stunned look on my face.

Speechless, I held up the paper I'd been staring at. "Eve called and said they'd received this. She said the envelope looked pretty official, so I told her to forward it here." He took the letter out of my hands.

"A draft notice? What the hell is this, some kind of practical joke? I wouldn't put something like this past Les."

I took the letter back. "No, man. This is real. Not just a draft notice, either. I think I've already been drafted. Listen," I said as I read to him.

"'Greetings, you are hereby ordered for induction into the Armed Forces of the United States.'"

I sat down at the little table in my room. "Says I have to report to somewhere in Long Beach with three changes of clothes." I rubbed my forehead in disbelief. "Can you fucking believe this? We've got our first record coming out; I'm on the hook for three grand for my new B3. We have a chance to finally make it to the big time—and all of a sudden, I'm in the goddamn army?"

51

INDUCTED

*For what is it to die but to stand Naked in
the wind and to melt into the sun?*

— Kahlil Gibran

*June 15, 1967
Downey, California*

THE BAND WANTED to talk about my induction orders, so, after the first set, we gathered in the Pink Carousel's backstage dressing room. If I thought it was because they wanted to commiserate with me because I was so down in the dumps, I was mistaken.

"Bad enough they want to draft you," Les said, "but this thing says you've got to show up at six thirty in the morning."

"Yeah. I noticed."

"So, what are you going to do?"

"Well crap, Leonard, I guess there's nothing I can do but go get in the army." I hated sounding so scared and frustrated. Truth was, I had no idea what to do. "Fuck, fuck, fuck, fuck, and double fuck."

"Hate to be the first guy to bring this up, but what's the band gonna do?" Craig didn't waste a moment getting to the band's problem. "Get somebody to replace him, right?"

My heart dropped to my stomach. I was becoming history already. My world was crumbling, dominoes falling one by one. I had to get out of there.

It was noisy and crowded out in the club. I didn't really want a drink, but I needed something to deaden the deepening pall of dread falling over me. I pulled a barstool up to where Mark Anthony, our bartender friend, was dealing glasses of exotic-looking liquor and beer.

"Hey Larry, what can I get you?"

"Something strong. Whatever you recommend, I guess." He was back in a minute to sweep a rocks glass filled with ice and bourbon onto a napkin in front of me. "None of my business, but you don't look so great. Something bugging you?"

I appreciated the genuine concern on his face. I took a slug of whiskey and grimaced; stuff tasted like medicine.

"Yeah, something's wrong all right. I got an induction notice from the army. Orders say pack a bag, do not pass Go, get your ass down here, you're in the army. Fuck, I can't believe this is happening. Just when things were finally starting to roll."

"Wow. That's tough. Kind of surprising, though."

I roused from my growing despair. "Surprising?"

"How old are you?"

"Twenty-five. Twenty-six in December."

"You're kind of old to be called up. Way I heard it, they're drafting younger guys, guys who won't affect the work force so much. You get caught in this kind of call up now, you'll be a ground pounder for sure."

I shook my head. "Ground pounder?"

"Infantry. The grunts. College guys get deferments; maybe do a couple of years of ROTC." He pronounced it *rot-see*. "Do their hitches as officers. The recruiters promise them no combat, stuff like that. Sounds like you'd be going right to rifleman, though; combat almost for sure."

"If you're trying to cheer me up, it's not really working." I frowned at him.

Mark pondered me for a moment. "Look, I might know somebody who can help. Come by the bar after your last set."

I was too horrified by the size of the hole opening in my life to think much about what Mark had told me. I'd thought with Jack gone, my place in the band was finally secure. How could this disaster have picked now to happen?

I got through the night in an alcohol-anesthetized daze, smiling vaguely and excusing myself from conversations. I rushed out of the club at the end of the night to marinate alone in my misery. At our mini-apartment complex, dozens of people drifted between many of the rooms' open doors, carrying beer cans, drinks in plastic glasses, and puffing lighted joints or cigarettes in the tropical night air. The majority seemed to be female, many wearing amazingly skimpy mini-skirts with boots or pumps, some in jeans, sandals, and tie-dye.

I recognized most of the crowd from the Carousel; they'd migrated over here after the club closed at two. Between our forays down to the Hullabaloo afterhours and what was happening here, a little of the vaunted "rock and roll legend" excitement seemed to be developing around us. But the floating party only reminded me of the direction our band was headed, and how it was going there without me.

Dave's room was packed with people, while a Mothers of Invention album, *Absolutely Free* moaned in the background of the herb-choked atmosphere. It added an otherworldly vibe to an atmosphere already strange. In a corner easy chair, Mark Anthony held sway. His eyes glistened with blitzed excitement as he spoke in portentous tones, as if reciting Khalil Gibran. A fascinated audience oohed and wowed at every pronouncement.

"So here I am looking out my bedroom window, I didn't know what was real, might have been a dream, but maybe not. I can see a gigantic spider hanging right outside, and it's spun this enormous web that covers our whole house—even most of our property, as far as I can see, anyway. Scattered all around in the web are these wrapped-up bundles—about the size of cocker spaniels—and then I remember several neighborhood dogs have been reported missing. The spider, well, it turns those bunches of beady eyes toward me, like they do, you know, and says . . ."

He looked around at those who stood or sat at his feet. "So, got any idea what the giant arachnid says to me?" Several crazy suggestions were yelled out that Mark fielded with quick one-liners.

Mark held up a palm, head bowed, until the only sound was Frank Zappa's monotone chant, *Brown Shoes Don't Make It*. "The spider says"—he raised his head with great dignity, and spoke—"crowded elevators smell different to midgets." His audience groaned and moaned as he laughed along with them.

An entranced young girl, sitting near the front, said with the exaggerated concern of the highly stoned, "But what does it mean?"

"Sweetheart," Mark said with a beatific smile. "I can't say for certain, I have no idea how spiders think. It's just what the spider said."

Spotting me, leaning on the doorframe, he extricated himself from the laughter to come over to me.

"Larry. Glad you're here. Missed you at the bar." His grin had a manic tinge. I was able to summon a weary grimace.

"Listen man, don't get too down. Got a friend coming in tomorrow night. He thinks he knows somebody who can help, so just wait until we talk to him." His wild eyes scrutinized me, reading my expression. "Yeah, you're right, I'm wasted, but I got a feeling about this. When I get fucked up just right, not too much booze or too much weed, a channel opens up between the weird part of my brain and my mouth. Never sure what's going to come out, but I just know certain things. I can tell what's going to happen. Hard part's finding the balance." He teeter-tottered his hand, slipping into that special place. "Oh, but I'm feelin' right tonight my friend, so listen, I know this problem of yours is going to come out okay. Have faith."

He swept an arm around my shoulders to hug me so fiercely I nearly got a contact high.

"Tomorrow night. You'll see," he said, returning to his throne to accept a freshly lit joint from one of his admirers.

I vacillated wildly between trying to believe Mark wasn't entirely crazy and pure panic as I climbed the concrete stairs to the second floor and my room. After the frenetic atmosphere of a nightclub, I normally liked to get high, to relax and read, or sometimes wind down to mindless television after work. But I couldn't do that when I was upset or depressed. The blessed weed only seemed to make a downer worse. I crawled into bed, trying to ignore the muffled party noises and the assorted knocks on my closed door. Much later, I drifted into a tortured sleep.

When I woke the next day, it took a moment to remember I was on borrowed time. I struggled through a late breakfast, and then did something I knew I shouldn't do. I called Marie.

"Larry?" she asked, hearing my voice. "God. I'm so glad to hear from you. I was worried I never would."

"You probably shouldn't have."

"What does that mean?"

"Marie, I'm being drafted. Into the army. In about four weeks."

"Omigod. To Vietnam?"

"No way to know, but I guess that's where everybody goes. What sucks is one of the songs we recorded is being released any day now, and, well I don't know . . . I just needed to talk to someone, so I called you."

"I'm coming down there. You're in LA somewhere, aren't you?"

"Downey, we're at the Pink Carousel."

"I can leave on Monday. I'll take the train. You pick me up, okay?"

"It will be good to see you, Marie."

"Be even better to feel me, baby."

Saturday night at the Pink Carousel was even more of a madhouse than the night before, starting the moment we walked in. Mark waved from the already busy bar, looking as if he was working with four hands. As I walked by, he said, "My friend Thom will be in around eleven." I nodded.

George Simone happily observed the line of people waiting, which ran down the stairs into the parking lot. At least the gig was going great; it seemed we could do no wrong here. I looked forward to the two new songs we'd finished this week, both of them fun to play and sing: *You Keep Me Hangin' On*, a down and dirty version of Diana Ross's hit by Vanilla Fudge, and the funky *Expressway to Your Heart*, by the Soul Survivors. Hopefully, I could forget about what was happening for a few minutes while concentrating on playing them. Maybe I was oversensitive, but I felt as though the guys were avoiding me, treating me like I was already gone, a walking ghost.

At the third break, Mark came out from behind the bar to take me to a back table where a man in his thirties with a goatee and moustache sat next to a slender girl with straight, white-blond hair held in place by a beaded headband. She fitted a filtered cigarette into a short holder as the man rose to shake my hand.

"Larry, meet Thom Keith," Mark said as I sat down. "A good friend of mine. He's a film producer and director. I'll let Thom introduce the young lady."

"Ah, yes, this is, ah hmm . . ." Thom looked disconcerted for a moment.

"Diane," the girl said smoothly with a slight frown for Thom as she turned to him for a light.

"Your band is excellent." Thom smiled graciously. "We're really enjoying your music, the whole ambiance. It's like a rock concert in a nightclub."

I nodded. Appreciated, of course, but compliments weren't what was on my mind. "Thanks for coming. I guess Mark has mentioned my problem to you. I hope I'm not being too direct in bringing it up right away. I'm kind of anxious."

Thom turned to the girl. "Sweetheart, would you mind finding the women's room and doing what women do for a few minutes? Thanks."

Diane ground out her barely started smoke and rose gracefully to turn away. She was tall to begin with and easily topped six feet in her skyrocket heels. We took a moment to appreciate what her loose, long-legged stroll did to her tight, white jeans as she swayed into the crowd.

"No, not too direct at all." Thom dragged his attention back to me as if we hadn't paused. "Mark tells me you may have a problem with the draft."

I laughed bitterly. "Not just 'may,' it's totally a problem. I received an order to report for induction. In less than a month."

He examined me closely before going on. "Not everyone knows that draft boards are local. I'm led to believe there's a number of influential people in Hollywood who oppose the war in Vietnam. They're especially against risking the lives of our young men to fight some dirty war in God-knows-where, you know."

I didn't know, but my fears receded a little.

"I know of an attorney who has mentioned in passing he knew of ways to reach these people. I've never had occasion to use his contacts, but we've done business funding films and so on. That's worked out well. If you'd like me to, I would be willing to contact him on your behalf."

An attorney? How could a lawyer help? Maybe I was grasping at straws.

"It's my understanding," Thom Keith went on. "Something might be done for only a few thousand dollars or so."

"What?" My heart dropped off a cliff again. "I wouldn't have a clue where to find a thousand dollars. I play in a nightclub band." I swept my hand toward the stage. "I make about a hundred and eighty bucks a week, and that's when we're employed." The faint hope I'd allowed myself began to fizzle away.

"Perhaps you should go to Canada. It would cost far less to get you on the underground railroad to Vancouver."

I shook my head stubbornly. "I'd still have to leave my band. That's what's crucial to me. I couldn't care less about the war." I hadn't had much interest in politics since the Kennedy assassination.

My thoughts drifted inward as I spoke, my chagrin obvious. "We're just about to have a record released, *Billboard* magazine is mentioning us. We're going back to Las Vegas soon, we're getting really popular there. I've been with most of these guys since we came out here from Indianapolis, some for years before that. This feels like a once-in-a-lifetime moment, and I'm going to miss it. I need to find a way to stay in my band." My desperate whining was embarrassing, but I didn't care.

"Well, why don't I talk to my attorney friend?" Thom gave me a gentle smile. "Maybe he will have some ideas."

Mark walked toward the stage with me before he went back to work. "Look, let Thom find out what he can. There's always a way. Don't lose heart, just keep singing. I'm bringing Thom and his dolly over to the place tonight. We'll find out more, we'll figure something out."

52
THE PROPHET AND THE LAWYER

> *I have exposed myself and am not ashamed to stand there
> Naked. "Shame" is what we call the monster that attached
> itself to men when they aspired beyond the animals.*
>
> — Friedrich Nietzsche

June 17, 1967
Downey, California

AS MARK RODE over to the apartments with me after work, he told me there'd never been such wild times at the Carousel since he'd been there; everyone seemed as excited about being at the after-party at the apartment building as being at the club.

"I've been to some craaazy Hollywood parties, pal. One time Natalie Wood and I got drunk and sexy together under a kitchen table at a Hollywood party. I know that's hard to believe, but it's true, tell you all about it one of these first days. Seems like we're building up to some legendary status here, too." He laughed and flashed a wide smile.

Like the night before, the place was hopping on both floors and down around the pool, despite the early morning hour. Everyone who lived here must be night owls; no one complained.

People were gathered around the open door to Mark's room door on the first level in front of the central swimming pool. I hadn't realized that he had a mini-apartment in our building, too, as did several waitresses and another bartender from the club. A round of applause from people waiting nearby and inside greeted him as we walked up. His after-hours performances were becoming well known. In Mark's sitting room, Thom Keith sat comfortably enthroned in a chair, his girlfriend Diane perched on the arm, long legs crossed.

"Come on, prophet," somebody called, "tell us what the spider said." I walked over to Thom as Mark made his way through the crowded, smoke-hazed room. Grinning in anticipation, Mark accepted a proffered water glass filled halfway with a smoky amber liquid and a lit joint. He knocked back a healthy swallow and inhaled deeply.

Leaking weed smoke between his teeth, he grunted out, "If six out of ten people suffer from constipation, does that mean the other four are enjoying it?" Laughter followed as more people crammed themselves into the room. Somebody hollered, "Mark, tell us about your girlfriend again."

He beamed as he inhaled, held in the smoke, and exhaled before he spoke. Squinting down into the joint's glowing tip, he began. "Ah yes, I know the girl you mean, the one with only one tooth." He looked them over in a bemused beatitude.

"Whenever she smiled the tooth showed up in a different place. I kissed her and it turned out to be a Chiclet." A round of laughter.

"I took her home to meet my dad. He's a tall-complected man, talks with a limp. He says to me, 'Son, she sure is a pretty little thing, why she's no bigger than my hand.' I said, 'Yes, Dad, but she's a lot more fun.'"

Mark went on a nonstop gallop with lines from his stand-up routine, so I slipped upstairs to my room for a quick shower and change of clothes. By the time I returned, Thom's girlfriend had disappeared, but he didn't seem to notice. He held a half-empty bottle of Old Grand-Dad by the neck and whispered intimately to a pretty brunette with thick calves and ankles who hung on his every word. I interrupted to thank him for coming to the club, hoping he'd tell me when I could expect to hear from him. Thom's vacuous smile held no sign of recognition. Mark was no help, either. Much of his audience had drifted away. Smiling at something only he could see, it was obvious he'd crossed the threshold into incoherence. I wouldn't be getting any answers from either of them tonight.

"Two thousand dollars?" I exploded in frustration. "Where in hell would I ever find that kind of money, Mark?" We were outside by the pool the next afternoon, after Mark had talked with Thom. Surprisingly, Mark didn't seem the worse for wear from last night's indulgence.

"I know, I know." He nodded. "But now we've got an idea of what it costs to keep you from dying in a Vietnamese jungle." He put a mournful smile on his face. "I don't mind telling you that's not the way I'd want to go. Personally, I plan to die peacefully in my sleep, the way my grandfather did. Not screaming and yelling like the passengers in his car."

"God damn it, Mark." I laughed in spite of myself. "That's not funny."

"Don't I know it. It's why I'm still working as a bartender and not as a comic. Look, at least we know there's a way out for you. Any way you figure, a lot more than we knew a week ago."

I nodded reluctantly. "You're a twisted guy, Mark Anthony, you make me laugh at the worst times."

"If God's watching, least we can do is be entertaining."

His expression got serious. "Thom's made an appointment for you to meet this attorney Crozier next Wednesday. You should keep it. Take the next step, we'll figure out the one after that somehow."

Charles Crozier's upscale office was on Melrose in West Hollywood. Ushered into a long office furnished more like a luxurious living room, I was confronted by a stocky, older man hunched into an expensive suit. I was immediately struck by the unnaturally wide-set eyes gouged into his severely cratered face; the ice-blue irises and deep dark pupils made him appear reptilian and predatory. He must be a terror to face in a courtroom, I thought. He gave me a quick, unnatural smile that looked like a paper cut, and pointed me to a leather wing chair, while he took a spot on the facing love seat. I tried not to look like prey.

"Let's see," he said, the supernally alert eyes in his ruined face studying me. "You are Larry Dunlap, I believe, a friend of Thom Keith." He spoke in the raspy voice of a life-long smoker. His taloned hands held an encased legal pad he didn't open.

I nodded.

"I understand you've been sent a form by the Selective Service. You brought it with you?"

I handed over the offending letter, wrinkled from obsessive folding and refolding.

"Um, form 252," he said, smoothing the paper and examining it closely. "You are being ordered to an intake station in Long Beach, according to this." He glanced up at me solemnly. "You are aware that this form presupposes you are already under orders to be inducted into the United States Army?" I nodded. "And you understand, when you arrive at this location, your ass will belong to the United States Army, under the authority of the United States government, henceforth to do whatever the hell it pleases with it, until forced by law to give it back?"

I whispered, "I guess so."

He rose abruptly and walked to a humidor on a breakfront to remove a cigar. While he clipped and prepared it for smoking, he spoke, almost to himself, but loud enough so I could hear.

"The idea of our government spending the lives of our youth and the treasure of our nation to pulverize one half of a tiny, backward country halfway around the world leaves me speechless—fortunately, however, not helpless."

I couldn't think of any appropriate comment in the following pause.

"So tell me, Larry." My name sounded odd coming from his mouth. He took a moment to make sure his stogie was properly lit before turning back to me. "Are you, or have you been, married?"

"Yes, I was married, we have two sons."

"Really," he said conversationally. Taking his time, he returned to the love seat and sat, crossing his legs at the knee in a disconcertingly feminine way. He rocked his leg, studying me through the blue smoke as if I were a five-legged dog.

"And your divorce was finalized?" I nodded, and he did, too. "And you gave your children up for adoption?"

I stared at him.

"Yes, I check things out, young man. I know your situation. Much better than you do, I'm afraid. You've been fucked." His cheeks hollowed as he drew on the cigar again.

My eyes opened wider.

"Oh don't act like such a naïf. I know you're in a band. You know what 'fucked' means, I'm sure." He blew out more smoke. He seemed pleased in some way.

"You have been fucked because someone, somewhere, hates you enough to get you conscripted, and apparently that someone either hopes or doesn't give a good goddamn if you are killed in some particularly terrible way by savage jungle fighters in southeastern Asia." His lips curled back from yellowish teeth into a shark smile.

"Do you know they put their own shit on sharpened sticks they drive into the ground to poison our troops?" His bared-teeth smile, which he probably thought was jovial, froze me.

He waved his cigar in a tiny circle in the air. "You haven't said much so far, but I assume you've come here because you're under the impression I can make this induction order go away. Am I right?"

"Yes. That's why I'm here. But I never realized . . ."

"I used to be a personnel officer in the Air Force, you see. I was a captain, I know my way around the Pentagon. I understand how the armed services work, how the Selective Service runs. By all rights, you should never have been called up. I know what the unspoken criteria for conscription are right now, and you don't fit the bill, my friend. You were married and have children. The army isn't taking men with children, even ones whose children have been adopted, even though you're unable to pay child support." He smiled his shark smirk again. "You must explain that adoption business to me sometime," he said as an aside.

"And there's more. You have some college, which means, by their thinking, you are probably a productive member of the economy. You had some ROTC training where you went to school in Kentucky—even though you didn't finish the required two years, no reason to waste you as a common grunt. At twenty-five, you're barely within the upper age limit for conscription. And I'll be frank: you are not of the right race. These target ranges change depending upon how badly they need warm bodies, of course, but that's what it is now and has been for the last several months or so." He tipped ash into a heavy cut-glass ashtray.

"So there's the situation in a nutshell. You'll be sleeping in a bunk in Fort Hood, Texas, in"—he glanced at the order—"three Monday nights from now."

"Mr. Crozier, I do want you to save me from being drafted if you can, especially since I shouldn't have been called up, but I don't have two thousand dollars."

"You can call me Chuck." I didn't think I could actually do that.

He considered the glowing tip of his cigar.

"You aren't interested in emigrating to Canada, which is not extraditing American youths protesting their induction? No?"

"No. The important thing to me is staying in my band. We're beginning to achieve the dreams we've fought so hard for. I think it will kill me to get left behind."

"I'm going to make another exception in your case." He considered his words for a moment. "Though you'll have to take my word for it, I have already made one concession to offer you this service for two thousand dollars. Though I may be able to waive my fee, some people in this chain either cannot or will not waive theirs. So there is a minimum expense you must meet."

His pale blue eyes drilled into mine. "If you can find fifteen hundred dollars, I guarantee you will not spend one day of service in our armed forces, all accomplished entirely legally. Do you believe me?"

"Yes sir. I do."

"Then get the money together. It is not an impossible feat. If you have to suck some dicks to get this money, do it, as it will most likely save your life. When you have it, call me, and we'll get started. But you've only got a week; there are things that must be set in motion."

53
GAY IN LA

*Acting is all about honesty. If you can
fake that, you've got it made.*

— George Burns

June 28, 1967
Downey, California

BACK IN MY rooms in Downy later that afternoon, I sat on the short couch with Marie and Dave, describing my meeting with Charles Crozier. "He is one scary son of a bitch," I finished. "But he's right. Somehow I have to find the money."

"Crap man, I gotta couple hundred bucks you can have." Dave scratched his head. "Probably just gamble it away in Vegas anyway, and this sounds like it might be a real shot."

I grinned at him. "I'll bear it in mind, brother. If I feel it could make a difference, I'll let you know." He nodded his head decisively.

"Larry," Marie said. "I still have a little bit of the money left . . . I could give you two hundred dollars, too."

I walked over and leaned down to kiss her. "Same deal as with Dave," I said, but it wasn't true. I couldn't take any money from her. I was glad she'd come to stay with me, in fact, I didn't know what I would have done without her in the night. But we both knew I was taking advantage of her feelings.

"Maybe we should try to hit up the band?"

I gave Dave a wry smile and shook my head. I could accept money from him because he was my best friend. I was sure I could get the money back to him if I accepted his offer, but if for some reason I couldn't, our friendship wouldn't be damaged. A loan between us was just something between two friends. I couldn't ask the other guys: it could create a difficult situation for those who might want to, but had other mouths to feed, or for those who didn't want to, who might feel coerced or resentful.

"Mac's contacted Glen Hughes from the Casinos," Dave said. "Wants him to come out here to replace you."

I could feel the bile bite in my stomach. I'd always knew Mac wanted someone who could move around on the stage better than me. My shoulders slumped. Now he'd get his wish. Glen was Mac's best friend from his old band, and he had a good voice, too. Maybe everybody would think he was an upgrade, maybe I'd be replaced no matter what happened. I understood they had to think of the band first, I got that. I didn't like that it was happening so fast, though.

Mark popped his head in and knocked on the open door. "Am I interrupting? Just wanted to hear how things went with Crozier."

"Well, he asked me to call him Chuck, and that's not going to happen."

He laughed. After I'd told him what the attorney had offered, Mark grinned at me. "Well thank God for small favors. I've been talking a little with George. I think he's willing to swing a thousand bucks for you."

"What? Wait now. You said a thousand dollars? He'd give me a thousand dollars?" I jumped up and grabbed Mark and bounced him around. Dave was hugging and bouncing Marie around.

"Yeah, yeah," Mark stuttered until I let him down. "But we still got to find five hundred somewhere."

"I'm putting up two," Dave said, grinning. "We're damned close." Dave was right. With what I would earn in the next few weeks, there would be enough money.

The Psychology Center was a single-story building south of little Santa Monica in west Los Angeles. The reception area was a narrow room with the east wall, all windows, facing a residential street. The receptionist checked her list and smiled at me. "Yes, Mr. Dunlap, Mr. Crozier's office told us to expect you." She stood and took a few steps to point me at a room down the corridor.

A polite older lady there had me sit opposite her at a table. Vines grown over the edges of the windows created a light and pleasant atmosphere, reminding me, for some reason, of kindergarten. She administered a battery of tests that included some innocuous questions about what kind of food I preferred, attitudes I expected from friends, how many drinks I had per week, how I felt about politics, and whether I smoked. Then she gave me multiple-choice questions where I chose things I agreed with, or didn't, on a scale of one to five. The tests finished with me fitting wooden shapes into a board with carved-out matching holes while she timed me.

Within an hour, I was on my way back to Downey without much comprehension of what the tests had accomplished.

At six thirty, the Monday morning designated in my induction orders, I stepped out of a cab in an industrial area near Long Beach Harbor. The sun struggled to lift itself high enough over the horizon to burn off the onshore cloud cover. A hulking, block-long, windowless building swallowed hundreds of guys of every size, shape, and color, carrying suitcases, duffels, even paper bags. The air from the ocean was cool, heavy with humidity and the smell of the sea as I paid the driver. A shiver passed through me in the dark morning that had less to do with the chill and more to do with the few anxious hours of restless sleep I'd gotten. Last chance, I could still opt for Canada, I thought, knowing I couldn't. I hefted my cheap sports bag with three sets of underwear, socks, a pair of jeans, and fresh tees.

Marie had cried last night when I told her I planned to take a cab. I was afraid I'd make an ass of myself if she dropped me off. Once I walked in this place, I might not see her, or anyone else I knew, for months. If I didn't come back, she'd have to pack up and drive my car to Northern California. But she believed, even more than I did, that I'd get out. She promised to wait by the phone, ready to come get me when I called. I shuffled reluctantly toward the cavernous door, remembering how I'd walked off the Pink Carousel's stage only a few hours ago.

Closing nights can be bittersweet, but this one was funereal. All the guys in the band had stopped by my room last night to say goodbye before they packed for the drive to Las Vegas.

"Think this Crozier guy's on the level?" Mac asked me.

"Man, I hope so. He sounds so certain." Everyone nodded and said things like, "No problem, we'll see you in Vegas, man." What I heard was, "Be realistic, man, maybe you should just resign your sorry ass to what's about to happen." I could tell none of them thought they'd see me anytime soon.

Glen Hughes had rehearsed with the band all last week. I'd offered to teach him my parts, but Les pretty much handled everything. Mac had already begun working on dance moves with Glen. *The band must already be halfway across the desert, on their way to Las Vegas and the Cat.*

Despite Crozier's instructions, I wasn't so confident. Last Tuesday afternoon, his office had called to set an appointment for me to come in. Just three days ago. I'd been nervous; he seemed to be cutting things very close.

"I waited until the last minute because I don't want you to over-think this," he'd said as we settled into chairs in the same room where I'd first met him. "You are going to be excused from the armed services because you are a homosexual man, which is not an accepted sexual practice in the army."

I sat dumbfounded, hearing this for the first time. "You're saying I have to pretend to be queer to get out of the army?"

"No, not at all. You are expressly *not* to act gay. This is exactly why I didn't want to discuss this with you until the last minute. The last thing I want you to do is to pretend to be a homosexual. I want you to look at me. Do you think I'm gay?"

I wasn't sure how to answer correctly. Charles Crozier didn't seem swishy. In fact, he seemed pretty macho and intensely scary. A couple of little inconsistencies, I supposed, effeminacies, perhaps, that could be true of anybody if you were looking for those kind of clues. I was leaning toward answering no, but still uncertain whether this was a trick question, when he spoke.

"You are over-thinking your answer. If you saw me on the street, or in conversation, or in a casual or public setting, would you automatically think I was a gay man?"

"No sir, I don't think I can imagine you as a gay man, actually."

"Sorry to disabuse you, but I am, in fact, very gay, though I do not advertise my inclination, and I will thank you not to, either." His piercing eyes chilled me.

"The point is, one cannot 'act' gay. The only difference between hetero- and homosexual men is gender preference. You are who you are; if you happen to prefer men over women, then that's who you are. If you try to act like some simpering fool, you'll completely mess this up." He stopped to light a menthol cigarette with a gold lighter. "This is the most crucial aspect of our endeavor. Do you grasp this concept completely?"

"Sounds like you just want me to be myself."

"Precisely what you must do. Now, I'm going to ask you some questions and I want to hear your answers."

"First of all, are you queer, gay, homosexual?"

A trap, of course.

"Yes."

"Tell me. Tell me what you would say if someone asked you."

"Mr. Crozier, I am a gay man."

He smiled reluctantly. "Okay. Good enough. Tell me where you go to hang out in Hollywood."

"Hm. Well I don't actually hang out in Hollywood, but sometimes we play at the Hullabaloo afterhours, and we've played at the Red Velvet and Gazzaris."

"Where would you go after performing at these places?"

"That's easy. Cantor's Deli on Fairfax. They're open twenty-four hours with a huge menu, and I love good deli food. The place is jammed on weekends after midnight."

"Perfect."

We went on in this vein of me describing various aspects of my life, none of them earth shattering. When he thought I was prepped enough, he handed me a plain envelope containing the results from the test I'd taken at the psychologist's lab with a final admonition.

"None of this will make any difference if you don't get the psychological profile in this envelope to the on-duty psychiatrist at the Induction Center. This is the part only you can do, and it's crucial. You must get the sergeant in charge to let you go to the psychiatrist no matter what it takes. Otherwise, you will shortly be on a bus to Texas. However, accomplish this task, and I guarantee you will be free of your indenture."

As I entered the warehouse-like building, I frantically ran Charles Crozier's final instructions through my mind. I passed by two tough-looking soldiers at each side of the wide double doors, their attention focused into the dim interior, probably to keep anyone who'd already entered from changing their mind. The closest soldier looked at me dispassionately, as if I were a cow on the way to the sledgehammer.

More soldiers funneled us into two lines. We handed in our orders and received a canvas bag with a drawstring, a small bag with a wrist strap and a piece of paper. I added my psychological profile to the paper they gave me. Except for the shuffling sound of shoes on concrete, gruff reminders to "keep moving" and "follow the arrows," and occasionally, "no talking," the area was unnervingly quiet. Big red arrows were painted on the walls. *Thousands of men and boys must have passed through here.* For the first time, I considered an aspect I hadn't thought of before. *How many of them are still alive?*

I continued with everyone else through gloomy tunnels formed by canvas walls, where I sensed, from an occasional soft cough and the sounds of movement, there were many more men here. The atmosphere reeked of tension; my anal sphincter puckered. A soldier stood in front of us, directing us to the left into a large expanse with a couple of hundred other men. Two soldiers were lining us up into rows. I was in the front row near one end.

"You men," shouted out a sergeant who stepped in front of us. He sported three chevrons on his arm. "Form up to the man on your left so that your line is even, and form up to the man in front, so your column is straight. You men in the front row, starting on my right, extend your left arm until you are an inch away from the man on your left. Not you, you idiot. You are the first man in the row; there is no one to your left." This was directed to the poor slob who was on the opposite end of my row. When we were all finally standing in the required formation, the sergeant continued.

"Drop your suitcases, backpacks, bundles with your fresh clothes on the floor." He paced up and down in front of us. "Now disrobe. Disrobe down to your underpants and socks, people. Every other stitch of clothing must come off and be placed in the large bag. The contents of your pockets, rings, wrist watches, jewelry, valuables of any kind, must be placed in the small bag." He continued pacing and peering down each column. "Do not, I repeat, do not, leave any valuables in your belongings. Put them in the little bag." Two other sergeants worked between the rows to expedite matters.

"The large bag will remain here with your other belongings until you are returned here. The small bag with your valuables must be attached to your wrist by the appropriate strap. If you lose this bag, you will not get it back. When you finish disrobing—you in the back, all the way down to your skivvies, mister. No tee shirts. When all your clothes are in that sack, look for the sticky number on the paper you were given. Peel the number off and stick it onto the bag. Stand up straight when you are finished. I am only going to warn you once not to lose that paper in your hand. If you somehow manage to lose it, you'll not only lose your clothes, but you may end up in this man's army for the rest of your life. If we don't have a record of you being in the army, we damn sure won't let you out of it."

I guess he thought he was being funny, at least to himself.

"Okay. Now turn to your left. Everyone. Even you, that dumbass that turned to his right. Turn to *your* left idiot, not mine. Now follow the man to your left or, if you are on the end, follow the man in the row ahead of you as he passes by, through this opening." He pointed to where the dark green canvas had been thrown back to reveal a room similar to the one we were leaving.

In a serpentine unwinding, the group of us followed one another like ants into the new room. Was I going to be able to get up the courage to do what I was going to have to do? I often got butterflies before performing, but this felt like horses galloping through my guts. It would be so much harder if I lost my stomach contents out either end in the middle of this.

We stood stoically, as a group of doctors, or so I supposed they were, came into the room to give us each a cursory physical. This included checking our pupils and pulse, pulling down our underwear, grasping our testicles with cold fingers and asking us to cough, and then marking on our papers. The humiliating experience was over in about half an hour, but afterward, we were forced to continue standing in our underwear and socks, holding our paper and the little wrist bag for some interminable amount of time. We probably stood in place for about an hour; if so, it was one of the longest hours of my life. Cold seeped up through my socks into my feet from the smooth concrete floor. I hated standing here in my underwear, and I'm sure every man jack of us felt the same. Many of my companions stood woebegone with hands crossed, clutching their genitals as if they were afraid they'd fall off onto the floor.

Eventually, a different sergeant came into our room, formed us up, and moved us into a vast area already full of men. We filed into the front. I couldn't get a full view, but I was sure there were several hundred men in this much larger area. As we lined up, my mouth went dry as the Nevada desert the guys were probably crossing about now. I shut down the sudden last-minute fear that nothing Crozier had told me was true, and croaked out, "Sergeant, sir."

No one said anything to me, no one looked at me. Maybe I hadn't actually said anything, only thought I had.

I spoke up again, "Sergeant, sir," listening to be certain I was speaking out loud, but still no response.

I stepped out of line and screamed desperately, "Sergeant, sir!" Everything stopped. Probably because I'd stepped out of line.

The sergeant walked up to me, looking at me as if I was something vomited on the floor. *I bet someone has done that here before.*

"Did you have something to say to me?" He looked at me like, *Say anything and I'll chew your ass from here to Southeast Asia.*

He clearly did not want me to speak, but before he could turn away, I said, voice quavering, but clear, "I want to see the psychiatrist, sir."

He turned away as if I hadn't spoken. I heard Charles Crozier's voice in my head: *You must get to the psychiatrist. If you don't, the buses in the back of the building will take you nonstop to Fort Hood.*

Where was my band? I thought wildly. *Were they in Las Vegas yet? Only one way to get back to them.*

"I need to see the psychiatrist!" I screeched. All the men around me stopped breathing. Nobody moved, but I still felt them shrink away from me. The sergeant slowly returned to face me.

"And why, pray tell, do you need to see a psychiatrist?" That's what his voice said, almost gently. What his face said was, *You fucking pissant sonofabitch, shut the fuck up and get back in line before I ream you up the ass with a baton, which I will surely do once I get you alone.*

I couldn't have felt more exposed had I been singing the national anthem buck-naked at the Super Bowl. And the situation was about to get worse. I didn't dare glance toward the person next to me. My view narrowed down to the sergeant's collar point as I felt the heat rise on my face.

"I'm gay, sir." Crozier said to use the word gay, which was becoming the accepted label, not the more clinical term, homosexual. Gay, he said, would be less inciting. *Of course, he's not here with me though, is he?*

"What did you say?" The sergeant marched up into my personal space, only inches separating us. I clenched my eyes and put all my fear and frustration into my declaration. "I said, I am a gay man, sir."

It was deafeningly silent. Except for the sound of quiet breathing, I might have been all alone. The whir of a distant turbine started up, probably to power the whispering fans moving air above the tented partitions throughout the gigantic building. *Maybe everyone had heard me, from one end of the place to the other.* I opened my eyes because I was getting a little unsteady. The sergeant stood right where I'd left him. He spoke in a normal voice.

"Go through that opening." He gestured. "The soldier there will direct you." He turned, excising me from the human race, no longer worthy of his attention, as he shouted directions to the rest of the men.

I staggered on stick-rotten legs through the opening where another sergeant stood in a narrow space between the canvas-created rooms. He had only one chevron. "Wait here" was all he said, though without rancor. It was cold, and I began to shiver and then I almost fell down. I was reacting to the experience I'd gone through. *It's not over yet*, I reminded myself.

In a few minutes, the new sergeant appeared, with my sports bag and the large canvas bag. At an empty bench, I put my clothes back on. I was walked to the back of the building and left where an open stairwell led to a suspended second story. A receptionist at the top of the stairs took my paper and the psychological profile I'd brought, and invited me to sit on one of the empty couches in a waiting area. Behind her, a corridor extended away with office doors on each side.

I prepared myself for a Perry Mason-style cross-examination meant to discover my deception. A polite civilian gentleman with a friendly smile asked me into one of the offices, where a pebbly glass skylight with embedded screening let in soft light. He accepted my papers and asked questions similar to the ones I'd been asked before, in Crozier's and the psychologist's office. When I mentioned frequenting Cantor's Deli, a confirming nod from my interviewer made me feel as though I'd delivered some sort of secret code. He inked and pounded a stamp into a box on the paper I'd gotten downstairs, before stapling the psychological profile to it. He smiled as he handed them back to me. The receptionist slapped the papers into a file tray, made a couple of checkmarks on a green card, then signed and handed the card to me. She gave me another warm smile and directed me through a door on the other side of the suspended floor. I was afraid to look at the card. What if I was marked for life as some kind of sexual deviant? Maybe I should have gone to Canada? Maybe I'd still have to.

I felt drained as I pushed through the metal door that slammed behind me with the solid thunk of a fire door. I looked around, confused. I was all alone on a long metal landing; the only way down, naked iron steps to a narrow, dimly lit corridor. I turned back to the metal door—locked. I considered knocking, but my capacity for confrontation had been exceeded. With no other choice, I descended. Finding another metal door to the right, I pushed into brilliant California sunshine. It cascaded onto my face. A few steps to the sidewalk and I was fifty feet from the doors, now closed like the gates into Mordor, where I'd entered the building at dawn. The card I'd been handed was a temporary draft card. I was rated 1Y. I didn't know what that meant, but it wasn't 1A, and unless someone came rushing out to get me, the nightmare was over. I got out my wristwatch; nearly eleven o'clock. I'd been in the clutches of the army for four and a half hours, though I felt as though I'd been there all day. I thought for a moment about all the guys still inside, and the entirety of the experience hit me in a rush.

Maybe I hadn't truly believed I'd get out. I hadn't considered how I was going to call Marie. I spotted a pay phone across the street at the corner. It was impossible to express how beautiful her voice sounded when she answered. I was still sitting on the curb, confounded, when an endless train of dull green buses began pulling out from behind the building, rumbling away toward the Long Beach Freeway.

54
GET ME TO THE CAT ON TIME

... one of those fortunate men who, if they were to dive under one side of a barge Stark-Naked, would come up on the other with a new suit of clothes on, and a ticket for soup in the waistcoat-pocket.

— Charles Dickens

July 18, 1967
Downey, California

I STOOD FOR A moment outside my room. I turned to Marie, taking her, the sky, the sun, and the sparkling perfect day, in with the unfettered eyes of the newly saved. Once inside, my first thought was to call Las Vegas.

"Holy shit. I can't believe it," Dave said. I heard him pull the receiver away from his ear to yell, "Hey you guys, it's Larry. He's not in the army."

"And I'll be in Vegas tomorrow, Dave—you hear me? So don't let Glen-fucking-Hughes on the stage. Protect my gig, okay?"

"Ha ha. Okay, I'll tell everybody. Hey great news, man. Now you'll be able to give me the two hundred bucks I lent you so I can lose it on a blackjack table where it was meant to be wasted."

I dialed Charles Crozier's office. He was in a meeting, but his secretary promised to pass on the news. Next was George Simone, whose genuine pleasure heartened me. He told me he wanted the band booked back into the Pink Carousel as soon as possible. I knocked on Mark's door on our way up to my place but no answer. If I didn't see him before

I left, I'd leave a note asking him to thank Thom Keith for me and letting him know how to contact me in Las Vegas.

After the calls, and inhaling a fast-food sandwich for breakfast, I couldn't sleep until I'd showered the army induction center off my skin. Marie waited between the sheets for me, and soon, though not right away, I fell off the face of the world.

Marie was needed back in Fremont to help with her grandfather's failing health, so I took her to the train station and lit out for Vegas. I'd called her, hoping she would come, because I'd never felt more alone. I thought about the way she stood by me, knowing all the while I couldn't match her feelings. I appreciated having her with me with all my heart, and hoped that would be enough.

Accelerating onto the I-15 east from the San Bernardino Freeway, up the switchbacks into the high desert toward Nevada, I realized how disconnected I'd become from my family. It wasn't just being out of sight, out of mind, eighteen hundred miles and two time zones away, or even the difference in lifestyle. Somehow, I'd lost all connection to my little boys, along with any communication with Pat, who, besides being my wife, had been the rock I'd built my life on. I didn't feel as though there was anyone in Indianapolis with solely my interests at heart. In that moment, the place where I felt the truest sense of kinship was with the guys in my band. I got shivers realizing how close I'd come to losing that. I'd be on stage with them at the Cat tonight if I had to fight somebody.

I pulled into the Pussycat parking lot in under five hours, stopping only for gas and to check the radiator in Baker. My dependable little Ford Falcon might be ugly and basic, but it had gotten me across the Mojave again, this time in the height of summer. I rode most of the way with the windows down, broiling in the dry-sauna wind to save the little engine. Unkinking my legs, still dusty and dirty, I rushed into the nightclub, where the band waited for me. My eyes stung in the barrage of congratulations and welcoming hugs, until I noticed Craig's sour face.

"Well, glad you got here, but what about the money we spent to fly Mac's buddy out here? Do I get my money back?"

"Hey jerk-off," Mac said, rounding on him. "That money come out of the group fund, and it's just for shit like this. Ain't yours or anybody else's. We couldn't have counted on Larry pullin off a damn miracle like he did. Had to have us a backup." Craig was not making himself a lot of friends.

At a table apart from the others, Glen Hughes sat, legs crossed like a yogi in the seat of a chair, smoking a cigarette with a highball glass in front of him. He'd let his hair grow out into a wild afro since I'd last seen him. Even more wiry than Mac, he had bright, tiny dark eyes that always seemed as near to anger as laughter. He looked to me like a pale kewpie doll. He flicked ash in the general direction of an ashtray.

"Who'd have believed you'd beat the fucking draft? Well, you got your job back, but I woulda kicked your ass if it had been a competition." His teasing cut too close to the bone.

I fixed a plastic smile on my face. I didn't feel like I'd beaten anything. I didn't have a political position or care about any of that. The army induction meant nothing to me other than an obstacle I had to overcome to be with these guys, my guys, to win back my place in the band.

"Did you get my suits cleaned?" I asked Leonard. "You didn't have them altered or anything, did you?"

"What? No man, course not. Wouldn't do that unless you weren't coming back for sure," Leonard said. "How'd you do it? Hoped you would, but we didn't think there was any way."

The residue of anxiety and lack of rest began catching up to me. I slid into a chair and pulled out a cigarette. I sat for a moment wondering where to start while I lit up and expelled a lungful of smoke.

"Scariest, weirdest thing I have seen or done. I don't ever want to go through anything like it again. Had to stand up to some goddamned gorilla sergeant in front of a huge warehouse full of guys, all of us in our underpants, and tell 'em I wanted to see the psychiatrist because I was a queer. Had to yell out, 'I'm a gay, homosexual man.'"

A couple of guys chuckled. They didn't really get it, of course. If they had, they'd realize there was nothing funny in that fresh memory I had.

"After I got out of this huge building, I sat on the curb outside waiting for Marie to come get me, just digging the sunshine, you know, and thinking about how soon I could start for Vegas. A few minutes before she got there army buses started flying out of the alley next to the big warehouse I'd been in. One after another, turning down the block from where I'm sitting across the street. I knew where they were going: right to the freeway and all the way to Texas."

I thought about all those boys who'd stood next to me inside, now riding in those buses, and how I could've, maybe even should've, been with them. *Goddammit*, I thought, *why didn't you guys yell out, too?*

"Bus after bus after bus, out of the alley, still turning toward the freeway as Marie drove me away in the opposite direction. Out of more than a thousand guys, I was the only one, far as I could tell, who got out. I mean there I sat, all by myself on that damn curb, while those poor bastards rode off to war." I gazed down, swept a palm across the table.

"Thought about them while I drove here, wondering what will happen to them, how much danger they're in." I glanced up at my friends' faces.

"And look at me. Here I am in fucking Las Vegas with you guys, with my brothers. Did what I had to do, you know." I was choking, trying not to break out in manic laughter, trying to keep the desperation I'd felt from spilling out.

"Had to get back here, this is where I'm supposed to be, where I need to be." I gritted out a pained smile, through misty eyes.

"You got that right man," Mac said, leaning over to clap me on the shoulder. "We're family." Dave smiled and nodded; murmurs of assent from everyone except Craig. He sulked off by himself somewhere.

Little by little, I fell back into our old routines, sliding into the leader responsibilities again, and the relative easiness of our way of life: singing and playing at the Cat at night, rehearsing new songs, or working on a tan at one of the hotel swimming pools during the day. But I tried to hold onto a newfound appreciation for how much this life and my bandmates meant to me, for as long as I could. It would be a long time before I could put my experience at the induction center behind me.

A reference copy of our new single arrived by mail via Eve, from Eddie. The artist name printed on the record label read "S.N. and THE Ct's". What in hell did that mean? Another case where our name jumped up and bit us, like Caesars? Worse, the record itself disturbed and disappointed us. *The Pleasure of Your Company* was the A-side, while *Maria, Love and Music*, the song we'd had the most hopes for, had been banished to the B-side, where it would probably never be heard. On both songs, Eddie's final mix buried the background harmonies we'd worked so hard on in bottomless echo and countless overdubs. Dave's voice came across as strained and uncomfortable in many places, especially at the end of *Maria*, and for some unfathomable reason, Eddie had added weird, extraneous instrumentation to both tracks. I hadn't been crazy about *The Pleasure of Your Company* to begin with, but I'd hoped our voices and the arrangement would shine through, at least. What could Eddie have been thinking?

At least we have a record coming out, I tried to tell myself, *maybe something will happen. Nobody knows what makes a record a hit.* We didn't say so to each other, but instead of expecting our creative and smooth vocals to guarantee us a hit, we'd been reduced to hoping to get lucky.

A week later, Eve sent a page cut from *Billboard* magazine picking *The Pleasure of Your Company* to hit Billboard's Hot 100 chart, and a bunch of notices from around the country about how well it was being received by the deejays.

Les got us together for a half-hearted attempt to learn *Pleasure* and *Maria, Love and Music*, for live performance. We found it impossible to reproduce the deep, layered harmony live. In the studio, we'd used Dave's voice to thicken the harmony, as well as for the lead. Even with four background voices, we couldn't cover the top harmony part, and the rest of our vocals sounded thin. And Dave still hadn't figured out what to do at the end of *Maria*. After a few futile attempts, we gave up the effort. That was something we should have realized then; if we didn't want to play our own recorded songs live, something was radically wrong.

We'd learned from the rounders that you didn't have to be a guest to use the pools at the hotels, just wear shorts with a bathing suit underneath, find a bathroom to slip out of the shorts, and walk out to the pool, where attendants came by with towels and took drink requests. It wasn't a coincidence that the pool attendant taking care of us at the Flamingo was a fan from the Pussycat.

Mac and I lay out on towel-covered redwood recliners in the shade of giant umbrellas, sipping margaritas on the house, watching bikini-clad foxes strut past. Though the heat index was well over a hundred, it was comfortable where we were by the pool. I asked Mac about a couple of things that were making my brain itch. One was why he hadn't held out for Glen to replace me even though I'd managed to avoid the army. I told him I'd always thought that he would've liked to replace me with his best friend. This had been his best chance.

"Nah man, ain't so. Always your gig far as I'm concerned," he said, adding a laugh. "Guess there ain't no doubt you want it."

"Thought I might have to give Glen a knuckle sandwich, or wrestle the both of you, to get my job back," I said with a chuckle.

His eyes crinkled when he smiled. "Love Glen like a brother. Like brothers do, though, we fought a lot, even in the Casinos, mostly about stupid shit. You, you're my newer brother, and the thing about you is, you care about the band, always trying to do the best you can for it. Don't always agree with everything you do, but always feel I can trust you cause of that. Can't say that about Glen, much as I love him. Even straight up, I'd have to take you over him to work with." That warmed my heart.

We sipped our drinks and considered the poolside scenery.

"Funny, the things you chew over when you're driving across the desert alone. I got to thinking about how Pat and Bunny became girlfriends back when you joined the group, how they went off to Cincinnati together that night. I feel kind of guilty about it, I never should have let her get into that situation—she was not prepared for Bunny."

Nothing had prepared any of us in the group for Mac's live-in call girl. We referred to Bunny as Mac's girlfriend because we didn't know what else to call her. They seemed like a couple, but I couldn't grasp the idea of a guy letting his girlfriend have sex with other guys for money.

In the years since we'd met in high school, Pat had either sung with my group or had naturally been friends with everyone in it, and by extension, their girlfriends, because we all hung out together. So, I shouldn't have been surprised that before I'd figured out a way to explain about Bunny, Pat had cultivated a friendship with Mac's girlfriend without reservation. I just didn't notice she had—and I didn't know Mac was leading a double life.

One night Bunny phoned Pat to ask her to go on a field trip to check up on Mac. Jealous by nature anyway, she'd begun to suspect he was sneaking off to see someone in Cincinnati. The girls planned the excursion on a night when the group had scheduled a rehearsal, so Mac would be occupied. I can't say for sure that Pat kept it a secret from me, though I'm pretty sure if she told me she planned a trip to another state with Bunny, it wouldn't have slipped past me.

They left in late afternoon, and the expedition didn't turn out well for anyone. Bunny, unable to restrain her anger, confronted Mac's other love interest, who turned out instead to be his wife. The scene that resulted shocked all three of them. Bunny drove the hundred miles back to Indianapolis like a bat out of hell, giving Pat time to call me before rehearsal ended. Shaken by the near fist fight between the two women, and realizing the real relationship between them, she wanted me to warn Mac that Bunny was waiting for him, dead set on mayhem. Pat felt bad for both Bunny and Joan, and had no recriminations for Mac. Her generous nature was one of the many things I loved about her.

"Bunny damn near killed me after that, you know, twice with a knife and once with a gun," Mac said. "And that weren't nothin compared to what Joan wanted to do to me. But you're right. Never would've forgiven myself either if somethin had happened to Pat that night."

"Can I ask you a question? Kind of personal?"

"Sure. Why not?"

"I never understood about you and Bunny. I mean how you two got together."

"Wasn't no Bunny and me, not like you mean, not really." Mac's brow wrinkled in dismay. "Like you know, I got in a fight with Glen before I left the band, but it was his brother, Gene, wantin to take over the band and make the rest of us sidemen that pissed me off. Fought with Glen 'cause he let me down, not standin up to Gene with me like he said he would. Bunny was with Gene then, not me. Yeah, she'd made it clear she had eyes for me, but that big house of hers"—he shook his head—"just sposed to be a place to stay in Indianapolis when the Casinos went back to Cincy." He shook his head in irritation with himself. "Just plain stupid that things got further than that, and then she got all possessive."

"Well, she did buy you a lot of clothes and jewelry and stuff. Seem to recall you cruising around in a new Pontiac Bonneville you told me she bought you. And, oh"—I grinned—"there was the money she gave you . . ."

"There was that, sure. See, we had an understandin. She wasn't sposed to put no hold on me, though. To me, it was more of a job. I got money and things like that so she'd look like she had herself a man when she was out in public. Kept the pimps off her, she said. She wanted arm candy, didn't want me out on the street if I wasn't turned out. I always had to look good so she'd look good, even if she wasn't with me. That's why she got me them things. Guess after a while she figured she'd bought me with 'em, though I never thought of most of that shit as mine. Left it all behind when I left Indianapolis. I didn't expect her to get so attached."

"Guess things must have been pretty messed up between you and Joan back then."

Mac sighed and closed his eyes before he spoke to me. "It was a real confusing time, we was trying to figure out a lotta shit."

"Thing is," I said, "soon as the band got going out here, even though its future was kinda shaky, you sent for Joan and Dani—first thing, man."

"Damn straight. We always planned to make it outta Cincy together when I hit the big time. We promised each other when we first got together in school. Nothing's ever going to change that."

I thought about Mac and Joan, and looked inside myself.

"I wanted that with Pat, you know. I didn't want things to end the way they did, her and the kids gone, all that. She said she'd move out here to California with the boys, but I wouldn't let her, didn't believe it was the right thing to do. But I wonder about it sometimes, like when I was driving here from LA. I think about ways we might have been able to make it work, if we could have gotten some help from my family, maybe. Or if we had planned it out, somehow. Maybe if she would've been willing to go back to Indiana until we got more stable. If we'd talked about it when I was better able to think." I closed my eyes for a minute. "And then I think about all the reasons why I know it was the right decision." I looked at Mac. "But I'll always wonder . . ."

55
LARRY LAMB

I don't mind being Naked.

— Nicole Kidman

July 27, 1967
Las Vegas, Nevada

THERE ARE FEW cooler moments in life for a singer than when you hear your own record on the radio for the first time. I heard *The Pleasure of Your Company* from a radio tuned to a Las Vegas rock station on a side table a few feet away from where I was laid out poolside at the Sands. You expect everyone within hearing distance to realize the world has changed in that moment, though the difference is only in you.

When the big vocal harmony began, even through the tinny little speaker, I could tell that it was us. Despite the muddy, yelling way our voices sounded and the other problems, I heard our signature sound. *Nobody else sounds like that except us*! I glowed inside.

Hearing us on the radio like this was very different from the first time I heard *In the Still of the Night* on a radio. For one thing, I realized now how difficult it is to create a quality record, find a record label to release it, a distributor to distribute it, and then getting radio stations to play the damn thing on the radio. I realized with new appreciation what amazing luck we'd had two and a half years ago. Everything had gone so fast and been so unexpected back then, it had seemed like magic. We'd never even heard our record played on the radio until the weekend we went to Chicago to promote it. We heard ourselves announced as the Reflections and then heard our song on a car radio on the way to a WLS sponsored sock hop. Though all the Chicago stations were playing *In the Still of the Night* in regular rotation, and everyone there seemed to know who we were, no station played it in Indianapolis. Back in Indianapolis, the whole thing had seemed like a group hallucination. Not being able to share that momentous event with our friends and family only heightened the Twilight Zone sensation. By the time we'd come to understand that we might actually become nationally known recording artists, it was over, like waking from a month long dream. Just as we realized what could have been, it had slipped from our fingers, and the anonymity we fell into was even deeper because of it.

Here in Las Vegas, in this international Mecca of entertainment, our record was being played for everyone to hear. Even when I didn't hear it, I knew it was in the invisible radio waves all around me. Someone, somewhere in Las Vegas, was listening to us every time it came on their radio. Having people at the Cat tell us at night how much they liked hearing our song on the radio, and the big crowds made us feel more comfortable with our growing celebrity.

One night, Mac brought a guy to the stage to meet the band. As usual, Mac had managed to meet everyone in the room.

"Guys, this is Larry Lamb. Wants to buy the band a drink."

The gangly young man with a big, goofy grin on his face standing alongside Mac wore jeans, a checked woolen shirt, and scuffed cowboy boots. He might've just thrown his reins over a hitching post outside, maybe left his hat and spurs at the bar.

"Yup I do. You boys are the gol-damndest best band I ever heard, and I heard a lot of 'em. Grew up in this town, never missed anybody good that came through here. Seen Paul Revere and the Raiders, and the Checkmates in this joint. Them boys is good, but you kick their asses." He was wild-eyed, obviously having put away more than a few drinks already. I didn't know yet how normal that was for him.

Up on stage, Mac pulled us aside. "You know who this Larry Lamb guy is? Ever check who signed your Sheriff's card?" To work in any capacity where there's gambling in Las Vegas, you had to be fingerprinted, pass a background check, and keep your Clark County Sherriff's photo ID card with you at all times.

"Never mind, you don't need to look. Card's signed by Sheriff Ralph

Lamb, Larry Lamb's big brother. Another Lamb brother's a state senator and another a county commissioner. We need to stay right with this guy."

When a tray of shots appeared at the stage's edge, Mac thanked Larry Lamb from the stage, and we gave him a salute. I set my shooter aside for one of the other guys. So did Les and Leonard.

Our closing week passed quickly. We had time to add a couple of Young Rascals songs to our play list, *Good Lovin'* and *How Can I Be Sure*, along with Van Morrison's laid-back and very cool *Brown-Eyed Girl*.

Howard King put us out on a two-month road trip at very good money after the Pussycat. We would have preferred to be promoting our record, but it had fizzled out on the East Coast, after a promising start. It was still in regular rotation in Las Vegas when we left for four weeks in Vancouver, Canada, but the label's PR machine had gone silent. I doubted it was being heard anywhere else.

Oil Can Harry's in the west end of Vancouver was an extravagant three-floor nightclub. An elegant restaurant and small piano lounge filled the main floor; a large showroom where we played, the second; and a dance room called the Back Door on top. Every day, the restaurant laid out a gigantic freshly poached salmon on a serving table at lunchtime, refreshed as needed and free to patrons and employees. Whenever we were in the club for rehearsal, we flaked off platefuls of this amazing feast.

We rearranged our song list into three one-hour shows, repeating a few of the most popular numbers for each show, and adding a three-song Beatles medley that went over big at Oil Can's. I'd grown to accept and appreciate the Beatles loose and easy harmony, which sprang from the newer, more modern concept of a group of singer/songwriters, each backing each other up when they sang leads, a style quite different than ours. We were built around a primary lead singer backed by tight, blended harmony. And we hadn't learned how to be songwriters.

Vancouver was Canada's San Francisco, though this city seemed even more international, the way I imagined a European city would be. When I couldn't find anywhere to buy American cigarettes, I asked a clerk at a tobacconist near our hotel why. She made a clucking sound and said with pity, "American cigarettes? First off, don't be so arrogant, Canadians are Americans too, eh? And second—buy the English Ovals—they're better cigarettes than you can get in the States anyway."

The audiences were enthusiastic and friendly. Danny Baceda, the owner, made sure we had fun and told me we'd be welcome back anytime, an offer we would have loved to accept if Vancouver hadn't been fifteen hundred miles north of LA—two full driving days from Las Vegas. I wouldn't have minded another month in the fantastic atmosphere of Oil Can's and the beautiful city and countryside of British Columbia, but we were booked for four weeks at the Lemon Tree Lounge in Sparks, Nevada, just outside of Reno, before we returned to the Cat.

One Thursday at the Lemon Tree, before our last set, the dressing room went quiet.

"Say that again," said Les, frowning.

"Ron's got a friend in the club who wants to see if we'll actually go out on stage naked," I repeated. Ron Stevens was the club owner. "Ron will give us six one-hundred-dollar bills if we do. Says the guy has some kind of terminal illness or whatever, and he wants us to do this as a favor for him."

"Weird favor," Les said. "You guys do whatever you want, but I'm not going out there naked."

"At least you can hide behind your guitar, Les. What are Mac and I supposed to do?" Dave glanced in apprehension at Mac.

"I'm not worried," I said with a complacent grin. "If I don't wiggle around too much, my B3 should be big enough to keep me covered. I am a little worried my butt might get cold on the bench, though."

"An extra hundred dollars," Leonard murmured. The money meant more if you had a family. "Think we can we negotiate this some way?"

I hadn't really considered Ron's offer seriously. But it was after one o'clock—it would be a relatively short set. It had been an especially chilly night, so there were probably no more than fifty people in the place.

"Maybe. Want to talk to Ron with me?"

At the bar, Ron Stevens and an older, slender man sat in genial conversation.

"Ron, Leonard would like to talk to you. We're having a mini-crisis in the dressing room over your offer. Some guys are less concerned about being naked on stage than others, especially the lead singers, who would have to let everything hang out, so to speak. They're worried it might frighten some of the ladies." Ron and his friend laughed out loud.

"See, we'd like to make the extra money," Leonard told them, "but some of us can't very well play a set naked. I mean, imagine me sitting back there on the drums and some of my stuff flops up onto the snare." Leonard let his rubbery face slide into a woeful expression. "My wife would never forgive me putting our future children at risk. So suppose we do the set in our underwear. That's pretty naked."

Ron glanced at his friend, who smiled and nodded. "Okay, you're on. Finish out the night in your Jockey shorts, and you'll get six crisp hundred-dollar bills."

While it was a wild set and everybody had a lot of fun at our expense, our genitalia stayed unexposed beneath boxer briefs and Jockey shorts. Somehow the word got around town, though: Stark Naked and the Car Thieves were playing naked at the Lemon Tree. The publicity didn't turn out to be bad for the club or the band if Friday night's standing-room-only turnout was any indication.

In gratitude for our willingness to go along with his strange request, Ron invited us to a soul-food restaurant in downtown Reno after the club closed Saturday night. As we mowed our way through the plates of red beans, rice, and ham hocks and various other Cajun foods, Ron mentioned something to me.

"You know, there's a Lemon Tree Lounge in Honolulu, Larry, right on the beach in Waikiki. I know Stan Alapa, guy who owns the club. They'd love your band in the islands. Want me to let him know about you? I could have Stan contact Howard King if you want? I'll call him, but you've got to promise here and now, you'll play my club again next year. For a big Las Vegas act like yours, Reno's off the beaten track. This way I'd be sure of getting you back."

"Sounds interesting, Ron." I frowned a little. "I don't know a thing about Hawaii, though."

"I do," Leonard broke in. "I was stationed there for two years when I was in the Navy. I'd go back in a heartbeat."

"You'll love the place," Ron told me. "You do have to go for at least a couple of months, though. Stan will pay your airfare over and back, but he's got to have enough time to make his costs back."

Reno was an interesting little city, but the blasted landscape of northern Nevada and the rough cowboy action in the gambling mills downtown made me happy to get on the road south to our home in Vegas.

56
BONNIE SPRINGS RANCH

*My wife was afraid of the dark—then she saw
me Naked and now she's afraid of the light.*

— Rodney Dangerfield

October 12, 1967
Las Vegas, Nevada

A FEW DAYS AFTER we'd returned to the Cat, Mac told us Larry Lamb was in the club. "Him and his friends want to take us to some place where we can get us a special ranch-style breakfast after the gig."

Larry, still dressed as if he'd ridden in off the range, smiled his whacked-out smile and waved to us from across the room. I waved back.

"Place is called Bonnie Springs Ranch. Larry says you get a big Porterhouse steak, three eggs, biscuits and gravy, and the best, crispiest hash browns ever made in the West," Mac went on, selling us. "And after breakfast they got horseridin'. I say we do this."

"Hell yes, love horseback riding," Craig said. "Let's go."

"Know you love eatin, too. Be surprised you don't kill the damn horse," Mac said, referring to Craig's hefty size and getting a black look from him.

"Place opens about six AM," Larry said, when we gathered near the bar at the end of the night. "So you boys got time for another drink with us"—as if they needed another—"before you change clothes."

We skipped the offer and went back to our rooms to change into jeans. When Leonard stopped by his room to confer with Paula, she decided he wasn't coming. Craig emerged resplendent in a white-and-purple cowboy shirt with matching bandana, and tooled cowboy boots to go along with black Levis, a tall black Stetson cowboy hat perched on his head.

A sliver of red outlined the horizon to the east as we pulled out of the Cat's parking lot. Most of the band had piled into Dave's red Cadillac convertible, while Craig drove alone in his Chevy Camaro. Larry, behind the wheel of a brand new 1968 Cadillac, loaded in his three friends and peeled rubber, squealing and fishtailing out onto the Strip, accelerating south down Las Vegas Boulevard. There wasn't anybody on the road, but even so, this guy was turning out to be plenty crazy.

By the time we got through the light at Flamingo, the Cadillac had disappeared.

"Ain't no problem," Mac said to us as Dave tried to catch up. "He told me the way. We turn at Blue Diamond Road. Ain't far after that, he said."

Where Las Vegas Boulevard turned into a two-lane highway as it lifted out of the valley Larry impatiently revved his Cadillac at the country-road turnoff. The desert was filled with long shadows bending away from us in the quickening dawn as we tried to keep up. Larry took little detours off into the desert that seemed likely to ruin his suspension before pulling back in front of us. Before long, the three cars pulled off onto an unmarked dirt road that went on for about a quarter of a mile before ending under a gigantic spreading oak tree.

Sheltered in its shadow, a large stone ranch house, which must have had its big front room and porch converted into a restaurant, slumped comfortably on the circular drive behind rough-hewn hitching posts. Ours were the only cars there as we parked in the gravel lot. Inside, the restaurant centered around a fireplace enclosed by a wide hearth, set with heavy paving stones, and big enough to roast cows. Two of the tables, made from irregular-shaped rough-cut planks, pushed end to end, sat us all. Through floor-to-ceiling windows, the western mountains unveiled themselves in the morning's glorious golden-red rays as the desert floor wakened in front of us.

Billy, one of Larry's cohorts, told us a little more about our host while the kitchen behind us came to life.

"Larry is most particularly well known for the night he put soap powder in the Caesar's Palace fountains. Well actually there was four of us . . ."

"Allegedly, now," Larry interrupted with a big lopsided smile. "Allegedly. Wasn't no conviction."

"Yup, allegedly, o' course, so anyway there was four of us—allegedly. We had this van jam-pack full with boxes of dish-soap powder. We figured we'd need a lot 'cause them fountains are so goddamn huge, as you can plainly see."

"Man, there was a lot more soap suds than anyone coulda ever guessed. Whoever done it must've used too much soap. Happened in the dark of morning, and when the sun came up, somebody had turned them fountains into the world's biggest bubble bath." Larry did his best to look puzzled, then he smiled. "Man, it was fucking great. Most fun I ever had with my clothes on. Ralph beat me with a switch he cut special for that one." I tried to picture what those huge fountains shooting sudsy water forty or fifty feet up into the air outside of Caesars must have looked like.

While we were waiting for steaks and eggs and more breakfast than I could ever eat, Larry leaned over to me and gestured Mac to come into a little huddle with us. "You think I could talk to you boys private-like for a minute, say over on the other side by the bar?"

When we'd settled and he'd gotten some orange juice for us all with a vodka wake-up in his, he spoke to me. "I mentioned this here idea I got to Mac, and he said you, being the leader and all, were the person to run this by." He hitched his stool closer and spoke with the confidence of the youngest son of a family that practically ran southern Nevada even though they didn't own a single hotel. Rumor had it that the Lamb family held the exclusive licensing rights to the bar dispenser guns used everywhere in Clark County.

"See me and some boys I know have us an idea of starting up a nightclub on the Strip, somewhat like the Pussycat, you know. Of course I know what makes the Pussycat go is you guys. Jesus Christ, that club ain't been the same since you guys come to town and rocked the place. I mean not only are you fucking great, you sing great, you play great music, you look great, and you're nice guys—everybody loves you. I mean you're great performers but you do rock and roll. Hell of a combination I'd say."

I humbly waved off his effusive compliments.

"Anyway, we figger if Stark Naked was to open this place our consortium"—*con-sore-she-um*, as he pronounced it—"is fixin' to buy, we will get it kicked off as good as ever could be. I asked Mac, what would it take to get you guys to open the place for us?"

Uh-oh. I didn't like what I was hearing. Our rising star in Las Vegas had already taken a couple of body blows. First, not getting our contract renewed at Caesars and then getting dumped out on our ear at the Thunderbird. What would the hotel entertainment buyers think if we played some rinky-dink, half-assed joint in the heart of the Strip? We might never get back into a high-paying job in one of the Strip hotels. What would the Cat think? Jack Turner or Bob Hirsch might not like us playing in a competitive club near theirs. On the other hand, wouldn't be good to have the sheriff's little brother pissed at us, either. Diplomacy was required.

"I don't know, Larry," I said, letting him believe I was seriously considering his proposition. "You're asking us to burn a lot of bridges with the hotels and clubs."

He nodded his head. "Well, maybe. But I think my connections could do you a lot of good, too. I can help you get work in the hotels, especially downtown, stuff like that. Plus, if you're worried about the Pussycat"—he gave me a complacent grin—"I can make sure that's not a problem." He didn't go into any detail, and I didn't ask for any. A gambling club on the Strip, not associated with any hotels, would have their gaming license examined very closely. I expected the Lambs could make the process easier or harder if they wanted to.

"And let's not forget about the money," Larry said, sipping his potent juice. "If you don't mind my askin', what'd they give for you at Caesars?"

Delicate stuff, asking what an act made. I looked him straight in the eye and lied, "Four thousand a week to start. Of course if you could find out what happened to the three-year three-hundred-thousand-dollar contract we were supposed to have there, that'd be a big incentive."

"Crap, can't pay that kinda money. We ain't even got our bar license yet, probably not for a couple of weeks. Trying to get my brothers to help me get a gambling license for table games. Slots ain't no big deal, but table games is where the money is." He scratched his jaw, glaring at me.

"I can't very well fuck with Jay Sarno or Nate Jocobsen and them Chicago boys over at Caesars any more. They didn't take too much of a shine to my shenanigans, you know. They don't appreciate that my family are just fun-loving, high-spirited country folk. Reckon you're shit outta luck on that contract. Sorry."

He considered me for a moment. "However, we could pay you what the Pussycat does. What do you get from them?"

Without a quaver, I said, "Twenty-four hundred a week."

He gave me a little laugh. "Well, I reckon that's more like two grand but tell you what, suppose I were offering twenty-five even. Would you consider that?"

I did a mental checklist of the people this deal would be likely to anger, starting with Jimmy and/or Seymour, Howard King, and the Pussycat. I looked at Mac, who shrugged; he was leaving it to me. I knew he was thinking we could cut out some of the commissions. Didn't anybody realize if you want to get somewhere in this business, you need allies? Sometimes you got to pay them for what they don't do so they'll produce other opportunities.

"When are you thinking of opening your club?"

"We'll be ready when you close the Pussycat in three weeks." I did a double take.

"Damn, we couldn't be available that quick."

"Well, tell you what. Lemme get this breakfast and the horse ride we are about to take, and you figure out your schedule over the next few days. If you can give me the answer I want by the end of the week, then I'll getcha another five hundred a week."

I looked at Mac, who shrugged again. "Lot of people to talk to about this so I'll do my best," I said, "But I don't want you upset with us if we can't make this happen that quickly." I was already hoping we could figure out some way we could get out of this without upsetting anybody.

Larry stared into my eyes, trying to read me, then shook his head. "I believe you. And long as you promise you'll play in my place soon's you can, even if you can't do it right away, then I'll be happy with that. 'Cept you won't be gettin that five hundred kicker," he said with a gleam in his eye.

I have never had a better or more generous breakfast: the steak was huge, delicious, and could have fed three of us; the eggs so fresh they must have still been in a chicken when we drove up, and hash browns as crisp as promised. I stayed with the virgin orange juice and coffee to wash down the meal.

While the rest of us went out to the stable behind the restaurant, Craig stopped by his car before rejoining us, wearing a black leather double-holster set, filled with two chromed, pearl-handled single-action revolvers.

"For rattlesnakes," he said.

Amazing that he traveled around with this cowboy stuff, I thought, but then, I lugged a steamer trunk of books and games with me, so who was I to judge.

I thought Larry might not be able to stay on his horse. He and his friends had put away a lot of booze with breakfast, even after drinking all night. He'd had a hell of a time just getting into the saddle, falling once all the way over the animal into the dirt, laughing the whole time. He didn't seem to care, said falling on his head just got his brain working right.

Somehow, as we milled around in the saddling area, Craig got jostled and lost his immaculate Stetson. In the same reckless way they'd gotten here in his new Cadillac, Larry and his buddies shot off into the desert at full gallop, whooping and hollering and hanging on for dear life. But not before trampling Craig's black hat into the dust before he could retrieve it. Though he was thoroughly irritated, I thought the hat looked a lot more authentic beat up.

There were no trails. Once mounted, we just headed out in whatever direction suited us. The stable simply charged for however long you stayed out. The five of us in the band rode much slower into the breathtaking morning than Larry and his pals did. Within moments, we were out of sight of any sign of civilization, left to ourselves in the utter silence and beauty of the deep desert.

Joshua trees overtopped low-growing mesquite, creosote, and other shrubs and bushes. Around us, cacti of various kinds sported colorful little flowers on their tops. We'd been warned of rattlesnakes, warmed to life from nighttime torpor in the rising morning temperature, so we tried to stay in sunlight and kept our eyes out for them.

After a couple of hours, I felt as if I'd gone back in time to the Old West and we were a million miles from nowhere. The air was so clean and clear I could catch delicate hints of desert aromas, gone too soon to identify. I hadn't felt so relaxed since my brush with induction into the army. Craig spotted coyote or bobcat tracks. We startled an occasional jackrabbit, and overhead a red-tailed hawk checked out the menu along our meandering path.

The morning was still cool when the sun reminded us that even though it was October, it was going to get hot, so we decided to head back. The stable was nowhere in sight, but we didn't need to know where the ranch was, the ranch hand had told us. "When you're ready to come on back just give the horse his head, he knows the way."

As Dave's horse scrambled down one of the broken ravines we'd come across, it twisted as if it was going to fall, caught itself, and lurched, scrambling up out of the gully. Dave, freaking out, jumped off the horse, afraid it would fall on him, and backed away cursing and yelling. The horse, lifting his tail as all four hooves hit the ground running, never gave him a second look. He was out of sight in no time. Dave stared after the disappearing beast in astonishment.

"That was dumb," Craig said. You'd think the guy had been around us long enough to know not to tweak Dave when he was embarrassed.

"Yeah, so what the fuck do you know?" Dave growled.

"I know you don't ever let go of the bridle when you aren't riding your own horse. Horse tricked you into letting go. They'll always try to do that so they can take off for the stable."

"Well you can kiss my rosy red ass, asshole. Doesn't help when the fucking hayburner is long gone. Mighta said something when it counted."

I guided my horse near Dave. "Hey man, slide on back of me, we'll ride double. We were getting ready to go anyway."

"Get that fucking fleabag away from me. I'm not getting on one of those goddamn things ever again. I'll walk back on my own two goddamn legs." No question, he was steamed.

Craig dug around in his man bag and pulled out a camera. "Got to get a picture of this," he muttered, popping the lens cap and fiddling with the settings. He was out in front, so he turned his horse around to face Dave walking toward him and aimed the camera. Somewhere, there's a photo of Dave with his middle finger raised, frowning into the camera.

Surprisingly, no one at the Cat seemed to care if we played at a new club a couple of blocks south. Jack Turner laughed at the idea that anyone would think Stark Naked and the Car Thieves was what made the Pussycat so popular.

"Even if the Colonial House does well, we'll pull more people out of the hotels into both clubs, going back and forth between them. If that Larry Lamb character can find that much more money to pay you, go get it."

We continued to feel like the toast of the town during the following weeks at the Cat. Major artists and celebrities were in the room nightly. Bill Cosby had become a regular, coming over between his shows at the New Frontier across the street. I'd first learned of him from his hilarious standup comedy albums when I lived in Indiana. Now he had a hit TV show and drew huge crowds in Las Vegas. He was funny and personable, and could make you feel like you'd been friends forever.

The first time he came into the club, his head appeared out of the drapes as he hopped out onto the stage from the dressing room door. "Hey you cats got any bongos, or something I can bang on? Can't just sit out there when you're playing this great music."

Dave found him a tambourine, and pretty soon his lead tambourine rang through everything we played. He would come back after his midnight show sometimes and hang with us until closing. He loved music, and made us feel like we were the best band he'd ever seen.

He seemed like a great guy to me.

57
THE COLONIAL HOUSE DEBACLE

Art can never exist without Naked beauty displayed.
— William Blake

November 2, 1967
Las Vegas, Nevada

"WE ARE SO fucked." I frowned in disgust at the caved-in space where a stage was supposed to be, maybe in a month from now, the way it looked to me. Larry Lamb had agreed to let us drop by the new nightclub on the Thursday of our last week at the Cat. The Colonial House's interior resembled a barn, rat's nests of dust visible in the corners of the open rafters above. The only things presentable about the place were the dingy white antebellum-style columns outside that ran along the building's entryway, as if the structure had been lifted here through a time warp from the Civil War South.

"Ain't that bad," Mac said. "But does need some work."

"He needs a full construction crew in here right now to have a prayer of having this place finished in time to open in four days, Mac. No way will the stage and PA, let alone the dance floor, be ready."

"Hear you're worried about the condition of the place," Larry Lamb said, jaw jutting out as he swaggered up to us. He'd been doing something out back with the cracked and weed-choked pool. The Colonial House had previously existed as a restaurant with a long row of motel rooms out back. Its aspirations of becoming something grander had failed, and the place had fallen into serious disrepair.

"Don't worry so much. Our monkeys will be here building yer stage in the morning. We'll have a final coat of paint on her Monday. You'll be loving this place when you set up Tuesday."

We didn't love the place Tuesday. Though the electricity worked, the PA sounded atrocious, and the clangy, obnoxious wooden acoustics of the room made the bad sound system sound worse. Instead of advertising the new Colonial House nightclub on the radio, in street-flyer giveaways and newspaper ads, promotion had degenerated into Larry sending some of his friends around to the clubs and hotels to tell people where we were playing. I guess customers had been expected to flock in based on the tiny marquee with Stark Naked and the Car Thieves on it in tiny letters where Steak Lunch $4.95 had previously appeared.

Unsurprisingly, we opened to a sparse crowd in the unfinished room. Over the next few days, the few workmen who showed up during the day didn't seem to improve anything.

Our dressing room was up a flight of stairs in a second-floor attic. We pushed piles of broken chairs, tables, and other useless bits of restaurant rubble into corners to clear as large a space as possible. Our clothes hung in makeshift closets made from pieces of wood and wire strung wherever we could find a spot. Musical equipment cases stood along a casement-windowed wall. We found most of a full-length mirror and leaned it against a junk pile; we fished out some usable chairs from the trash and set them in a circle, as if around an invisible campfire.

All of us hated going downstairs to the embarrassment waiting below. At first, nobody complained to me. After all, we'd been in on the decision together, and circumstances made it difficult to turn down. As morale sank and frustration rose, I tried to remind the band, and myself, how great the money was, and that at least we hadn't had to travel out of town after the Cat. This place was proving Jack Turner's contention that we weren't the straw that stirred the Pussycat's drink. Bill Cosby wouldn't be visiting us here. I hadn't put much credence in Larry Lamb's belief that we were what made the Cat the hottest rock club in Las Vegas, but I thought we'd draw a lot better than we had.

The Colonial House got the best of us right up to the end. Before we were halfway through the gig, Larry Lamb had begun to make his disappointment with the crowd we'd drawn obvious, blaming us for his missteps. I couldn't remember another time when all of us were this bad-tempered at once. By closing night, everybody was irritable, and because shit rolls downhill, as they say, it felt like most of it landed on me. I didn't have any solutions, other than longing for this horrible experience to end. Rumor had it that bitter disagreement had risen between the partners of Larry's "consorsheum," and apparently money was short. Instead of showing himself to quell the rumors, Larry remained invisible during the final days. It was strongly suggested that since I was the leader, and ultimately responsible for this debacle, I should stay behind on closing night, to pick up our final check and make sure it cleared the bank on Monday, before joining everyone in LA. Just to be on the safe side.

My emotions finally got away from me and I snapped back during a couple of hot discussions late in an evening spiced with a few too many Jack and colas. It didn't take many; I drank so little my tolerance for booze was low.

Feuding with the band achieved nothing except leaving me the onerous chore of packing up the B3 and speakers by myself and sullenly wrestling them out to the van without the usual assistance. There, Leonard and Dave made a resentful effort to help me get them into the van. Eager to put the Colonial House behind them, Leonard led the caravan to California and the Rag Doll into the early morning darkness.

No matter how much money we'd gotten for this job, taking it had been a disaster though I don't know how we could have avoided it. Playing here had further damaged our reputation, already dinged at two of the Strip's major hotels. And now, after resuscitating our reputation at the red-hot Pussycat A' Go Go, this fiasco. *Something must be lacking in me as a leader, or us as a band, to have blown so many opportunities in this town*, I thought, shuffling back into the club to pick up a few final things, including our check.

An odd sense of abandonment stole over me. I was intimately familiar with Las Vegas—it was as much home to me as anywhere—but without the band and an engagement to play, I felt like a stranger. I wished we'd been able talk things out before they left. *I'll just get some sleep*, I told myself, *get to the bank first thing in the morning, and hit the road early.*

I might have gone out to my car and gotten a room then if a couple of the waitresses and the late bartender, Steve, hadn't offered to buy me another drink as I came in out of the dark. Though depressed and a little lonely, I wasn't sleepy, and welcomed the company, commiserating with some of the servers and bartenders over the uncertainty of who might or might not get paid, or laid off, until everyone had drifted away except Steve and a pretty long-haired blond girl, who'd joined us somewhere along the line. Somehow, my glass had never gotten empty. The room seemed a little tilty, and I realized I'd accidentally gotten pretty drunk. That seemed okay with me, so I giggled and took another sip.

I heard Steve say, "Kathy, my shift's over, got to close the bar. Can you help get Larry home or something? He's pretty wasted."

"Sure," she said. "I'm in a motel just off Paradise. Sunday night, I'm sure they've got rooms available. Can you help get him to my car?"

"No, now wait a minute," I blustered, momentarily panicked. *Can't be without transportation, gotta get to LA.* "Just get me out to my car, awright?"

"You're not doing any driving." Kathy waggled a finger under my nose. "You can come get it in the morning. You'll only be a little ways away."

I tried to think of another argument, but before I could, a dark world was slipping by outside an open window. Like a dog, I stuck my head out into the cool breeze, which felt so good, I forgot about opposing the idea. I looked to see who was driving, hoping it wasn't me because we were going pretty fast. Kathy, the blond girl from the bar, was at the wheel. *Kathy. Must not be that drunk, I remembered her name.*

"Yeah? What's up, Larry?"

"Unh?"

"You said 'Kathy' just now. Did you want something?"

"Oh. Dint realize I said nothing, something. Out loud, I mean. Just thinking it was good I knew your name." I smiled in her general direction.

"Yeah, that is good. We know each other's names. Always a good start I'd say."

With a bump, we whooshed into a parking lot, and before I could focus, the car had parked head-in to rooms that ran along the wall in front of me. *Red doors,* I noticed.

"Right, red doors. Not colorblind, another hopeful sign."

I had to stop saying things I was thinking. Probably meant I was more fucked up than I realized.

"So, we got lucky," Kathy said, before opening the car door, "That red door right there, number 118, is mine. Never got a spot this close before." She pushed the door open and turned back to me. "Why don't you come into my room and we'll ring up the office about getting you a room from here. No sense staggering down there yet, right?"

"Right, right. Good." It was tiring trying to figure out which things to do next. *Be nice to just rest for a minute.*

"That's what I was thinking. You come in and relax for a minute." I was thinking out loud again.

"Come on, let me help you."

In a couple of minutes, we were through the door, and I lay spread-eagled on my back across the queen-sized bed, feeling much more secure now that I was gripping the mattress beneath me. *Takes lots less effort to stay horizontal compared to staying vertical. A big improvement.* My eyes began to close, and I started to curl up before I stopped myself. *I'll fall asleep for sure if I do that. That would be rude.* I forced my eyes open and scooched myself up against the headboard. I opened my eyes real wide and looked around. I was an expert at motel rooms; while pretty much the same functionally, some were much nicer than others. This one was pretty good, roomy, with a nicely finished little table and solid wooden chairs near the front window, and a new, probably twenty-four-inch television, high in an open armoire. Water running in the bathroom shut off, and in a moment the blond girl walked out in her bra and panties—and the game changed.

"Oh," she said a little sheepishly. "I thought you'd gone to sleep. I figured, what the hey, it's already four in the morning, why pay for another room when for two hours, you could sleep here." She tossed her arms out, seemingly a little embarrassed.

"Falling asleep would be pretty bad-mannered after, you know, after you were so nice to take me in, here, from the bar." I was pretty drunk but not feeling sick or anything. And she looked great out of her clothes. Not that she didn't look great in them. *Actually,* I realized as I thought further, *she looks pretty great either way, in or out of them.* "I'm willing to go back to sleep if you'll let me stay."

"Don't think that'll be necessary, but I'm feeling a little exposed. Either I need to put more clothes on or you need to take some off."

I struggled with my shirt buttons, until I realized that she was kneeling on the bed, helping me. I slid off my shoes with my feet and by that time she'd started on my pants. I shimmied out of them, and she looked down at me and giggled in pleasure, before pulling back the covers.

Kathy looks best of all, I decided, *with her bra and panties off.*

58
TWO BRICKS AND A HUNDRED-DOLLAR BILL

*We don't have to have sex, let's just get
Naked and see what happens.*

— unknown

December 4, 1967
Las Vegas, Nevada

I WOKE SPOONED BEHIND something wonderfully girl-shaped. To be certain, I ran my hand along a waist that swelled into nice girl hips. This has got to be the best way in the world to wake up, I thought. I didn't open my eyes, I just lay there, quietly feeling good about things, not allowing anything in that might disturb the moment. Not even the horrible month we'd just endured. It was finally over and here I was with . . . um, Kathy. I opened my eyes and looked around the room. Even in a room darkened by blackout drapes, you can always tell when the sun is high and bright in Las Vegas.

Beneath me, Kathie wriggled and snuggled her backside into me. That always gets me. After celebrating waking up, we went out to the Silver Slipper for the $1.99 breakfast special in her new Ford Mustang convertible. Though well into the afternoon, we weren't the only ones ordering breakfast. That's Vegas.

"So how do you feel?" She munched toast she had dragged through egg yolk and gazed at me with a sweet, innocent smile. For a moment I felt like a boyfriend, some weird memory of playing hooky on a school day that had never been.

"I should feel terrible, but I feel surprisingly great. I would be a horrible ad for AA."

"But maybe a decent one for Jack Daniels." We both laughed easily.

I chased eggs around on my plate with a forkful of hash browns and followed my last bite with coffee heavily laced with cream and sugar. I looked up, satisfied, and patted my tummy.

She pushed her plate away and put her elbows on the table. "So what's your plan, Stan?"

"How'd you know my real name was Stan?"

"It was embroidered in your underwear." She giggled. "No, on your socks. No wait, I know. I saw a tattoo on your . . . part that rhymes with sock." We both broke out laughing.

After we got our breath, I told her I had to find a Bank of Nevada, and after that, I admitted, I had no plan.

"How's this for coincidence. I don't have anything planned, either. Do you want to not do anything with me?"

We stopped down the street at the Colonial House parking lot so I could pick up and drive my car to her motel, and then to the bank. Happily, the check cleared without drama, and I converted the cash into a cashier's check to take back to LA. When I got back to the motel, I phoned Dave to let him know the check had cleared, and asked him to call the Mid-Valley office and move my reservation back—I would be staying in Vegas a little while longer. Kathy giggled and clapped her hands.

With business complete, Kathy and I decided an afternoon in bed with the television on was well earned. All the moodiness and anxiety I'd let build up was being wrung out of me as the day disappeared into a cool October evening.

Kathy, in panties only, was stuffing chips in her mouth and laughing at a comedian on television when I turned to her. "I want to tell you something."

"Oh yeah, and what would that be, masked man?"

"I'm taking off my mask for a moment. But you're going to have to stop laughing, your breasts jiggle and distract me."

"Ooooh," she squealed, "I love this part. Is this where we're going to do sex again?"

"Maybe." I grinned. "Okay, well, probably. But not for a minute. I want to tell you that being here with you is so lucky, so fortuitous, so synchronistic."

She squealed again. *This girl is just not going to let me be serious.*

"Look, I just want to say something. Today—well beginning with last night—has been like a day out of a story. We meet and everything in this little crack in time is so perfect, I almost can't believe it. Things have been a little crazy for me recently, and I can feel all the crunchiness smoothing out, being here with you."

From behind a pillow where she was unsuccessfully hiding a big grin, only her laughing eyes showed. "So, now that I've said that, yes, we can have sex." She moaned in apparent anticipation, and after a while I did, too.

We called Leaning Tower Pizza on the Strip to deliver dinner and soft drinks, and it was shaping up into a nice comfortable stay-at-home—in a motel-room, in a bed—kind of night. About seven thirty, as I lay dozing, I heard the shower running, and a few minutes later Kathy walked out to start getting into a nice dress. I didn't say anything, but I thought it was a little strange. In a few minutes, she was back from the bathroom after putting on lipstick and makeup.

"Well I'm surprised you haven't asked me what I'm doing so I suppose I'm going to have to pretend you did. Here goes," she said, pinning in earrings.

"I've got to go out for a little while tonight. I promised someone I'd meet them before I knew you'd be here with me." She looked at her wristwatch. "I have to be there at eight thirty, but I'll probably be back by ten. You'll keep the bed warm for me until then, won't you?"

"Sure. Of course you had a life going on here before I dropped into it like a drunken sailor."

"More accurately, I shanghaied you for nefarious purposes." I got her million-dollar smile. She pulled on her jacket against the cooling desert air. "Will more nefarity later tonight be okay with you?"

I watched the end of *Laugh-In* and fell asleep for a while in the middle of Bill Cosby's *I Spy*. The room had gotten kind of chilly, and I thought about crawling under the covers. I glanced at the clock; it was well after eleven. I got up and pulled my well-wrinkled jeans on over my underwear and slipped on shirt and shoes. I didn't have any other clothes—I'd expected to be in California with the van and my steamer trunks by now. I stepped out into the desert night. Cars hummed along Paradise Road; other than that, it was clear and quiet, save for the muted sound from television in the room.

Stupid of me to worry about what Kathy's doing. She has her own life. For all I know, she might have a boyfriend or something. Be realistic, this is just a momentary fling. I would be leaving for LA soon, I couldn't make any demands on her, I argued. It didn't help; I was still a little concerned. It got nippy enough to drive me back into the room to turn up the window heater. I'd hardly gotten onto the bed when Kathy walked in.

"Glad to be home to my now-properly masked man again."

The room and my mood lightened immediately. "Glad to have my sidekick back."

She dropped a shopping bag on the floor, threw her coat onto a chair, and jumped on the bed to give me a warm, wet kiss. She pouted for a minute and then sat back on her knees.

"I want so bad to tell you something but I'm so afraid you'll be angry or disappointed, even though there isn't any reason to be. I can't stand the idea of you being mad with me." *She is so cute*, I thought, but I could tell she was serious.

I smiled. I had to admit to being glad she cared about what I thought. "Kathy, I don't own you. I'm not going to be disappointed no matter what you tell me."

She got off the bed and turned partly away from me, smoothing out her dress. "I had to go out to meet a man tonight." She looked over at me and my open mouth.

"I know him, and it wasn't to have sex or anything. Nothing like that. But he does give me money." I closed my open mouth and tried to give her a brave smile.

"Now stop it, Larry. You said you wouldn't be disappointed. I can tell you're not going to be angry, but you are also not allowed to look like a kicked dog. I would've much rather been here with you, but I'd given my word. Plus he gave me a thousand dollars." This time, I was unable to get my mouth closed.

"Not to get sidetracked. And, believe me, you don't have to say anything if you don't want to, but I can't help but be curious. Why did the man give you all that money?"

She went to her purse and fanned out a bunch of one-hundred-dollar bills.

"He gives it to me for going out to dinner with him and his friends. He's an Arabian prince, and his religion doesn't let him have sex with infidels. That being me. Usually it's just dinner, but tonight he and his friends decided to go see Shecky Green at the Riv, and he wanted me to go. I could have come back here to you after dinner, I guess, but gee, I mean, a thousand dollars."

"Right, right." An Arabian prince. "Well, I'm glad you're an infidel. I've been considering infidelity myself. Just been waiting for the right opportunity."

"I didn't used to be an infidel, but there are these pills that can help." She nodded cheerfully. We were back on more comfortable ground.

"But you're not a hooker though, right? Because technically, if you don't have sex with people for money, I don't think that's a hooker. You're being sort of, I don't know what exactly? Maybe an escort?"

She thought about it. "Well, maybe," she said as a small frown line appeared just above and between her eyes. "But I think escorts tend to have sex for money, too, only I don't think you have to unless you're okay with it."

She sat on the side of the bed. "It could be that's what I am, an escort, I'm not sure. I came to Las Vegas looking for something and I haven't figured out what. I kinda sorta fell into this, and though I don't know where you apply for this exact position of dinner partner at a thousand bucks a night, if this keeps up, I'm likely to stick with it."

I didn't know what to say. While I was thinking, she jumped off the bed. "And that's not all, my good friend. Not at all, all. Look at this." She dumped the contents of the shopping bag onto the bed. Two rectangular blocks, a little bigger and flatter than cigar cases, tightly wrapped in shiny black plastic, fell out. One of them had been slightly wounded at a corner and taped back up. I wasn't sure what I was looking at.

"It's marijuana, silly. Two kilos of grass, one for you and one for me. Isn't this neat?"

"Damn. I mean, wow." I'd never seen more than a baggie of grass before. "So this is how weed looks in the wild, huh?" I picked up and hefted one of the bricks. I rapped it with my knuckles—rock solid. "I see one of them has had a bite taken out of it."

She dipped into her purse and pulled out a nearly full baggie. I eyeballed it in comparison to the tiny nibble out of the block and realized how tightly compressed the block was. This was fascinating, I had to admit.

"So out of my thousand dollars I got a really great deal. I only paid two hundred bucks for two bricks." She gave me a childlike smile, as if she'd gotten all the marbles back in the bag. This was a lot to handle.

"I don't know if I can take this from you, Kathy. One of these is worth a lot of money."

"Well, tell you what. I was going to say the baggie's contents was out of my kilo, but if it will make you feel better, then you can have the brick that's been broken into. Since it's yours, so is the baggie. So how about rolling us a doobie-doobie-do?"

She handed me a packet of papers, and I started to work while she took a second shower and soon came out, toweling wet hair and wearing nothing but her beautiful tight young body.

"I have been laid by this beautiful woman several times in the last twenty-four hours so I am somewhat sated. That's the reason I'm not already all over you."

"I'll let that excuse stand for the moment. But hand me that lighter before I change my mind."

We laughed and smoked, and in a few minutes disappeared into sexual congress that transported us into enhanced states of ecstasy. We fell asleep like we belonged to the same pack of puppies.

I awoke again in Kathy's bed, but this time I knew right where I was. I felt her warmth against my thigh as I slid up to put my back against the headboard. It was Tuesday, but we wouldn't be opening at the Rag Doll until tomorrow night. If today was going to be anything like yesterday, I wondered if I could find some way to stretch this amazing fantasy out a little longer.

Kathy kicked out her slender arms and legs in a full animal stretch. She knew I was watching and put on a full performance. She gave me a secret smile and rolled over to disappear into the bathroom.

We decided to splurge and break a hundred-dollar bill for two full breakfast buffets at the Frontier Hotel.

"After breakfast, though, we have to get me some underwear," I said.

"I didn't know I was going to be here this long. In fact, you should probably be insisting on the underwear."

"I was thinking you should just go commando. Solve a couple of problems at the same time. Maybe I could, too." This girl was unbelievable.

"That is a commendable suggestion with a lot of merit. I first want to say, I have inferred from your comment what 'going commando' means. I am loath to admit I had never heard that term before, but I promise I will never forget it."

We jabbered like idiots, drinking each other in, while feasting on the extravagant smorgasbord the Frontier laid out for us. We visited the mall south of Sahara to get me underwear and socks, and Kathy found a nice little undershirt thing she called a blouse. We looked at dresses and perfumes, walked by Frank Sinatra and the Rat Pack on velvet pictures with a glittery Sands Hotel marquee in the background. We talked about driving up to Mount Charleston to visit the snow, but remembered in time that snow was cold, so we retreated to our room again to smoke, watch old *Lucy* reruns, and test our sexual stamina.

It was with some surprise that I once again heard Kathy slip into the shower at around seven o'clock. I went to the bathroom door and leaned in.

"You have to go out again tonight?"

"Yes, one more dinner with the prince. He flies back to his country tomorrow."

"When were you going to tell me?"

She popped her head out of the shower. "When I was walking out the door. I don't like goodbyes. I wanted to wait until the last minute. But the good news is this should be a very short evening. Perhaps I won't get the whole thousand dollars, it will be so short. I meet him at eight at a Moroccan restaurant, and I might get home before ten."

By midnight, I'd gone nearly out of my mind with worry. While I was enjoying this casual romantic vibe we had going, for me it was just put on. I was playing a part, like in a Cary Grant movie or something. As for her, I wasn't so sure. She seemed to be a true nature's child. I worried about what kind of trouble she might get in. As I suffered in this protective mode, the television tuned to something I couldn't follow, the telephone startled me. It took a moment to turn down the TV and locate the phone beneath a couple of damp, discarded towels.

"Hello?" I said cautiously.

"Hi. It's me, Kathy."

"Are you okay?" I knew I sounded worried, but I didn't want to just come right out and say it. "Couldn't help being a little worried," I blurted out anyway.

"I'm fine. Well, in a relative sort of way. Listen, no time, so don't talk. Just listen to me, okay?"

I nodded, realized, and said, "Yeah, sure."

"I've been busted by the Vegas police. For hooking. You have to get everything incriminating out of that room and get out of there right away. You got that? You have at most fifteen minutes. Do you understand?"

"Yeah, okay. But Kathy, you used your one phone call to call here and tell me this? Do I need to find you a lawyer?"

"No, silly." I heard her smothered laugh. "Technically, I got busted for being underage. You're not allowed to illegally hook until you're twenty-one. How do you like them apples?"

"You're underage," I said faintly.

"No, I'm not underage to have sex with you, you loon. Just to do sex work apparently, which I wasn't doing anyway, as you know. So, they called my parents, who are already on their way from Northern California to get me. So, I don't need another phone call."

"What do I do with your stuff? I mean your brick? How can I get that back to you? Can you give me an address or anything?"

"You have to take it with you. You're in a band. I can find you when this is all over. Another thing, I put a hundred-dollar bill under a glass on the dressing table. I wanted to give it to you before you left anyway. I think you are the coolest, sweetest guy ever. Only you're not the masked man, sweetheart, I am. I've got to go, just get out of there right now with the stuff, don't leave anything for the cops to find."

To be on the safe side, I was on the road in seven minutes. I had both bricks and the bag of weed in the trunk, and the hundred-dollar bill Kathy had left in my pocket. My trusty Ford Falcon carried me south on Las Vegas Boulevard toward the I-15, North Hollywood—and reality.

59
VIKING

> *"I think you'd look good in a body bag." "Yeah? Well I think I'd look good as your parole officer, asshole."*
>
> — Overheard in Claremont Square

December 7, 1967
North Hollywood, California

I SETTLED EASILY BACK into the Mid-Valley Motel, and within a few days, Marie joined me. We were comfortable with each other. She was a great companion and a generous lover. In her heart of hearts, I knew she believed she could convince me to make a full commitment to her someday. She couldn't. Marrying again would be the ultimate betrayal of Pat. I'd never find anyone so perfectly matched to me as Pat had been. We'd practically grown up together, from two fresh young teenagers to parents of two young children of our own. An unrepeatable experience. I would never be so close to anyone again, even if I wanted to. Which I didn't. If I ever found myself thinking I could, I'd run like a scared rabbit, rather than risk repeating the pain that had been exacted on us.

The Rag Doll and the rooms at the Mid-Valley always felt like home. Mac kept the running party going at the club, the fame of Leonard's conga line was spreading, and girls lined up at the door to hear Dave sing, on occasion screaming when he stepped to the mic. Famous guitar players like Joe Pass and Wes Montgomery stopped in to listen to Les. He just kept getting better and better, and the word was getting around. Top studio musicians around town often dropped in, usually on Sunday nights, to sit in with us. One of Les's earliest heroes and influences, Nokie Edwards of the Ventures, came in and tongue-tied him when he told us in front of Les how impressed he was with him; they ended up jamming together on stage after the club closed. Les seemed so driven, I couldn't tell if he realized or had gotten much satisfaction from how far he'd come as a guitarist since those Bouncin' Bill Baker sock-hop days not that long ago in Indianapolis. He'd even begun to develop his own little entourage of followers.

One afternoon, Les asked me to take a drive with him. As we cruised along Lankershim Boulevard, between high-crowned fan palms, convenience stores, and garages, he told me he had something to tell me.

"Larry, I've been asked to join the Lettermen."

I gripped the wheel, speechless.

"Bob Engeman is leaving and Tony Butala has seen us play several time in Las Vegas. He contacted me, asked if I'd be interested. I had to say yes, it's such an incredible compliment to even be considered."

"The Lettermen." I tried to wrap my mind around a group I liked so much as a fan being interested in tagging one of us. They were crooners, not rockers, but they had a huge following, and such a smooth, cool sound.

"So you've, like, auditioned or something? I mean, it's not like they're just showing some interest?" My head whirled. What would we do if this really happened? Les had a special knowledge and understanding of us as vocalists, as had been made obvious when he'd rejoined the band last year, and it was more true than ever now.

"I've gotten a solid offer from Bob's brother, Karl, who manages them. They're willing to give me full membership, including royalties from some of their old hits, and I'd own my own compositions if I write any songs the group records."

"Les, the Lettermen have always been one of my favorite groups. Yours, too, I know. While I can't imagine what we'd do without you, I completely understand if you decide to go with them. But they are a vocal group. I don't imagine you'd play guitar." He nodded and we rode quietly for a few minutes.

"Have you made up your mind yet?"

Les looked out the passenger window. "I'm leaning toward taking their offer, Larry. But I wanted you to know first. I've promised Karl and

Tony an answer by next week, so I'll let you know for sure by then. If I decide to go, I promise I'll give you plenty of notice."

I talked over the situation with each of the other guys, one by one. None of us had any idea what to do if Les left. He was more than a guitar player and voice, he arranged our vocals, he was our musical leader. And most of all, he was our friend. How do you replace somebody like that? Difficult to believe that one of us from the original Midwestern group might leave.

Before we'd gotten ourselves worked into full panic mode, Les pulled me aside a few days later. "Just can't leave Stark Naked, man."

"Thank God," I said in selfish relief. "What happened?"

He shrugged. "I just felt like we weren't done here. I still think we can have hits, big hits. I think Stark Naked could be bigger than the Lettermen. I talked to Eddie. He thinks so, too. So I'm staying."

"Glad to hear it, Bear, don't know what we would've done if you left."

But we still weren't writing songs, though, not even bad ones. We weren't being creative, inventive. It seemed so obvious: without a whole lot of luck, we would never control our own recording career until we composed our own material. At our next meeting, I gave the guys something to consider.

"We've got to find our creativity, so we can write our own original songs. We've got the voices." I gestured toward Les. "We've got the arranger, and we know we can get studio time. We just need to discover our own music."

Most everyone nodded. "I'm going to suggest something outrageous, something you'd never think I'd propose." I paused to reconsider what I was about to say.

"Due to an unexpected but enjoyable encounter in Las Vegas recently, about which I've already told you as much as you're going to hear, I've got more smoking dope than I know what to do with." I heard some laughs. "Even with Mac and Dave's help, and some of the rest of you, the kilo of grass I brought back from Vegas still looks like it hasn't been touched. I know we've always agreed we shouldn't get high on stage or at rehearsals, and we've stuck to it most of the time." There were a few hoots and comments. "But we've got to do something to change things, slap ourselves in the face some way. What if we let the righteous influence of the beneficent herb inspire us, see if that might help us come up with some ideas for original songs?"

Mac required no convincing, and Dave was on board. I was surprised when Les, the most opposed of any of us to being impaired on stage, agreed as long as we limited the experiment to a specific length of time. It wasn't that he was so sure it would help, he said, but if it didn't, at least we'd have some fun. Leonard was never going to be a smoker, his mind just wasn't wired that way, but he went along with the concept. As far as Craig, who knew what he'd actually do, even though he agreed.

Mac volunteered Joan to help Marie in organizing a rolling party, which Paula signed up for, though I didn't know what Leonard's wife thought about getting high. The next night, before getting in the shower, I came to the dining table. The television stood silent as the girls happily chattered away, their hands busily breaking apart the compressed block of marijuana and spreading it out on the table.

No one but Dave knew about the second plastic wrapped brick I'd brought back from Las Vegas yet. Those few days with Kathy had been precious. I hadn't shared everything that had happened between us with these barbarians I worked with. I kept her kilo tucked away in the back of my closet, hoping she'd contact me someday and I'd get to see her again—but that seemed more unlikely every day.

When I left for work, the crumbled-up grass covered the entire table, six inches deep, and most of the brick remained unbroken. They'd begun straining out the seeds and stems, and collecting the clean grass into a big bowl. When I got home with the rest of the band, who stopped by my unit to pick up supplies, more than a hundred J's stood stacked into glasses and cups. Considering the carpet of cuttings remaining on the table, there'd be many more rolling parties in the days ahead. Some of the guys pitched in to roll, too, whenever we could.

So began our hazy winter days of late 1967 in LA. Juice glasses and sugar bowls full of joints stood at every table in our rooms, including nightstands, for cannabis mornings. We carried joints with us everywhere, and I worked at staying high. Mac, the new Johnny Appleseed of pot, handed out joints like M&Ms to everyone he met. But none of us had produced an original song idea by the time the end of the year rolled around.

We did, finally, fire Craig. It was almost a foregone conclusion after a dramatic performance one night when he rolled around in the parking lot pretending to be sick so he could skip work. Just the final straw after the tiresome name-dropping, pretensions, bad temper, and general lack of respect he'd shown all of us at one time or another. Removing him from the band went right to my front burner after he sold me his car.

He'd grown further and further from us in recent weeks. To be fair, we were all bummed during the month we spent at the Colonial House, but his insular and ill-tempered attitude had only made it that much worse for all of us. Since we'd returned to the Doll, he'd avoided the rest of us as much as possible, missing rehearsals to hang out with his friends. He'd begun dropping hints, bragging about secret projects he was involved in with Gary Usher and Nick Venet, another producer at Columbia Records, which, of course, didn't include us. He treated us as though we were his day job. One afternoon, he showed up in a new Jaguar XKE he said Gary Usher had given him.

That was the day he broke his trust with me for good. Craig offered me his Chevrolet Camaro if I would take over the payments on his auto loan, since he'd have to make the payments on the Jaguar. To take immediate possession, all he needed from me was ninety-five dollars to make the current payment on the Chevy, he said. I put my trusty Falcon up for sale that day and sold it the next.

He knew how much I admired his Camaro, with its all-black leather interior and bucket seats, but after acquiring it, I fell in love with its fantastic sound system. I bought my first eight-track cassette tape to play in the car, the Mamas and Papas' *If You Can Believe Your Eyes and Ears*, and for four days and nights, I rode around for hours, mellowed out behind the herb, listening to the album as loud as my ears could stand it. Different songs made me think different things, but every time I heard *I Saw Her Again Last Night*, I thought of Marie, and hot tears of guilt and affection rolled down my cheeks.

On the fifth night, while we were at work, the Camaro disappeared from the parking lot in back of the Rag Doll—it had been repossessed—along with my new tape in the tape deck. When I called the bank to explain that I was taking over the loan, they told me the car loan was more than three payments behind, and that had triggered automatic repossession. Craig had been informed in writing and by phone weeks ago. He'd known when he'd let me take the car. They also told me the ninety-five dollars I'd given Craig had never been posted to the account. In fact, once the car was in repossession no payments could be accepted. And the bank wouldn't be giving me my Mamas and Papas tape back, either.

We'd been lazy, or maybe just high, over the last few weeks, waiting for the right guy to walk up and replace him. Why did the final piece to our puzzle always seem to be the bass player? Beginning the week following Christmas, my twenty-sixth birthday present to myself was to present Craig with his two-week notice.

Howard King had gotten wind of a bass player in San Jose who was interested enough to drive down to LA to audition. Originally from Minnesota, Mickey Borden had traveled nationally with his family, playing steel guitar from the tender age of five. That accounted for his thunderous style of playing bass with finger and thumb picks. He and his sister had continued the family tradition with their own band, Sandy and the Vikings. He'd been the leader, while Sandy, a much prettier, and very female, version of Mickey, sang lead. Though the band was successful, Sandy decided her roving days were over, and Mickey decided he'd like to find a new band.

Mickey's boyish, chipped-toothed grin crinkled his eyes. He was a broad-shouldered Oregonian lumberjack carved from a redwood tree, who wore his naturally blond hair like a Norwegian god. We welcomed Mickey into Stark Naked and the Car Thieves, while Craig finished out his two weeks with the expected poor grace. With that, Mickey became the band's fourth, and I prayed last, bass player.

Our final week at the Rag Doll would be Mickey's first on stage with us, then we'd return to Las Vegas to mend fences at the Cat. I hoped we'd found our final Car Thief.

Though it meant saying goodbye to Marie when she left for Northern California, I welcomed our return to Las Vegas. Each time we arrived at either the Pussycat or the Rag Doll, I felt a comfortable sense of anticipation, security, and homecoming. Mickey absorbed our song list with little difficulty and quickly fitted himself into the band. Leonard and Mickey both took the same brute-force approach to rock music. Our rhythm section definitely defined us as a full-on rock band.

Craig had skipped so many rehearsals before we were rid of him, we'd fallen behind in learning new songs, so Les suggested dropping many of the tunes we were sick to death of immediately, even if we had to repeat songs, as we began feeding new material into our song list as fast as possible. Mac picked Wilson Pickett's *Funky Broadway,* and Sam and Dave's *Soul Man* along with Dave. Les brought in *Build Me Up Buttercup* by the Foundations in the first week. I was a little jealous at first; I would have liked to have sung that song but in a couple of week, I got *Kind of A Drag*, by the Buckinghams, a good tune I enjoyed singing. And Leonard decided he wanted to come out from behind his drums for a song. We watched with some trepidation as he comically mutilated the Classics IV, S*pooky* while Dave did some very basic drumming, but it was usually funny. We were enthusiastic about the future, sounding good, and a lot of the star performers dropped in regularly to see us at the Cat. The late night sit-in sessions with some of the best main-room and lounge musicians during our later sets often turned into legendary jams that brought everyone to their feet. It felt great to be home.

60
MISSING MORRISON

*Actually I don't remember being born, it must
have happened during one of my black outs.*

—Jim Morrison

January 29, 1968
Las Vegas, Nevada

WITHIN DAYS OF being back at the Cat again, Dave met a gorgeous, five ten, curvy, and very sexy glamazon showgirl named Nikki from the Lido de Paris show at the Stardust. She'd been blessed with a robust figure and stood almost as tall as him. She introduced me to her friend Jan, who was short for a Lido girl at five seven, but almost as tall as me. She was willowy, limber, and, though not quite as glamorous as Nikki, every bit as sexy. Nikki was a US citizen, but Jan was English. They'd become friends in Paris, where both girls had gone for tryouts, signing onto the show before th*e current* version rotated to Vegas. Jan's visa would run out in a few months, and she worried about being forced to return to England soon. As one of the most popular extravaganzas to ever play in Las Vegas, Lido de Paris had been running here since the fifties.

The show paid its entertainers well, even for Vegas, so the girls shared an elegant townhouse well away from the Strip. They insisted they were happiest when we were with them, so Dave and I spent most of our free time with them, and little at our motel.

Lido almost always sold out, but sometimes the girls found us seats for the late show. At first, I resisted, not sure how I'd feel about seeing Jan nearly naked on stage, but both girls really wanted us to go, so I agreed. Jan's beauty was undeniable, but the first time I saw her in full makeup, proudly strutting bare-breasted in a gigantic feathered headdress and alluring costume that still managed to leave a little to the imagination, I couldn't believe this stunning creature was the same girl. My first impression, watching her do a sassy showgirl stalk down the runway out over the crowd, brought on an uncomfortable, angry possessiveness opposed by an odd sense of pride. Something like, "Hey, stop staring at her! I should be the only one salivating over those gorgeous breasts," countered by, "Okay, look all you want, but that beautiful woman sleeps with me every night." The acts in the show were terrific, and there was an overall elegance to the extravaganza that made me understand her pride in being part of it.

The girls loved showing off their "rock and rollers" to their girlfriends around town as much as we enjoyed being seen with them. The four of us became inseparable in our weeks together.

Things had really begun to heat up in LA. Before, to get news, I would have to call Howard or a club owner to find out what was happening. Now, I was hearing from Jimmy O'Neill every few days. Most recently, he called to confirm a photo shoot for album pictures after we closed the Cat and returned to the Rag Doll, and to let me know our contracts were back for our engagement in Honolulu. Eddie would be sending new songs for us to learn, and more recording sessions were being tentatively scheduled. Jimmy heard some of us—me—mention we'd like to play an engagement at home in Indianapolis. While Howard King hadn't quite gotten it signed yet, Jimmy said, he'd gotten avid interest from the Holyoke Club for four weeks following Hawaii. There was an entirely new feeling about how things were going.

"And Larry," Jimmy said, and I could hear the smile in his voice. "Remember I told you we were working on some television appearances? When you get to LA, you'll be filming a television special with Billy Joe Royal. So brush up on *The Pleasure of Your Company* and *Look Back in Love*."

Halfway through our engagement at the Cat, Jim Morrison of the Doors came to see us on a Monday evening. Unfortunately, we were off on

Mondays. Morrison and his friend Robert Gover, a well-respected novelist and columnist for the New York Times Magazine, drove from Orange County that afternoon to meet friends in Las Vegas before coming to the Pussycat.

It's not unlikely we crossed paths with individual members of the Doors at the Hullabaloo afterhours, when they were still getting their band together, or later, at Gazzarri's, about the time they'd become the house band at the Whisky A Go Go up the street. Now they were the fastest-rising rock group of their generation. I was surprised and flattered to hear Morrison had come to see us.

Afterward, Jim's writer friend would write a famous essay, "A Hell of a Way to Peddle Poems," about that night. What happened to them, especially to Jim Morrison, was shocking, but over the months we'd played at the Cat, I was coming to find that this kind of bigotry wasn't as unusual as I would've thought. Most people would never have expected that kind of violence in a club on the modern, world-famous Las Vegas Strip of 1968; after all, we weren't living in the Bugsy Siegel era of the forties.

Based on Gover's account, I can easily visualize the scene that night: Jim Morrison, waiting in the entryway to the Cat, using a Pall Mall cigarette to mimic smoking a joint. When confronted about smoking grass in the club, he pretended to blow smoke on the security guard. More than likely, the guard was Scottie, the club's bouncer, who we'd come to consider our protector and friend. I can see how that would set Scottie off. Morrison's gesture, along with his party being racially mixed and the fact that he and his contingent were obviously "hippies," as Gover wrote, would have earned them close scrutiny at this club anyway.

The Pussycat was a wonderful place to entertain, the only place, in fact, for many of the most famous rock and R&B bands to perform in Las Vegas. But there was a strict, undocumented, rough and violent code of conduct in a club that was still a part of the old western town of Vegas. We'd seen hints of the brutality and prejudice there before, and we'd see it again. It was only the celebrity of Jim Morrison to the rest of the world that made this particular incident famous.

While I'm certain that the management of the Pussycat had no idea who Jim Morrison or the Doors were, Gover and Morrison also didn't realize the Cat's owner, Bill Hirsch, was a retired deputy police chief, and Scottie had been one of his trusted deputies. After Morrison was beaten severely and repeatedly in the head by the security guard, Gover says, the Vegas cops arrived almost immediately. The local cops always responded in a New York heartbeat to any call that came in from the Cat, and they were always there to back up the club's actions.

Morrison and his writer friend were roughly bundled into police cars and brought to the station, where a number of indignities and threats ignited Jim Morrison's demons to—as Gover describes—grow ever worse and more intense. As Morrison's berserker rage continued to build, Gover reports, officers raised their level of menace to threats of deadly beatings and great bodily harm to Morrison following the end of their shift—12 AM. Eventually, Gover's girlfriend got them out just before midnight, charged only with public drunkenness.

The unspoken understanding between the rich hoteliers and old Vegas, including local law enforcement, made the cops' responsibility keeping the streets quiet paramount above all else. The resort owners needed winning gamblers to feel secure anywhere in town so they'd come back to the tables, knowing the odds would eventually favor the casinos. They recognized crime of any kind was bad for business, and advertising the winners, by extension safety, was good. In return for blanket police cooperation, they turned a blind eye to the means, the various tricks and schemes used by law enforcement to intimidate and harass "undesirables"—usually, people who broke one of the forty-seven or so broad vagrancy laws the statutes maintained. It left open a door for individual prejudices of people of influence. Too often, hippies, druggies, and people who just looked different, such as mixed-race couples, were persuaded, sometimes violently, to leave businesses, and sometimes, leave town.

Some people believe that the ordeal Jim Morrison experienced at the Pussycat, and later at the hands of law enforcement, was so brutal, that it affected what remained of the rest of his life as it spiraled in a deep depression downward, to end in a Paris restroom three years later. I don't know how true that is, but I wish we'd been playing that night; maybe we could have defused the situation. I would have liked to have met the Lizard King and his friend Robert, and maybe it would have turned out much better for everyone. Las Vegas of the 60s was an amazing city of lights, a city that never slept, offering an unending sense of adventure when you had money to risk. But if you didn't, and you didn't fit the right profile, the illusion was likely to be pierced and the city reveal itself as a dark, dangerous, and gritty place—especially if you made the misstep of looking out of place.

A couple of weeks later, I made a random stop by my motel room to check for messages on the way to work, and got a shock. My dad, Malcolm Dunlap, had left a phone message with a return number in San Jose, California. My breath caught when I heard my father's voice in the receiver.

"Dad, great to hear your voice. Is everything okay? You're in San Jose?"

"I'm fine, Son. Here for an IAA conference. Can't get over the weather here. Pretty damn cold when I left Indianapolis, I can tell you."

"Too bad you're not closer. Wish I could see you."

"That's why I called. When I flew out here, the plane stopped in Las Vegas, and I remembered your mother telling me your band was playing there. So I checked around and found out you're appearing at the Pussycat club. I got this telephone number from them."

"Gee, wish I'd known, I would have run out to the airport to be with you for a few minutes at least." I smoothed a hand over the cover on the motel room bed; it hadn't been turned back for days.

"I may have a better idea. I think I can extend my layover there on the way back to Indianapolis on Sunday."

"That would be fantastic. That will be our closing night. Do you want me to pick you up at the airport?"

"No, no, I'll just catch a cab. Can't extend my layover for longer than twenty-four hours, so I'll just blow into town, grab a room near the airport, and catch a plane out early next morning. If you agree, I'll be there Sunday night."

61
MY FATHER AND THE CAT

I wasn't really Naked. I simply didn't have any clothes on.
— Josephine Baker

February 11, 1968
Las Vegas, Nevada

CLOSING NIGHTS COULD be emotional, but Sunday night was over the top. My dad, the first person in my family I'd seen since I'd left Indianapolis three years ago, would be watching me perform in the band for the first time ever. I'd also be saying goodbye to Jan tonight. We'd become attached over these few weeks, but based on our upcoming schedule, it would be months before the band would be back to Vegas.

A power trio named Flower Garden were doing a creditable, if deafening, job on Cream's *The Sunshine of Your Love* when my father walked into the Pussycat a little after eleven thirty. One of the waitresses pointed me out with a smile. The gray window-patterned suit he wore with a white open-necked dress shirt made him look like the insurance salesman he was. Watching him work his six-foot frame through the floor to the table I held for him was wrenching but cool. I thought his wavy hair looked a little grayer along the temples, but he still had the same angular, craggy good looks. His head swiveled from side to side, taking everything in. As he came up to me for an embrace, Old Spice aftershave brought home the incongruity of him here, with me, in Las Vegas.

Dave, Mac, and Les came over to give him a warm greeting. We were always excited to have family from home come to see us. Dave's mom and stepdad, and Mac's sister had already visited in the last few months. I introduced Leonard and Mickey, who joined us, pulling up chairs around my father, who loved the attention.

"Fantastic to see you, Dad. I've kept an eye on the door since we started tonight," I told him once the guys had cleared off. "Any trouble getting here?"

"None at all. Cab driver helped me find a place to stay over near the airport." *And made a few bucks for himself at the same time*, I was certain. "The hotels along the main street on the ride are amazing. I guess I didn't understand what Las Vegas looks like." *Damn. I should have pulled some strings to reserve a room for him at one of the Strip hotels.*

"Listen, Dad, the band's got to go on in a few minutes, but Jan, a girl I've been seeing, is coming in when her last show at the Stardust closes. I'm going to ask her and her girlfriend, who Dave's dating, to sit at your table. Keep an eye out for them, will you?"

I think it hadn't crossed his mind I might have a girlfriend, but he was quick on the uptake, and nodded. "How late do you play?"

"We trade sets with the trio playing on the small stage behind you twice more and then play the final two sets. Entertainment shuts down at four, but the club doesn't close until six AM, so they can clean up."

"Oh boy," he said. "Late nights—and they keep selling booze at the bar, I suppose."

"Right up 'til closing."

In a few minutes, our band milled around on the darkened stage, readying a little trick we'd stolen from the Checkmates Ltd. We stood with our backs to the audience as if we were tuning and adjusting our equipment. When Les stepped into a spotlight to begin the tricky little guitar intro to *Five O' Clock World* by the Vogues, the stage lights flashed on. Dave, Mac, and I danced up to our mics from each side of the stage to start yelling the "Hey" vocal hits that began the song. Leonard and Mickey joined in with Les on Leonard's downbeat. Once Dave jumped into the lead lyric, and Les and Mickey were rolling into the rhythm, I leaped to the B3 just in time to dig my thumb into a low growly E and rip my fingers up the keyboard while flipping the Leslie switch to rotate the amplifier horns. It always came out kinda cool and flashy.

After the opener, we zipped into Gary Puckett and the Union Gap's *Young Girl*, a song so in Dave's wheelhouse, he should have been the one to record it. He ripped through the performance. Open amazement beamed on my dad's face, and I knew he'd been caught up in the show. *Come Si Bella*, an Italian love ballad, brought all our voices to the front mics next. We performed this song almost a cappella; the old Reflections had sung it back in my parents' living room during my high-school days. We'd recently learned it for our act, and I felt the connection to my father in the pit of my stomach right up to the big chord at the end. When Jan arrived, she came to the edge of the stage, and I pointed out Dad's table. He stood as the girls took chairs. He tried to be cool, but it was more than he could manage. Rare fun to see him intimidated by anyone or anything. It was obvious he thought they were pretty spectacular looking. Which, being fresh from their performances, they were. We continued through our best set of the night, ending with *Shout* and the high energy it always produced to bring down the house.

The lights went off on our stage as the trio started up across the room. We gathered coats and ties, and exited into the dressing room. After hanging my coat up for the next set, I pulled on a white cardigan and went out, anxious to hear what Dad thought.

"Why young man, Larry, dammit, your band is . . . well, it's nothing short of magnificent." The shock and awe on his face touched my heart; this moment meant everything to me, something I would never forget. I'd been more nervous and excited singing in front of him than any other time I'd been on stage.

"I had no idea. I wish your mother and your sister could have been here." His voice had gotten husky with emotion. "I just don't know what to say, Larry." I couldn't speak, either; my voice would have been husky, too.

I leaned over to Jan for a quick kiss and introduced her to Dad. All through high school, my father had charmed every girl I'd been interested in, including Pat. Nothing had changed. Dad immediately fell for her British accent—like father, like son. She lapped up his attention like a cat served cream in a saucer. His enthusiastic praise to each of the guys as they stopped by the table was heartwarming. I had a moment, as I had many times before, but especially just then, when I felt an indescribable sense of pride in my band brothers, realizing how much we'd grown and accomplished by sticking together. I loved and treasured each of them for who they were, warts and all, and I hoped they felt the same way about me. Jan noticed the expression on my face.

"You look positively enraptured with something. Are you okay?"

I smiled back at her. "You know, this will sound kind of trite, but there's something very special about singing for your father. I don't think my dad ever thought I would amount to much. He always considered me a dreamer, a wasted opportunity. For a moment, I saw us through his eyes and felt so proud of the band, above all, those of us from Indiana—we've come so far together. Yes, I'm very okay. Except for you and me, and this being our last night together before we leave for LA."

She patted my hand on the table. "We'll make it a night to remember when we get home then, won't we." She sealed her promise with a smile, but I sensed a wistful something she was holding back.

"What's the matter, sweetie?"

She looked in my eyes for a moment. "I love when you call me sweetie in your cute American accent."

Her eyes were downcast as she told me she'd heard tonight the entire cast of their show would probably be rotated back to Paris in the next few weeks. They did that sometimes to keep whole casts together, she explained. The dates on exit visas got staggered over time, and this would bring all the *Lido* performers' visas back into sync. Even though her visa didn't expire until the end of the year, she would be forced to leave because of the limits of her work permit.

"I can't guarantee when, or even if, I'll ever get back to the US again."

It was a bittersweet moment for my dad to be here and also find I might never again see this girl I'd come to care so much about. A subtext lay beneath what she'd told me. If she married a US citizen, she wouldn't need to leave with the show. *Given more time, I might come to love her enough, our compatibility made it seem possible. But no, even if that were true—no, never again. Even if I felt deeply enough about someone to consider marriage, I would never risk it.* I couldn't speak to Jan from the heart here in the club, so I tried to set my feelings aside and concentrate on the few hours I had left with my father.

We finished with a powerful closing set. We had a strong list of songs these days, enough for four excellent sets. The strain of being up so late had begun to show on Dad, but a couple of Irish coffees seemed to revive him. Dave ended the night with *Cara Mia*. We tried to reserve these kinds of songs for peak hours, before Dave's voice tired. But he wanted to sing it for Dad, and we'd retained a good-sized crowd. His presence earned us a standing ovation at four in the morning.

The equipment had to be broken down and loaded into the van for the trip to Southern California before the night was over for us. I kissed Jan and told her I'd be home to the townhouse as soon as I could, trying to compartmentalize my feelings.

Dad noticed my expression when I turned back to the stage. "You seem a little down, Son."

"I like Jan a lot, Dad. She just found out her show is being transferred back to Paris. Things are starting to move pretty fast. Our schedule is taking us back to LA to do a TV special, we're going back into the studio, and then halfway around the world to Hawaii. We seem to be going in two different directions. I may never see her again after tonight."

"I'm sorry, Larry. I can offer you only one piece of advice, though you may already be wiser than me in this. There will always be regrets at the end of your life, can't be helped, but the ones that sting the worst will be for the things you didn't do, rather than the things you did."

I smiled at him. "Dad, don't go yet. We still have some time to be together while we get everything loaded up. If you're not too tired, we could get some breakfast afterward." He clapped me on the shoulder and put a hand behind my head to grasp the back of my neck and beamed.

"I hoped you'd let me stay. I'd love to help you pack up. By God, and John Henry, I wish I could be in the caravan traveling back to California with you boys. But I better pass on the breakfast idea. My plane leaves in"—he checked his watch—"less than five hours."

No roadies for us. We were pretty well organized, and Leonard had a plan for where everything went in the van. Dad rolled up his sleeves and carried equipment along with everyone else. He also thought it was pretty cool to order a highball at four thirty in the morning. By five thirty, job done, everyone came by to say goodbye to my father before he left.

"Look, this isn't going to be a long goodbye. You said your band's coming to Indianapolis in a few months, maybe after Hawaii, right?" I nodded. "Okay then. I'll tell your mother and sister you're doing fine. In fact, I'll tell them you're doing goddamn great. You take care, Son. I'm proud to pieces of you, and love you very much."

I hugged him and let him go out to the cab that Scottie had called for him. I was pretty choked up. It had been a long time since my dad told me he loved me.

"Pretty great your old man being here. Got the feeling he was ready to go on the road with us." Dave and I rode the back streets to Jan and Nikki's condo out near Sunrise Mountain. I nodded, still cherishing the special moment I'd had with my father.

"Did Jan tell you the news about the *Lido* show?" The distressing reminder of my future with her jolted me into reality.

"About the show going back to Paris? Yeah, she told me."

"Bummer, huh?"

I thought for a moment. "Dave, if Nikki was from outside the US, like Jan, would you consider marrying her, you know, so she could stay in the country?"

"You mean actually marry her? For real?"

"Of course for real. You can't pretend to get married so she could stay here. I don't think there's any special Las Vegas temporary marriage license. I mean you'd have to marry her right now, before we left for LA, for it to work." I slowed and stopped as the light at the empty intersection ahead turned red.

He turned to study me. "Has this got something to do with Jan?"

"Not the point. I asked what you would do. If it was Nikki."

"I think the world of Nikki. I mean, look at the girl's body. Lord, she's an adult jungle gym!" He leaned back in his seat. "And she's not like most of these hard-ass showgirls we've met. She's very, very cool. But even if I thought about her that way, I just don't think I'm ready to be married. Actually, I don't think she is, either." He glanced at me as we sat idling in the cool Las Vegas morning before going on. "I've thought about being married, but then I also think about when I go to the gig at night and look out at all these amazing, available women who want to be with me. Something attracts me to a different one each night."

"Big tits," I observed.

He grinned, "Yeah, that happens real often. Anyway, I feel like I've just got to see if she wants me to jump her bones. Not something I could do and be married. And I have never met the girl, no matter how spectacular, I could marry and still not want to do that. So, my answer to you, young truth-seeker, is, until I meet her, the answer is no."

"So you're never getting married then, either?"

"No sense buying the dairy," he said with a smile.

"Fuck you, man. You say bullshit like that, but I know you better than that. I think what you're saying is you don't want to be like Mac." I accelerated through the green light and the empty cross street.

Dave's expression turned serious. "You know Mac is like a brother to me, to both of us. But sometimes it's hard for me to watch what he does when he's around the girls in the clubs. I think the absolute world of Joan, but sometimes I get mad at her for letting him get away with it. I just know I could never live like that. You know how I feel about my mom and my real dad. I'm not going into the whole thing, but I don't ever want that to happen to a wife of mine."

I'd never heard Dave talk about what had happened between his parents. Eileen, his mom, had been like a second mother to me after we'd begun singing together. I didn't meet his father until we'd decided to try being a band, when he bought the singers our first matching suits. I liked Ralph. We were grownups now and understood that forces and emotions beyond our control sometimes caused good people to do things they wished they hadn't, but Dave, in many ways, remained a constant. Once he'd made up his mind about something or somebody, moving a mountain would be easier than getting him to reconsider.

"Sometimes I find it difficult, too, Dave, but I also think Joan's a pretty smart, and pretty tough, cookie. I'm sure she knows more about what Mac's up to than she lets on. She's nobody's fool. The two of them have made their peace over this. To be their friends, I think we've got to try not to judge either of them. Their early life was pretty rough. Despite what Mac may say or how he acts, I believe down deep he needs Joan, and they both know it—and I know he loves her. I have a suspicion they'll always be married unless Joan ever decides she doesn't want to be. So we should respect the way she makes her own decisions."

"I get that, I do," he said. "But I still have trouble with it. It can never be like that for me."

Jan and I clung to each other in desperation after making love. The taste of her was still on my lips when I began to hear words I couldn't believe were coming out of my mouth.

"Have you considered getting married to stay in the country?"

With a deep sigh, she rolled away onto her back. I heard her breathing, and I knew she was looking deep into the darkness above us. "I wondered if you'd say that, I did. You're so sweet I thought you probably would. I even wondered how I would respond. Now I know." The bed moved as she turned toward me.

"Considered. Odd word, that, don't you think? I did consider us being married, just for a moment, but we can't. Neither of us would ever know if we really meant to, or if it was just an expediency of the moment. No, my dearest. You are my sweet American love, and I shall remember you and our lusty adventure always. But this has to be the end for us. I do so thank you for the offer, though. I will add it to the treasure of our relationship."

"How you do go on," I mimicked lightly, masking unspoken relief that I'd shown the courage to at least broach the idea, and also relief she'd refused me—followed by an unexpected twinge of disappointment.

62
SERIAL MONOGAMY

*It's easy to take off your clothes and have sex. People
do it all the time. But opening up your soul to
someone, letting them into your spirit, thoughts, fears,
future, hopes, dreams... that is being Naked.*

— Rob Bell

February 13, 1968
North Hollywood, California

AFTER MOVING BACK into the Mid-Valley Motel, I steeled myself against calling Marie, as I normally would, to arrange for her to come to North Hollywood. It wasn't just that Jimmy had so many things planned for us before we left for Hawaii. After all that I'd sworn to about avoiding entanglements, I was shaken by my proposal to Jan in Las Vegas, and even more troubled by the sharp ache I'd felt when she refused me. What was going on? I didn't understand my own feelings. One thing was certain: things couldn't stay the same between Marie and me. I didn't know what I was going to say to her, and by not calling, I could put off the painful confrontation I knew was ahead.

Thursday night as I stepped off the stage after the first set at the Rag Doll, Marie stood there waiting for me. She looked sweet and sexy, and she smiled that secret smile people do at the big moment of a surprise party.

"Marie. What are you doing here? When did you get in? I didn't even know you were coming."

"You shouldn't be so shocked. It didn't take long to get here."

"Are you kidding? From Fremont?"

"No, from Van Nuys. It's only about a fifteen-minute drive. I got an apartment here in the Valley a few weeks ago." She practically wriggled with pleasure at the astonished look on my face.

"Can we get a table or something?" she asked.

Once I was past the shock of her move to Southern California, we fell into a familiar pattern during the evening. At the end of the night, she invited me to see her new apartment, and I couldn't think of a way not to, or more likely, I just seemed to be unable to resist sleeping with her.

It was surprising to see how settled she'd become in her new place, knickknacks all around, and the rooms nicely furnished. Our proximity soon led to the inevitable, and in the cigarette-hazed, post-coital conversation, she invited me to make her new apartment my home.

"It would be perfect for you here, honey. Whenever you're in LA, you'd have a comfortable place to stay instead of that cruddy motel. You could keep your books and things here instead of lugging them around when you travel."

I didn't want to hurt her feelings, but now I understood why she'd moved. Marie still hoped she could change my mind about marriage or, at least, a committed relationship with her. My fault, of course. We'd been breaking up, on and off, for nearly three years. Each time, I'd let us—no, encouraged us—to fall back into our easy and sexually comforting intimacy. At least Dave was honest with his one-night-only girlfriends. My relationship with Marie was dishonest, based on my own insecurities and needs, keeping her from finding the someone she needed and deserved. Though we never discussed it, she knew I was with other girls when we were apart. But in proposing to Jan, I'd crossed an invisible line. I could no longer convince myself that I was being honest just because I didn't lie to her about the other girls. It was too deceitful knowing I'd offered marriage to someone other than Marie, and still slept with her whenever it was convenient and needful for me. This time I'd gone too far.

There were tears and recriminations and disappointment over the days and nights that followed until Marie came to accept that this wouldn't be like our previous separations. Our relationship was really ending. The band would perform in Honolulu for nine weeks. Once I got to Hawaii, twenty-five hundred miles of Pacific Ocean would separate us. This was my best chance to make our breakup stick.

In the end, Marie only requested that I stay with her in her new apartment during the remaining weeks before the band closed at the Rag Doll. When the time came for me to leave, she said, "I should just go, no goodbyes." We spent our nights together during these last few weeks in sometimes-gentle and sometimes-frantic lovemaking and quiet retrospective moments. If there were tears, Marie held them in check the final morning I left for my flight. I hated hurting her, it was the last thing I wanted to do. It chilled me, too, knowing the security blanket she provided me no longer existed. I took what comfort I could in believing we'd ended our relationship like adults.

I had to make a change, be smart about how I dated girls so this wouldn't happen again. I spent a lot of time thinking about it. As any healthy young single man would, I enjoyed relationships with girls I met, but there could be no more Maries, no more implied promises of a future I couldn't and swore I wouldn't deliver on. It was my nature and temperament to be happiest when I was romantically involved with only one person, even for a limited time. I was uncomfortable with feeling that my actions could hurt or deceive, even by omission, someone else. In my heart I understood that unless I was willing to meet my own standard of honesty, the honesty I'd want from someone else, I wasn't taking the responsibility necessary to allow me to enjoy these relationships.

I decided that the most practical solution was to date one girl at a time, or none at all, wherever we played, and only for as long as we played there. To accommodate my nomadic lifestyle, I would compartmentalize and enjoy each relationship in its own temporal geography—in its own time and place. Once, and only if, I met the right girl, I wouldn't look further. No commitment beyond that. If I didn't meet anyone like that, so be it. The band would soon be on to the next place. I gave this kind of relationship a name, *serial monogamy*.

Certain other advantages existed in this plan. Most of the girls I met accepted the fundamental reality of how limited our time together would be. It tended to compress the awkwardness of first dates—decisions about what would happen between us had to be made quickly—often in one night. Before the bloom was off our time together, we'd separate without promises, perhaps with hopes we might meet again if the band returned to play in that city. I'd already met several girls who preferred things this way, and if it was all aboveboard and honest, this should work out to be less hurtful to everyone's feelings, including my own. And, for good measure, I redoubled my pledge to never marry again, to never let marriage sneak up on me again, the way it nearly had with Jan.

During most of these days in LA, I spent a lot of time with Jimmy, and Seymour, who'd begun to take significantly more interest in us. With Howard King virtually our fulltime agent, the Pussycat and the Rag Doll as home bases, the highest-paying clubs in LA available, and short road trips along the West Coast thrown in to spice things up, we'd developed the security of a solid work circuit. And soon, we'd return to our hometown where several of us would get to play in front of family and friends for the first time.

Seymour told me he planned to check on venues for a national tour during his upcoming trip to the East Coast with Liberace. Especially for top clubs in New York and Florida, where he had connections through other acts he managed.

Though *The Pleasure of Your Company* hadn't hit big nationally, it had apparently shown enough promise with sales and radio stations back East that Eddie and his partner, Ray Harris, expected great things from *Look Back in Love*, our next release. I was assured that Eddie had done a masterful job on the final mix. Ray told us Bell Records, the famous New York City label who distributed our record label, Sunburst, had committed to a big promotional and marketing push for the song's release.

Jimmy had us bring our stage clothes down to the office in Hollywood early one afternoon. He'd hired one of Hollywood's top photographers to take an afternoon of photos for the album we'd release following *Look Back In Love's* near-certain success. We hustled over to a nearby park that featured a photogenic tree, some small hills, and abundant greenery within about a half acre. We wore our Nehru jackets and white boots while reclining, jumping, and running through this tiny area. He had big plans to use his connections to get us into the top Hollywood nightclubs to promote our new single once we were back from the islands. While they didn't pay up to our standard, the entertainment press coverage was priceless with a record on the charts.

One Saturday afternoon, we stepped out onto a sound stage surrounded by bleachers full of screaming teenagers, ready to play in front of several television cameras. We thought we'd be performing *Look Back in Love* and *The Pleasure of Your Company* for a TV special to be broadcast in the future but it turned out we'd only be lip-synching, and instead of sharing the stage with Billy Joe Royal, it was the Seeds who'd just proceeded us. We never even saw them, not even in the dressing room.

Afterward, as Jimmy hustled us off to change clothes, he filled our heads with the potential television variety and talk shows he was pursuing. Eddie was begging Seymour, he told us, to find more studio time for us. The only odd thing I noticed was that Burt Jacobs, Jimmy's partner in B-J Enterprises, who we'd met the first time we'd come to the office, was no longer around. Jimmy's cards now read "Jimmy O'Neill Management," just above, "Seymour Heller and Associates."

With top-flight personal management, a hot and famous record producer, and a committed label, our star was rising. Our future success seemed golden, inevitable. The sneaking suspicion I'd felt, about us maybe being imposters, just some lightly regarded Midwestern guys from the Hoosier state posing as rock stars, was about to be refuted. We'd fly off to Hawaii, recharge ourselves in these coming weeks, and come back refreshed and eager to take our place at the *top of the top* among the pantheon of rock and roll stars that included Frankie Valli and the Four Seasons, Brian Wilson and the Beach Boys, Bobby Hatfield from the Righteous Brothers, Gary Puckett and the Union Gap, and so many other of our idols. And soon, our lead singer, Dave Dunn, and our band, Stark Naked and the Car Thieves, would no longer be a joke name.

ACKNOWLEDGEMENTS

BOOKS ARE RARELY written in a vacuum and this one is no different. I'm grateful for the help I've received from so many people I will not be able to name them all. I have to begin with David Dunn, who has read everything I've written over the years, including the hundreds of thousands of words discarded during the process. Though there are surprisingly few details we remember differently and none of them that directly affect our adventure, he's been my rudder, helping me stay on course. I appreciate that Mac and Joan Brown, the seventh member of the band, whom I treasure, have read everything, and recognize this entire story is a *look back in love*, and that we'll be connected forever through our journey together.

June and John Clair have provided invaluable insight and review as my first editors. I cannot thank them enough for their selfless help and honest appraisal, especially for my Indianapolis chapters.

Rick Stepp-Bolling, my critique partner has been the leader of the beta reading, which includes Chris Tunnah, John Lamb, Johanna Long, Kevin Keefe, Rob Reiter and others on the TWLitN Updates mailing list. Rick's a stalwart supporter who thinks I write better than I actually do. My appreciation goes out to Jan and Jim Seagrave, and Sheri Moline, who were notably generous with their time in digging out facts from various archives in Las Vegas. Avoiding many of the perils of publishing has been due to valuable and generous help and advice from publishing professional, Marion Gropen of Gropen Associates, and to Carla King and her very effective Self-Publishing Boot Camp.

I want to mention Christine Marie Bryant, president, organizer, and den mother of the Coffee House Writers Group of San Dimas, California, and the following members: Rick, Elizabyth Harrington, Edward Owen, Cliff Ashpaugh, Elena Smith, Michael Ian Churchman,

Stephen Hamilton, Heather Lyons, Eric Van Mizener, Lauren Candia, Cherisse Yanit Nadal, Keiko Amano, Mike Hacker, and Janis Hawkridge who gave me a forum to figure out where to begin writing after months of research. I appreciate their continued support and encouragement, and remain an active online member of CHWG.

I've received great marketing support from Sandy Beckworth at Beckworth Communications, and invaluable help and advice from Mary Farragher from the Independent Book Publishers Association, whose organization has been a constant resource.

I'd like to thank the team that has helped me bring this book to publication, including Andra Vacaro, intellectual property attorney and avid reader, Andrew Turner for his assistance, the design team, including Damon and Alisha at Damonza.com, and Katie Stirling at Eschler Editing.

I want to acknowledge the inspiration that certain writers have provided me in writing this particular book, Cheryl Strayed, Kaui Hart Hemmings, Diablo Cody, Kiana Davenport, Marisha Pessl, and Dennis Lehane. There are far too many more to mention who have inspired me to write at all.

My greatest thanks go to my wife Laurie. Even when writing drives me into obsessive seclusion to pound on the keyboard, she pitches in to help, to read, to suggest (or demand), and love me no matter how obnoxious I become. It would have been impossible to complete this book without her constant loving support.

BEFORE YOU GO

Thanks for reading *NIGHT PEOPLE*, Book 1 *of Things We Lost in the Night, a Memoir of Love and Music in the 60s with Stark Naked and the Car Thieves.* and for spending time with me and my friends in the spectacular Sixties!

I hope you're enjoying the story. I've spent many, many hours reliving the events and revisiting friends in writing this book—it has been a return to a seminal time in my life, that feels as though it happened in a distant past sometimes, and in others, as though it were yesterday.

I'd like to ask an important favor. Reviews by readers like you are so powerful, perhaps even disproportionally so, that they can make or break a book—especially for independent writers competing with traditional publishers. I understand that asking you for this help could be an imposition. However if you have the time and are willing to help I'd love to see even a single line of what you thought or felt about *Things We Lost in the Night*; even if it's just clicking on the stars at Amazon, Goodreads, or any other book review site.

If you would like to contact me, I'd love to hear from you. Tell me what you liked, what you loved, even what you hated. You can write me directly at **larry@larryjdunlap**.com and visit me on the web at **www.larryjdunlap.com** for much more about the book, the people who populate it, and other news.

I hope you're looking forward to the conclusion of my memoir in Book 2: *ENCHANTED*. Since *Things We Lost in the Night* was written as one story before being separated prior to birth, I expect few delays in preparing it for publication. If you'd like to keep track of progress on the next book in the links below. I'd love to have you with me.

IMPORTANT INFORMATION:

Below are several links if you'd like to help or stay in touch. The most important one is the page for readers who have finished either one or both of the books that make up *THINGS WE LOST IN THE NIGHT*. But there are several other useful ones you can copy into your Internet browser that you might be interested in as well.

1. larryjdunlap.com/readers - Information and current information of all kinds about the music and people of *THINGS WE LOST IN THE NIGHT*.
2. amazon.com/author/larryjdunlap - Amazon Larry J. Dunlap author page.
3. goodreads.com/larryjdunlap - Goodreads.com review page for NIGHT PEOPLE.
4. http://eepurl.com/UMbdj - Join me for all the latest news and interesting stories that didn't make it into the books and premiums and prizes.
5. facebook.com/larryjdunlap.author - Join our Facebook community and make your voice heard.

With gratitude,
Larry J. Dunlap

www.ingramcontent.com/pod-product-compliance
Lightning Source LLC
Chambersburg PA
CBHW031400290426
44110CB00011B/222